For Mahendra Gonsalkorale and Bill Sang
in friendship, gratitude and admiration.

Contents

Acknowledgements

This book owes its existence to the enthusiasm and encouragement of Jacqueline Korn of David Higham Associates, my agent, and of Toby Mundy of Atlantic Books. Toby it was who suggested the title of the book. Many thanks to both of you.

I am even more indebted to Louisa Joyner for her brilliant editorial work. Her eye for detail, combined with her clear understanding of the big picture, has resulted in countless suggestions that have dramatically improved *Hippocratic Oaths* from the original manuscript. Louisa, I can't thank you enough. Louisa's work has been complemented by the superb copy-editing of Jane Robertson, to whom I am enormously grateful for much judicious textual liposuction, vital structural changes, an intelligent scepticism that has tempered some of my more passionate outbursts, and an unremitting attention to important minutiae.

Finally, thanks are due to my secretary, Penny Essex a) for putting up with me not only during the period of gestation of *Hippocratic Oaths* but also for wonderful support over the preceding decade and a half and b) for chasing up many elusive references often on the basis of vague and/or misleading information.

I

A (Very) Personal Introduction

Nothing could be more serious than the care of ill people, nor more deserving of intelligent discussion. Few topics attract such media coverage; the National Health Service is never far from the top of the political agenda; and most people regard good health – and access to first-class care when they fall ill – as supremely important. It is, therefore, regrettable that discussion of medicine – of medical science, of clinical practice, of the profession itself – is frequently ill-informed. Comment is often shallow, even when it is not riddled with errors of fact, interpretation or emphasis. Reactive, piecemeal and disconnected from the big picture, much analysis lacks historical perspective and ignores the complex reality of medical care.

Notwithstanding all the books, column inches, air-time and screen-time devoted to it, therefore, the practice of medicine remains virtually invisible. *Hippocratic Oaths*, which contemplates the art of medicine from a broad perspective while not losing sight of the details, aims at making medicine more visible. This is worthwhile not only because scientific medicine is one of the greatest triumphs of humankind; but also because illness is potentially a mirror, albeit a dark one, in which we may see something of what we are, at the deepest level. Making medicine truly visible may cast some light on the greater mystery of what it is to be a human being. That mystery is the starting point of this book.

Medicine, objectively, has never been in better shape. Its scientific basis, the application of this science in clinical practice, the processes by which health care is delivered; the outcomes for patients, the accountability of professionals, and the way doctors and their patients interact with each other – all have improved enormously even during my thirty years as a practitioner. Yet the talk is all of doom and gloom: short memories have hidden the extraordinary advances of the last century.

The danger is that endless predictions of crisis may become self-fulfilling by making the key roles of doctor and nurse deeply unattractive. This would be a disaster, given that further progress will require more, not less, medical and nursing time.

The curious dissociation between what medicine has achieved and the way in which it is perceived originates outside of medicine itself. While medical practice is continuously improving, it has not kept up with patients' rising expectations. Many things are much better than they were, but few things are as good as people have been led to expect. Changes in patients' expectations reflect changes in the world at large. What is more, there is a tension between the consumerist values of society and the values that have hitherto informed medicine at its best; values that have driven its gradual transformation from a system beleaguered by fraud, venality and abuse of power[1] to a genuinely caring profession whose practices are informed by biological science and underpinned by clinical evidence.

Hippocratic Oaths does not pretend be a comprehensive account of medicine or even of its current troubles. I have aimed at depth rather than breadth. I examine the institutions of medicine and their present discontents in a series of essays – in some cases prompted by particular events or personal experiences. The book is a triptych: the large middle section deals with present discontents. It is flanked by panels that deal, respectively, with the origins and the destination of the art of medicine.

Though many of its reflections are cast in an impersonal form and address matters of public interest, *Hippocratic Oaths* is deeply personal. I believe that medicine is in danger of being irreversibly corrupted. This threat comes not from within (where its values are struggling to survive) but from society at large. The most serious dangers emanate from those for whom the moral high ground is a platform for self-advancement, many of whom have never borne, or have been willing to bear, the responsibilities that weigh on the daily life of practitioners. The unthinking voices of those who have a shallow understanding of the real challenges of medicine (and an even shallower appreciation of its achievements) will make patient care worse not better. Their influence already threatens to bring about a disastrous revolution in the values and attitudes of health-care professionals: if we are not careful, the patient-as-client will receive service-with-a-smile from a 'customer-aware' self-protecting doctor delivering strictly on contract. If the current debased public perception is not challenged, medicine may become the first blue-collar profession, delivered by supine, sessional functionaries. This will not serve the longer term interests of people who fall ill.

Everyone agrees that we need to rethink medicine; in particular its relationship to society at large. This book offers an introduction to that rethink. We need to take a long view and to unpeel the layers of second-order discussion that takes so much for granted and has hidden the reality of a deeply human, and humane, profession. Only on the basis of an appreciation of what has been achieved, and a better understanding of the ends, aims and ultimate limitations of medical care, shall we be able to begin an intelligent examination of the present discontents and the future path; and arrive at a clearer understanding of what might be expected of medicine and of those who deliver medical care.

This book is dedicated to two of the many admirable people I have worked with in my thirty-two years in the NHS. Mohendra Gonsalkorale has been a consultant colleague for sixteen years. His many patients and colleagues, including myself, have benefited from his energy, cheerfulness, clinical expertise and wisdom, moral support and conscientiousness. Bill Sang is a manager whose ability to keep the larger vision in view while attending to the small details has been an inspiration. It is such people who keep the NHS afloat despite the misguided interventions of those many ill-informed individuals who wish to 'save it'. However, neither Mohendra nor Bill would agree with everything in the pages that follow: both would be more philosophical about many of the things that cause me to bite the carpet. But they share my passion for public service and for the supremely serious calling of medicine – a passion which, over the years, has prompted them to work all the hours God made and some He has not thought of yet.

Perhaps this book should have another dedicatee: the students of Manchester Medical School, which still attracts the best and brightest. It is upon such people that the future of medicine will rest. If their sense of medicine as a calling is not destroyed, they will be doing their best for sick people in the dark hours when the hostile critics of the profession are chattering away at their dinner parties or safely tucked up in bed.

PART ONE

Origins

> Nor dread nor hope attend
> A dying animal;
> A man awaits his end
> Dreading and hoping all;
> Man has created death[1]

From 'Death' by W.B. Yeats

A crushed beetle pedals the air for a while before expiring. A wounded snake slithers to a dark place and dies. A sick dog mopes, eats grass, vomits, and waits. A cat with a damaged paw licks it incessantly. Chimps are a little more sophisticated: they sometimes dab leaves on a bloody wound. This is as far as 'animal medicine' goes. If medicine is 'the provision of special care to a sick individual by others',[2] there are no examples in the animal kingdom. The closest that non-human creatures get to physicianly attention is picking ticks off each other's backs.

William Osler's ironical definition of man as 'the medicine-taking animal' is therefore justified inasmuch as it captures something distinctive about humans. It is, however, inaccurate for interesting reasons. First, taking medicine is only a recent characteristic of the species. While hominids started parting company from the beasts several million years ago, taking medicine might not have begun until 10,000 years ago. We cannot be sure of this, of course. The behaviour and institutions of our ancestors prior to the invention of writing can only be guessed at. Evidence about the beginning of medical care is bound to be tenuously inferential. For the taking of medicines is not just a matter of ingesting material of therapeutic benefit as when a dog eats grass. And this is the second reason for qualifying Osler's assertion: there is a vast cultural hinterland to the popping of the most ordinary pill.

I

The Medicine-taking Animal:
a Philosophical Overture

Medicine-taking has roots in many different quarters of individual and collective human consciousness. Swallowing a safe pill makes sense only in the context of a recognized system of knowledge and belief, which encompasses many things: the significance of the suffering that prompts the search for relief; the structure and function of the human body and the means by which they may be changed; and numerous sciences, such as organic chemistry, pharmacology and industrial chemistry. What is more, it is part of a tapestry of social arrangements ensuring the dissemination of expertise in the prescription and administration of medicines, involving the division and sub-division of labour, the development of institutions, the creation of numerous forms of material infrastructure, and networks of agreements based on trust or contracts. The least-considered therapeutic action draws on fathomless aquifers of implicit knowledge, understanding, custom and practice.

In the next chapter, I will sketch the long journey that led us to this point where humanity began to pop its pills. For the present, I want to focus on the beginning of the journey. While whatever it was that made us takers of medicine sits at the heart of the difference between ourselves and animals, the science which gives scientific medicine its efficacy comes from seeing sick persons as if they were stricken animals. There is therefore a paradox: as medicine-takers we are not organisms but complex selves; but the effectiveness of the medicine we take is owed to a view of ourselves as organisms.[1] If we are to place medicine and its present discontents in perspective, and understand both its achievements and its limitations, we must bear this paradox in mind: medicine's triumphs are rooted in a biological understanding of sickness while the science, the art, the humanity of medical care is a supreme expression of the distance of humans from their biology.

Humane, scientific medicine is a (very) recent manifestation of the special nature of a creature who, uniquely among sentient beings, has *knowledge*. Knowledge – articulated or propositional awareness formulated into factual information and abstract general principles – is utterly different from the sentience that all conscious animals (including human beings) possess. Medical expertise is a peculiar development of knowledge: it is directed upon the body of the knower, who is in the grip of the least mediated form of awareness, namely bodily suffering. It is hardly surprising, then, that truly scientific medicine is less than a hundred years old. It has taken a long time for 'the knowing animal' to look dispassionately at his own body, the place where knowledge first awoke.

No one, I expect, will count it a revelation that the practice of medicine is a manifestation of the special consciousness of human beings; that the reason sick ducks don't go to quacks is that they have a fundamentally different relationship to the world in which they live. This special consciousness, however, is worth examining because it contains not only the seeds of medicine but also the origin of the tensions that have always beset medical practice.[2]

At the root of the innumerable differences between animals that merely live (and suffer illness) and human beings who lead their lives (and, for example, seek help from doctors) is a difference in their relationship to their own bodies. The animal lives its body; the human being not only lives its body but also explicitly and deliberately utilizes it, possesses it and *exists* it. (The awkward transitive is intended to reflect the active expropriation of the human body by its 'owner'.) This difference originates in the emergence, several million years ago, of the full-blown hand which acquired the status of a tool. This proto-tool has a wider instrumentalizing effect: it makes both the hominid's body and the surrounding world into a potential tool kit. Several other consequences follow. The hand tool, which instrumentalizes the body and its world, awakens not only a sense of agency but also suffuses the organism with a sense of 'am'. The consciousness of the organism is transformed into a subject: the subject is 'within' the body, not entirely merged with it (as in the case of a sentient animal) but, in a sense, 'owning', 'having', 'possessing', 'utilizing' it. As subjects, we experience our bodies as objects as well as suffering them as more or less invisible destiny. This is not to imply that we are separate from our bodies as Descartes imagined. Human consciousness can never be entirely liberated from the flesh; on the contrary, humans *assume* their bodies, or parts of them, as themselves and use other parts of their bodies to serve their purposes as tools, as means to action.

Within the human body there are many layers of subjects and objects, of agents and tools. These primordial corporeal tools are, of course, supplemented by extra-corporeal tools of ever greater complexity, requisitioned for a variety of purposes. The proto-tool that is the hand instrumentalizes not only the body but the world outside of it. As the philosopher Martin Heidegger said, the world with which the human subject engages in busy everyday life is, to a greater or lesser degree, a nexus of tools or of potential tools – what he called 'the ready-to-hand'.[3]

The sense that those tools are 'objects', that they have properties in themselves that are not entirely dissolved into their relationships with the user, lies at the root of science. The fundamental intuition of science is that the things that lie around us are only partially open to direct scrutiny: they have something 'in themselves' that is beyond the direct deliverances of our senses; and there is, therefore, more sense to be made, more to be known. What John Dewey called the 'active uncertainty' of human enquiry – systematized in the multifarious enterprises of science – owes its origin to this feeling that objects have a reality beyond their immediate appearance.

The world experienced by the merely sentient animal has no objects (objects in themselves) because the creature is not fully developed as a subject. Consciousness of self – which is not present, except perhaps fleetingly, in other animals[4] – makes apparent to the human creature the incomplete transparency of its own body. A human being's encounter with its own body as an object lies at the origin of object knowledge: the intuition of one's own body as being only partially available to oneself, intensified by an increasing awareness of oneself as a subject, awakens the uniquely human sense of living in a world comprised of objects of incomplete scrutability. Incomplete identification with one's own body lies at the basis of the intuition that eventually gives rise to objective or factual knowledge.

As knowledge grows, its relationship to sense experience becomes less direct. This is in part because knowledge is a collective or collectivized form of awareness: whereas sentience is solitary, knowledge is always actually or potentially shared. The collectivization of awareness is most obviously underpinned by language. Language, however, is a relative newcomer: the socialization of awareness, and the transformation of the spatial cohabitation of beasts into the more complex modes of togetherness of human societies, was originally mediated by the tools that were suggested by, or extensions of, the proto-tool that is the hand.

There are obvious ways in which tools might facilitate socialization, indeed collectivization, of human consciousness; for example, they are held in common and they are publicly visible. More fundamentally, they symbolize the needs they serve, making problems and solutions visible in shared space. More fundamentally still, they embody and signify those needs in a generalized way. Tools are consequently proto-linguistic; forerunners (by several million years) of the signs of language. It is no coincidence that the demands made on the brain by tool use are similar to those that are required for language.

This philosophical excursus is meant to underline the wide, deep gap between man, the medicine-taking non-animal and non-medicine-taking animals, between leaf-dabbing chimps and pill-popping humans. While medicine has much in common with many other complex human practices, it is rather special. Although the body apprehended by the human subject may have been the primordial object, or the primordial bearer of object-sense, treating the body itself as an object among objects, an object like any other – the necessary precursor of systematic medicine – was a late development. The collectivization and intellectualization of human consciousness was well advanced before there arose the fully developed notion of the human body as an object – and subsequently as an object of care to which abstract knowledge might be applied.

The transition from sentience to self-awareness, from sense experience to object knowledge, is the ultimate source of the medical gaze in which our bodies are objects of knowledgeable care. It seems doubtful that any animal 'worries' about falling ill or interprets abnormal sensations or bodily failings, with or without an evident external cause, as 'symptoms'. Animal suffering is present experience and not a sign of possible future experiences, or future bodily states. Conceiving of her body as a vulnerable organism, with an endangered future as well as an uncomfortable present, requires an individual human being to be at once outside of her body and identified with it; to be its subject and at the same time see it objectively; to suffer it as her being and know it as an object.

This is what lies at the bottom of Yeats' seemingly paradoxical assertion that 'Man created death'. The animal who created death also invented disease, labelling decay, or the heightened possibility of it, with the names of sicknesses, and invented medicine to postpone the one and ward off and treat the other.

The cognitive pre-history of medicine is, of course, unwritten. The written record shows how long and difficult was the subsequent journey to scientific medicine. We shall examine this journey very briefly in the next chapter, with the primary purpose of demonstrating that it was by no means inevitable that it should have reached its present remarkable destination. If the phenomenon of human knowledge is 'the greatest miracle in the universe',[5] medical knowledge – pre-scientific and scientific – is one of the most extraordinary manifestations of that great miracle. It required much cognitive 'self-overcoming' on the part of humanity.

2

The Miracle of Scientific Medicine

These conquests have been made possible only by a never-ending struggle against entrenched error, and by an unflagging recognition that the accepted methods and philosophical principles underlying basic research must be constantly revised... Disease is as old as life, but the science of medicine is still young.

Jean Starobinski[1]

The long journey to biomedical science

I have described some conditions necessary for the emergence of *Homo therapeuticus*. They are not, of course, sufficient in themselves nor are they specific to medicine. Indeed, the process of placing medicine on an objective basis is not complete even today.[2] While we do not know how recent medicine-taking is, we do know that scientific therapeutics is little more than a century old.

It is hardly surprising that the objective inquiries of *Homo scientificus* should have been directed rather late to the human body – to the body of the inquirer. Since it is out of our special relationship to our bodies that knowledge has grown, the pursuit of objective knowledge about the body and its illnesses requires a return to the very place where knowledge first awoke. Somewhat less esoterically, we may anticipate that the body 'we look out of' should be the kind of object we are most likely to 'look past'. It is something that we *are* as well as something we know or use; mired in subjectivity, it was a late focus for systematic objective inquiry. Humans found it easier to assume an objective attitude towards the stars than towards their own inner organs: scientific astronomy antedated scientific cardiology by thousands of years.

Scientific medicine required the assumption of an attitude to the human body similar to that which physical scientists had adopted towards other objects in the world: a 'depersonalization' and ultimately 'dehumanization' of the human body. (None of these terms is meant pejoratively: they are all necessary conditions of effective – humane and non-fraudulent – medical care.) Progress was neither smooth nor swift. Even less was it inevitable. 'Physic' had to extricate itself from a multitude of pre-scientific world-views. Other sciences had had to negotiate such obstacles: the heliocentric theory and the notion of the elliptical orbits of the planets, for example, faced opposition from theologically based ideas about the proper order of things, and how, consequently, God would order them. They had to displace more intuitively attractive notions of the principles governing the movement of objects. In the case of knowledge of the body and its illnesses, resistance to objective understanding was particularly intimate and adherent. The brief observations that follow are not intended even to outline all the steps leading to the forms of medicine we know today. Their purpose is solely to emphasize what had to be overcome during the passage from the first therapeutic intuitions to scientific practice.

In the earliest recorded phase of medicine, sickness was attributed to ill will, malevolent spirits, sorcery, witchcraft and diabolical and divine interventions. Illness and recovery were interpreted in providential and supernatural terms.[3] Illness was about *persons* rather than bodies and was often seen as punishment.

The secular world-views postulated in early Greek science opened up the possibility of a naturalistic understanding of illness. 'Natural causation theories which view illness as a result of ordinary activities that have gone wrong – for example the effects of climate, hunger, fatigue, accidents, wounds, or parasites'[4] began to displace 'personal or supernatural causation beliefs, which regarded illness as harm wreaked by a human or superhuman agency'. The so-called 'sacred disease' – epilepsy – was nothing of the kind. It was caused by phlegm blocking the airways and the convulsions were the body's attempt to clear the blockage.[5] Crucially, the body was seen to be subject to the same laws as the world around it: it *was* a piece of nature. The theory of the four humours (blood, phlegm, choler and black bile), which corresponded directly with the four elements of nature (fire, water, air and earth), and dominated thinking from Hippocrates in the fifth century BCE to Galen in the second century CE, expressed this naturalistic approach. The aim of the doctor was to restore the balance of humours when it was disturbed. Analogous ideas held sway in Indian and traditional Chinese medicine.

The replacement of transcendental by naturalistic (though still intuitive) ideas of illness was an enormous step. It did not, however, bring real progress, except in so far as it removed a justification for inhumane attitudes to sick people. The step from intuitive theories of illness to science-based ones was as great as that from transcendental to naturalistic accounts of disease. It built on the Hippocratic denial of the 'sacred' nature of disease – and of the body that suffered from it – and allowed a new conception of illness, upon which European medicine was founded. In the sixteenth century we see this new conception active in the pursuit of the anatomical, physiological and pathological knowledge which eventually led to European medicine becoming, on account of its singular efficacy, world medicine.

Two events are crucial: the publication of Vesalius' great anatomical textbook, *De Humani Corporis Fabrica* (1543) and William Harvey's *De Motu Cordis* (1628). Both authors described how the body looked when exposed to the unprejudiced, undazzled gaze, what its structure was and how it, or part of it, might function. Cartesian dualism, which separated the spiritual from the natural in the human person, endorsed the mechanistic view of the body that was implicit in the work of proto-biomedical scientists such as Vesalius and Harvey. The idea of the body as a carnal machine emerged as an intellectual framework for a systematic investigation of its component mechanisms. The development of physics and chemistry from the seventeenth century onwards furnished the concepts, insights and facts necessary to translate general ideas about bodily mechanisms into specific accounts of how various parts – organs, systems, cellular components – worked. (The verb is itself illuminating.) Metaphors from the technology of the time – mechanical, hydro-dynamic, and later electrical – fed into the modelling process.

This desacralization, which permitted the body to be examined as a set of mechanisms and understood illness in terms of disorders of those mechanisms, was supported by another, not entirely distinct, intellectual trend: that of de-animation. Underpinning de-animation was the discrediting of vitalism – the assumption that living tissues and non-living matter belonged to irreducibly different orders of being. The demonstration that organic substances, such as urea (the end-product of protein metabolism in many species), which was derived from living creatures, could also be synthesized out of inorganic substances was a crucial step in the development of organic chemistry (a revealing hybrid) and eventually its mighty offshoot, biochemistry. The examination of non-living components of living tissues (isolated organs, cells, individual chemical substances) emerged as the high road to understanding health and disease.

While it was accepted long before Darwin that human health and disease could be illuminated by studies and experiments performed on animals, *The Origin of Species* provided blanket justification, if it was needed, of extrapolation from animals to humans. Since *Homo sapiens* was the product of the same processes as other species, there could be no principled limit to the applicability of animal research to human beings. While there were differences between species, similarities were more important. Biomedical sciences, which could progress faster on the basis of animal experiments, envisaged human beings as organisms like any other. The physiological or biochemical parameters that signified sickness or health were similar in monkeys and monarchs.

The sick body, a damaged carnal machine operating in accordance with the laws of physics and chemistry, is a far cry from the man or woman punished by the gods for some private peccadillo or ancestral wrong. Scientific medicine minimized the personal element in illness: disease was a manifestation of general biological processes. Illness, which could ultimately be understood in biochemical, chemical or even physical terms, was not only impersonal but in a sense inanimate. The component mechanisms were remote from the living, breathing, animate whole organism, and even more remote from the suffering endured by the whole person.

Each of these steps – desacralization, de-animation, dehumanization, and depersonalization of illness – which of course overlapped both conceptually and temporally, represents a huge collective leap of understanding. The consequences have been entirely benign: not only treatments that are effective to a degree unimaginable by our predecessors but also humanization of medical care. Priestly authorities, supposed representatives of vast invisible forces, and bearers of terror, were banished from the sickbed. Gratuitous cruelty inflicted by those pretending to intercede on behalf of the sick, often justified by the ill person's supposed responsibility for her illness, had no place in scientific medicine. Healing (notwithstanding the complaints that will be discussed in later chapters) was separated from amorphous or pervasive power – the power of priests and shamans and of the social order they support. The obverse of this was the increasing accountability of healers – a trend which led to the establishment of regulatory authorities which policed the behaviour of healers and monitored their procedures and outcomes against collectively agreed professional and ethical standards.

One of the healthiest features of scientific medicine was the separation in time between the acquisition of knowledge (of the body and its ailments) and the ability to use such knowledge to effect cures. Biomedical science did not at once translate into science-based medical practice. It was recognized that true science was full of disappointments while only charlatans hit the jackpot every time. The disappointments were salutary: they undermined the intuitive certainties that had arrested progress. Uncertainty as to whether even robust knowledge would lead to effective treatments dissolved the priestly 'knowledge-healer-authority' complex. There was also disciplinary separation: the rise of the *non-clinical* biomedical scientist meant that those who generated the knowledge were not necessarily those who applied it.

Medicine, as Jean Starobinski pointed out, is still a young science. The dissolution of the 'knowledge-healer-authority' complex is not yet complete. Even now, effective practitioners have something of the charismatic healer mixed with the scientific doctor. A doctor brings personality as well as knowledge to the bedside. The rise of scientific medicine, however, put the instilling of confidence on the basis of personal authority in its proper place. Decreasing personal authority is healthy, and unique to modern Western medicine.

Another, equally profound, consequence of the rise of scientific medicine was the increasing distance between knowledge of the body and of sickness and intuitive or common-sense understanding of disease. Science, as Lewis Wolpert has pointed out, is deeply counter-intuitive, to the point of being unnatural.[6] To import that 'unnatural' standpoint into the body, where knowledge and understanding began, was an extraordinary achievement. A striking example is the understanding of the circulation of the blood. The beating of the heart is something we all experience; whereas the surprising fact that the blood circulates around the arteries and veins and through the capillaries had to be realized by an individual of genius. For less than a ten-thousandth part of the millions of years that hominids have been aware of the beating of their hearts have they known that the blood that is set in motion by these pulsations is circulating around their bodies.

From modest counter-intuitive beginnings such as this, a vast continent of knowledge about the body and its blood has grown. The dependence of my well-being upon, for example, my blood pressure or the level of potassium in my serum will not be something I can perceive by means of introspection. Biomedical science knows things about me in general that I could not directly intuit. 'The heart', Pascal said, 'has reasons that reason knows not.' Scientific medicine has taught us that the body has mechanisms that the embodied know not. It undermines both personal and socially mediated preconceptions.

The discrediting of common sense as a guide to understanding ill-health has profound connections with one of the most impressive and powerful engines of knowledge acquisition: scepticism and a willingness to live with, indeed to prolong, uncertainty. The sceptical physician is no less passionate about bringing the quest for cures to a successful conclusion than the traditional healer, but he is able to separate his passion from his procedures and his conclusions. This preparedness to expose ideas and claims to objective testing gradually permeated clinical medicine. (Though, as we shall see, only recently has it become ubiquitous.) Nietzsche's aphorism that 'convictions are greater enemies of truth than lies' identifies by default the drivers of true progress At its edges, scientific medicine is in constant quarrel with itself. Unlike traditional medicine, it does not take the antiquity of its ideas as independent evidence of their truth and efficacy; on the contrary, every assumption and assertion is to be tested and re-tested using ever more ingenious methodologies. Its cumulative body of reliable knowledge is the product of permanent civil war.

While scientific medicine had to advance in the teeth of prior (theological and other) convictions, it had also to overturn immediate ('common sense') and mediated ('cultural') intuitions about the nature of health and disease. What is more, these intuitions were often supported by systems of thought, themselves backed up by institutions with authority, power and menaces, and by the less organized forces of deception and self-deception. On top of all this, it had to insert longer and longer chains of argument, knowledge, and expertise between the body and its care for itself. Medical science has transformed the self-consciousness of the hominid body into a vast corpus of mediated understanding. Let me illustrate this with a personal example.

A little while back, I came to believe that I had dyspepsia due either to a stomach ulcer or to a reflux of acid into my oesophagus. I arrived at this seemingly straightforward conclusion as a result of accessing a body of knowledge and understanding that had taken many centuries to assemble. The first intimation that this might be my problem was noticing that my recurrent discomfort had a certain pattern. I was able to match this pattern against a variety of conditions whose naming has been the outcome of a vast effort of conceptualization and empirical research. My interrupted interior monologue as to what the pain might mean drew on facts and concepts emerging out of the cooperative effort of many thousands of people scattered over widely disparate times and places.

In order to test my diagnosis, I undertook a therapeutic trial of lansoprazole, a drug for dyspepsia. This seemingly simple act was not, of course, at all simple. Inserting the pill into my mouth was an act whose rationale drew on many disparate realms of intellectual achievement and human endeavour and indirectly involved many institutions, professions and trades. The manufacture, packaging and transport of the pills (which, I see, have been imported from Italy) engage many kinds of expertise, each of which incorporates and presupposes other forms of expertise. Some of these lie outside of strictly medical knowledge: the technologies of invoicing, lorry manufacture, the synthesis of plastic capsules, automated packaging, quality control in mass production, all meet in this tablet. James Buchan reflects that a banknote is 'an outcrop of some vast mountain of social arrangements, rather as the little peaks called *nunataks* that I later marvelled at in Antarctica, are the tips of Everest buried under miles of ice'.[7] This applies a thousand times over to the capsule that I swallowed in the hope of curing my discomfort. While it is true of any manufactured item, as Adam Smith pointed out,[8] the distinctive miracle of this example of science-based technology deserves more attention.

Lansoprazole belongs to a class of drugs called 'proton pump inhibitors'. They prevent the active transport of hydrogen ions (that is to say, atoms of hydrogen minus their electrons) across the semi-permeable membrane that constitutes the lining of some of the cells that coat the stomach wall. The point of proton pump inhibition is to switch off the secretion of hydrochloric acid. While hydrochloric acid has a role in creating an environment favourable to the first stage of digestion of food, it may also attack the lining of the very organ from which it is secreted, causing peptic ulcers, or alternatively wash up into the oesophagus, causing reflux oesophagitis. Each of these terms – proton, active transport, semi-permeable membrane, hydrochloric acid, digestion, reflux oesophagitis – is a node in a web of countless concepts, and the product of discussion spread over vast numbers of papers and presented in numerous scientific meetings and letters and corridor conversations. The pill is a meeting point of many hundreds of nunataks, the tips of Everests of discovery and their technological application.

In order to appreciate the complexity of the scientific discourse I have glanced at, consider some of the terms I have employed. For example, the notion of 'a proton' comes from fundamental physics; the concept of a semi-permeable membrane from physical chemistry; that of active transport comes from biochemistry; of acid secretion from physiology (and some famous experiments); and the esoteric idea of proton pump inhibition from the pharmacological application of biochemistry. I have not even considered the many layers of the drug delivery system which ensure that it arrives in the right quantity and in good condition at the places in my body where it does its work. Nor have I examined the dovetailing of the different components of the system – the capsule, the blister pack, the cardboard box, the pharmacist, the prescription, the educational institutions that enabled me to prescribe the right tablet – necessary to present the drug to my acid-scorched mucosa.

Scientific medicine delivers – life expectancy

While it is entirely proper to be impressed by the science, technology and sociology of medicine, it is equally proper to ask what it has done for mankind. An account that did any kind of justice to the achievements of science-based medicine would occupy many volumes. I shall settle for a few observations.

The most direct measure of success is postponement of death, and on this medicine has delivered handsomely. Global life expectancy has more than doubled over the last 140 years.[9] Nearly two thirds of the increase in longevity in the entire history of the human race has occurred since 1900.[10] If we narrow our gaze for a while and look simply at the data for England and Wales in the first fifty years of the NHS,[11] the news remains pretty extraordinary. Infant mortality fell from 39/1000 to 7/1000 for girls and from 30/1000 to 5/1000 for boys; and the proportion of people dying before reaching 65 from 40 per cent to 7 per cent. Life expectancy at birth increased by nearly a decade – from 66 to 74.5 for men and from 70.5 to just under 80 for women – during the second half of the twentieth century. If we look at the last century as a whole, the changes are even more amazing. Whereas the proportion of deaths that occurred between 0 and 4 years of age was 37 per cent in 1901, it was 0.8 per cent in 1999; and while only 12 per cent of deaths in 1901 were in people above 75, 64 per cent of all deaths in England and Wales in 1999 were among people over the age of 75.[12]

Much of this may be attributed to factors beyond medicine narrowly understood. Increasing prosperity, better nutrition, education, public hygiene, housing, health and safety at work, the emergence of liberal democracies protecting individuals against exploitation and abuse, and social welfare policies have all played their part. It is easy, however, to underestimate the contribution of medical science.[13] Admittedly, much of the fall in mortality at all ages during the first half of the last century was due to declining death rates from infectious diseases, especially at younger ages, to which the contribution of specific treatments was relatively small. For example, reduced mortality from respiratory tuberculosis (which alone accounted for 20 per cent of the increase in life expectancy of the UK population between 1871 and 1911) occurred before effective treatments and specific preventative measures such as BCG immunization had been discovered. Perhaps as little of two out of the twenty-five years of increased life expectancy between 1900 and 1950 in USA and UK were directly due to medical treatments.[14]

It is easy to misunderstand the significance of these facts. The public health measures that reduced premature deaths from infectious diseases were shaped by the rationalistic understanding of disease that owed its origin to an emergent medical science: successful public health is informed by medical as well as social science. It is no coincidence that the steepest declines in deaths from infectious diseases came in the wake of the final decades of the nineteenth century in which Robert Koch and Louis Pasteur raced each other to the identification of the micro-organisms causing tuberculosis, cholera and other decimators of humanity. They placed the germ theory on a firm footing and created a scientific framework for public health measures. The importance of the scientific approach to public hygiene is dramatically illustrated by the contrast between the success of Western attitudes to infectious diseases and the catastrophic and continuing failure of traditional approaches based upon theological and moralistic notions of purity and impurity (for example those that underpin the caste system in India).[15]

In recent decades, moreover, when public health infrastructure has been a constant and reliable factor, the proportional contribution of specific medical treatments to improved life expectancy in developed countries has risen. The American physician and commentator J. P. Bunker has estimated that about half of the gains in the UK since the inception of the NHS have been due to medical treatments.[16] The absolute increase in life expectancy in the developing world and the contribution to this of medicine in the widest sense – medical science, medical practice and what we may call 'scientific medical intelligence' or 'a medically informed outlook' – is even greater.

More telling still is the fact that life expectancy has continued to rise sharply in older people long after public health measures and social policies have been fully in place: life expectancy at birth increased in the last two decades of the twentieth century by 4.7 years for man and 3.5 years for women;[17] male life expectancy at age 65 in England and Wales increased from just under 12 years to just under 15 years between 1970 and 1995 – a little more than in the whole period from 1900 to 1970. (Similarly encouraging figures apply to females.) During this period, estimates indicated that the percentage of people in England and Wales surviving to 85 more than doubled: in males from 11.4 to 24.2, and in females from 27 to 41. Perhaps most telling of all, life expectancy in the UK in both males and females increased by nearly a year in the first half of the 1990s, when the malign impact of a decade of Tory assault on state welfare was at its height.[18]

So while scientific medicine is not acting alone, its contribution – once the foundation stones of public hygiene and a welfare state are in place – is proportionately greater. Unless a new politician with Mrs Thatcher's destructive fervour comes along, this proportionate contribution of medicine to health gains will continue to rise.

Scientific medicine delivers – quality of life

If medicine prolonged life without alleviating suffering, this would scarcely be cause for congratulation. However, the impact of medicine on the traditional sources of discomfort and misery – pain, itch, nausea, immobilization, decay – is even more impressive than its impact on life expectancy. This is true even in old age in developed countries, as we shall see in Chapter 8, where many have (incorrectly) suggested that increased life expectancy has been bought at the cost of increased suffering. The example I want to give here, however, is a recent (and not atypical) triumph in a developing country.

In 1999, the World Health Organization announced the virtual elimination of onchocerciasis, 'River Blindness', in much of its West African home.[19] This was the result of a programme of control inaugurated in 1974. Blindness is caused by dead microfilarial larvae of *Onchocerca volvulus*, produced for up to 15–18 years by adult worms inside the eye. The disintegrating bodies of the worms damage the cornea. The beneficial results of the elimination programme are both immediate and long-term. It has saved 100,000 people at immediate risk of contracting the disease and prevented the potential infection of nearly 12 million children. In addition, 1.25 million people have lost their onchocercal infection through the programme. Removing the threat of infection has allowed people to farm the 25 million hectares of fertile land, capable of feeding 17 million people a year, that had been abandoned as a result of infestations of the black fly that carried the filaria.

Thus was eliminated a scourge that had literally darkened the lives of many millions of Africans since time immemorial and had had catastrophic effects on the economic well-being of entire villages, indeed, entire populations. This triumph was the outcome of advances in a multitude of medical sciences, of dozens of cognitive nunataks, all of which are taken so much for granted that they are almost invisible.

First, recognition of the disease as a specific entity, distinct from other conditions causing blindness, such as trachoma and vitamin deficiency, was a *tour de force* of descriptive clinical science. Identification of the correct insect carriers (the black fly) in a habitat teeming with thousands of candidates was equally remarkable. It built on the notion of insects as 'disease vectors'. This presupposed a grasp of insect anatomy and physiology, speciation and parasitology.

The incrimination of the filarian worm as the cause of the disease also required knowledge and wisdom to interpret, observe, identify and inculpate micro-organisms in the blood of sufferers. Further, stringent criteria for separating innocent bystanders and secondary opportunist infections from primary causative organisms had to be applied with unremitting vigour. The identification of the dead larvae as the cause of the blindness – as the result of an immune, inflammatory reaction – required a further leap of understanding.

Equally, the development of drugs to treat the organisms without causing harm to the sufferer relied upon numerous bodies of knowledge: not only of the physiology of filarian worms and the kinetics, dynamics, hepatotoxicity, nephrotoxicity of potential pharmaceuticals, but also of the appropriate way to monitor the clinical, physiological and bio-chemical impact of the chosen drugs. The invention and assessment of Ivermectin – the cure developed in the late 1980s and the first appropriate drug that could be dispensed widely without fear of serious side effects – was an extraordinary achievement even if one overlooks the organic chemistry, chemical engineering and analytical techniques necessary to ensure mass production to a high standard of purity. On top of this, there was the practical knowledge necessary to overcome the obstacles that stand in the way of a rational public health initiative in a terrain where adverse climatic conditions (a hell of moist heat), disease, corruption, the threat of war, endemic poverty and malnutrition and, above all, application of traditional magic and superstition to thinking about disease and its causes, predominated.

Scientific medicine delivers – but only so much

The terrible story of AIDS occasioned another striking triumph of recent medicine. The recognition of AIDS as a specific disease, the identification of Human Immunovirus (HIV) as its cause and of the synergistic effects of other sexually transmitted diseases, malnutrition and other factors promoting the transition from HIV carriage to the full-blown disease; the development of rational policies to reduce spread through the population, and of drugs to prevent transmission of HIV and to treat AIDS – all this took a mere fifteen years. One only has to compare the 600 years it took for the cause of the Black Death to be understood to appreciate how scientific medicine has transformed our ability to respond to new diseases.

In many places, however, scientific triumphs have not translated into the alleviation of human suffering. The unremitting catastrophe of AIDS in sub-Saharan Africa is due not to the deficiencies of medical science, but to the failure to apply it because of irrationality and a misplaced national *amour-propre* which has delayed acknowledgement of the problem until it is too late. The effects of this delay have been compounded by the endemic sexual abuse of women, war, famine, poverty, and corrupt governments headed by murderous kleptocrats.

By contrast, quality-controlled medicine is effective because it is based upon a rational, though counter-intuitive, understanding of the pathophysiology of disease. This is remarkable not only on account of the science but for the way in which the community that has generated the science has been able collectively to overcome a multitude of weaknesses, frailties and temptations. Wishful thinking, superstition, corruption and deception are ubiquitous features of human life, and while biomedical scientists, clinical scientists and clinicians are still prey to them, they are nevertheless able to resist them collectively to a degree that is unique in human affairs.

The rewards for this have been immeasurable. Unlike most human beings in history (indeed, unlike most organisms), I did not die before reaching adult life. My survival to what is now called 'late middle age' makes me part of an even luckier minority. I have not brought to my middle years the heritage of chronic childhood disease. My own children are not the survivors of a permanent natural massacre of the innocents. I am not riddled with numerous undiagnosed and incurable infestations. Even if the illnesses that I eventually develop prove to be incurable, they will be significantly alleviated or at least palliated.

In this, and many other respects, I am privileged beyond the wildest dreams of my ancestors – thanks to those of my predecessors who were able to see past their dreams and look dispassionately at the object that, more than any other, is infused with subjectivity: the human body.

Scientific medicine has made the human body more human by acknowledging its intrinsic animality, its lack of divinity. It is this that has made it possible to displace the inhumanity of the body to the edges of human life.

3

The Coming of Age of the Youngest Science

It is hardly surprising that medicine is 'the Youngest Science'.[1] The furthering of our understanding of the human body had to await the maturation of natural sciences such as chemistry and physics. Scientific medicine also requires us to adopt an objective approach to the material basis of our existence and to treat dispassionately the horrors which engulf the part of the world with which we are most closely identified. That the body – the object at the root of objective knowledge – should have been the last to be illuminated by objective knowledge is precisely what might be expected. We humans have to make sense of disease from within the bituminous darkness of the relationship we have with our own bodies.

Between the sick human body and the gaze of the scientist, there have intervened many distorting lenses – authorities, prejudices, and preconceptions, both theological and secular. Scientific medicine is a triumph of human knowledge over superstition and irrationality, over intuitively attractive ideas, and over the temptation to exploit the fears of the sick and abuse the trust of the vulnerable.

The great sociologist, philosopher and anthropologist Ernest Gellner spoke of reason as 'a Cosmic Exile'.[2] Rationality has the weight of culture, custom, tradition and traditional authority lined up against it:

Reason is a foundling, not an heir of the old line, and its identity or justification, such as it is, is forged without the benefit of ancient lineage. A bastard of nature cannot be vindicated by ancestry but only, at best, by achievement. (p. 160)

And when reason is applied to something as terrifying, intimate and engulfing as illness, even 'achievement' is sometimes insufficient vindication.

There are inescapable tensions built into the very nature of science-based medicine. Unresolved and probably unresolvable, they bubble just under the surface, feeding the discontents that will be the central theme of this book. But before I discuss them, let us look at the steps that had to be taken by medicine before it could become a fully 'grown up' science.

The permanent self-criticism of scientific medicine

One of the arguments mobilized by alternative medicine practitioners (of whom more later) against orthodox medicine is that the latter is constantly changing while alternative medicine has remained largely unaltered for hundreds, even thousands, of years. This decade's favourite orthodox remedy, they point out, is next decade's also-ran.

This is true; there is a fringe of development at which medicine is indeed changing, but this is not the result merely of the fluctuation of fashion but a consequence of the discovery of new treatments that are more effective and have fewer side-effects than remedies previously on offer. Change reflects strengths rather than weaknesses in conventional medicine: it is not a question of replacing one useless drug with another but of replacing a useful drug with one that is more useful. This places the claim that alternative medicine remedies belong to 'an ancient tradition' in an interesting light. The lack of development in 5,000 years can be a good thing only if 5,000 years ago alternative practitioners already knew of entirely satisfactory treatments for conditions that orthodox medicine has only recently started to be able to cure or improve, or cannot yet cure or improve. (If they did, they have kept remarkably quiet about them.) The argument that venerability makes evaluation unnecessary[3] is based on a confusion between 5,000 years of use and 5,000 years of accumulated evidence of usefulness.

Unlike traditional medicine, which is deeply self-satisfied with its knowledge and what it believes to be its effectiveness, scientific medicine is driven by an active uncertainty that is sceptical of received ideas and of authority and is continually seeking to improve on the status quo. The contrast between the stagnation of alternative medicine and scientific medicine's dissatisfaction and constant transformation – resulting in ever more effective and, for the most part, less unpleasant treatments – is often misunderstood. A discipline which is marked by a carefully nurtured scepticism towards itself is sometimes seen as arrogant or in disarray.

The greatest of all the obstacles medicine has had to face in its journey towards a fully developed clinical science has been the overthrowing of its own authority. In an act of collective humility, it has cultivated a routine distrust of its own practices. This humility has been almost as important in the development of effective therapies as biomedical science. Let us examine its evolution.

The first step towards genuine evidence-based medical practice was the formal clinical trial. It is not enough for me to say of a treatment that 'I know it works' or (even) that 'My patients know it works'. It is not even good enough that those in whom I have faith – Aristotle or the Queen's physician – believe or assert that it works. The duration of the faith and belief makes no difference, either: just because a treatment has been prescribed with enthusiasm for many centuries doesn't prove it is effective. Tried doesn't mean tested. The humility of shaping clinical practice in accordance with the unmanipulated outcomes of therapeutic trials is also connected with another layer of scepticism: that what looks good in theory (irrespective of how good the theory is) may not benefit patients in the real world.

Perhaps the most remarkable facet of this humility is the willingness of doctors to enter patients (with the latter's consent) into trials run by other clinicians. Submission to the authority of such trials means sub-ordinating one's own personal authority to that of other professionals, many of whom (such as statisticians and biomedical scientists) do not even belong to the medical profession. As Marc Daniels pointed out:

[for clinicians] to be willing to merge their individuality sufficiently to take part in group investigations, to accept only patients approved by an independent team, and to submit results for analysis by an outside investigator involves considerable sacrifice.[4]

The design of the modern clinical trial assumes that, unless numerous safeguards are put in place, results will be distorted by wishful thinking. Clinical trials are 'double-blind': neither the patient nor the doctor knows whether the patient is receiving the new treatment or the old (where two treatments are being compared) or the new treatment or a placebo (where the new treatment is being compared with a dummy) until completion. In order to avoid bias that might come from entering patients with a better prognosis in the group that is receiving the new treatment, patients have to be allocated randomly, for example by means of computer-generated random numbers. This ensures that like is being compared with like.

The danger of bias was strikingly illustrated when I was in Nigeria. There I observed an involuntary trial comparing snake-bite treatment by the local hospital with the community's traditional healer. Most snake bites are unpleasant but not life-threatening and the majority of patients either seek no treatment or go to the traditional healer. Where snake bites settle, no more is heard of them: they are therapeutic successes. A small number of patients develop serious, and sometimes fatal, adverse consequences; they are the ones that go to hospital usually after an unsuccessful visit to the traditional healer. The traditional healer unsurprisingly had much better results in treating snake bites than the hospital did. Many of our patients died, whereas the healer's outcomes were almost invariably excellent. The greater apparent success of the healer was manifestly due to case selection: cases that went well remained on his list; those that went badly ended up in hospital.[5]

In order to guarantee that the results of a study are generalizable to the relevant population of patients, sufficient numbers of people have to be entered into the trial. This will avoid either a false positive outcome (an apparent benefit which is merely due to chance) or a false negative outcome (in which a real benefit is overlooked.) The calculations that guard against these errors are complex and have nothing to do with the opinion of physicians running the trial. Equally, when the data is analysed, the analysis must be guided by the prior hypothesis. 'Data dredging' to identify *post hoc* a sub-group of patients who seemed to have benefited is allowed only as a means of generating hypotheses for future studies. It cannot be regarded as a source of robust knowledge. The retrospective discovery that patients of a certain age or sex did better than those of a different age or sex cannot lead to the conclusion that such sub-groups of patients are particularly likely to benefit from the treatment, any more than the discovery that patients whose surnames began with 'R' did better implies that the treatment should be particularly directed at such individuals.

The complexity of clinical trials may be illustrated by one to which I contributed patients myself. The aim was to determine whether aspirin would be useful in patients who had had a stroke due to a clot in one of the blood vessels in the brain – the so-called 'ischaemic stroke'. Aspirin would seem to be a good thing because it reduces the propensity of blood to clot, and so might prevent extension of the thrombus after the stroke. However, it might also cause bleeding in the area affected by the stroke and so make the stroke worse. Only a properly conducted trial could determine the balance of risk and benefit. Power calculations indicated that it would be necessary to recruit about 10,000 patients to each side of the trial – aspirin and placebo – in order to avoid either a false positive or a false negative. This required that the study should be multi-centre (somewhat of an understatement: in all, 467 centres in 36 countries participated). About a decade after the study was first planned, the results were published in *The Lancet*:[6] aspirin produced a small – but clear-cut and worthwhile – reduction in mortality if given early. The following week *The Lancet* published another study of aspirin administered to acute stroke sufferers,[7] carried out in China, also requiring 20,000 patients, with an equally rigorous design, which came to an identical conclusion – illustrating how international good science is, and also the robustness of the results derived from it.

Mega-trials such as these were introduced in the 1980s and it is remarkable how short a time separates them from the period when prescribing was largely governed by tradition and personal opinion. My first boss in the early 1970s remembers his bosses – two titled grandees of British medicine – arguing over whether one or two spoonfuls of arsenic (a favourite remedy for many conditions) was the appropriate daily dose for tuberculosis.

Mega-trials also illustrate how medical science is a cooperative discipline. I was one out of perhaps a 1,000 physicians participating in the aspirin trial. As clinical scientists we are often merely ants contributing to the ant-heap of knowledge. This reflects a revolution in the sociology of clinical medicine: even those of us who aspire to be leaders of the profession (opinion leaders even) are embedded in a huge collective enterprise from which consensus about best practice is forged. As I look back at my own contributions over a quarter of a century of active medical research, I see that even those things that I regard as 'discoveries' add only a little to the body of collective knowledge and understanding, were arrived at in cooperation with others, and sometimes simply replicated findings that had been demonstrated in preliminary studies.

Notwithstanding the power of mega-trials, many clinicians and clinical scientists still feel that guidance from single trials is not sufficient for true evidence-based medicine. There are several reasons for believing this: the most important is a publication bias which means that (exciting) positive results are more likely to be written up, published and publicized than (disappointing) negative ones. There is also the problem of dealing with conflicting results: when one trial shows that drug A is more effective than drug B and another trial contradicts this, which trial should we believe? Until recently, clinical opinion was shaped or led (for those physicians who kept assiduously up to date) by 'expert' reviews: the reviewer would look over the literature and, where there was conflict, give an opinion as to which papers should carry the most weight. This is now regarded as insufficiently scientific – more like a student essay than a true research synthesis. Expert reviews have been displaced by 'systematic reviews' using a variety of techniques that limit bias in the assembly, critical appraisal, and synthesis of all relevant studies on a specific topic.[8]

Such techniques include 'meta-analysis', which permits the pooling of results from different studies, even though they may have slightly different designs. This is enormously labour-intensive and often involves going back to the raw data on individual patients. (A colleague of mine has spent nearly three years on a collaborative synthesis of trials comparing the efficacy of a handful of anti-epileptic drugs.) The overviews not only take into account the results of all the appropriate published trials but, in addition, search exhaustively for data from registered trials that have not been published. Searches have to encompass all publications irrespective of the languages they are written in. Systematic reviews are usually overseen by bodies that control for quality, scrutinizing both the proposals before the work is carried out and the final product, using stringent tests of validity. Two such bodies in the United Kingdom are the National Health Service Health Technology Assessment Programme and the Cochrane Collaboration.

The latter, which has achieved world-wide recognition and is, indeed, a multinational cooperative, was named after Archibald Cochrane, a visionary thinker. He observed, in an essay published in 1979:

that it is surely a great criticism of our profession [medicine] that we have not organized a critical summary, by speciality or sub-specialty, adapted periodically, of all relevant randomized controlled trials.[9]

This is what is happening in the Cochrane Centre, established as a result of the work of other visionaries, such as Iain Chalmers. His endeavours in establishing the methods, creating the institutions and fostering the collective will to fulfill Cochrane's vision, have made an enormous contribution to ensuring that effective treatments are made maximally available and ineffective ones discredited. (He has most certainly saved more lives than any other doctor I have met.) Systematic reviews, which have relegated 'expert opinion' to a rather low level of evidence (below systematic reviews, individual double-blind controlled trials, and open trials), are the bedrock of evidence-based medicine and the rationale for the numerous guidelines now available to clinicians who wish to offer their patients the best possible treatments. The GOBSAT (Good Old Boys Sitting Around a Table) sounding-off has been placed on permanent notice of dismissal!

The effectiveness (and side-effectiveness) of treatments is not the only consideration in clinical trials. There are limited resources, especially in a publicly funded service, and it is appropriate that those resources should be used for the greatest possible health gains. Cost effectiveness is therefore an issue. In England and Wales, the National Institute for Clinical Excellence (NICE) was established in the late nineties to determine whether new (and indeed some existing) treatments should be made generally available. It has become a model which is now being copied world-wide.

For three years, I was a member of one of the appraisal committees advising the NICE executive. The rigour and the complexity of the analysis of the scientific, clinical and economic data, and of the human and ethical issues, was extraordinary. Which is not to say that the decisions were unassailable: there was a margin of judgement. Even so, it was more rigorous than anything available in pretty well any other human institution.

Needless to say, the scrupulous and sustained application of science to delivering medical care has not met with universal acclaim. NICE has, for example, to distinguish between treatments that represent value for money and those that do not, so that the former can be made universally available and the 'post-code prescribing lottery', determined by the accidents of history and of local advocacy and the availability of expertise as well as the whims of those who commission services, is corrected. Its decisions have often provoked outrage either from those who feel that money is being wasted on insufficiently cost-effective treatments or from those who feel that patients should not have been deprived of such treatments.

In some cases the attacks on evidence-based medicine and on NICE and other sources of evidence-based clinical guidelines are intended as reminders that medical decision-making can never be automated. All patients are different and it is sometimes necessary to depart from conventional practice. The recent emphasis on narrative-based medicine, taking account of individual characteristics of patients, is a healthy corrective to the notion that medical practice can be reduced to a series of algorithms. While evidence-based medicine is a *necessary* condition of good medical care, it is not a *sufficient* condition. The evidence and the guidelines and protocols that are based upon it do not take the doctor all the way to the decision in an individual case. There is room for judgement, for application of common sense, and for modifying practice in the light of the patient's priorities. Those who depart from the guidance, however, should do so in full knowledge of the guidelines and document the reason for deviating from recommended practice.

Thanks to recent meta-analyses under the aegis of the Cochrane Collaboration, I think I have a better idea when, in general, to start anti-epileptic drugs in an elderly patient and which drug to try first. I shall still be guided, however, by the patient, in determining whether preventing a further fit is a greater priority than avoiding the side effects, however slight, of anti-epileptic drugs. A patient may prefer a minor seizure once a year to falling asleep every time she starts watching her favourite soap on TV.

Guidelines supported by meta-analyses, moreover, do not spare clinicians the necessity for courage in making and sticking by 'best guess' decisions in what are often 'probabilistic' situations. Since this seems obvious, why has evidence-based medicine sometimes been mocked as the abrogation of responsibility or of common sense? The resistance even of some physicians to maximizing the input of science, of reliable knowledge, into their decision-making shows that even they are not always immune from the 'regressive temptation'.[10] Reasons and numerical evidence are often unsatisfactory to work with: they have no connotative odour; they do not seem one's own. And this, of course, is their glory and the true power of evidence-based, science-based medicine.

There is a profound irony in the fact that, when medicine is increasingly willing to put to the test the validity of authoritative opinion, those who wish to carry out high-quality research are regarded with mounting suspicion and are faced with more and more obstacles to their endeavours – in the name of patient protection. And yet, of all the signs of the maturity of medical science, the most impressive, and the most important for patient welfare, has been the insistence on testing all new treatments in ever more rigorous clinical trials. This often meets with profound hostility. The very words 'research' and 'drug trial' are associated in the public mind with 'experimentation' on 'human guinea pigs'. It is not appreciated that the use of treatments that have not been fully evaluated is not only an experiment but one from which one will learn nothing of benefit to other patients.

When Dr Spock, with the best of intentions, gave the evidence-free advice that babies should not sleep on their backs, such was his authority that he probably caused thousands, if not tens of thousands, of avoidable sudden infant deaths.[11] And yet anyone who had suggested testing his advice by randomizing babies to be nursed on their backs or their fronts would have faced a storm of abuse. Iain Chalmers quotes a *Lancet* editorial published in 1990 which notes the paradox that:

the clinician who is convinced that a certain treatment works will almost never find an ethicist in his path, whereas his colleague who wonders and doubts and wants to learn will stumble over piles of them.[12]

The widespread failure to understand clinical uncertainty, and the fact that it is uncertainty that justifies clinical trials, can make life very difficult for those who want to advance medical knowledge. Without that understanding – that the medical community genuinely does not know whether Promising Treatment A is better than Routine Treatment B – the purpose and ethical standing of double-blind controlled trials will not be apparent. The recent persecution of Professor David Southall indicates the risks all clinical researchers run.[13]

Professor Southall is a paediatrician who carried out a study comparing two ways of ensuring that premature babies receive sufficient oxygen after birth: the standard approach and a new type of ventilator machine. The study was approved by the ethics committee and all babies in the trial were entered with the informed consent of the parents. The mother of a child who developed cerebral palsy following a bleed into the brain (as frequently happens in the case of marked prematurity) decided that it was due to the experimental treatment and also claimed that she did not know that the baby was in a trial. When presented with the original consent form that she had signed, she asserted that 'it looks very much like my signature. All I can say is that if I signed the form I did not know what I was signing for.' Despite this, the paediatrician (along with his colleague) was suspended, was pilloried in the press, (unfounded accusations were reported),[14] every aspect of his research was crawled over by lawyers and journalists, his family (as is the way) was threatened, and he was the subject of several inquiries. He was compared by one aggrieved parent, whose views were widely reported in the media, to Josef Mengele.

A report by the West Midlands Regional Health Director Rod Griffiths was presented in the press as giving Southall 'a good kicking', although a study of this report, published in the *British Medical Journal*[15] concluded that 'almost every statement made about the design, conduct and reporting of the neonatal CNEP trial in [it] was ill-informed, misguided or factually wrong.' The Department of Health subsequently retracted parts of the Griffiths report and acknowledged that the clinical trial was, for its time, of a high standard. The Minister responsible, however, stated in answer to a question raised in the House of Lords, that 'he had no reason to believe that the review was not conducted properly'.[16] At the time of writing, Southall and his colleague still have to face the General Medical Council. As the *Guardian* comments, one lesson of this disgraceful episode is that doctors should be allowed 'the common privilege of not being considered guilty until they are convicted'. This will not, of course, be possible until the default assumption that courageous, imaginative and energetic researchers are akin to the Nazi Mengele is regarded with contempt and disgust.

Iain Chalmers' observation is pertinent here:

People not infrequently raise questions about the ethics of well-controlled randomized experiments designed to address uncertainties about the effects of inadequately evaluated policies and practices. They would do well to consider the ethics of acquiescing in professional promulgation of the same policies and practices among recipients who have not been made aware either of the lack of reliable evidence of their effects, or of the real reasons that they are being recommended to accept these interventions.[17]

The commitment to minimizing the role of chance, of bias, or of wishful thinking, is what scientific medicine requires. Avoiding beliefs guided by delusive hope, unfounded authority, superstition and plain stupidity, it cultivates an attitude of healthy scepticism towards itself to prevent its practitioners from misleading themselves or their patients. Its permanent strategy of active uncertainty, and the humility this implies, is the distinctive virtue of scientific medicine. In the world outside of scientific medicine, however, humanity has had little time to adjust to this almost inhuman scrupulousness.

PART TWO

Contemporary Discontents

The purpose of the first section of *Hippocratic Oaths* was two-fold: to make the extraordinary nature of medicine visible; and to highlight its inevitable tensions. These tensions may be expressed as discontents with medical care and it is these that are the focus of the second, most substantive section of the book. The connection between present discontents and fundamental tensions is not always straightforward. It is certainly not the case that every 'scandal' or 'crisis' in medicine is the direct result of the incompleteness of our liberation from our organic basis, the human body. Even so, without this background it will be difficult to make useful sense of the troubled surface of contemporary medicine and of the direction it is taking. At any rate, it may help us to separate those troubles that are truly superficial from those that are connected with enduring problems, and to address these problems with the depth of understanding they deserve and rarely get.

The chapters that follow try to cover the noisiest issues without the agenda being determined solely by the volume of noise they have provoked: communication, time, power (of doctors and of patients), trust and distrust, the enemies of the progress that medical care should and could make, the influence of the law and of journalism, and the appalling burden of responsibility assumed by doctors – all have a significance that is not encompassed in the tabloid agenda.

4

Communication, Time, Waiting

Making sense of illness

'Poor communication' is the most commonly reported reason for dissatisfaction with, and complaints against, doctors.[1] This is hardly surprising. Communication between patient and doctor pervades all aspects of medicine: not all doctors carry out operations but every physician spends most of his or her time communicating with patients. Concern about communication also touches on many other discontents: the paternalistic attitudes of 'god-like' doctors, time pressures, and the question of trust. Communication, as we shall see, also illustrates the extent to which current discontents are or are not remediable.

In 1993, the General Medical Council, the regulatory body overseeing medical education in the UK, issued new guidelines to medical schools. *Tomorrow's Doctors*[2] advocated a shift from passive rote-learning and fact-dominated courses to more active problem-based, student-led inquiry, focusing on core knowledge and general principles. Mindful of the high level of complaints from the public, it also directed that there should be an emphasis throughout training on communication. It could no longer be assumed that a well-informed, motivated, respectful student would come out of medical school equipped to communicate well with patients.

Teaching good communication skills now figures prominently in the curriculum and such teaching is no longer left to senior doctors: educationalists and lay people are also involved. Students are tested not only on their ability to take a history, to conduct a physical examination, and to arrive at a diagnosis and a management plan, but are also assessed on how well they communicate with patients. This is taught and examined in minute detail. The student's demeanour, his or her ability to place the patient at ease, the initial use of open rather than closed questions, checking with patients whether they have been properly understood, exploring underlying beliefs, fears and concerns about the illness, are all scored. Students are instructed in the posture of 'active listening' – making eye contact, murmuring 'aha' at intervals, leaning forwards, mirroring the patient – and all the other verbal and non-verbal apparatus of the process of reception. They have to know not only how to be good listeners but also how to signify their good listening to the patient. They are invited to consider what lessons they might derive from their own experiences as patients. They also observe each other interviewing patients (or simulated patients) and discuss the performance afterwards, carefully adhering to the rules for feedback, specifying first what went well and then what might have been done differently, after having allowed the interviewer and the interviewee to give their views.

In short, they are taught how to *perform* the role of a good – listening, caring, empathetic – doctor. Some find this a bit unnecessary. The notion that listening sympathetically and intelligently to someone telling you their troubles should have to be taught weakens the assumption that it is fundamental to being a decent human being; making it an acquired skill seems to undermine sincerity. And, of course, it does; because sincerity is beside the point. Most people's sincere emotions on hearing of the troubles of strangers are not helpful and may in fact be negative. When the number of strangers runs into ten of thousands – as in the case of a general practitioner who will have between a quarter and half a million appointments in the course of a forty-year career – then the normal reaction will certainly be inadequate and possibly damaging. Doctors have to be taught to exhibit superhuman empathy and attentiveness if they are not going to appear inattentive or even inhumane. A doctor who brought to his or her practice behaviour considered normal in the world outside of medicine – if he or she had not been cured of at least some of the tactlessness with which most humans are born – would be a disaster.

If poor communication is still the subject of a rising number of complaints this may not be because doctors are especially bad communicators but because they are not sufficiently better at communication than the great majority of their fellow human beings. They must act out, or develop, a manner consistent with intense empathy, irrespective of whether they feel empathetic. Otherwise they will leave their patients dissatisfied, upset, or even shocked. The thirtieth patient of the day is as entitled to a faultless performance as the first.

This is a tough challenge and some doctors meet it very well; so well in some cases that they evade judgement of their medical competence. People rarely sue a doctor who smiles a lot, it used to be said. Avuncular, kindly doctors who look tired and concerned are more likely to get away with technically poor medicine than a brusque, technically competent doctor will get away with failing to show that he or she cares. The *process* often weighs more in patients' judgement of their care than the *outcome*, particularly if the outcome is good.

CASE 1 **The General Practitioner**

I remember the time [Dr X] gave to my Dad. He would come round at the drop of a hat. He was a marvellous GP.[3]

This is the patient's son speaking. Dr X had all the characteristics of a 'good' general practitioner: avuncular, kind, and very tired-looking, weighed down by the burden of caring for his community.[4] He also happened to be one of the most prolific serial killers Europe has known. The people of Hyde refused at first to accept the charges against Dr Shipman. Their belief that he was wonderful was based entirely upon the impression he gave of tireless commitment to their well-being; his manner, his visibility, his availability. The appalling death rate among his patients, and the frequency with which he was present at their deaths, would – one might have thought – have raised questions about his competence, even if it was unthinkable to question his motivation. But his outcomes did not seem to weigh in the community's assessment of his 'goodness' as a doctor.

CASE 2 **The Consultant Surgeon**

And then he spoiled it. He said it was unusual to find gallstones in someone so young – I was in my mid-twenties – since sufferers are normally 'the four F's: fair, fat, fertile, and forty. You're certainly not three of those but hopefully you're still fertile!' I was mortified.[5]

The patient (who described herself as 'mortified') is a woman who had a painful and potentially dangerous condition – gallstones – diagnosed first time round, despite the fact that, as the consultant was trying to point out, she didn't fit the stereotype. She was subsequently treated successfully with advanced, minimally invasive technology that enabled her to leave hospital in two days and resume normal life shortly after, as opposed to the usual ten-day stay and six weeks off work. An excellent outcome. But where the communication is judged by the patient to be poor, the excellent outcome is (it seems) irrelevant and neither gratitude nor mercy is to be shown. The article was headlined 'How I fell foul of the NHS'.[6]

It seems that, ten years after *Tomorrow's Doctors*, much remains to be done, not only to ensure that doctors communicate better with patients, but also to ensure that doctors create a setting in which patients are enabled to engage with the doctors effectively.[7] Complaints against doctors are increasing, with communication still flagged up as the leading ground for complaint. This suggests that the new training is not having the desired impact. Nor has the feminization of the profession – women are now in the majority among doctors under thirty – made much difference, notwithstanding that women are said to be better communicators than men. So what is happening?

Communication about an illness begins, long before the patient sees the doctor, with patients' internal dialogue about what their bodies seem to be saying. This will colour the description and interpretation of their symptoms and determine which of those symptoms, and which aspects of them, they will count as relevant. Description, analysis and interpretation – and the beliefs to which they give rise – will have been modified and elaborated by conversations with family and friends, and by what they have heard or seen in the media. The story they find themselves narrating will often seem to be only one out of a large number of possible stories.

The doctor will be quite a late entrant into this ongoing conversation. To make things worse, the doctor is himself or herself a mass of stories about illnesses, their mechanisms and their presentation, derived from studies and from personal experience of treating patients. The interview will be an attempt on the part of the doctor to find in the patient's story a pattern that fits with one of a portfolio of medical stories about illness. The doctor will discard some of the things the patient says – even though they may be of great personal importance – as extraneous, and upgrade other things that the patient may regard as of minor significance. This 'narrative incommensurability'[8] may make the seemingly gentle pastime of history-taking into something of a tussle.

The medical profession has long been aware of these conflicts and good doctors will do their best to deal with them. They will, if there is time, try to make sure that they have identified all the patient's beliefs about the significance of the symptoms, so that unexpressed worries may be brought to the surface and addressed. Nevertheless tension will remain. This will most clearly manifest itself in the different ways in which patient and doctor summarize what has happened to the patient. The medical retelling of the patient's story – although intended to translate it into terms that will determine the appropriate course of action – will seem something like a 'defoliation', removing all that is truly personal about the story. The passage of the history-taking from open to closed questions, presages the transition to physical examination, in which patients largely cease to be speaking subjects and become instead the silent proferrer of the body-as-object. This licenses another transition – to investigations which go beyond the visible surface of the body, with which the patient is entirely familiar, to the inscrutable (though rather general) interior, remote from the person.[9]

In short, the possibility of a breakdown in communication, or at least of the two parties talking past each other, lies at the heart of the consultation between patient and doctor. Some doctors exaggerate the extent to which the diagnosis can be made solely from the uninterrupted story told by the patient, and regard the passage from open to closed questions as a defeat.[10] While this is an important corrective to the impatient approach of some doctors, who ride roughshod over patients' stories and so miss vital clues, it remains at best a half-truth. Effective medicine requires the patient's history to be guided by questions – and by prompts whose significance will be unclear to the patient.

There have been numerous studies of the time patients need to 'say their piece' and feel that they have been heard. One study of 'spontaneous talking time' in an out-patient clinic observed that uninterrupted patients talked for only a minute and a half.[11] The authors concluded that 'doctors do not risk being swamped by their patients' complaints if they listen until a patient indicates that his or her list of complaints is complete.' This overlooks the difficulty many patients have in marshalling their thoughts in

47

an opening statement; they often remember new complaints during the consultation or in response to prompting, and listing complaints is only a small part of the entire process. A great deal of time is required to clarify, explore and understand the symptoms, and to link them to a diagnosis and plan of action.

Inevitably many commentators trained in the humanities, and remote from the responsibility for making and acting on correct diagnoses, see the tussle or tension between stories as a hermeneutic power struggle, with the omnipotent doctor crushing the powerless patient with his version of events. (The doctor in this scenario is usually assumed to be male and the patient female.) I will say more about the supposed omnipotence of doctors in future chapters, but for the present, I note simply that the knowledge the physician brings to the consultation is not personal knowledge and, equally, that the exercise of diagnostic skills on the basis of such knowledge is directed towards solving a problem that the patient has brought to the clinic. And this knowledge has itself been shaped by the outcomes that are seen in, and reported by, patients. While it is usually necessary to spell this out only to those who have engaged in advanced studies in the humanities, it does explain how the dialogue with a doctor may seem unsatisfactory however effective it may be in guiding suitable action. It illustrates well Roy Porter's observation that 'Medicine has offered the promise of the greatest benefit of mankind', but 'not always on terms palatable to and compatible with cherished ideals'.[12]

The emphasis on giving patients the space and time to have their say is, of course, absolutely right; as is the feeling that they are sometimes overridden – though it is easy to exaggerate this. But it is not the only consideration. As Polly Toynbee pointed out in the *British Medical Journal*:

If asked to choose qualities, most patients would probably rather be cured by a brusque doctor with up to date skills than be listened to and respected by one who had hardly looked at new treatments in the past 20 years.[13]

She made this comment in response to her own observation that, in the list of 'the duties of doctors registered with the General Medical Council', the injunction 'to keep your professional knowledge and skills up to date' comes in seventh after a series of what she calls 'touchy-feely' modish qualities such as politeness, consideration and respecting a patient's dignity and privacy.

It should not be a question of either/or, of course; but the GMC list makes it just as incumbent on doctors to be graceful under clinical pressure – however appalling – as not to place a patient's life at risk by incompetent treatment. The way in which doctors communicate with patients, what they communicate – both verbally and non-verbally – is therefore being placed under closer and closer scrutiny.

The tensions inherent in the very process of eliciting from patients accounts of their illness would seem to make the ideal of jargon-free, transparent communication a remote one. It becomes even more remote when the doctor starts explaining the problem to the patient, its significance, and the course of action that should be taken. How much should the patient be told? How much technical explanation can the patient comprehend? How much knowledge does he or she want? How much can they cope with?

There are many people who are confident that they know the answers to these questions. Very few of them are doctors who meet patients day in, day out. Among them are patients' advocates, representatives and champions. They assert, for example, that when it comes to bad news, 'patients value honesty, frankness, directness'. This does not square with what some of my patients have indicated, nor with the requests I frequently receive from relatives of patients, not to tell him/her if it turns out to be cancer. What will be experienced by one patient as honesty may be experienced as another as brutal frankness. Directness valued by one patient will be regarded as crassness by another. All patients are entitled to be protected from information they do not want, however much mysteriously omniscient 'patient representatives' believe that they always want it or ought to do so. Likewise, they are entitled to the information they *do* want, even if their closest supporters would prefer them to be kept in the dark. My own rule is this: no patients should be lied to; and no patients should be force-fed information they would rather not have. Finding a humane and honest middle course that is right for an individual patient is not easy.

There is no set limit to the extent and range of information that some patients will want, require and expect. Ms Kendall, whose angry response to her (totally successful) treatment for gallstones I referred to earlier, expected quite a lot of information from the surgeon who recommended a gall-bladder operation:

The consultant said I'd need a scan to confirm his diagnosis. He told me I would have to have my gall bladder removed using keyhole surgery (although I might have to be opened up if there were complications) and that he would refer me to an appropriate surgeon.

On the way back to work... I started thinking about all the questions I should have asked. I had been given very little information about my condition or the operation. Why not? It was my body that was going to be cut open.

What does a gall bladder do? Why does it go wrong? How does the body cope without it? What happens during keyhole surgery? What are the potential risks? Who was the surgeon I'd been referred to and what was his track record? Shouldn't I be told all this as a matter of course? Or are patients considered to be too stupid to understand what's going to be done to them?[14]

The tutorial on the function of the gall bladder and the pathophysiology of gallstones alone would have been quite a major undertaking in the absence of any prior knowledge of biology. Information about the track record of the surgeon who was going to do the operation would take some finding, given that the name of the surgeon would not necessarily be known until shortly before the procedure. For Kendall this was unacceptable, a 'lack of information, choice, and control that I simply wouldn't tolerate in any other part of my life'.[15] Had this information been provided at the time, the clinic (which was overrunning – she complained of having been kept waiting for an hour) would have overrun further and the next patient would have been kept waiting even longer.

I have singled out this case of a patient whose (wholly successful) treatment apparently warranted a full-page philippic in the *Observer* to illustrate the rising expectations some patients have for information and explanation. Ms Kendall's expectations may be entirely appropriate but meeting them would have added to already unbearable time pressures on the clinic. The rate at which one can communicate with a patient is (or certainly should be) determined by the rate at which that patient can receive and retain information and, in the case of individuals with sensory impairment, cognitive problems, or limited education or simply in an anxious state of mind, this may be quite slow. Many patients who learn that they have a disease are encountering a huge amount of biological information for the first time.

Ms Kendall's article demonstrates just how many dimensions

mandatory communication can have: listening to what the patient has to say is only the beginning. Adequate communication of a diagnosis is an elaborate exercise in description, explanation, education and exploration. The receipt of a diagnosis has been correctly described as the beginning of a journey of understanding. The patient quite properly expects to be told not only the diagnosis but what it means, the range of treatment options and their respective merits, and the possible impact of the disease and its treatments on every aspect of life.

Nevertheless the General Medical Council would agree with Kendall's expectations: doctors have to 'respect the right of patients to be fully involved in decisions about their care'.[16] It has been suggested that the requirement for formal consent – that is, explicit and documented as opposed to implied consent – should be extended to many more procedures than those that currently require it: to non-invasive investigative procedures, injections and even aspects of the bedside examination. The problem is, nobody can give a foolproof specification of truly informed consent. There has been much discussion of late about how much information one should have for consent to be truly informed.

My own Trust (Salford Royal Hospitals Trust) has recently issued a twenty-page Consent Policy.[17] The spirit behind the document, which reflects 'guidance' from the General Medical Council and other statutory bodies, is entirely laudable; whether it is implementable in practice is another question entirely. The objective of the Trust (it states) is 'to encourage the active participation of individual patients in decisions relating to their treatment, and to promote patient education regarding the risks and benefits of clinical procedures'. The Trust therefore 'seeks to ensure that relevant information is provided to all patients, in ways that each patient can understand, about proposed treatments, including any alternatives'. This information 'should contain an estimate of the relative risks and benefits of proposed treatments, and should be sufficiently detailed to enable patients to arrive at a balanced judgement, having had the opportunity to put their own value on the relative risks and benefits described'. Moreover, 'decisions to recommend particular treatments should be based on transparent criteria, with individual clients' own needs and interests having primacy in the decision-making process.' Finally, it has to be appreciated, 'consent is a total process and is not merely effected by the signing of a consent form.'

Even if they had time to meet all these requirements, clinicians would themselves need more information than they presently have. Whereas it may be possible to state that a procedure is, on the whole, of benefit and carries greater benefit than other procedures, it is not possible, for example: a) to quantify precisely the relative risks/benefits of the proferred procedure compared with alternative procedures (many procedures – especially surgical procedures – will not have been compared in head-to-head trials); b) to state how those risks will apply to the patient in front of one who may have additional illnesses which will increase risks; and c) to know what is currently available down the road, elsewhere in the country, or abroad. The further demand that:

clinicians should be prepared to give details of both national and Trust figures for the proposed procedure, in addition to the clinician's own outcome figures, and the clinician's own assessment of risk in the light of the patient's condition[18]

cannot be met. Even clinicians who spent 50 per cent of their time trying to inform their patients to the level demanded by the Policy would not succeed.

Even more demanding is the requirement that 'the patient's explicit and written consent' should be be obtained 'for any procedure that carries significant risk'. Most prescriptions and nearly all intravenous injections carry 'significant risk'. Hitherto, it has been customary to disclose any significant complications occurring at a rate of 1 per cent or greater, and discuss in all cases serious complications such as death or neurological damage, no matter how low the rate of occurrence. Such percentages, established in custom and practice, have now become irrelevant since the law requires clinicians to consider, when determining what information to give to the patient, any risks which would have affected 'the judgement of a *reasonable patient* in the situation'. A disappointed or angry patient may quite retrospectively consider a piece of information – for example, about a very rare side effect – as something that would have altered his or her decision.

The changed situation has been summarized as follows by Peter Marks (citing a recent judgment), who points out that:

whether the patient has been given all the relevant information to choose between undergoing and not undergoing the proposed treatment is not a question the answer to which depends upon medical standards or practice.[19]

If it is no longer up to doctors to determine what information should be given, it follows that doctors can no longer *know* what information should be given.

These are not merely theoretical anxieties, as the pharmaceutical industry knows only too well. A four-page spread in the *Mail on Sunday* Review illustrates this.[20] Jo Knowsley, who happened to be a journalist on the *Mail on Sunday*, was admitted to hospital for a laparoscopy, a very common procedure in which, through a small incision and using a cleverly designed scope, the operator is able to inspect the abdominal cavity for diagnostic purposes.[21] It is essentially a safe procedure and much less invasive and dangerous than earlier approaches. In her case, however, the bowel was perforated and a larger incision had to be made so that it could be stitched. The patient's stay was prolonged from one to five days and it took her a few weeks to get back to normal. According to Ms Knowsley's own account, the consultant told her what had happened as soon as she woke up, visited a few hours later when she was fully awake, and apologized. Nevertheless, she remained very angry.

She informed her readers that she was contemplating legal action because she believed the consultant should have told her of the risk of bowel perforation. He said that he had not done so as he had estimated the risk as 1 in 2,000 procedures. She argues that the figure could be 'as high as 1 : 200'. Even Ms Knowsley's figure would not have reached the traditional cut-off. Her retrospective demand to have been informed of the very small risk of bowel perforation may now be judged to fall within the entitlement of 'a reasonable patient'. It would be a brave man or woman who tried to hint to an angry Ms Knowsley that he or she was not being reasonable.

The Consent Policy for my own Trust document says that 'best practice' in obtaining informed consent requires the doctor to 'ensure that even remote risks are recognized as important, and therefore disclosed, where the interests or vocation of an individual patient make this appropriate'. Being off your feet for longer than you expected because of a complication will affect every patient's interest and/or vocation. This underlines the point that there is no *principled* way of distinguishing between information patients ought to have in order to make an informed decision from that which they do not need to be given. The conversation around informed consent is potentially infinite.

The time taken to inform patients depends not only upon the amount of detail in the disussion of risk but also, as we have noted, on the patient's ability to absorb the relevant information. If it has *not* been established that the patient consenting to a treatment or investigation fully understands its benefits and risks, consent is not valid. A significant proportion of the population may have difficulty in fully grasping everything the doctor is now required to tell them.[22] More time will now be required for doctors to document what has been said and the evidence that the patient has understood it.

Preoccupation with communication is also connected to a general distrust of the medical profession.[23] The default position that the doctor will usually have the patient's best interests at heart when recommending a treatment has in many cases been replaced by its antithesis. Patients are now frequently encouraged to arm themselves to the teeth with information and documentation to protect themselves against uncaring, negligent practitioners on the lookout for guinea pigs upon whom to experiment or hone their skills.

The absurdities to which this may lead is illustrated by an experience my mother had when I accompanied her to hospital after she had had a massive heart attack. Her care at Stepping Hill, our local district general hospital, was impeccable: thoughtful, compassionate, tactful and technically faultless. When she arrived in the casualty department she was given urgent diamorphine (heroin) immediately to relieve her pain, and clot-busting therapy. Before she received the therapy, a junior doctor, in exemplary fashion, explained the treatment and then recited a long list of benefits and risks. This was a legal requirement. My mother, who had left her hearing aid at home, was in some distress and drowsy from the effects of diamorphine. She was unable to follow this list nor was she able to make a choice on the basis of the information given to her. I told my mother to say 'Yes', she did so, and the infusion proceeded. It was important to get on with things because the benefits of clot-busting treatment are greatly influenced by the 'door-to-needle' time delay in giving the treatment, i.e. the quicker the better. In a sensible world the doctor would have been trusted. After all, the use of this treatment, demonstrating net benefits (many lives saved), was based on studies involving tens of thousands of patients and agreed national guidelines. The sham of getting fully informed consent could have cost my mother her life. After all, if the default position is not to trust the hospital to provide evidence-based treatments that will be of net benefit, why should one trust the doctor – an employee of the hospital – giving you the information upon which consent was based?

The problems of informed consent may be deeper than many clinicians appreciate. Certain words mean different things to different people. For example, some of the anger felt by the parents of the children whose organs were removed and retained in the Alder Hey affair[24] may have been because, when they consented to 'tissue' being removed from their children's bodies, they did not appreciate that this meant the removal of organs. This opens up an entirely new requirement for what counts as informed consent and, more widely, what counts as adequate communication. Doctors must not only speak clearly, sympathetically and comprehensively, but also in a way that recognizes the very different idiolect of different patients – especially when complex procedures are being described. As the Kennedy Report following the inquiry into paediatric cardiac surgery at Bristol observed, 'informing patients... must be regarded as a process and not a one-off event.'[25]

It has been suggested that every clinic and GP's surgery should include 'information brokers' on the staff – people who will tell patients what they need to know and, if necessary, help them to arrive at informed decisions about their care. But it is not clear who these individuals might be and how they might be trained, or indeed why they should be better communicators than the 'information brokers' we have at present (doctors and nurses) and how they will acquire a sufficient body of knowledge to deal adequately with the patients' questions. Ms Kendall would, I suspect, soon make short work of an information broker and, sooner or later, there would be reference back to the doctor for further clarification and explanation and for putting the information into some kind of perspective. Most people, for entirely sensible reasons, would like to get the information about treatment from the person who is going to prescribe it, or, in the case of an operation, from the person who is going to perform it and has spent many years thinking about its indications, its benefits and its adverse effects.

In the end, given that understanding the nature of disease and its treatment, and the rationale for treatments, requires quite a bit of training, and given, too, that the rational assessment of risk is not very well developed in many of us, there will be an irreducible element of trust in agreeing to a treatment. This is viewed with distaste by some, but it is not the only reason why (as is quoted in the Kennedy Report) the

Royal College of Surgeons of England has acknowledged communication as 'the area of greatest compromise and the source of most
complaints'. It will probably remain the source of most complaints, not
because things cannot be improved but because they will never reach the
ideal envisaged, or assumed, by medical ethicists for whom the notion of
the autonomous (that is fully informed) patient is taken for granted. The
number of complaints in this area will also be fuelled by lawyers whose
livelihood depends upon a steady stream of individuals who feel that,
when things haven't gone as they had hoped, they had not been
adequately informed. The failure to achieve this ideal must not be
treated as a scandal or as specific to medical practice: it is simply a
feature of human affairs.

The ideal of informed consent, seemingly the least contentious
principle of medical practice, and one of the most closely examined
aspects of doctor–patient communication, runs into trouble as soon as it
has to be realized in the real mess of the real world. It looks increasingly
like an aspiration, which can be only approximated – to a degree that
will depend on both the informant and the informed – and less like an
unassailable starting point for good practice. In the real world there is
always a limit to our ability to foresee immediate outcomes or long-term
consequences. As Socrates pointed out to the ferryman who had taken
him across the river, he did not thank him for his services because he had
no idea whether his action might have brought him closer to his doom.

The problem of communication between patient and doctor – and
incremental improvements will never lead to an absolute ideal of
communication that will satisfy everyone – has many causes, ranging
from the incommensurability of the personal experience of illness and
the scientific understanding of it, to the impossibility of defining a limit
to what should be communicated. The limit in practice is determined by
available time and this, the greatest barrier to communication, is itself
increasingly becoming a problem.

How much time does a patient need?

Many discontents with health care both within and beyond the United
Kingdom revolve around a perceived lack of resources. The nature of
this lack varies from country to country. Where basic care is

underdeveloped, the most serious shortfall is of equipment and consumables – surgical instruments, antibiotics, bandages. In relatively affluent Western countries, it is lack of time with the doctor (and the attention that goes with it) that is the most bitter source of complaint. This is hardly surprising, as medical time is the common constituent of pretty well every aspect of medical care. Moreover, as Michael Balint pointed out many years ago,[26] the doctor's attention is a potent prescription, for which there may in some cases be unlimited demand. Even without pathological dependency, available medical time (and, indeed, available nursing time and available physiotherapy time), falls short of what is required. Doctors have to do things at a gallop.

I do not recall any time since I qualified when I have not been in a hurry. My rush has rarely taken the classical form of a dash towards a mortally ill patient whose life depends upon the speed of the medical response. More commonly, it has been that of a person with too much to do; who is being perpetually interrupted; upon whom are made several simultaneous demands.

If the Inuit have twenty different terms for kinds of snow, doctors should have words for an equal number of kinds of time pressure. I have known every allotrope of hurry, from that of a houseman trying to complete the clerking-in of a dozen patients in time for the ward round in the face of a mounting impatience in the Accident and Emergency department where the admissions are piling up, to that of the consultant trying to complete a ward round without junior staff, with half of the results missing, in time for a crucial planning meeting about the development of services, or to catch a train for a conference at which I will present some research. I have also known every intensity of hurry: the chronic tension that results from falling behind in an out-patient's clinic because the first patient had many more problems than anticipated, through the anguished feeling that one is simply losing track of everything as one literally gallops from one commitment to the next.

Over the last decade, it seems the quickening pace has virtually eliminated a sense of community within my hospital. Unscheduled, corridor conversations with colleagues are almost a thing of the past (indeed, many of us will often pretend not to see each other in order not to get caught up in a conversation that politeness demands). The consultant's dining room is deserted, as lunch for most is often a few sandwich crumbs sprayed into a telephone receiver while the speaker-eater signs letters and skim-reads documents or medical journals.

Many readers who have been patients will read this unmoved. This may be because doctors manage not infrequently to conceal the hurry they are in and the irritation they feel. More likely, it is because patients do not want to be fobbed off by sob stories. Indeed, being busy is dismissed as the alibi of a doctor who could not be bothered and does not care. The complaint that the doctor did not spend enough time is sometimes indirect: 'she was in too much of a rush.' The busyness of a hard-pressed doctor compounds rather than mitigates his or her crime of neglect.

The hurry, scurry and worry of the life of a doctor hardly fits with the image of a 'god-like' physician. The patient's indifference to the cause of the doctor's hurry – not infrequently the needs of another patient – points to something that has rarely been noted. In a condition of scarcity, every patient is the direct or indirect enemy of every other patient. The current demand for time (and the attention that goes with it) is potentially limitless and the quantity available is finite. Over the last few years, the gap between expected and available time is widening – and it will get wider.

Let us look first of all at the increasing demand for medical time. Serious illness, which brings fear as well as suffering, is inevitably associated with a demand for attention – for reassurance, for explanation, for compassion and witnessing of one's suffering – as well as for effective medicine. The importance of clinical time and attention increases as diseases become less curable and more chronic – in short as specific treatments become less effective. The increasing presence of *chronic* disease in medical practice therefore brings time pressures in its wake.

Some doctors seem to have the knack of making patients feel as if they have received enough attention within very severe time constraints. This may be illusory and temporary, however. The patient who leaves satisfied often later reflects, feels short-changed, and grumbles. General practitioners are apparent experts at delivering satisfaction in a very short period of time, but here, too, things may not always be as they appear: GPs often deal with one problem per appointment; frequently they do not examine their patients. They set aside a longer visit for a full hearing, and a further short encounter for a second or a third problem and when they are stuck may refer on to others.

Other factors than communication come into play as well when we consider what is happening to medicine as a whole. For example, the volume of activity is rising inexorably. In hospitals, there has been a massive increase in both emergency and planned care such as elective surgery. The population is ageing and elderly patients tend to have multiple problems. As a result, both numbers of patients and numbers of problems per patient are rising. Moreover, the pressure on hospital beds, and the development of large numbers of hospital-avoidance schemes, has meant that only the most acutely ill patients are admitted. The increased range of possible treatments and the appropriate expectation that these will be offered to the patient further multiplies the clinical workload associated with each admission. In the acute admissions ward, it is unusual to find a patient without a drip and a cardiac monitor. Shorter stays put greater pressure on staff, as it is the landing and take-off – admission with its complex clerical (bureaucratic, legalistic) procedures, and discharge planning – that are most labour-intensive. The average length of stay has fallen year on year – from 11.7 days in 1980 to 6.8 in 1999–2000.[27] Over the last twenty-five years, while the number of hospital beds fell by over 50 per cent, the number of hospital in-patient admissions and discharges has doubled.[28] Discharge procedures can often be unduly protracted when, for example, plans for discharge (welcomed by the patient) are contested or even blocked by relatives who for a variety of reasons are not willing to accept the risks that may attend the return of a frail elderly person to their home.

The pressures on elective admissions for surgical procedures have been widely discussed in the press and in government policy documents. Under-investment in the health service over the last thirty years and ageist assumptions among policy-makers have resulted in a huge backlog of patients with orthopaedic, cardiac and other problems. Waiting lists remain long despite the often misdirected efforts of governments to reduce their size. For many clinicians, in particular surgeons, the pressure to meet waiting list targets is becoming unsupportable: it is analogous to clearing the snow from a front path in a blizzard.

Clinicians are being incessantly nagged to do what they would like anyway to do, if they were given the resources: that is, to provide a service that is flexible, accessible and precisely tailored to the circumstances of the patient. Nothing would please a surgeon more than that patients should be able electronically to book their operations at a time convenient to both parties. Physicians would be equally delighted were patients able to be treated in the comfort of their own home at a time of their choosing. This, however, has huge resource implications: the safe provision of care at or near the patient's home means an expensive duplication of resources. At the very least there would be loss of economies of scale. The consultant who is driving to the patient's home or to an outreach clinic is seeing fewer patients per session, ignoring his or her in-patients, and spending time in traffic jams listening to Radio 3 instead of listening to patients or teaching and supervising juniors. Patient-centred care is what clinicians (and front-line managers, I ought to add) always strive for, but it comes at an unsustainable cost.

The time taken to maintain and monitor standards of care is growing exponentially. Doctors have to participate in audit, in clinical governance, and in critical incident reporting schemes. They have to meet targets for 'Continuing Professional Development' (CPD) and provide evidence for this.[29] There is an annual appraisal which involves the collection of a vast amount of information about one's own practice compared with national benchmarks, a list of ways in which one is intending to improve one's knowledge, skills and attitudes in the coming years, and how one is going to contribute to developing the capability of the service in the forthcoming year to achieve local and national targets. The appraisal folder should also include a full account of any complaints and how they have been dealt with, and copies of letters of thanks from patients.[30] All of this is intended to build towards the much greater documentation that will support the case for five-yearly revalidation, to be introduced in 2005. The time this supposedly worthwhile activity will take is incalculable. At present doctors are willing to carry it out in their off-duty periods. This may not last.

These are just some of the factors that increase the need for clinical time. There are many others: the education, teaching, training and mentoring of undergraduate and postgraduates; pressures on clinical academics to deliver research that will make their parent institutions look good in the Research Assessment Exercise;[31] the expectation that clinical care will be delivered by consultants and not by their juniors, whose training increasingly takes place 'off the job' and, indeed, off-site; the increasing need to document everything that is done and said and to do so legibly.[32]

The point, however, is sufficiently made: there is a widening gap between the time required to deliver what the nation is being encouraged to expect of a Health Service and the time available to deliver it.

This gap will continue to widen – and the tension between the priority to deliver on quality and on quantity will get worse – because the amount of clinician time available for patients will be reduced. The pressure to be involved in management – in the development and well as the delivery of services – will become greater. At present only 37 per cent of consultants perform major duties in management outside of their own work, or work for the postgraduate dean, BMA or the Royal College of Physicians.[33] This number will increase not only because there will be more work to do but also because consultant pay in future will almost certainly depend upon doing more managerial work. The time spent in professional development will also increase.[34] The expectation of consultant-delivered (as opposed to merely consultant-led) hospital services will further reduce clinical input from trainees. Consultants in teaching hospitals will be expected to contribute to an ever-more demanding (for teachers that is) curriculum provided for student-consumers who will no longer accept learning by osmosis and observation, or fitting into existing clinical activity, but will expect personal attention in a timetable increasingly shaped around their training needs. Objective-setting and objective-monitoring meetings with trainees and increasing documentation of their training and their mentoring is an additional unwelcome burden, however valuable it is in itself.

Under such circumstances, the number of patients who can be seen will be rather less and they will be competing for attention with postgraduate trainees and undergraduates.

Sooner or later doctors will rebel against their increasing workloads: productivity per hour will fall. Newcomers to the medical profession will anyway have had a less pressured life than their predecessors. As a recent appointee has discovered, being a consultant 'means that I often work harder and longer hours than I did as a junior doctor'.[35] Already the Royal Colleges are setting out guidelines for the maximum number of patients a consultant should see in a clinic, the number of patients they should have under their care at any one time, and the number of patients they should see in a 24-hour take. Although they have the laudable aim of protecting both patients and doctors against the minor and major disasters that come in the wake of hurry and tiredness, they are daunting, given the standard of care patients expect to receive and doctors want to give. Even so, they are utopian compared with the present workload.

While intensity of work – or productivity per consultant per hour – will fall[36] the hours worked by consultants will also diminish, possibly quite dramatically. Despite repeated claims to the contrary, there is consistent evidence that consultants do a great deal of unpaid overtime. A survey of over 6,000 physicians in the UK showed that they worked an average of 29 hours a week over and above their contracted 37.5 hours.[37] This is disappointingly at odds with the idea of consultants as (to use the image of Jeff Rooker MP) 'dividing their time between the golf course and their private patients' and has therefore received little press coverage. It has, however, huge implications for policy-makers. The European Working Time Directive, due to be implemented by 2009, will limit the working week to 48 hours. This will increase the number of consultants needed to deliver even the present level of service. For example, a recent report estimates that the number of cardiologists alone in England and Wales will have to increase by 900 to offset the effect of this Directive, quite apart from any increase in demand.[38] (This will still leave the numbers of cardiologists per head of population well below the European average.)

While hitherto most consultants have despised clock-watchers and have stayed on duty for as long as it takes to deliver the care they believe their NHS patients are entitled to, this seems likely to change. There will be a sea-change in attitude towards the career of medicine.[39] The New Deal, which limits the number of hours junior doctors are at work or on call to 56 has resulted in shift-working. This is a pattern that profoundly alters one's attitude to the job: a professional who feels a continuing personal responsibility for his or her patients becomes a functionary who does a certain number of hours. A survey in 2003 showed that in only 2 per cent of Trusts were all posts 'New Deal compliant' and in over 40 per cent of Trusts about half the posts failed to comply with this edict.[40] From August 2004, another European Working Time Directive requires 11 hours unbroken rest within any given 24-hour period. This will make shift-working universal. It will create insuperable problems for those trying to ensure safe cover for patients.[41]

Quite independently of alterations in employment law that will change being a doctor from a way of life to a sessional commitment, there are shifts in attitudes to work that point in the same direction. New recruits to medicine will be wanting to work fewer hours than their predecessors. The welcome and long overdue feminization of the profession – approximately 60 per cent of newly qualified doctors in England and Wales are women[42] – also has worrying implications for available medical time. So long as women carry the greatest burden of child-care, most female doctors will spend a significant proportion of their professional life working part-time.

Women now constitute about 75 per cent of general practitioners under thirty. A recent study of trainee general practioners – the choice of about two thirds of medical graduates – showed that only 30 per cent of women planned to work full-time.[43] Current NHS policy, however, envisages an increasing role for general practice in providing more complex medical services.[44] Even more startling is that 25 per cent of men also intended to work part-time.[45] They are willing to take a reduced salary because it seems that, like the specialist registrar Dr Melanie Powell, who turned down the first version of the new consultant contract, they don't want any more money; they want 'a life outside of medicine'.[46] The changing work commitment indicates that it will be necessary to train a minimum of 150 new entrants to general practice to replace 100 retiring principals, even if the expectations of patients for doctor time were not raised.

Finding these extra doctors is not proving easy. The promise made in 2000 that there would be an additional 2,000 general practitioners by 2004 has not been met. According to the Department of Health's own figures, the net increase in GPs measured according to the hours they work was about eighteen by 2002. This rather modest gain will have been cancelled out many times over simply by the amount of hours devoted to appraisal, preparation for validation, clinical governance and other activities that do not show up as direct patient contact. The number of GP vacancies increased from 1,214 to 2,464 between 2000 and 2001. There are shortages in all specialities: it is estimated that nearly half a million patients are waiting for an X-ray, a scan or some other radiological examination at any one time in the UK. This is in part due to outdated equipment which is slower and less reliable but mainly due to a shortage of radiologists: approximately 15 per cent of consultant radiology posts in England are vacant. The knock-on effects on other aspects of care are enormous: many patients wait in hospital beds for radiological investigations because there are not enough staff to carry them out and report on them.

It was always going to be difficult to create new doctors fast enough to meet government promises: it will be a long time before the 58 per cent increase in medical school places between 1995 and 2005 delivers fully qualified doctors. But things are even more difficult than might have been anticipated. Medicine has become less attractive as a profession, especially to men. The supply of medical students may not meet the demands of medical school expansion.[47] There has been a sharp drop in applicants per place from a peak of 3.5 to the present level of 1.55. The pace of decline has quickened: as recently as 1995, there were 2.11 applicants per place. Even if this trend is halted and the number of applicants remains steady, there will be a mere 1.2 applicants per available place in 2005, when all the new places are available. Virtually everyone who applies will be accepted.[48]

One way of reversing this trend will be to lower the entrance criteria. This would please those who have argued that doctors have in the past been too academically well qualified for the rather homely job they have to do. I disagree with this: medicine is complex and requires intelligence of a high order. There is plenty of evidence that, for example, A levels predict performance in finals and postgraduate medical examinations:[49] if the entry bar is lowered, there may be an increased drop-out rate, unless students are given more support and supervision than today's generation of very bright, academically confident and self-motivated entrants.

This additional support is unlikely to be forthcoming; for the increase in planned student numbers has coincided with a crisis in academic medicine. There are problems of funding and problems of recruitment to funded posts. In the wake of the 2001 Research Assessment Exercise (RAE), many teachers have been lost from medical schools.[50] Because of the low esteem in which applied clinical research is held compared with basic biological research, many medical schools have done very badly thus reducing funding. London medical schools have had to shed hundreds of staff whom they can no longer afford to pay.[51] Excellence in teaching has relatively few obvious fiscal benefits for the host institution. It is undervalued compared with excellence in research, which attracts considerable funding to the institution that hosts it. With fewer academics doing more and more teaching, and NHS consultants, who have hitherto contributed significantly to teaching, increasingly turning their attention to delivering on NHS priorities, the pressure on the remaining teachers engaged in this low-status activity is increased.

The competing workloads – clinical work for the NHS and teaching and research for the university, increasing the average working week to 64 hours – also make academic medicine profoundly unattractive. It is therefore not surprising that there is a major problem in filling those academic posts that have been retained. Nearly 20 per cent of medical academic posts that have not been cut remained unfilled at the beginning of the planned 60 per cent increase in medical school places.[52]

Despite initial public denial, the Department of Health is aware that there might not be enough medical time to meet the public's expectations of medical care and attention. It has responded to the current problems by a series of hasty initiatives, some of which may have long-term adverse effects on the quality of doctors produced in the UK (for example fast-track undergraduate courses) and some of which are simply ludicrous.[53]

Much more dangerous – and liable to cause lasting damage – are plans to reduce drastically the duration of consultant training.[54] This may ease workforce problems in the medium term but it has unpredictable long-term consequences. One should anyway be suspicious when it is 'discovered' that junior doctor training is 'too long' at a time when there is a political imperative to get more hands on deck. A recent study has indicated that, whereas in 1995 a trainee could be expected to work over 30,000 hours between becoming a senior house officer and getting a consultant post, this will fall to 8,000 hours with the implementation of the European Working Time Directive.[55] Recent 'reforms' in training proposed by the Chief Medical Officer will further reduce this to 6,000 hours. As Joanna Chikwe and colleagues point out, 'to become a competent surgeon in one fifth of the time once needed either requires genius, intensive practice or lower standards.'[56] In fact, for reasons already discussed, there has been a reduction in the intensity of teaching. It looks as if lower standards are on the menu. No wonder that, in a recent poll of consultant surgeons, two thirds of respondents stated that they would not wish to be operated on by a consultant colleague trained under the present arrangements.[57] The Royal College of

Surgeons, meanwhile, is seeking a change in the law to enable trainees to make up for the shortfall in experience on human beings by operating on animals such as pigs.[58]

The failure to address satisfactorily the lack of clinical time is of particular concern as many doctors are seeking to leave the NHS, and indeed medicine, as soon as they can afford it. Approximately 50 per cent of doctors have claimed that, if given their time over again, they would choose another occupation.[59] A recent census of consultants indicated that only 10 per cent say they will work until sixty-five (compared with 16 per cent in the previous year). Just under 40 per cent of the consultant workforce will reach sixty in the next ten years.[60] There is a similar picture in general practice. The proportion of doctors intending to quit direct patient care in the next five years rose from 14 per cent to 22 per cent between 1998 and 2001. The rise was almost entirely due to lack of job satisfaction.[61] The promise in the NHS Plan[62] to increase the number of full-time consultants or their equivalent in part-timers by 7,500 or 30 per cent looks hollow.

The only strategy available to the Government is to fudge. Statistics will be generated showing a rising number of consultants, 'roughly on target' and those statistics will be in part supported by a redefinition of what counts as a consultant and a reduction of training.[63] Meanwhile, the gap between the time needed, deserved, demanded by patients and that which is available to them will grow.[64]

Why are we waiting?

When patients complain of poor communication it often has less to do with the competence of the doctor than with the difficulty of reconciling different ways of understanding disease: the subjective experience as opposed to objective knowledge of illness. Bringing together the physiological and the personal aspects of an illness takes time; and medical time is, as we have seen, in short supply. The shortage of time is especially resented if patients feel they have spent too much time waiting to see the doctor.

Concern with waiting, of course, extends far beyond the encounter between patient and doctor. It permeates every aspect of health care and has consequently prompted more policy initiatives than any other issue.

There have been scandals, claims and counter-claims connected with all kinds of waiting: waiting to see a general practitioner; waiting for an out-patient appointment with a consultant; waiting for investigations; waiting for ambulances; waiting (on and off trolleys) in accident and emergency departments; and, of course, waiting for operations. Waiting times account for five out of the nine top targets the government has set for the NHS.[65]

I cannot resist a brief digression on targets. Clinicians have lived with targets for so long that many have ceased noticing their arbitrariness or resenting the adverse effect they have on the rational use of health care resources. Built into the notion of the 'target' – with its factory farming approach to medical practice – is the assumption that, without external pressure, clinicians and their immediate managers wouldn't care about keeping patients waiting.

A decade ago my hospital was granted £700,000 on condition that the latest ministerial waiting list target would be met. The managerial and consultant body was assembled to meet the chairman of the North West Region to be warned that the money would be withdrawn if we failed to meet the target *even by a single patient.* He favoured us with a homely analogy: if you miss a train by one minute, he said, you have still missed the train. Since the £700,000 had already been spent, and the Trust was in debt, the withdrawal of the funds would have meant yet more cuts in those services which were not the subject of government targets, such as the rehabilitation of elderly people. Most of the 'long waiters' were orthopaedic patients requiring joint replacements. Our fate therefore lay in the hands of certain orthopaedic surgeons, most of whom were already over-stretched, but who were, nevertheless, entitled to holidays. One orthopaedic surgeon had booked a skiing holiday. If Mr N had an injury and was unable to operate, the targets would not have been met and the £700,000 would be lost. An ill-advised expedition off-piste could have resulted in my elderly rehabilitation patients being punished.

Targets produce 'collateral damage'.[66] Highlighting one problem and throwing resources at it, means lowlighting other problems and depriving them of resources. This is particularly damaging if the highlighted problem has been picked out as a result of tabloid rage, or the strutting of an opposition politician, rather than because of the scale of its contribution to human suffering. But even where prioritizing is medically justified, it may still cause collateral damage – quite apart from the costs of realigning services to meet the target. The emphasis on cardiovascular disease and falls in *The National Service Framework for Older People* (Department of Health, 2001) for example, means that chronic respiratory diseases, one of the greatest sources of misery in old age, will be comparatively neglected. Cardiologists have found that *The National Service Framework for Coronary Heart Disease*, while stimulating investment in resources for coronary artery operations, has resulted in other cardiac conditions such as heart muscle disease, complex heart rhythms and valvular heart disease, being neglected.[67] The edict that all women concerned about breast cancer should be seen within a fortnight has in fact increased overall waiting for radiotherapy for those who actually have breast cancer.[68] Where there is overall scarcity, the prioritization of one problem means the 'posteriorization' of another.

'Collateral damage' is an expression of the wider problem of 'moving the bump in the carpet'. When you have a carpet that is too big for the floor on which it is laid, flattening a bump in one place results in its emergence elsewhere. What is more, the new bump that is created by central directives is often greater than the one that has been flattened. Waiting time initiatives generate some of the most glaring examples of 'collateral damage'. The insistence that the ambulance service should respond to all 999 calls (whatever their reason) within eight minutes means that GPs cannot raise ambulances to take sick patients to hospital. The requirement that patients who worry about a lump in the breast should be seen by a specialist within two weeks means that patients worried about a lump in the stomach move to the back of the queue. Introducing a triage nurse into the A & E department to ensure that patients were seen within five minutes of arrival not only used up resources but simply extended the time between first being seen and being definitively treated.[69] When priority is given to patients who have been waiting over a certain arbitrary time for operations, individuals with more serious and dangerous conditions have to wait longer. The adverse impact of the obsession with surgical waiting lists on the allocation of resources for patients with chronic diseases such as asthma and diabetes has now been acknowledged and new policies are being put in place. Another time-consuming U-turn.[70]

Why are so many distracting and disruptive targets centred on waiting – beyond the obvious fact that when you have a painful illness or a worrying symptom you want to sort it out as soon as possible?

The meaning of waiting

A symptom makes you suffer but it also turns you into one who waits. At first it is a matter of waiting for this peculiar or unpleasant feeling or sensation to go away or, failing this, to become interpretable. Is it something or nothing? If it is something, is it serious or trivial? As a doctor, I can impose all sorts of complex interpretations on the odd feelings my own body serves up to me. Take, for example, the sensations I have had in my left leg over the last week or two. These have nothing to do with my day's timetable or indeed the chosen course of my life. At the least they are a minor interruption, a distraction; at the worst, a shark's fin in calm sea on a sunny day: a reminder, anyway, that the body, though closer to being what we are than any other part of the world, is subject to laws that are hidden from us. Our Mondays and Tuesdays, our workdays and holidays, our commitments and responsibilities, our plans and plots, are mistbows on a hidden waterfall of cellular activity. The symptom reminds us that our bodies were not designed with our busy, ordered, important lives in mind. It reminds us of the unchosen corporeal basis of our daily lives; of the fact that the body that we are is also something that we are not. The symptom says 'You are not the master of your destiny.' It says 'Stop'. It says 'Wait'.

Waiting is woven into the very fabric of illness: waiting for a spontaneous resolution; waiting for a (hopefully reassuring) explanation – perhaps from a friend or family member; waiting for relief from suffering; waiting for the end of interruption.

If the symptom doesn't go away and my rationalizations look thin, I seek help. This translates my inner, private waiting to public spaces and enmeshes it with public time. My first port of call is my general practitioner. I make an appointment and wait for the day and hour of my appointment. I wait in the surgery, pretending to read the magazines. I have joined my first queue. I tell my story and wait for the verdict. The doctor suggests what the problem might be. Perhaps I leave the surgery with a prescription and continue waiting for the symptom to go away. It gets worse. I make another appointment and enter another period of waiting. This time the doctor orders some tests and I wait for the results. They are inconclusive. Another appointment, another wait, another queue. I am referred to a specialist. The specialist has a longer queue.

Eventually I am seen. Meanwhile the symptom continues and my life is warped into a question mark.

The specialist has a few ideas about what the problem might be but is not too sure. More tests are needed. These are more complex and more expensive than those ordered by the GP: there is a waiting list for them. In due course, I attend for my tests, waiting in the ante-room of the radiology department for my turn to come, pretending to read more magazines. Then I wait for the results, and for my appointment with the GP to get the results, and for my appointment with the specialist to have the results interpreted and a course of action planned. It turns out that I have a condition that needs more complex treatment.

New kinds of waiting begin: waiting for the treatment to work. Or, if an operation is required, several new kinds of waiting: waiting for the appointed time for my operation; waiting to recover from it; waiting for the wound to heal; waiting for the results of the biopsy; waiting to recover my independence; waiting to be 'signed off' to go back to driving and to work; ultimately waiting to feel 100 per cent so that I can put the interruption behind me and resume normal life.

The interruption of illness is resented. One feels powerless and the source of the powerlessness is intimate: it is one's own body that has imposed this narrative of doctors and tests, and operations and tablets. This radical assault on my freedom arises because the body, the very ground of agency, has properties and propensities that have nothing to do with, and indeed cut across my very status as an agent. Nothing could demonstrate the profound impertinence of illness more clearly than the peculiar sensation of waiting idly on a busy workday morning in an out-patient clinic. Or finding oneself in a hospital ward which is halfway between a bedroom and a street.

Sooner or later, powerlessness may be blamed on those who are supposed to help. The journey from bodily question to medical answer, from the emergence of illness to its resolution, is extended by delays at each step of the way, and by the zigs and zags of the referrals and re-referrals necessary to co-opt all the diagnostic and therapeutic forces of modern scientific medicine. The prolongation of the waiting imposed by the illness resulting from negotiating the services designed to deal with illness exacerbates the feeling of powerlessness inseparable from illness. People whose daily life is minutely self-determined will bitterly resent this powerlessness. The disempowerment of illness is sometimes blamed on the institutions – and above all the individuals who work within them – who, because they are not instantly available and cannot provide instant answers, keep one waiting in ignorance.

The knot of waiting, impotence and uncertainty at the heart of sickness contributes to many patients' standing discontent with medicine. In a recent article, a medical ethicist described (with extraordinary candour) how being kept waiting for a few minutes in a casualty department to be seen after a minor injury made him 'grumpy, foul-mouthed, and ill-tempered'.[71] The injury was unscheduled: the appointment with the hospital was not in his diary.

A recent survey of 14,000 patients carried some bad news for a government that has taken patients' impatience very seriously. A third were dissatisfied at having to wait forty-eight hours to see a GP (a target that looks anyway unachievable without interfering with other priorities, for example, developing specialist GP clinics and carrying out preventive work) and almost a fifth were dissatisfied at having to wait even twenty-four hours to see a particular GP. (Patients were satisfied only if they could see their own GP a lot of the time.) More alarmingly, a third were dissatisfied at being detained in the waiting room for more than five minutes while 71 per cent thought a ten-minute delay unacceptable. [72] The possibility that the delay may be because the doctor is attending to another patient hardly appeases impatience or slows its evolution towards anger. This anger is exacerbated by the ancient connection between power and making someone wait.

As lovers, prisoners and servants know, to be made to wait is, short of being physically abused, one of the most naked experiences of being in the power of others. '*To make someone wait*: the constant prerogative of all power', as Roland Barthes said. It is the 'age-old pastime of humanity'.[73] 'Waiting is an enchantment: I have received *orders not to move*.' The patient waiting in the surgery or the clinic is frightened to move lest he or she lose his or her place. It is difficult to believe that this power is exercised by no one, that it is the result simply of one's being just one of many. As anger builds up, so it becomes more and more focused on the people seemingly in control in the institution; in particular at the doctor whose closed door is an apparent symbol of authority and power. The waiting room becomes an ante-room and the patient feels like a petitioner, seeking an audience, awaiting his or her share of privileged time with the physician.[74]

The deep significance of waiting as an expression of comparative powerlessness and its intimate connection with the very nature of illness explains why, of all the sources of dissatisfaction with the medical profession, the fact that they make you wait is the most pervasive. There is an understandable anger that comes from the knowledge that there is succour and it is being denied; but there is equal anger that the very process of receiving succour, the business of diagnosis, treatment and recovery, takes time. There will always be problems arising out of waiting. They will not be solved by telling doctors to increase their productivity, by reducing the time they spend with individual patients, or by dividing consultant clinics into slots as small as three minutes, as has been recently recommended.[75] This will simply generate more dissatisfied patients whose need to communicate and be communicated with will be unmet.

In fact, an instantaneous consultative and diagnostic service ('appropriate to our 24/7 society') may not benefit patients. They would still spend as much time waiting for answers as they proceed from clinician to clinician and from test to test. The impression that something was being done would be offset by the inconvenience or more inconclusive activity. After all, the only waiting time that matters is the interval between the onset of an illness and its resolution – something that no one has yet got round to measuring. There is another reason why a rapid response service might actually cause harm: in the case of many conditions, the earlier it comes to medical attention, the harder it is to diagnose. That may be one of the reasons why instant access services, such as NHS Direct, a phone advisory service, and walk-in clinics, have not taken the pressure off slightly less instant access services, such as GPs and Casualty departments.[76]

That warm feeling in my left leg I alluded to earlier – which could have orginated from the nerve roots, the spinal cord or the brain – and might have had all sorts of serious or non-serious meanings, has now (a week or so later) passed away. If I had presented myself a week ago to my GP or even to a neurologist friend, I would have been none the wiser. A mixture of good sense, apathy, busyness, professsional pride and self-reassurance – or denial – prevented me from taking it any further. If I had demanded instant investigation, I should have been put to great inconvenience, public resources would have been squandered, and I would have been no closer to a diagnosis. Worse, doubtful abnormalities on one test and borderline results on another would have simply multiplied the diagnostic possibilities.

The point is this: it usually takes time for an emergent illness to assume a distinct enough form for it to be recognized; for the serious to be differentiated from the trivial; and for illness to be distinguished from non-illness. In a society that associates waiting with the failure of a system to serve its citizens' needs in a timely fashion, this is no longer understood or accepted. The suggestion by a GP that one should 'wait and see', that it 'doesn't seem serious' (which in the overwhelming majority of cases will be true), that one should first try such and such a simple remedy before being referred to a specialist for expensive and invasive tests, is greeted with suspicion. The patient feels 'fobbed off', 'not taken seriously' or 'patronized'. In that small minority of cases where this results in a delay in the diagnosis of a major illness, this may retrospectively be held against the doctor.[77]

Waiting, in other words, can often be the most sensible – patient-friendly as well as cost-effective – response: time itself is a most powerful diagnostic tool. If this goes down very badly in certain quarters, it is because it is interpreted as a mixture of incompetence and the improper exercise of power. Meanwhile, as medicine becomes more beset with bureaucracy, and more and more demands are made on doctors, and doctors themselves will feel less and less inclined to deal with these demands in their spare time, waiting will get longer (though it may be made less visible) and the accusations of abuse of power through making people wait will become ever louder.

5

Power and Trust

The god-like consultant

The NHS doesn't need more money, it needs total reorganization – and consultants need to realize that they are not gods but fallible people who should be accountable for their mistakes.[1]

The notion of the 'god-like' consultant awakens a complex image. He is a white, male, late middle-aged, upper middle-class character. He browbeats and humiliates the staff with whom he works: the deferential, terrified, and handmaidenly nurses, therapists, social workers, managers and, above all, exploited, cowed, junior doctors who do the work for which he is himself paid out of taxes. He talks past, or over, silent, compulsorily grateful patients whose views are neither sought nor welcomed and who are denied the respect due to equals. He organizes the world around his advancement, convenience and comfort and blocks any reforms in health care lest they impinge on his privileged status or slow his passage through the public hospital on his way from the golf course to his private rooms. His pronouncements about everything from the diagnosis of the patient in front of him to the way care is organized in the hospital in which he is on the staff and occasionally works are listened to with deference, never challenged, and immediately become law. When, as frequently happens – because his idleness and arrogance discourage him from keeping up to date – errors occur, he is not held to account.

This caricature is at least thirty and probably fifty years out of date and even back in the 1950s it was unfair to the vast majority of hardworking consultants who built up and developed an under-resourced NHS. Moreover, rather than being a manifestation of a uniquely class-ridden society (as is often asserted), British medicine seems to be far less hierarchical than elsewhere. Those of us who have trainees from continental Europe or from the Commonwealth sometimes find their deference disconcerting. For their part, the trainees are often nonplussed by the informality of ward rounds and teaching sessions and are wrong-footed by sincere requests to question the diagnoses and management plans of the seniors.[2]

It would be foolish to deny that there have been, and are, consultants who exploit their position – cheating on the taxpayers, abusing their juniors and harming patients physically or psychologically. Such individuals – for example, Rodney Ledward, a gynaecological surgeon whose arrogance and incompetence damaged so many women until he was stopped from operating – are occasionally exposed by the press and there are others almost as bad who are not. But it would be equally foolish to infer from this that consultants routinely engage in such psychopathic behaviour; more foolish, because the actions of doctors are more closely regulated than those of any other profession, and such individuals comprise a minority of the profession. Disappointingly, as has been noted, survey after survey has shown that consultants, far from playing truant, work 30 per cent over their contracted hours for the NHS.[3]

As the erstwhile Secretary of State for Health, admitted in his final speech (to the General Medical Council): 'The overwhelming majority of doctors do a quite brilliant job for patients. They work long hours, show huge commitment and deserve our support and appreciation.'[4] The content of those long hours is far from god-like.

The real issue is the power, or apparent power, of doctors and the uses to which they put it. Gods are all-powerful. It is ironical that this image has come to the fore at a time when doctors are relatively *dis*empowered – more cog-like than god-like. Gods are also unaccountable, so it is a further irony that the claims that doctors are unaccountable grow ever louder at a time when they have been closely regulated as never before.

This paradox reflects a consumerism that originates in certain assumptions: that all providers of goods and services will cheat unless they are exposed in a transparent world to the disciplines of the market and to full legal liability; and that professional groups who provide services primarily serve their own interests. Consumers have a right to know what their service providers get up to. It is in the spirit of transparency, therefore, that I offer this portrait of a consultant at work.

The cog-like consultant

The first thing to be pointed out is that the consultant is, with increasing frequency, a woman.[5] The second is that much of her professional life is passed in a tense hurry, scurrying between clinical work, teaching, research, administration, local, regional and national committees. Her ward rounds are carried out faster than she finds comfortable; overbooked, under-resourced clinics are 'got through' at a speed incompatible with giving patients the time and attention they need and the consultant would like to give them; the endless paperwork is disposed of at a gallop; teaching is squeezed in; reading journals to keep up to date is snatched along with lunch.

This may not be evident to the casual spectator. Since she feels her patients are entitled to at least the appearance of unhurried attention, our consultant will do her best to make sure her hurry is invisible. She will not always succeed, though woe betide her if she does not. The accusation that the doctor was, or seemed to be, in a hurry is a grave one and carries numerous implications: that her mind was elsewhere, that her performance was perfunctory, that she failed in her duty of care, or in her obligation not only to care but also to show that she was caring.

Our typical consultant will worry about the often difficult decisions that she has to make. She is not, of course, free to act with unchallenged authority: most of what she does is shaped by the evidence base mediated through textbooks, lectures, national and local guidelines. Clinical freedom – the freedom to invent one's own solutions to medical problems in ignorance of the best evidence that is available, to value one's own opinion over the guidance that comes from the body of knowledge that belongs to no one – has long been jettisoned by consultants.[6] Clinical judgement, however, has *not* been jettisoned; nor can it be. However closely drawn is the mesh of the evidence base, medical decision-making is a probabilistic skill.

For example, the conclusion that there is something serious underlying apparently banal symptoms is in part intuitive. Trying to avoid dependency on intuition by having a permanently low threshold for suspecting that something is seriously amiss will not be best for patients as they will be made to undergo the inconvenience of multiple referrals and tests, in order to rule out possible conditions. Therapeutics, like diagnosis, remains an art. The decision to recommend one treatment rather than another is never absolute: the balance of risks and benefits is not the same for all patients.

Since medicine is a probabilistic art, in order to get most things right the consultant will inevitably get some things wrong and occasional things seriously wrong. The sense of the probable – informed by knowledge (better than ever before), experience, and clinical judgement – will underpin the advice offered but is often hedged with uncertainty. Our consultant is usually quite frank about this admission of non-omniscience.

Admission of uncertainty is not readily tolerated by some patients. A recent survey[7] revealed just how little patients appreciate honesty about their own limitations that is enjoined upon professionals. 'Let's see what happens', 'I don't know', asking a nurse for advice and 'I think this might be...' are the top four ways of denting a patient's confidence in the doctor. 'Let's see what happens' is, as we have discussed, actually very sensible: given that both rare serious and common non-serious conditions begin with indistinguishable symptoms, time is a powerful diagnostic tool, though many patients are deeply unimpressed by it.

Much of the life of a consultant (and even more of a GP) is about handling and living with uncertainty. This is not easy in a culture of 'zero tolerance' of error, especially when honest disclosure of error no longer seems to satisfy many patients in an increasingly litigious environment. The new statutory 'duty of candour' will in many cases be seen 'as an invitation to pursue a claim'.[8] Each claim will involve a huge amount of work on the part of the doctor, even where the error is accepted by all as a non-negligent example of human fallibility.

The pressures of clinical life exact an iron self-discipline of our consultant, especially as she will be exposed to many other challenges to her self-control and good behaviour. Medical practice requires an almost superhuman grace under a multitude of pressures. If sometimes that grace fails and impatience and rudeness result this is regrettable but at least understandable. In the present climate it will be taken as evidence of the constitutional arrogance of consultants, and she will be marked out for complaint, irrespective of the value of the advice and treatment she offers. A moment of ill temper will not go unpunished. The unforgiving patient may find it difficult, as we have noted, to forgive even hurry, as it suggests that the doctor's attention is directed elsewhere – perhaps to another patient.[9]

The frustrations of ordinary hospital medicine are manifold. Doing a ward round or a clinic is like trying to perform a can-can in a marsh. While the archetypal consultant has a tail of admiring acolytes, the actual consultant is likely to come to the ward and find that there is no registrar (off on a training course), no house officer (down in Casualty dealing with emergencies or asleep because he has been on the night shift), and no nurse who knows what has most recently happened to the patients (just back from a period off-duty). The results of tests will not be available: they have not been done; or if done are not yet available; or if available, filed away in foot-high case notes. Patients are often hard of hearing, or anxious, and will find it difficult to give a coherent history; with an ageing hospital population, some patients may have cognitive impairment and the relative who is able to give the history is not present. (Other relatives of other patients may, however, be present and will expect to speak to the consultant in the middle of her round and may interpret her request to make an appointment when she is less busy as unacceptable unapproachability.) Teasing out a multitude of complaints connected with several different illnesses is especially difficult – and dangerous – to hurry, however great the pressures are to move quickly from one patient to the next.

If the consultant is accompanied by a group, it will be comprised of students and postgraduate visitors, who will expect to be taught and will be unhappy if they are merely observers: they expect instruction tailored to their needs. The ward round is therefore a balancing act in which the needs of patients, colleagues and students have to be weighed against one another. If this were not challenging enough, there will be interruptions by bleep and by telephone, many of which cannot be ignored.

It might be expected that there would be places where our consultant could escape from interruption and exercise her skills unimpeded by distractions and obstructions; an out-patient clinic, for example. Not so. Clinics will invariably be overbooked.[10] Patients will not necessarily arrive at the appointed time. If they arrive early they expect to be seen early. If, as often happens – because they travel by unreliable ambulance or because they hit traffic or got lost in the hospital – they arrive late, there is a sudden influx after a period of thumb-twiddling. Not infrequently there are computer errors, so that all the patients are booked in at the same time. There will always be patients who have more, and more difficult, problems than expected and require more than the allocated time. Some patients may need assistance to undress and dress and the nurse who was due to provide this help may have been called away. A patient who has just been diagnosed with a serious illness will properly expect information, support and comfort, which are difficult to fit into the scheduled time.

Under such circumstances the consultant cannot nowadays count on understanding, or even forgiveness, from the patients kept waiting. Another patient may require urgent admission, so there will be the hunt for a bed and conversations with the admitting team – if they can be tracked down. Numerous other, almost comically homely factors add to the viscosity of the medium in which our consultant tries to perform her duties: more interruptions, missing investigations – and wrong or engaged numbers obstructing the search, missing request forms, the wrong kind of writing implement to write on investigation request forms, missing sticky labels with the demographic information about the patient the forms require. Sooner or later, she will fall behind and then will have to face someone in the waiting room, sighing or pointing to his watch, pantomiming his anger at being kept waiting, for her benefit and that of his fellow patients.

These obstacles are not a reflection of the special inefficiency of our consultant. A recent study of a surgical out-patient clinic[11] found that consultants spend only half the time in consultation with patients that they spent in 1988. The most conspicuous waste of time was in searching for missing case notes or investigation results, 17 per cent on administrative duties and 15 per cent on disturbances from the phone and other staff. The study concluded that doctors' hours are getting longer and longer because of non-clinical work.

Amid all the distractions our consultant has to bear in mind what medicine is about: frightened, suffering people who may be facing disability or death. She has to maintain a quadruple vision that encompasses the pathology of the illness, the symptoms experienced by an individual patient, the unique impact on the patient's life, and the meaning the illness has for the patient. Of course, if our sample consultant cannot maintain that quadruple vision while she is fussing over complicated blood tests or a technically difficult procedure, if she is sometimes irritable, abstracted or less than understanding, it is especially hurtful to a patient who feels helpless and is deeply worried.

Although this does not justify classifying her behaviour as malpractice, any slip-up is likely to confirm the view that consultants are arrogant, rude and poor communicators – and bad experiences are more likely to be reported while ordinary or even good ones are not. Just as those many occasions in which her reassurance turns out to be wise will be overshadowed by the one occasion in which it is proved wrong, so one moment of rudeness will outweigh any amount of forbearance and kindness. A headline in the *Observer* ran, 'How doctors deliver the curt words that mean life or death' and much of the page was taken up with a photograph of a patient whose 'battle to communicate with doctors has left her profoundly disillusioned'.[12] The article began with a story of a consultant in 'a tiny office' (one can be criticized for not being god-like enough) who broke bad news in a way that seemed manifestly unsatisfactory. Much of the rest of the article was taken up with a survey carried out by a medical charity. Its findings scarcely reflected the negative picture suggested by the headline: specialist support nurses giving patients additional information; special diaries issued to patients setting out what they might expect; between 94 per cent of patients (seen in the best hospitals) and 69 per cent of patients (in the worst hospitals) reporting that they had received enough information; and five out of six patients stating that they *had* spent sufficient time with the consultant when the news was broken. The actual content of the article hardly supported the angry conclusion that 'It will take a culture shock to turn Government's rhetoric about patient choice into reality.'

What explains this dissociation between the image of the consultant and the reality of her working life? By the very fact that they are 'playing a home match' and that they keep people waiting, doctors seem powerful, although this is not a power they actually exercise or want. It belongs to the structure within which they work and of which they are a part. The hurry that some patients interpret as deliberate devaluation is imposed upon, rather than chosen by, the consultant: in short, our consultant is less god-like than cog-like. If she is sometimes disempowering, it is because she herself is disempowered.

Some medical power goes beyond the unwilled and unenjoyed power transmitted from the structures within which doctors work. There is a benign power arising from their medical knowledge and their skills rooted in knowledge and experience. It is the desire to exercise such a power that brought most of us into medicine in the first place. Without admittedly sometimes romanticized ideas of 'doing good' it would be difficult to see how anyone could stand being a doctor.

Even this benign exercise of power through acquired expertise is regarded by some with great suspicion: the very idea of an individual with special access to knowledge (especially knowledge expressed in technical terms, which are seen to be instruments of mystification) is unacceptable. While all are agreed that 'doctor knows best' is no longer acceptable, for some 'doctor knows better' is just as outdated and paternalistic. The assumption that the doctor's knowledge is deployed to ends that are of benefit to patients is treated with suspicion, especially by those attracted by the notion of a 'postmodern' challenge to expertise and professional authority – though even Michel Foucault, the patron saint of postmodernist attacks on the professions, sought conventional, hi-tech care when he fell seriously ill.[13] In practice, the appropriate expectation that one has (some) answers is experienced by doctors as a burden rather than a privilege. And there are benign uses of knowledge and of the power that comes with it, as a lawyer who is acting on behalf of a client mismanaged by an ignorant doctor will be the first to point out.

The powerlessness suffered by our consultant extends beyond the experience of caring for individual patients. She is unable even to bring about those changes that would enable her to get things under control. She will usually feel impotent to implement the improvements she wants to see in the service she provides. The things her patients complain about are things she, too, complains about. Like many consultants, she spends hours of her free time helping to draw up documents in support of what in NHS jargon is called 'the business case' for urgently needed equipment or a new building or a new clinic session.[14] In my own hospital, in my last year as a full-time consultant, we have just had the annual round of 'cost improvement programmes' – that is, cuts – which I have known every year since I became a consultant in 1982.[15]

Between 1997 and 2001, in addition to my clinical and academic duties, I was Project Director overseeing a much-needed reorganization of neurosciences services – neurosurgery, neurology, neurological rehabilitation and support services like neuroradiology – in Greater Manchester. During this time twenty or thirty consultants (working with managers, nurses, therapists, social workers and patient groups) spent hours of their own time drawing up plans for a better service for people with chronic diseases such as epilepsy and multiple sclerosis and Parkinson's disease. The only obstacle to what should have been an unstoppable combination of managerial and clinical wisdom was lack of funds. (It took us two years of ceaseless argument and discussions to get a further £2 million extra funding to enable a Neurosciences Centre to serve a population of 3 million to be located in a new building and not in refurbished Victorian stock.)

The Neurological Rehabilitation Units had been agreed as a top priority with patients and their representatives and acknowledged by the relevant Health Authorities as integral to the scheme. The relevant Service Design Group (who took advice from patients) put in a huge amount of utterly tedious work making and remaking the case for each of the components of each of the Units. For nearly four years this yielded no result: squabbles between Health Authorities over who should bear the costs of the units that served more than one district, uncertainty as to where the power to make decisions lay, and so on, left everything stuck in the sand. For example, three years were spent drawing up, submitting, revising, resubmitting the job description of a consultant neurologist that everyone had already agreed was imperative to address the unmet needs of the people of Rochdale, and an equal amount of time – long after agreement had been reached – to track down the actual funds for a social worker essential to support patients with desperately severe neurological problems and their families.[16]

The difficulty we experienced in implementing the neurosciences reorganization under apparently optimal circumstances – close working of hospital managers and clinicians, political and patient support – in bringing about things that were universally regarded as being of the highest priority gives some indication of the frustrations facing consultants who are simply rooting for their own service and have to place them in a long queue of priorities battling for attention and resources.

Yet the Healthcare Financial Management Association, one of countless organizations remote from patient care that have sprung up over the last few decades or so – the god-like consultant may be dead but the god-like consultancy is not[17] – has declared that it is now up to doctors and their like to deliver on the government's promises:

The government has defined the standards and targets and now promised the funding [in the wake of Wanless]. It is important that staff now take ownership and responsibility for delivery. This may well cause annoyance in the profession, with many doctors arguing that they have long been putting in the effort in the absence of decent funding, and that it is not up to them to meet the Government's politically motivated targets.[18]

One of the non-accidental consequences of the interminable structural changes in the NHS over the last twenty years has been a shift of the power to change things *away* from senior clinicians to central government. The assumption has been that clinicians are not to be trusted with power and that, in the case of consultants, they have abused it. In practice, despite obstacles, the vast progress that the NHS has made in the half-century since it was founded has largely depended upon reforms and innovations led by clinicians, that have required ingenuity, vision, insight, negotiating skills and often a willingness to be personally exposed to risk.[19] These doctor-led innovations have been across the board: new operations, new drugs, new investigations, and changes in the way the services are shaped and delivered.

Here are a few examples, selected at random from a list that runs into many thousands:

a) Surgical treatments: joint replacements, coronary artery by-pass grafting and angioplasty, organ transplants, heart valve replacements, minimally invasive surgery, fertility treatments.

b) Non-surgical treatments: drugs for infections, high blood pressure, hypertension, raised cholesterol, peptic ulcers, for cancer; kidney dialysis; devices to break up kidney stones.

c) Investigations: the choice is overwhelming but it includes catheterization to diagnose cardiac disease, arteriography, ultrasound, CT and MRI scanning of the brain and body, bacteriological, virological tests, biochemical tests and hormonal assays.

d) Service delivery: doctors have always been interested in the way services are organized as well as what they deliver, and some of the doctor-led innovations include: formal appointment times to see general practitioners, diary dates for admissions, all-day ward visiting, admission wards, day surgery, home-based hospital care, peripatetic rehabilitation teams, specialist nurses in, for example, diabetes, chronic mental illness and epilepsy, audit, confidential inquiries into maternal and perioperative deaths, peer review of services.[20]

The list, it will be noted, includes not only headline-attracting advances such as heart transplants and cancer drugs but also more homely, patient-friendly developments such as bringing services nearer to patients' homes and all-day ward visiting.[21] Such innovations in therapeutics, surgery, intensive care, rehabilitation and service delivery that change the actual business of care, and indubitably contribute to the health and happiness of the people, often lie beyond the ambitions, visions, time-scale and competence of politicians.

The respective contributions of consultants and the government to improving patient care may be judged by comparing this list with the innovations introduced by government:[22]

a) Repeated reorganizations of the management structure of the NHS, which have cost huge amounts of time and effort and have been pronounced failures by succeeding administrations.[23]

b) The internal market, fund-holding practices – ditto.

c) Progressive reduction of hospital bed numbers, and a consequent inability to deal with acute admissions and disastrous reduction in capacity for elective surgery.

d) Setting targets for in-patient waiting lists, out-patient waiting times, and trolley waits while restricting resources including beds, with distortion of clinical priorities, and much dangerous distraction.

e) League tables, star systems, performance indicators, cash-limited budgets, none of which has been evaluated and all of which have had huge opportunity costs in terms of switching of focus.

Several things distinguish doctor-led from government-led innovations. The former are based on evidence and have a clear rationale, where this is relevant, from science. They are evaluated in the light of practical experience and, on this basis, they are often withdrawn. Governments cannot afford to wait for evidence or will not seek evidence to show that their reforms are working, in case they do not. Doctor-led innovations have little support behind them: they will not usually be in line with government thinking, which is always behind the times. A doctor trying to introduce a new service will encounter the full resistance of institutional and bureaucratic viscosity.

The transformation of health care for older people from back-wards warehousing to a modern comprehensive care for acute, rehabilitation and long-term problems, is a case in point:[24] there was no central support for this because at the beginning of the NHS (and still to some extent now) people over working age were seen as being a lower priority than younger adults.

Far from being blockers to reform and innovation, then, consultants have been the prime movers. It is obvious anyway who are the innovators and 'modernizers' and who are the 'wreckers'. Where there is overlap between government-led and clinician-led innovations, it is interesting that the former are often a cruder more distorted version of the latter – for example the profession's detailed audit of particular services being replaced by star ratings and league tables based upon inappropriate measures.[25] To have to respond to centrally inspired, ill-thought-through initiatives while having her own case for improved services sidelined, is a special cross for our consultant especially under New Labour.

If our sample consultant is senior enough, she may be invited by the Department of Health to join a working party reviewing some aspect of the NHS. Under the illusion that this may empower her to bring about the changes she has striven for, she may accept the invitation. She will find this a deeply scarring experience and it will leave her feeling even more powerless. The process of turning evidence-based medicine into civil-servant-acceptable prose and Treasury-approved guidelines is interminable.

Consider this real-life example of Department of Health practice. We have known since the early 1990s that properly organized care reduces mortality and severe disability following stroke by 30 per cent.[26] The evidence, gathered by the patient work of consultants and others, is so robust that you could jump on it without falling through. At present, however, it is a matter of chance whether, if you have a stroke, you will receive such care. As a result about five patients per day die unnecessarily and about seven per day become unnecessarily institutionalized. After years of discussion, the Department of Health eventually invited a group of individuals to draw up some guidelines for the management of this condition within the context of the National Service Framework (NSF) for Older People. Fortunately the Royal College of Physicians, in consultation with a variety of experts, including patients and their representatives, had already produced a comprehensive evidence-based set of guidelines for the care of this condition in hospital, in primary care and more widely in the community. The work of our small group was therefore effectively done, or so we thought.

In fact, producing the Service Framework took two years, during which another 3,500 patients died unnecessarily and another 5,000 became more severely disabled. These were some of the main themes of our deliberations, negotiations and explosions: the number of recommendations the Minister would allow us to make; given a limited number of recommendations, which aspects of good care we should throw out; how the Minister wanted us to structure the document underpinning the recommendations. Added to continual change of personnel, uniformly ignorant of clinical matters who had to be dragged up steep learning curves at high speed, and capricious behaviour by ministers, this led to a certain amount of anger among the clinicians who, after all, had day jobs.

After two years of work and lobbying – at weekends, in the evening, in the very early hours of the morning – the recommendations were published. Two years after the guidelines were published, a survey of stroke services has shown that, at the present rate of progress, it will be seventy-three years before the recommendations supposed to be universally implemented in 2004 are in place. Only 27 per cent of patients spend their hospital stay on a stroke unit, compared with 25 per cent before the guidance was published.[27] Moreover, no funds have been identified specifically for delivering on the promises in the National Service Framework. (That is why to the clinicians on the ground the acronym NSF means Nothing So Far or No Sodding Funds!)[28]

Sometimes powerlessness and the pressures of accountability will become unbearable and our sample consultant will behave badly. Occasionally she will be abrupt with a patient. More often her bad behaviour will be directed at a local manager, the other demonized species in the health service.

This is particularly regrettable as managers are, for the most part, as idealistic and as committed to the NHS as the clinicians. Many could have had a happier life in the private sector, with more resources, a more clearly defined and easily deliverable brief, better support, more salary and a few perks. They too work extremely hard and have their own, often frustrated, dreams of developing better services. They also have to bear the added burden of sometimes being treated badly by consultants at the end of their tethers while they are negotiating the constant white water created by ever-more numerous, ever-more complex, instructions from the Department of Health as one bright and unthought-through idea follows another. A survey of NHS Trust Chief Executives found that they were spending more than a quarter of their time implementing 'reforms' and that in 2001, after four years of continuous revolution, the majority were opposed to any further change – though there was much more to come. None, however, felt they could speak out.[29]

As for the claim that consultants enjoy god-like unaccountability, our consultant is accountable in at least five different kinds of ways: to the court of her conscience (which usually convenes at 4 a.m.);[30] to her peers (whose well-informed views of her competence will be inseparable from her self-respect); to the evidence-base and adherence to guidelines and protocols; to professional regulatory bodies, multiplying daily; and to the law. Every aspect of her work – the number and kind of patients she sees, her prescribing patterns – are recorded, monitored and to a greater or lesser degree regulated. Annual appraisals have to include evidence to back up statements about performance and about endeavours to keep up to date. Visits from the relevant Royal College and from the postgraduate dean's office monitor the quality of her training, appraisal and assessment of junior doctors working with her. The views of the junior doctors are sought in confidential interviews.

A consultant surgeon, who is also an academic, recently listed the bodies to which he had to report and all the ways in which he was assessed, noting in passing the huge amount of his time that this occupied.[31] The list included eight national bodies, starting with the General Medical Council; eight hospital bodies, ranging from the Clinical Governance Committee to the Pre-Registration House Officer and Senior House Officer Reviews for Post-Graduate Team; and six university bodies, including the Annual University Appraisal and the Research Governance Committee.[32] On top of these twenty-two regular reports, there are ad hoc investigations of clinical incidents, the assessment of individual research projects submitted to Research Ethics Committees, audit of particular aspects of practice, contributions to national surveys, and so on.

Because they are perceived to have unlimited power, consultants are held to account for numerous things over which they have no control. A few years ago, a child in Cambridgeshire with a very advanced leukaemia was denied funding for an extremely expensive treatment that was deemed unlikely to be cost-effective – as proved to be the case when she received it in the private sector supported by a private donation. Her father ran a very high profile campaign in support of the treatment. He singled out the consultant – a child cancer specialist and a dedicated doctor working under huge pressures in a very difficult area – for vilification. On one occasion, the oncologist wrote a letter to the patient's father about her daughter's treatment. It was sent out through the hospital post with a second-class stamp. The stamp was regarded as the final insult by the father, who informed the tabloid newspaper that was supporting him. 'SECOND CLASS DOCTOR'[33] ran the front-page headlines the following day, naming-and-shaming the consultant, who had made the correct judgement that the further course of expensive therapy was neither in the interests of the child nor an appropriate use of resources.

Medicine is more down to earth, much closer to the body, than other professions. There will be times when our specimen consultant may become aware that only sex-workers have to get as physically intimate as do health care workers with people they do not desire. She may find, as she inserts her finger up the rectum of yet another stranger or feels for a femoral pulse in another unwashed groin, or examines yet another pot full of the thickest and most purulent sputum, that she wishes she were in something more aseptic like the law. She may also find that a life of eternal interruption in a noisy ward, trying to hear heart murmurs in the midst of distractions, listening to the history being recounted by the house officer while she is waiting to get through to a GP, is just too much. If she does feel this, she will not admire herself for doing so. And she will continue her perpetually obstructed progress through her very ordinary – and extraordinary – and sometimes terrifying duties.

This, then, is the life of the consultant. What keeps her going are compassion, a sense of duty and determination to do a good job. The thespian swagger and bullying of Lancelot Spratt, the autocratic surgeon in Richard Gordon's *Doctor in the House*, is now a fiction. Unfortunately, as Marxists used to point out, social consciousness lags behind social reality.

The empowered consumer

Exaggerating the power of doctors goes hand in hand with exaggerating the powerlessness of the patient. The demonized doctor-perpetrator is linked with the canonization of the patient-victim as if decline in physicianly goodness must be compensated by an increase in patient saintliness.

The very suspicion which has sustained the attacks on the standing of doctors is that people are not trustworthy: that is why we are invited to believe medical power to be intrinsically malign and that, without ever-closer regulation of activities, doctors will behave badly. Left to themselves, they will be negligent, blundering, idle, uncaring, ignorant, fraudulent scoundrels who will damage patients by acts of commission or omission. But patients are people, too, and will share the faults of their all-too-human doctors. The emphasis on patients as 'consumers' is an inadvertent reminder that they are essentially self-interested.

For a physician to talk of the (necessary, understandable) selfishness of patients may be rather shocking. Despite all the cynical talk, it is still assumed that the patient–doctor relationship is one in which the doctors cares and the patient is cared for, the doctor is trustworthy and the patient trusts, the doctor respects and the patient is respected. In other words, the doctor is expected to have human qualities that consumerism cannot accommodate. And so we have a lopsided idealism: the patient is an empowered consumer while the doctor must altruistically treat the patient as an end in himself or herself. Most importantly, she will not pass judgement on the patient, whatever demands for treatment, time and attention he makes. She will certainly not judge the patient as harshly as would another patient, a fellow consumer, waiting in the same queue. Indeed, she will welcome the extra challenge presented by the patient-as-consumer because it is evidence of the empowerment of the hitherto powerless.

The implication that 'the empowered patient' is a new species created by politicians and other advocates implies that medicine overall is not patient-empowering. This a grotesque, indeed curious libel. The doctor who gets you back on your feet, relieves you of pain, helps you recover your independence, assists you in dealing with incontinence, or postpones your death, is empowering in a direct, fundamental and radical way that can be matched by few other professionals. Indeed, empowerment is what medicine is largely about. In some cases, of course, the treatment doesn't work; in a minority of cases, the treatment is worse than the disease. This will be disempowering but only incidentally so: the adverse effects of unsuccessful treatments are rarely the result of a direct intention to kill or maim. Even a doctor who cannot cure your condition, but at least shares with you his understanding of what is going on, is empowering. In some cases the attempt to communicate that understanding will fail and in other cases the understanding will be wrong: doctors make mistakes like other human beings.

For some critics of the medical profession, this will be beside the point: those who are preoccupied with the medical profession's power to disempower are often concerned more with the *process* – humiliating, undignified, inconvenient – than with the *outcome*. And there will indeed be cases where the experience of the treatment will be more disabling, humiliating, dependency-creating, than the illness. But this is not routine and certainly not intrinsic to the patient–doctor relationship.

Others who are preoccupied with the power of both individual doctors and of the medical profession will focus on 'medicalization': the translation of human unhappiness, foibles and faults – all the various ways in which humans may deviate from the stipulated norm – into medical problems. The profession has been criticized for medicalizing sexual diversity, grief following bereavement, hyperactivity in children, and childbirth, in pursuit of their ambition to be agents of social control. However, there have been equally vocal critics of profession's failure to acknowledge the same conditions as medical problems: doctors have been pilloried for freeing sexual deviants, who subsequently turn out to be dangerous repeat offenders, from institutions; for not diagnosing pathological grieving and withholding antidepressants; for failing to diagnose badly behaved children as having Attention Deficiency Hyperactivity Syndrome and not offering medical treatment; and for failing to intervene in childbirth.

'Medicalization' is often forced on doctors by the families of patients, as the following examples demonstrate.[34]

An old man has attempted suicide with digoxin. The psychiatrist finds nothing wrong with his psyche but writes that the patient's intentions to commit suicide were serious. The family, the social worker, and the legal adviser of the hospital concur that the patient should be restrained in bed. The physician is the one to write the order. On the day the patient is extubated [has the nasogastric tube removed] he tells his story. He is lonely, sick and in pain. His wife died and he is disappointed with his daughters. He wants to die. Because the physician fears litigation, he renews his order of constraint. He knows that he has done wrong.

The family of a sixty-year-old man with terminal metastatic cancer refuses to take him back home. His pains are well controlled, and they know that nothing more can be done for him. But we cannot conceive that he will die at home, they say. The task to comfort and cope with the dying man is left to the doctor who has known him less than a week.

Another aspect of medicalization is described by Roy Porter:

Thanks to diagnostic creep or leap, ever more disorders are revealed. Extensive and expensive treatments are then urged, and the physician who chooses not to treat may expose himself to malpractice accusations. Anxieties and interventions spiral upwards like a space-shot off course... Doctors and 'consumers' are becoming locked within a fantasy that *everyone* has *something* wrong with them, everyone and everything can be cured.[35]

As the authors of the paper from which these examples are taken, say:

These aspects of medicalization make doctors miserable. The bad things of life: old age, death, pain, and handicap are thrust on doctors to keep families and society from facing them. Some of them are an integral part of medicine, and accepted as such. But there is a boundary beyond which medicine has only a small role. When doctors are forced to go beyond that role they do not gain power or control: they suffer.

This is how 'medicalization' looks from the inside. It is more often imposed on doctors by societal expectations than imposed on patients by a power-hungry profession wanting to expropriate every human woe or variation for itself.[36] It is illustrated by the treatment of homosexuality as a sickness. An issue of the *British Medical Journal* on the thirtieth anniversary of the official declassification of homosexuality as a mental illness speaks of its medicalization as part of 'medicine's shameful past' and 'one of its many mistakes'.[37] This is unfair. From the standpoint of the twenty-first century, this does look barbaric; but from the standpoint of the 1950s and 1960s, this was comparatively enlightened and more liberal than the views in the population as a whole. After all, until 1967 in the UK and much later in other parts of the world, homosexuality was a criminal offence with jail as the standard management plan. What is more, it was the medical profession, against much internal and external resistance, that accepted that homosexuality was a personal choice rather than a crime or a sickness. In this respect the profession has been doubly enlightened: first decriminalizing and then demedicalizing what many – notably in the Catholic and Anglican churches and in Islam – still condemn as a mortal sin. The 'shameful past' is the past of society as a whole, not medicine in particular, which remains ahead of much disempowering public opinion.

The idealization of the patient as the marginalized, put-upon, disempowered victim of medicine, or of a system of care (the NHS) that 'seems to work for its own convenience not the patient's',[38] ignores the fact that the patient is primarily self-interested and how his or her self-interest is potentially in conflict with that of other patients. An anger that is not exactly selfless may none the less be moralized: in asserting their rights, in expropriating power for themselves, patients often believe they act on behalf of others; as victims they are striking blows for victims everywhere. Time and again one hears it said by a complainant that his only motive for suing for compensation is to protect others from the injustice/the wrong/the blunder in future.

The emphasis on the 'disempowering doctor' when clinicians have never been more able and willing to liberate patients from the intimate disempowerments of illness, reflects how technology and technological skill – in short, expertise – are taken most for granted when they are most effective: the hard-won, uncertain and limited benefits of the past were more appreciated than the massive advances upon which medicine presently stands.[39] Routine success ceases to be success.

In Chapter 4 we noted that, because illness is intrinsically disempowering, those who try to deal with its impact tend to be experienced as agents of disempowerment, even in those cases where treatment is entirely successful. The very processes of cure and care seem to compound the loss of volition resulting from illness. Clinicians, although they aim to restore the health and freedom of the patient, may seem to be part of the problem – a consequence of illness, rather than the solution. Anger at the disempowerment of illness is especially likely to be transferred to those who try to alleviate it where the process is complex, inconvenient and painful, and the treatments, notwithstanding their net benefits, have adverse effects.

The General Medical Council's list of the doctor's duties includes the command to 'listen to patients and respect their views'. This is more than giving the patient air-time to describe her symptoms: it includes acknowledging her expertise. A good consultation is a meeting between experts: while doctors are experts on medical problems in general, patients are experts on how they themselves experience these problems. Only the patient can determine whether she is finding a treatment of net benefit.

In my own clinic, I often leave it to the patient who has had only rare minor epileptic fits, to decide whether she wants to continue her anti-epileptic medication, with its side effects, or try doing without, knowing that this carries an increased risk of recurrence of fits, with implications for driving and other potential undesirable consequences. The same applies to the preference for medication: if the patient says tablet A is preferable to tablet B, then it would be absurd for me to contradict this, assuming that both tablets have the same general efficacy and range of indications. I can bring the recent pharmaceutical literature to the discussion and the patient brings her direct experience: we have the basis for a dialogue in which each of us respects the other's expertise. None of this is in the slightest bit revolutionary or even exceptionally progressive.

Patients with chronic diseases will certainly be experts. Providing that they have reflected responsibly on their experiences and acknowledge the limitations of generalization from a single case to others, they have much to give other patients with the same condition. If after fifteen years of living with diabetes I wasn't some kind of expert on it, there must be something wrong with me and/or my clinical advisers.

Expert patients are often employed to instruct, encourage and support others. What this brings to medical care is not as novel, or as subversive of the medical establishment or challenging to the hegemony of doctors, as is sometimes suggested. Doctors have for a long time encouraged patients to consult other patients, particularly when they are contemplating medical procedures about which they may be uncertain, such as amputations and colostomies. And support groups run by patients have long been welcomed by physicians. Moreover, it is routine in the research into the comparative benefits of treatments to include patient preferences, and quality of life measures, in a systematic way. The 'expert patient', in other words, is not new, except as a term of ideology: and here problems may arise.

A patient who is expert on his or her own condition is not always an expert on other patients, even those who have the same condition. This follows from the very fact emphasized by those who stress the expertise of the patient: that every patient is different. Extrapolating from one's own experience to that of others is rarely straightforward and this makes some expert patients a liability. A patient who, on the basis of her own bad experiences with medication, advises others that they should give up theirs may be well-intentioned but is dangerously irresponsible. She is setting her own experience of a single case against the experience of many thousands of other patients. Clinical advice is best rooted in rigorously conducted trials which tap into the experiences of patients in a way that minimizes bias and the play of chance. However, the use of expert patients as a new 'epistemic community', a special caste whose views have to be deferred to, should be evaluated as carefully as any other therapeutic ploy.

The same caution applies to 'patient representatives' who are being given an increasingly loud voice in NHS planning. While this may be a good thing in general, there are particular occasions when it is not. The notion of the patient representative itself is rather unclear. In what sense is the individual patient representative of a group of patients? They may be self-chosen, with a particular experience in the forefront of their mind. Perhaps they feel they have been cheated, let down, damaged or neglected by the 'system'. The satisfied are less vocal, so that the dissatisfied are disproportionately represented. They may not therefore be representative at all.[40] They will argue, however, that they are vocalizing the unexpressed anger of all those others who have been cheated, let down, damaged or neglected by the 'system'. Their rage, we are assured, is the tip of an iceberg of silent fury – of anger silenced by fear of the establishment and its powers of retribution. Reference to 'grateful' patients will be unwise; in the present climate, many regard gratitude as a pathological state, symptomatizing deference. Intense anger and grief, by contrast, are ascribed special authority, as if the intensity of an emotion were the guarantor of its cognitive value. And egocentric concern is repackaged as a selfless rage on behalf of those whose voices are unheard.[41]

It would be grossly unfair, however, to suggest that this is a typical outcome of patient empowerment. And the presence of patient representatives – or lay people – when services are being designed makes intuitive sense. It may require a patient to point out it is undesirable to start a geriatrics out-patient clinic at nine o'clock in the morning if the cheap bus passes do not allow patients who cannot afford the full fare to get there in time; or that the wheelchair assessment clinic is inaccessible to people who may need to use wheelchairs. The professionals may overlook things that would make the service user-friendly. There may even be a role for patients, or their representatives, in the design of services from the beginning.[42]

Unfortunately the value of the input from lay people has never been properly assessed. This may seem unnecessary when 'lay' itself becomes a qualification and 'professional' a disability. But it isn't: lay involvement in health care planning and management has significant up-front costs. Lay people will have to be brought up to speed on the nature of the problems being addressed. They will be at the bottom of the learning curve, not having yet made the mistakes that, properly reflected upon, are the engine for the continuously improved performance of the reflective clinician or manager. Meetings dealing with complex issues will be significantly slowed. Two systematic reviews (one of which searched through 337 studies of involving users or patients in development of health care) have failed to show any clear benefits.[43] In no case were the time costs taken into account, which means that, on the evidence so far, the involvement of patients in the planning of services may be deleterious overall. Of course, lack of evidence of benefit is not the same as evidence of lack of benefit; however, there was some preliminary suggestion that, in the case of mental health services, involvement of users in delivering services reduced client satisfaction. The jury, it would seem, is out: we are not yet justified in taking the patient, client or user as an oracle or for assuming the superiority of services into which patients have had a major design input. We should examine the contributions of patients to the design of services with the same cold objectivity as we should examine any resource-consuming practice in health care. A tide of antiprofessional rhetoric and unquestioned assumptions is not sufficient justification.

Behind the assumption that the patient viewpoint will make for better services is that experts will be blinded by their science to the things that matter to ordinary people, and will be unable, because of their positional advantage within the service, to see how things look from the putatively disadvantaged viewpoint of the user. Lay people and patient representatives will be free of the baggage of assumptions, habits of thought and vested interests that disable professional thinkers. None of this is necessarily true. While lay people may bring a modicum of common sense, they will not necessarily bring anything more. In many cases, generic lay members may be quite ignorant of some fairly basic facts. There is, for example, widespread confusion in the general population between stroke and heart attacks.[44] Many of my most upsetting miscommunications with patients have come from over-estimating people's understanding of the diseases I was talking about. Leaving aside lack of basic knowledge and understanding, it will be remarkable if patient's representatives do not bring their own prejudices to the table.

One such prejudice will be the assumption that the conditions they, their loved ones, or the group whom they are representing, suffer from are more important than conditions they may not have heard of, suffered by other patients. Many of the generally useful meetings we had with patient representatives when I was overseeing the design of neuroscience services in Greater Manchester were punctuated with the views of the husband of a patient who had a condition which, he felt, was not recognized by the medical profession and, even when recognized, not treated in the way he believed it should be. His interventions effectively removed air-time from those who were representing other important conditions such as stroke, Parkinson's disease, epilepsy, dementia and so on. While the representatives of sufferers from disease A may acknowledge the importance of diseases B, C and D, they will tend to leave the latter to look after themselves. This becomes rather nakedly apparent when what is at issue is allocation of resources.

This was particularly evident to me during my years as a member of one of the Appraisal Committees at the National Institute on Clinical Excellence (NICE). The appraisals, which determine whether particular drugs are sufficiently cost-effective to justify their being made available free through the NHS, were complex and involved wide consultation with a spectrum of stakeholders, including patient representatives and groups. For such groups, this was an opportunity to exercise their advocacy role. They sometimes discharged this with no regard to cost-effectiveness. Indeed, to have done so would have been a betrayal of the patients whom they represented; for, it was often argued, even if the drug were not cost-effective its availability would add to 'patient choice'. There was often little concern about the impact of funding of the drug on the resources available to other groups of patients. In many cases, when NICE concluded that a drug was not cost-effective, patient groups continued their advocacy work – in which of course they were supported by the relevant drug companies, and the media who bitterly criticized NICE's decision, often accusing it of 'disregard of expert opinion' and 'acting as the government's rationing agency'.

Patient representatives rarely see that in championing the apparent interests of their own constituency, they are sometimes acting to the detriment of other patients; that to highlight one disease is to lowlight all others. And yet it is very difficult to see past the notion of such individuals as 'doughty champions' for the disadvantaged against the faceless bureaucrats. To take one example: the Multiple Sclerosis Society's campaign in support of the drug beta-interferon would, had it have been successful, have resulted in the squandering of hundreds of millions of pounds on a treatment of doubtful cost-effectiveness and would have diverted resources which could have been invested in cancer and arthritis treatments.

Competition between patients is even more visible in the capillaries of the system. Any doctor who overruns in a clinic can expect an angry waiting room whose occupants care nothing for the special transactions, or kindness, or going the extra mile, that has taken place behind his closed doors. He can expect no mercy from those who feel dis-empowered by being kept inexplicably waiting. It is a little more difficult for doctors to hold on to the fundamental values of compassion and empathy if their exercise is usually resented by patients other than those currently benefiting from them.

As already mentioned, the GMC includes in its list of the 'Duties of a Doctor' to 'listen to patients and respect their views'. One must certainly listen to all patients and while, in most cases, their views are a) deserving of respect and b) of paramount importance, this is not always true.

What is more, the respect-worthiness of a patient's views is not necessarily proportional to the length or volume at which they are expressed. Patients expressing their views about their own needs should also respect the needs of other patients.

The contribution of the internet to empowering patients, by abolishing the inequality of knowledge between doctor and patient has been greatly exaggerated, even by those who should know better:

To a great extent the move towards the consumer-oriented society is itself being fuelled by the revolution in information technology. In medicine, this is changing the dynamic of the doctor/patient relationship – in favour of the patient – forever. A fundamental part of doctors' professionalism has traditionally rested on the unique body of knowledge and skill to which only professionals have access. But the internet has given every citizen direct access to the database of medicine. So the doctors' monopoly of information no longer exists. Of course, people still want, need and expect the help of a doctor to make sense of it all.[45]

It is alarming to observe that the writer, a doctor himself, regards 'skill' as coming with internet printouts and sees 'making sense of it all' as mere tweaking. This is connected with a widespread failure to acknowledge the sheer difficulty of medicine (never mind surgery), the central role of judgement, experience, practical wisdom, tacit knowledge, a sense of proportion and of perspective, that is no more available on the internet than it would be available in a magazine article. An 'e-hypochondriac' is no more sophisticated than one nourished on glossy magazines.[46]

Which is not to say that even the most competent and caring doctor cannot get things wrong. And a patient who has read something on the internet or in a magazine may usefully remind doctors of things they have forgotten or draw their attention to things they may be unaware of. But it is important to make sure that recall bias, focusing on those occasions when doctors get things wrong or when they were usefully updated by patients, does not lead to the default assumption that *everything* a doctor says or does has to be challenged, preferably with a printout from the net.[47]

It is not only doctors, of course, who are having to contend with decreasing respect from patients. The number of physical and verbal assaults on nurses rises annually. Ward nurses are particularly vulnerable because they are continuously, rather than episodically, exposed to abusive patients and their relatives, and hands-on care involves a considerable amount of physical closeness. It is very easy for a complaining patient, or a relative, picking on a nurse for everything that falls short of what is regarded as ideal care, to reduce that person to tears by unrelenting criticism. The most recent NHS survey conducted by the Commission on Health Improvement, with over 200,000 staff taking part, found that 15 per cent had been subjected to physical violence at work in the previous year and that 28 per cent had experienced harassment, bullying or abuse from patients or their families.[48]

One of the most memorable examples of disrespect I have witnessed, however, was in a totally different context. The Trust Board annual public meeting is the occasion when the Board informs the people it serves what it has been doing: for example, how many patients have been treated, what service developments are in hand, how the finances are working out. It is also an opportunity for the public to ask questions. One of the things we are particularly proud of is the internationally famed gastro-intestinal surgery service, which in addition to having a high standard of surgery pays a good deal of attention to after-care. This includes a club for young people who have had, or are about to have, colostomies, to help them to come to terms with this deeply upsetting procedure. This club was established by and is run (largely in her spare time) by a devoted nurse. She was persuaded, somewhat against her will, to give a presentation on the work of the club. She and her colleague put a huge amount of effort into their talk (this was the first time she had spoken in public). The talk, as well as being beautifully done, was very moving. After she had finished, the chairman asked if there were any questions. There were a few from the staff and stony silence from the public. The chairman therefore asked if there were any more general points. Immediately an individual who had been complaining about the rudeness of one of the surgeons in the Trust – and who had received an apology from the consultant and a visit at home from the chairman – resumed his complaints about the treatment he had received. It was evident from his tone that he thought that everything that he had heard – including the stuff about the club – was a mere smokescreen to distract us from his complaint. It was equally evident that he felt that, in drawing attention to his own complaint at the public meeting, he was acting as an advocate for all those who were served by the hospital. He was, he thought, empowering others.

There are some signs that the government is getting a little worried about increasing the role of 'the people' in shaping health services – but they are worried about political take-over. This is not merely a theoretical concern. Our Trust board will not readily forget the hijacking of one public meeting by a member of the Socialist Workers' Party (possibly the only member in Salford). The agenda item was the rationalization of fertility services in line with national recom- mendations. We were addressed, harangued, and argued with for the best part of an hour, about fertility services, the politics of the NHS, Western capitalism and the evils of globalization.

In order to ensure that Foundation Hospitals are sensitive to local needs, their ruling councils have to be elected by ex-patients, local resi- dents, and staff. Unfortunately, very few local people and ex-patients have registered to vote and there is a fear that 'Trotskyists and other extreme groups' such as the British National Party (who might have interesting views on the enhancement of services for patients from ethnic minorities) will take over.[49] It is all very well wresting power from the professionals and giving it to the people, so long as it is to the right people. Many advocates of democratizing the NHS and rolling out decision-making directly to the people are having to face the fact that, apart from an unrepresentative few (and the usual suspects – altruistic middle-class people with time on their hands), most people couldn't care less about the NHS except in so far as it impacts on themselves. A recent pamphlet from Hazel Blears (ex-Health Minister) has suggested estab- lishing a 'Citizen's Participation Agency' to get people a little more interested in exercising their new democratic rights.[50]

The suggestion that clinicians, too, deserve respect is now starting to feature a little in the press. In a recent article[51] prompted by a survey published in the *Reader's Digest*,[52] Cristina Odone points out that, if we really do believe that medicine has entered the market and patients are consumers, they must honour the obligations that consumers have. Odone lists some of them: 'politeness, or at least civility, cleanliness, and the willingness to try the treatment administered'. She quotes a south London GP:

I am here to treat any patient on my list. But it is a lot easier to do it properly if they keep their side of the bargain. I expect them to be punctual, sober and clean, to answer my questions politely and honestly and to take my advice seriously.

In short, to treat the doctor with the same respect as the GMC enjoins upon doctors, on pain of disciplinary action, to treat patients. Odone endorses this and also criticizes those who have replaced blind trust in the authority of doctors with 'wary suspicion': 'in establishing active interest in our welfare, we cannot elbow out those trained to safeguard it.'

The default assumption that doctors are constitutionally disempowering, that all patients who meet all doctors – or even most patients who meet most doctors – are disempowered by them is the profoundest imaginable expression of disrespect. It is certainly a very powerful force in health care planning at present. According to a recent report, doctors are being excluded from 'watchdogs, inspectorates, advisory and executive boards to oversee the modern quality-improved NHS' and they are being deliberately shunned in appointments to top jobs, including the Chair of the body that oversees postgraduate medical training, and NHS Professionals, the NHS's own locum agency. Most tellingly, the Healthcare Commission has no medical director on its board.[53]

There may be good reasons for this. Those who see patients day in and day out may not find it easy to support simple ideas: they will ask too many questions, be too aware of the complexities of patient care, and too cynical of the rhetoric of the quick fix and the global solution. They will be grit in the smooth machinery of initiatives that produce, and demand, more paper.

This disrespect for the profession, now being built into the very structure of the NHS may be something that the political class will come to regret. At any rate, when it is combined with a patient population increasingly encouraged to adopt an attitude of hostility towards their physicians, it will further reduce the good will of doctors and their commitment to the service as a whole. It will make them less willing, perhaps, to go the extra mile; already scarce medical time may become yet more scarce.

In this context, the following observation by Melinda Letts, chair of the Long Term Medical Conditions Alliance (a patients' organization), is of particular interest since it comes from an unexpected source:

I think [consumerism] has the potential to increase disdvantage. By widening the gulf between the strong consumer and the less strong; it adds pressures on stretched resources; it may feed people's sense of fragility, by indulging their wish to take medicines and thus institute a vicious circle of cost; and I fear it risks promoting self-interest rather than social solidarity, discouraging individual responsibility and pushing up cost.[54]

You bet.

Distrust as default[55]

People still seem to place a lot of trust in doctors – not only when they fall ill but also when they respond to opinion polls. Although this has been little diminished by the various scandals we read about in the press, the catchphrase 'trust me I'm a doctor' is now assured of a laugh.[56] It is seen as a symbol of the bygone era of *Dr Finlay's Casebook* and *Dr Kildare*. There seems to be a split in people's consciousness between their impression of individual doctors from whom they have sought help (who for the most part they have trusted and found helpful) and the idea of a 'scandal-hit' medical profession. 'Shipman', 'Bristol' and 'Alder Hey' are presented as symptomatic, even emblematic, of the profession as a whole. Yet a survey of 112,000 patients discharged from hospital with a diagnosis of coronary heart disease in 1998 found that 83 per cent had trust and confidence in their doctors – even more than the 79 per cent who had trust and confidence in their nurses.[57]

But for politicians, the assumed untrustworthiness of doctors supports the case for disempowering them and hence swinging the balance of power in their own favour: recent years have seen a supine medical profession offering little or no resistance to endless political interference. The supposed crisis of trust is not, however, all that it appears. As Onora O'Neill has pointed out, 'we still constantly place trust in many of the institutions and professions that we profess not to trust... we don't know whether we have a crisis of trust or only a culture of suspicion.'[58] After all, while the debate continues as to whether the public should trust doctors' skills, and they are being encouraged to challenge their advice, health care planners, presumably reflecting public priorities, are also preoccupied with reducing waiting lists for operations and increasing surgical throughput.

Moreover, the culture of suspicion extends far beyond the medical profession: it questions all forms of expertise, as we have seen, in particular in the theories of postmodernism with its global assault on authority of all sorts, including intellectual authority and expertise. Yet it can be noted that postmodern writers themselves underpin their position by claims to knowledge about huge areas of history.[59] Their authority seems miraculously immune from their own challenge. Beyond this, the loss of religious support for codes of ethics and, not unconnected with this, a pervasive consumerism with the attitude of caveat emptor have made suspicion and an explicit attitude of cynical distrust, seem as essential to self-respect as to self-protection.

If there were indeed a crisis of trust in the moral probity of doctors, how would it be addressed? Given that we have to trust in someone, to whom should we turn? Lawyers believe that we should seek their reassurance. Politicians want to take on the job of making doctors more trustworthy. Journalists think it is their job to bring doctors to moral account on behalf of the deceived public. Yet all of these groups are subject to even greater and more genuine suspicion.[60] Even the new breed of 'patient's champions' – lay people, managers, regulators being installed at various points in the NHS to watch over the welfare of patients – cannot be above suspicion. They have a job to do and to justify and to retain. If society as a whole lacks moral compass and suspicion is global and free-floating, there is no place outside of its corruptions. In short, if we withdraw trust from doctors, there is nowhere else to invest it.[61]

An alternative strategy is to invoke the triple-edged sword of transparency, accountability and regulation. O'Neill has pointed out that transparency will not deal with the real enemy of trust, namely deception. People understand this – and are suspicious of a deluge of information[62] – which may be why 'trust seems to have receded as transparency has advanced.' This is evident in the case of medicine: the more information people are given – through league tables, star ratings, audits, reports by regulatory bodies – the less confident they are that they know what is going on. This is in part because what they are told is not placed in perspective, because it is often distorted by interest groups and because there is always more information to come. As O'Neill points out, 'unless the individuals and institutions who sort, process and assess information are themselves already trusted, there is little reason to think that transparency and openness are going to increase trust.'[63]

So much for transparency. What about accountability and regulation? We have already examined the multiple layers of accountability of consultants and other doctors. They are being added to on an almost daily basis, with clinical guidelines and algorithms, patient pathways, service level agreements, quality standards, targets all mixed up together in an ever denser tangle of constraints. The regulatory framework of medicine – touching on everything from clinical management, through response times and throughput – is a very closely drawn mesh. Real crooks, however, will know what to do and, besides, will be more effectively concealed in a general cloud of suspicion.

Even so, there are those who wish to weave an even denser regulatory framework around medical practice. Jonathan Asbridge, who as the President of the new Nursing and Midwifery Council, has a vested interest in seeing regulation as the major force in building public trust (and an equal vested interest in assuming that it has to be built) asserts that 'Without regulation, of which the primary purpose is public protection… it is doubtful that health professionals could be trusted.'[64] Clara MacKay, in the same collection of papers in *Risk and Trust in the NHS*, concludes on the other hand, 'that regulation, whether it is self-regulation or external regulation, cannot instil trust or make people trust health professionals'.[65] Regulation cannot restore trust because without trust regulation will run into insuperable difficulties – not merely the problem of trusting the regulators (Do they do a good job? Is their work relevant to what matters? Do they have an agenda of their own?), but also of defining their own limits.

'The rise of regulation in the NHS'[66] is part of the growth of the 'regulatory state' or 'audit society'. The cost of regulation in the UK quadrupled between 1976 and 1995, by which time there were 135 different bodies overseeing the public sector.[67] The cost within the NHS has risen dramatically. By 2003, there were just under 20,000 staff employed in health quangos and watchdogs, consuming about £2.2 billion per year. This represents a rise of nearly 25 per cent since Labour came to power in 1997.[68] Uncontrolled proliferation of regulation (with the associated reporting structures and documentation and visits by regulatory bodies) will not only hamper everyday practice but also stifle innovation and frustrate the development of things that patients want. In the few years of its life – before it was replaced by the even grander sounding and menacing 'Commission on Healthcare, Audit and

Inspection' and recently renamed the Healthcare Commission – the Commission on Health Improvement (CHI) visited very large numbers of hospitals taking up time, disrupting management and clinical activity, prompting switches of priorities, and bringing considerable opprobium on some hospitals. We have no evidence that it has produced any benefit.[69]

Distrust-fuelled regulation is wasteful of resources. But there are more direct adverse consequences on patient care. Attempting to replace trust entirely by regulation looks particularly inappropriate in end-of-life decision-making. There, the replacement of judgement by regulation will force professionals to a precautionary attitude which will mean that many patients are subjected to protracted torment.[70] In a suspicious, over-regulated society, moral cowardice is the better part of clinical decision-making; prudence will be a higher value than compassion. There can be few doctors practising hospital medicine who have not subjected, or allowed patients to be subjected, to the grisly indignities of futile attempts at cardio-pulmonary resuscitation (CPR) in order to avoid the accusation by an aggrieved and ill-informed relative that the patient was neglected.

I can testify to the power of fear of reprisals myself. A while back, a patient came under my care as an acute emergency. He had a chest infection. He had been living in a nursing home for four years and for the last two years had been confined to bed, doubly incontinent, blind, speechless and severely demented. He was accompanied by his sister. He was so ill that I anticipated that he would die in the next day or so – a correct prognosis as it turned out. After I had seen him on the Sunday morning emergency admission ward round, I spoke to his sister, explaining the dire prognosis. Her only response was to say 'You will do everything you can for him, doctor, won't you?' with a little smile and a nod of the head. I explained that we would make him comfortable and treat his chest infection and ensure he had fluids but that it would be inappropriate to try to start his heart again if it stopped. 'I want you to try,' she said. And so began a conversation which lasted for over half an hour. During this time, she simply repeated with a sweet smile on her face variations of 'I want you to try', 'I want you to give him a chance'. That was why, she added, she had asked for him to be brought here: our hospital had a very good reputation for not giving up on people, unlike another hospital (which she named) down the road. I found myself spelling out, in starker and starker detail, the unpleasantness and the futility of CPR in her brother's case. At some stage during the conversation I became aware that this conversation – between a frail, eighty-year-old lady in a hat secured with a pin and a professor of geriatric medicine – looked like an unequal contest. What I had to say seemed like 'coercive discourse', and I felt like a bully. I was determined, however, not to subject this blind, speechless, confused, paralysed old man to the unimaginable horror of CPR. In the end, I compromised by saying that if 'something happened' the houseman would be called urgently but we would not try to start his heart. She was very unhappy about this. A couple of days later, the man passed away. For the next few weeks, I expected a long letter of complaint addressed to the Chief Executive about a doctor 'playing God', execrating an 'ageist professor of geriatric medicine', and a certain amount of unpleasant press coverage to which I would have no right of reply.

The consequences of the moral pressures by people ignorant both of the process and outcome of CPR upon clinicians are entirely predictable and it is little wonder that the right not to be subjected to 'inhuman or degrading treatment' (Article 3 of the Human Rights Act 1998) is so little respected. The situation is accurately summarized by John Saunders:

Cardiopulmonary resuscitation (CPR) is attempted on too many patients. At its best, CPR is the gift of life: chest compression, ventilation, intravenous medication and defibrillation followed by years of productive and fulfilled being. At its worst, it offers a scenario of vomit, blood and urine, then a confused, brain-damaged twilight, breathlessness from a failing ventricle, pain from rib fractures, until expiring in thrall to the full panoply of intensive care or forgotten in the long darkness of the persistent vegetative state. No humane doctor would consider this a good death, nor would any poet, priest, painter, musician or novelist use images of CPR to represent the Good Death. Rather, the images are more likely to be those of the factory: death in the industrial age.[71]

The reasons for this appalling travesty of clinical medicine – the opposite of humane care – are set out clearly by Saunders. Doctors are reluctant even to talk about dying, to move the dialogue with the patient, or the family, into another gear, for fear of being told that they are 'writing the patient off'.

In 1998, Age Concern claimed that elderly people were 'terrified' by reports of 'Do Not Resuscitate' orders being written in their case notes. This claim, based upon a handful of anecdotes, has made patients, their families and doctors even less able to discuss the pros and cons of aggressive and rarely successful treatments in terminal illness. A study in America (cited by Saunders) suggested that many doctors make decisions in favour of CPR because of fear of litigation or criticism, and most doctors admit to attempting resuscitation in full knowledge that such efforts would be futile.[72] As Saunders points out, this is morally indefensible: first, patients do not have rights to useless treatments nor doctors a duty to provide them on demand. Moreover, removing power from the physician by bureaucratic procedures surrounding 'Do Not Resuscitate' orders does not necessarily enhance the power of the patient.[73] Secondly, futile CPR reflects the immorality of defensive medicine for, as Saunders points out, 'it uses patients not as ends in themselves but merely as a means to the ends of others'.

In the end, we have to trust in trust: suspicion has to end somewhere for any profession to continue to function. Trust, like respect, also has to be two-way. If the patient's trust in the doctor is grounded in bodies that regulate him, rather than in his standing as a human being whose intentions are good, then the threshold for complaint and litigation will be lowered. This will alter the way doctors view patients: every patient will be seen as a potential litigant or complainant.

Some people seem unconcerned by this prospect. Clara MacKay (Principal Policy Adviser at the Consumers' Association and Chair of the UK Patients Forum) anticipates that the 'relationship between patients and professionals will continue to move towards one which is much more challenging, and perhaps more antagonistic',[74] adding that this 'is not necessarily bad'. As a doctor, and a potential patient, I think it could be catastrophic: not only would there be no limit to, or natural resolution of, the antagonism; but also the impact on medical care, and on caring in the wider sense, will be awful.

Medicine will become more defensive. 'Defensive medicine' is much worse than it sounds: it empties the patient–doctor relationship from within. It is a betrayal of the professional ethos because it apes extremely thorough, and hence extremely caring, medicine. The doctor will subject patients to endless tests and refer them to various specialists just so that patients will believe that 'everything has been done'. Even at its best, defensive medicine is clinically and morally lazy. The primary duty to protect the patient is overridden by the doctor's concern to protect himself. The Hippocratic precept of good medicine is 'First do no harm'; that of defensive medicine is 'First cover your ass'. In an unforgiving society that defines doctors by their mistakes and cannot acknowledge that medicine is a probabilistic art, doctors will be more likely to transfer the risk to the patient, under the guise of being thorough. If there is a one in a thousand chance of a sore throat being due to some serious underlying condition, the defensive doctor will put 1,000 patients to the inconvenience of throat swabs rather than risk being sued by the one patient who has something serious. The patient–doctor relationship will become a threefold relationship between a pre-litigant, the legal profession and the doctor.

Furthermore, distrust that leaves very little to the doctor's discretion, to clinical judgement, will squander resources:

A central authority not prepared to trust the way people carry out their tasks has an insatiable thirst for information, which it mistakes for understanding reality. Collecting this information requires the multiplication of records, and turns everyone into at least a part-time clerk. And by this process, every vocation turns clerkly.[75]

The danger of repeating the claim that patients no longer trust doctors – or, more cunningly, talking about trust having to be 'built' or 'rebuilt' – is that it may be self-fulfilling. People will start to feel that they would be foolish to trust doctors. MORI polls may not be as kind to the profession in future but it is patients, as well as doctors, who will have been the losers.

6

Enemies of Progress

Convictions

Convictions are greater enemies of truth than lies.

Friedrich Nietzsche

Sceptics dismiss individual experience as 'anecdotal', but when you are your own anecdote, it's hard not to be convinced.[1]

Rose Shepherd, the *Observer*

A necessary condition of an even better future for medicine is rational debate. When what is in question is the best means of preventing or treating illness, the most cost-effective uses of inescapably limited resources, or the scale and cause of a particular public health problem, or even the best configuration of services, such debate inevitably involves numbers. What a pity, then, that the opinions of the innumerate are being given increasing air-time. The attention they command is costing us dear in lost opportunities.

Not everyone can be equally expert on all things. In practice, this is usually accepted. My views on bridge-building are of no value to anyone, even myself, though I do not deny the importance of this topic. Even within medicine, my opinions are of variable value. The circumstances under which one should remove a brain tumour and how one should do it are things I am happy to leave to more expert colleagues. The treatment of heart failure is a bit closer to the sphere of my expertise, though what expertise I have derives from guidance developed on the basis of the emerging scientific literature. The only area in which I would claim to be an opinion-leader – so that I might expect other people's opinions to be influenced by mine – is in the very narrow field of epilepsy in older adults. Even then, while the value of my opinion has been (or should have been) enhanced by fifteen years of special interest, study and reflection, it is largely due to my familiarity with facts that others have unearthed and conversations and debate with other experts in the field.

My belief that I have worthwhile opinions on epilepsy in older people is no more arrogant than my rating my opinions on bridge-building as worthless is pathetically deferential. To imagine that, just because I once saw a bridge fall down – even if in doing so it killed my dearest friend – I am now an expert who should be consulted along with those of accredited experts, is absurd. All I am entitled to is sympathy. That my opinions are more likely to be listened to nowadays is based on the myth that proximity delivers expertise; that first-person experience somehow trumps objective knowledge.

In Chapter 3, we saw how the key to the great achievements of scientific medicine has been the progressive rejection of personal opinion as the basis for authority. Opinionated non-experts will be unimpressed by this; they will invoke fraud, the ruthless pursuit of profit by drug companies, and errors in science as decisive evidence of the fallibility and corruption of scientific medicine. While one could argue against this,[2] to do so would be to miss the essential point: that medical expertise, while imperfect, is based on research, and the synthesis of research, whose methods have been forged in centuries of debate about how to arrive at reliable general knowledge, how to universalize with minimal chance of error from the necessarily limited data one has, and how to distinguish causal relationships from chance associations.

Many of the voices given prominence today appear to be innocent of all that has been learnt in the last 250 years about the pitfalls of trying to move directly from personal experience to generalizable knowledge. The debate, for example, between the pressure groups and the medical scientists over immunization against mumps, measles and rubella (MMR) brought out all the fallacies medical science has struggled to escape since James Lind published his famous treatise on the treatment of scurvy. Lind remarked (in 1757) that 'it is no easy matter to root out prejudices' and that 'before the subject [the treatment of scurvy] could be set in a clear and proper light, it was necessary to remove a good deal of rubbish'.[3]

Again and again one hears a desperately unhappy parent of a child with severe learning disability explain why she believes her child's problem is due to what the media call 'The Triple Jab'. This illustrates the elementary fallacy that ensured that folk medicine remained resolutely pre-scientific: *post hoc, ergo propter hoc* (after this, therefore because of this). She may back up her claim with other observations: 'I know several other children who were never the same after the jab.' This illustrates another elementary fallacy: the belief that uncontrolled observations provide a safe basis for drawing general conclusions and, indeed, for adducing causal relations.[4] A profession whose expertise is based on massive datasets handled with increasing sophistication increasingly finds itself having to deal sympathetically and courteously with challenges from individuals who have not caught up with the methodological standards of the 1750s. As readers will recall from Chapter 3, there have been further developments in the methods by which causal relationships have been established in the succeeding 250 years.

One of the greatest sources of confusion comes from the notion of maintaining 'balance' in the media reporting of controversies. This results in equal prominence being given to views riddled with elementary fallacies and to the most considered and informed opinion. This is not, of course, balance at all: the opinions of an individual parent should not be regarded as equal to a knowledge-base summarizing the experiences of many hundreds of thousands of parents (who, incidentally, are also are individuals). We have been told that the views of parents with regard to the triple vaccine should be 'listened to', as if the views of (the overwhelming majority) of parents had been ignored in the scientific literature. To give special credence to the beliefs of a few angry parents is to devalue the experience of millions of others.

Medical expertise, as we have already noted, is not personal: it is informed by the authority of data gathered by countless anonymous strangers whose methods of avoiding bias and other pitfalls have been refined by the experiences and reflections of even more numerous strangers dead and alive.[5] The contrast of this humility with the attitude of the convinced lay person, the vox pop – who claims to have generalizable knowledge on the basis of her own experience – could not be sharper. It is ironical that something called 'the medical establishment' is accused of being arrogant, while the actual arrogance of 'the lone voice' is overlooked. When the scientific community offers data in support of an orthodox view, it is accused also of bullying, of silencing debate and steamrollering opposition with statistics (i.e. numerical facts).

Sooner or later the debate comes to be less about who is factually right and who is factually wrong than about who is deemed to be morally right and who morally wrong; or who is existentially in the right and who is existentially in the wrong. The very lack of factual support for the position adopted by the vox pop – 'this jab damaged my baby and it will damage other babies and therefore should be banned' – makes it seem unarmed and so 'plucky'. And even more plucky because the owner of the vox pop is taking on the 'combined might' of the government, the medical profession (unlikely co-conspirators in the present medico-political climate), and Big Business represented by the pharmaceutical industry.[6]

It will not escape the reader's attention that I have glided from general comments about the excessive deference paid to the ill-informed to a specific instance: the 'debate' about the MMR triple vaccine. This is a star example because it has proved desperately expensive, may turn out to be very dangerous, and has repeated the history of the opposition to the triple vaccine (for diphtheria, pertussis and tetanus) in the 1970s – a cautionary tale to which we shall return.

The MMR story begins in 1998 with a paper published by Andrew Wakefield and colleagues in *The Lancet*,[7] the most prestigious of British medical journals, describing twelve children who developed autism and bowel symptoms. Examination of the bowel wall showed inflammation. The authors hypothesized recklessly that the autism might be due to the inflammatory bowel disease. What was worse, they further hypothesized that, since the bowel symptoms had occurred after the child had received the measles, mumps and rubella (MMR) vaccine, this might be the cause. This was very alarming: if MMR causes inflammatory bowel disease and the latter causes autism, then MMR might cause autism. Given the large number of children receiving the vaccine, a public health disaster could be in the offing.

However, the paper was deeply flawed as an epidemiological study purporting to show a causal link between MMR and autism. The editorial team at *The Lancet* was aware of this but accepted it as a preliminary observation. Even so, they published an editorial in the same issue of the journal pointing out those flaws. What they had not reckoned with was the press conference held at the Royal Free Hospital to coincide with the publication of the article, at which Andrew Wakefield advocated, on the basis of his findings, the abandonment of the triple vaccine. To say that this was utterly irresponsible – because the evidence in his paper fell far short of justifying this conclusion – is the understatement of the century.

First, Wakefield and colleagues did not survey an entire population: their observations were confined to a small sub-group of children who happened to come to their highly specialized paediatric gastro-enterology unit at the Royal Free Hospital, which attracted patients with inflammatory bowel disease from all over the country. The selection criteria for referral to Wakefield's clinic were not made clear. [8] At any rate, Wakefield's data gave no indication of how commonly bowel symptoms, or autism, or the combination of the two, occurred in the general population compared with that in children who had received MMR. One thing was certain: the cases were not numerous enough and the children not sufficiently representative for any general conclusions about the relationship between autism and MMR, let alone a causal connection between the vaccine and these distressing conditions to be drawn. Given the status of the Royal Free as a national centre, the population from which referrals might arise was several millions – the number of children in the UK. This alone would make Wakefield's twelve cases unlikely to be in any sense representative.

To substantiate their conclusion, or even to justify suggesting it, they should also have compared the relative proportions of children within the population who had received MMR and subsequently developed inflammatory bowel disease and autism, with the proportion who developed these conditions in an unimmunized population. These data were not available. The claimed association was not therefore established.

Even if an *association* had been demonstrated, this would not have been proof of a *causal* relationship between MMR and inflammatory bowel disease or between the latter and autism: there might be all sorts of confounding factors, which could be associated with having had MMR and suffering from either inflammatory bowel disease or autism or both. For example, children who have been given MMR are more likely to be from upper socio-economic classes,[9] which would be associated with many environmental factors.

This is not to deny the value of case studies of the kind published by Wakefield et al. Controlled observations strong enough to establish causal relationships have to begin with uncontrolled, incidental observations. The problem arose out of publishing what were preliminary observations in a prestigious journal and then arranging a high-profile press conference through which to broadcast the most alarming news. Perhaps it was too trusting of the editor of *The Lancet* to imagine that the health warning in the accompanying editorial on Wakefield's paper would be heeded. Health scares emanating from prestigious journals are gold dust, especially where they seem to collide with Government policy.

In order to discredit Wakefield's fragile hypothesis it was necessary to demonstrate – in properly designed, population-based studies not susceptible to the ascertainment bias of Wakefield's twelve anecdotes – several things. First, that there was no excess of inflammatory bowel disease and autism in children receiving MMR. Secondly, that there was no defined temporal relationship between the onset of autism and the receipt of MMR. Thirdly, that there was no association between inflammatory bowel disease and autism. In a very short period of time, a series of massive studies, national and international, demonstrated each of these negatives.

Within a year, a UK study of autism and MMR, also published in *The Lancet*,[10] showed that there was no higher incidence of autism in children who had received MMR than in those who had not. A subsequent study[11] found no increased association between autism and bowel symptoms following the introduction of MMR in 1988. Next, a study from Denmark[12] of over half a million children – almost all the children born in the study period – confirmed that there was no increase in the risk of autism in children receiving MMR compared with those not receiving it. (Indeed, the risk was slightly *reduced*, though this reduction was not sufficient to rule out the play of chance. At any rate, the authors, with the proper caution of true scientists, refused to speculate that MMR might actually *prevent* autism!) Most impressive (in terms of numbers at any rate) was a Finnish study which followed 1.8 million children from the start of the MMR vaccination programme in 1982.[13] While there was an adverse incidence rate of 1 in 30,000 (mainly minor such as fevers), there was no excess of either autism or inflammatory bowel disease.

The Danish study failed to show any association between development of autism and age at vaccination or time since vaccination. This latter point was important because those who are wedded to the fallacy I mentioned earlier – *post hoc ergo propter hoc* – argued that the apparent temporal relationship between the vaccination and the onset of MMR was evidence of a causal relationship. Of course, the fact that something occurs after something doesn't necessarily mean that it is *because* of that something.[14] The incidental observation in the UK study that, in the case of several children with autism, the history given by the parent with respect to the same child changed, was of particular interest.[15] Before publicity about the MMR vaccine and autism, parents reported having concerns early in their child's life; subsequently they recorded symptoms as developing only after the vaccine. Observation bias means that we find what we seek, or we notice what we are prepared to find.

The final nail in the coffin of the Wakefield hypothesis was a study of 250,000 children born in the UK after 1988 which found no association between gastro-intestinal disorders and autism: bowel symptoms were found in 10 per cent of both children with autism and case-matched controls without autism.[16] There was a much stronger association, and evidence for a causal relationship on this basis, between autism and the possession of teddy bears than between autism and MMR, as was pointed out by Paula McDonald.[17]

So that should have been the end of the story. Millions of parents, whose experience was gathered up in the literature, testified to the safety of the jab, as against a handful who were convinced that an illness their children had developed after the jab was due to it. But of course it was not the end of the story. When a definitive overview of all the properly conducted epidemiological studies to date was published in the *British Medical Journal*,[18] there was some acknowledgement in the press – but it was grudging. For example, the headline in the London *Metro* newspaper (12 June 2002) ran: 'Doctors "prove" MMR jab is safe.' The inverted commas around 'prove' spoke volumes. For by now the science had become almost irrelevant, notwithstanding that the initial claim that had started all the hares running had itself been based upon scientific data. Under the influence of the media, who had to defend their original stories, the issue had become one of all-out war between unequal combatants: on the one side parents who had believed their children had been damaged by MMR and their brave champion Andrew

Wakefield; and on the other 'the medical establishment', aligned with a 'patronizing, bullying' Department of Health.

Much prominence was given to the views of Jackie Fletcher, spokeswoman of a group called JABS (Justice, Awareness & Basic Support). JABS campaigned on behalf of parents who, like Ms Fletcher, had children whom they believed had been damaged by MMR. She argued, in the absence of any data comparing the safety of these approaches, for the NHS to provide three separate injections instead of the triple vaccine. (This would of course increase the period when children were unprotected and increase the likelihood of some children remaining unprotected through failure to complete the course.) Ms Fletcher's views were sought whenever a new study appeared, and she was cited in the article in the London *Metro*: the overview, she said, was 'not new evidence. It's only old evidence rehashed.' The press supported her: the scale of her personal tragedy was such as to occlude the less visible experiences of many hundreds of thousands of other parents and children. It hardly mattered whether that tragedy had anything to do with the MMR vaccine. Convictions, especially angry ones, make better copy than data.

Other opinions were frequently cited in support of Wakefield's hypothesis, in particular those of individuals whose views carried weight not because of their track record in health care, epidemiology or microbiology, but because they were prominent. Vox pop idols have the equivalent of the old trades union block vote: the validity of their views is proportionate to their media significance, and they were given much greater air-time than those of the clinicians and scientists who had spent their professional lives considering the relevant issues. Ken Livingstone, speaking with the *gravitas* of a Mayor of London and a father-to-be, advised parents to reject the MMR vaccine: 'It seems to me that a child of fourteen months is incredibly vulnerable. Why whack them all [three vaccines] into a child at the same time?'[19] His own unborn child was going to have single jabs. Clive Lloyd, one of the greatest cricketers the world had ever known, believed his own son had had an adverse reaction to the MMR jab and this had destroyed his chances of playing for England. Mr Lloyd's experiences, which had been recounted on television and made the front page in the *Manchester Evening News*,[20] made him 'angry that the authorities claim it is perfectly safe when my son is living proof of the harm it can do'. In fact, his son had not suffered from autism, but from Guillain-Barré syndrome, an affliction of the nerves to the legs and arms. This is a well-described, very rare adverse effect of many vaccinations – which does not alter the fact that the risk-benefit ratio is still vastly in favour of vaccination. This rather important point was overlooked by the health correspondent of the *Manchester Evening News*.[21]

With such high-profile immunological advice, it was hardly surprising that parents were increasingly favouring sequential injections for their children (though the triple vaccine for diptheria, whooping cough and tetanus given to much younger children seemed to escape challenge this time round). Parents who could afford it opted to pay for single vaccines in order to avoid MMR while still giving their children protection. Private clinics, always on the lookout to make a buck or two, were established,[22] which provoked much criticism that something as basic as safe vaccination was being made available only to the rich. Liam Fox, the opposition spokesman on health, urged that single jabs should be made available for everyone – in the name of choice. Such political point-scoring was disgraceful, given that he was himself a doctor who had accepted the safety of MMR.[23] The fact that the prime minister (quite properly) did not disclose whether his own child had received the triple vaccine, that he refused to use his personal decision to support current health policy, also attracted criticism.

This marked an interesting phase in the 'debate'. As more and more evidence exonerating MMR came in, the media, far from apologizing for their assault on an important measure to improve public health, changed their tack and started to blame 'the authorities' – ministers, the Department of Health – for their arrogance, intransigence and bullying. The facts were now less important (especially since they had become less interesting) than how they had been communicated. There was perhaps a tinge of collective guilt at the damage irresponsible commentators had caused; for vaccination rates were falling, and measles was starting to return. In Mr Livingstone's London, the vaccination rates had fallen to just over 70 per cent from the 85 per cent levels they had reached just before Wakefield's paper.[24]

Even so, Lynda Lee Potter, commenting on the fact that Mr Blair had kept quiet about whether his baby son had had MMR, described it as a 'silence that's an insult to every parent'.[25] She asserted that 'if there is a measles epidemic Tony Blair will be to blame.' Few were quite so precise in their location of blame. Andrew Rawnsley,[26] reporting how he and his wife felt uncertain about what to do about their daughter, blamed the Department of Health and the Minister's 'patronizing bullying' for their 'agonies of uncertainty': they should not tell people what to do because, even if they did, this would only intensify uncertainties as governments are not to be trusted. Exhibiting an extraordinary capacity for association of ideas, Rawnsley reminded readers about the previous government's handling of BSE. He concluded that unscientific wisdom, such as his mother showed in refusing to take thalidomide, is to be preferred to any amount of science.[27] Despite being able to quote the reassurances of the BMA, the Royal Colleges, the World Health Organization, in favour of the triple jab, 'until I sound like a looped recording of Yvette Cooper' (the then Minister of Public Health), he was unpersuaded, not because of the data but because of the track record and patronizing manner of those who cited the relevant information.

An editorial in the same issue of the *Observer*, which also blamed the government, was even more confused.[28] Parents, it said, needed 'more information and choice'. The call for more information seemed a little puzzling since, as the journalist conceded, 'The overwhelming factual evidence is that there is no risk from MMR vaccine itself' and Dr Wakefield's 'unorthodox work has been confounded by more rigorous studies in Britain and elsewhere, which show no link between autism and MMR'. Nevertheless, 'the Government must now launch a massive educational offensive', presumably to get over these very simple facts. This should not, however, consist, 'of a recitation of the facts'. Moreover, parents should be offered the choice of a series of single jabs, while being told that this is less safe, given that there have been demonstrable problems with this option.

In the same issue of the *Observer*, there was also an extraordinary piece by the writer Nick Hornby, angered by the lack of support he and his partner received for their autistic child. He suggested (somewhat chillingly) that those parents 'who are engendering this panic, and whose fears prompted Andrew Wakefield's research in the first place – are really not feeling very public-spirited right now'.[29] In other words, don't expect the parents of autistic children, who feel they have been done badly by public services, to support the government line on MMR, irrespective of the facts.

One could be forgiven for believing that however good a job the Department of Health had done (and I believe that on this occasion they did a reasonable job), the media had collectively made it impossible for the complex voice of true, as opposed to folk, expertise to be clearly heard and understood.

The resolution of the crisis was also hindered by the scientist whose flawed study, reckless claims and misleading press conference had precipitated it. In Wakefield's own eyes, and in that of certain pressure groups, the failure of methodologically sound studies to support his hypothesis had enhanced rather than diminished his reputation. In pursuing the lonely path to the truth, you are, he says 'taking on your colleagues, the health department, and the biggest drug companies in the world'.[30] 'The question you have to ask is, "who do you represent?" ' The answer is, of course, the parents; and unlike his colleagues, he listened to parents: 'Everything I know about autism, I know from listening to parents.' This was not true: his claim that autism was associated with MMR was an extension of his earlier research supposedly demonstrating that inflammatory bowel disease in children was due to measles virus seen on bowel biopsies taken at colonoscopy.[31]

The cost of all this is yet to be counted. The direct costs to the Department of Health and to the doctors and nurses working in the NHS will have been enormous: time and resources spent on education, explanation and reassurance, diverted from other things, not to mention switching the research agenda (even within the field of autism)[32] to disprove a hypothesis for which there was no good evidence in the first place. In addition, there are the hidden costs of the 'agonies of uncertainty' referred to by Andrew Rawnsley and experienced by hundreds of thousands of parents. Most importantly, there are the potential costs of a measles epidemic. According to the *Evening Standard*, the uptake of MMR vaccine in London had fallen to 73 per cent by summer 2002[33] and the quadrupling of cases in the first quarter of 2002 compared with 2001 (admittedly from a very low baseline) had raised the possibility of an outbreak.

By 2002, a more serious tone was entering the press coverage. The *Evening Standard* article reminded its readers of the 'dangers of shunning the MMR jab': children who develop measles stand a 1:800 risk of dying and a 1:500 risk of severe brain damage; and when the vaccine was suspended in Japan because of production problems there were ninety deaths in a year, and huge suffering of children with non-fatal cases. The potential disaster could be much greater. If vaccination rates drop to 60 per cent population immunity will be lost and nearly all the vulnerable 40 per cent will get measles. Given an annual birth rate of 600,000 children, 240,000 children will get measles with an annual death rate of at least 240.[34] The *Evening Standard* was still sufficiently unmoved by these terrifying possibilities to give equal prominence to the views of a mother who believed her son had been made autistic by the vaccine. The triumphal progress of unsound logic and pre-scientific clinical reasoning was not to be short-lived. The triple vaccine continued to be referred to as 'controversial'.

The authority of scaremongers thrives on lack of historical knowledge and perspective. Two episodes illustrate the damage that the triumph of prejudice over reason may cause. In the late 1970s a group of articulate middle-class parents became convinced that their children had sustained brain damage from the triple vaccine against whooping cough, diphteria and tetanus (DPT). The whooping cough component was blamed. I remember this vividly, because it was when we had our first child immunized. The campaigners refused to accept, or perhaps did not understand, that sometimes children develop brain-damaging conditions spontaneously. The temporal relationship to the DPT vaccine was coincidental, as properly conducted studies had demonstrated this beyond reasonable doubt. The campaiguers were seduced by the same fallacy – *post hoc ergo propter hoc* – made more potent by the need to make sense of the terrible event that had happened to them. Nor did they take account of the overwhelming benefit of the vaccine. As in the MMR furore, they were supported by the press and uptake rates fell. By the time the safety of the vaccine had been reaffirmed, on the basis of a numerate appreciation of the data that were already available, there had been three major epidemics affecting 300,000 children and an estimated 100 avoidable deaths. Pertussis vaccine uptake took fifteen years to return to its previous levels.[35]

Giving popular opinion equal weight with rational, informed advice can carry an even more terrible price. In Stockholm, the population was persuaded by doubters to refuse 'unnatural' vaccination against smallpox. By 1872 vaccination rates had fallen to just over 40 per cent.[36] A major epidemic of smallpox in the city, which killed many thousands of people, restored an understanding of the comparative risks of vaccination and non-vaccination. Widespread vaccination, and an end to further epidemics, then followed.

One of the reasons why the evidence-lean opinions of non-experts command such a hearing is that public understanding of comparative risk is so poorly developed. It is further arrested by the constant undermining of legitimate expertise. As Theodore Dalrymple has said, consumer protection groups 'never recognize that they have any vested interest of their own to protect – vested interests being by definition interests which belong to someone else'.[37] A maverick researcher such as Andrew Wakefield is 'a lone voice' against the massed ranks of the establishment; and the rebuttal of his claims on the basis of huge accumulations of facts is 'an official whitewash' or (in view of the numbers of facts invoked and the range of authorities invoking them) cognitive bullying.

It is particularly apt, then, that the story of the MMR controversy took an extraordinary turn with the discovery that Andrew Wakefield, and some of the parents of the children reported in his original study, also had interests of their own that were not exclusively about science and the search for the truth. In early 2004, six years after the controversy was ignited, the *Sunday Times* revealed that Andrew Wakefield had received £55,000 from the Legal Aid Board several years before to carry out studies on behalf of parents who believed their children had been damaged by MMR and were seeking compensation. At least half of the children reported in his *Lancet* paper were amongst those in his legally aided study.[38] For the parents seeking compensation and for Wakefield acting on their behalf, *The Lancet* paper was a major coup. Wakefield had not declared his conflicting interest when he submitted the paper, although it is clear editorial policy that all interests should be declared. Suddenly the selection criteria for children referred to his clinic became clear: they had parents who believed that there was an association between MMR and autism and, in many cases, those parents hoped to secure compensation.

Even the press had to admit that the MMR vaccine should no longer be described as 'controversial'. But there was little evidence of repentance. The *Observer* editorial noted that 'the media and society needed to exercise caution in the face of claims from whistleblowers. Sometimes they, too, have an agenda.'[39] Its main article, however, still featured the opinions of Jackie Fletcher of JABS, that Dr Wakefield 'may have been the target of a smear campaign', adding that 'They seem to go all out to criticize the messenger.'[40] And the *Independent* wondered whether Andrew Wakefield was 'being attacked because of his findings or because of a potential conflict of interest'.[41] It featured the views of three women, none of them experts, who were respectively, for MMR, against it, and uncertain about it. The editorial questioned why the discovery of the conflict of interest should affect Wakefield's scientific findings and suggested that the response of the government and the Chief Medical Officer was an orchestrated campaign to distract from the real questions about MMR.[42]

Scientific data will cut little ice with those for whom truth is always subordinated to power and the refutation of the views of a lone whistleblower always the result of a conspiracy. Within medicine there are many examples of individuals canonized as opponents of the scientific establishment whose views have turned out to be wrong and whose disastrous impact has been amplified by their own sense of mission and by the refusal of the media to see the issues as in any way to be settled by facts: discussion of conspiracy theories and cover-ups are more attractive than numerate analysis of the facts. The most catastrophic example is Peter 'Lone-Voice' Duesberg who became convinced that AIDS was due not to a virus – which he saw as merely an innocent bystander – but to lifestyle factors such as recreational drug-taking and the use of pharmaceuticals such as AZT. As his scientific case fell apart, it turned into a cause, and his cause was taken up by sections of the media, notably, in the United Kingdom by the *Sunday Times*, whose editor Andrew Neil was, at the time, keen to demonstrate that heterosexual AIDS (which a viral cause would make a distinct possibility, while a lifestyle cause would make less probable) was a myth. Duesberg still clung to his theories when the causal role of HIV was demonstrated beyond doubt after anti-viral drugs had proved to be dramatically successful in the prevention of transmission of HIV and the emergence of full-blown AIDS in people infected with the virus, including individuals with conventional lifestyles, such as haemophiliacs, who had been infected through blood transfusions.

Part of the case for Duesberg's increasingly groundless hypothesis was that the viral explanation was not only the 'establishment' view, and therefore to be doubted,[43] but also it was of potential benefit to drug companies seeking to market anti-virals. The vast amount of time and effort spent refuting Duesberg's theories both in laboratories and in public arenas represented a huge opportunity cost. Many individuals, falsely reassured by his ideas, will have lost their lives. His true legacy, however, is to be found in South Africa where, as we shall see in the next chapter, they attracted the appreciative attention of Thabo Mbeki, with consequences that are unbearable to contemplate.

The popular media often point to errors made by scientists, and to what they regard as a politico-scientific establishment, to justify dismissing their views when they are backed up by governments. When the *Observer*[44] argued that we are not able to trust government advice any more, this was on the grounds of 'the BSE and foot and mouth fiascos'. The analogy, and the conclusion, is of course flawed. The uncertainties surrounding the proper handling of the suspicions about the transmissability of BSE from cattle to humans are of a totally different order from any uncertainties about the merits of MMR. Moreover, it is not clear that the government handling of these uncertainties was wrong: until the existence of new variant Creutzfeldt-Jakob disease was demonstrated in 1996,[45] the link between BSE and this (still) rare human tragedy was entirely speculative. It would have been grossly irresponsible of government to have ruined the livelihood of farmers and incurred billions of pounds of Exchequer costs on the basis of speculation. As for the management of foot and mouth disease, it is still not certain that alternative approaches – ring vaccination as opposed to culling – would have delivered a better overall result than the strategies adopted as the epidemic evolved.

For some, though, the two episodes justify wider scepticism about government advice. Some have even suggested that the controversy over MMR and the BSE 'scandal' might justify our 'interrogating... the usefulness of science (as reason in practice)' and asking whether 'science is simply a narrative among many competing others'.[46] This argument overlooks the fact that all parties to the debate are actually agreed on a large body of scientific facts: for example, the highly sophisticated notions of 'mumps', 'measles' and 'rubella' as viral diseases, the principles of safe vaccination (nobody in the debate opposes immunizing children against polio), and concepts of inflammatory bowel disease and autism, were all recently described by clinical scientists. The dispute is only about a *particular* scientific claim – that MMR immunization has certain adverse effects, and that these adverse effects are sufficiently frequent to outweigh its benefits compared with other approaches to vaccination – and not about science itself or indeed about government scientific advice.

So why is there such widespread profession of hostility to science? The combination of strong emotions – in particular moral indignation against, and suspicion of, 'the authorities' – and weak mathematics is very potent. One the most characteristic features of weak mathematics is numerators without denominators, a perfect recipe for 'panicdemics'.[47] The MMR panic is a perfect case: we had no idea of the population base from which Wakefield's twelve cases of inflammatory bowel disease and autism were drawn. Those numbers cannot therefore be translated into frequencies and therefore the frequency of occurrence in the MMR-vaccinated could not be compared with that in the unvaccinated population – or not until the large studies we have described were carried out.

Panicdemics are now themselves epidemic. The hallmarks include: citing numbers of cases without referring to the massive population from which they have been drawn (so that their rarity is overlooked); failing to distinguish between association and causation; and greeting with suspicion any reassuring facts that contradict the original concern. Theodore Dalrymple has given many such examples in his definitive *Mass Listeria*,[48] but one will suffice here. In 1986, it was found that alar, sprayed on to apples to prevent them from rotting, could, if injected in sufficient quantities, induce cancers in mice. Alar was denounced by consumer protection groups and 'apples were shunned as if they were the cast-off clothing of people who had died during the Black Death.'[49] Farmers were ruined. As Dalrymple pointed out, 'more people died of suicide because of the alar scare than consumers of apples ever died from the effects of alar itself'. Scares like this have been replicated world-wide at huge cost.[50]

The power of vox pops and panicdemcs to divert resources into the investigation of unquantifiable risks sometimes reflects the populist agenda of governments. As Bill Durodie has pointed out, responding to 'the activism of the lobbyist allows politicians to retain a semblance of accountability in an age when political participation is at an all-time low'.[51] The precautionary principle is a prudent response of governments unwilling to contradict the will of the people. This recipe for paralysis has been applied with particular vigour by the European Commission.[52] Where the science doesn't support consumer anxiety, the default position is to sympathize with the fact that 'consumers are not easily convinced by scientific evidence and advice' and that 'too great an emphasis on science is undesirable from the consumer's point of view'.[53]

Durodie points out that the precautionary principle is not 'zero-cost'. The banning of toys enclosed in food items as in Kinder Surprise eggs, which were said to be associated with three fatal chokings during a period when 218 million had been sold in the UK alone, diverts resources from real dangers. This cost is borne neither by the lobbying group nor by the politician, but by the consumers and taxpayers whose interests are supposedly being protected. And there are wider consequences. The concerns they raise 'have allowed the irrational ideas of unaccountable environmentalist and consumer advocacy groups to resonate more widely', and while 'their campaigns may take the form of radical critiques of business and governments', 'by encouraging mistrust and prioritizing feeling and emotion over thinking and reason, they are a threat to us all'.[54]

When, on the basis of the best scientific evidence, Michael Wilkes and Gavin Yamey argued that screening for prostate cancer, using digital examination and a test for a marker in the blood (PSA), may cause more harm than good, they were bombarded with e-mails orchestrated by a pressure group accusing them of 'having the deaths of hundreds of thousands of men on their hands'. The chancellor and dean of their university were overwhelmed with letters demanding that disciplinary action should be taken against them.[55] This did not happen but their experience is a clear warning to anyone who, on the basis of carefully analysed data, challenges lobbyist or editorial wisdom.

While minute risks are endlessly debated, real risks are forgotten. The unnecessary debate over the safety of MMR has diverted public attention from the terrible danger of a possible measles outbreak. Obsession with the negligible danger of contracting CJD from beefburgers overshadows the very present risks of life-threatening obesity from over-eating. Recently I overheard two seriously overweight pregnant teenagers gloomily discussing the dangers of BSE while exposing their babies to the cigarette smoke which will adversely affect their health and that of their mothers. Such smoke kills about 120,000 UK citizens a year.[56]

Meanwhile the MMR story runs and runs. A recent study[57] from the Cardiff School of Journalism found that half the public believe the scientific community is evenly divided over the safety of the triple jab. Only 23 per cent were aware that all experts, with the exception of

Wakefield and a few disciples, thought it was safe. Only 32 per cent of broadsheet stories about the MMR debate referred to this. The *Daily Mail* has turned its attention to a claimed link between the small amount of mercury in other triple vaccines – such as the triple DPT vaccine which has been so successful in wiping out the scourges of diphtheria, whooping cough and tetanus – and autism.[58] The Committee on Safety of Medicines and the US Institute of Medicines has found no evidence of any adverse effect; moreover the mercury-free alternative did not offer sufficient protection. Even so, the Chairman of Action Against Autism suggested that 'If the Department of Health is aware that the thiomersal [the mercury-containing component] is unsafe for childhood vaccines, then we may be looking at criminal medical negligence on a massive scale.' A further potential consequence of the sustained assault on safe vaccines is that pharmaceutical companies will be less inclined to invest in developing new products in this area or, once the patent has expired, to continue producing existing vaccines. A more devastating blow for world health would be difficult to imagine.

In December 2003, over five years after the publication of Wakefield's flawed paper, Channel 5 broadcast a play, *Hear the Silence*, in which the mother of a child with autism is treated with contempt by the medical profession until she finally meets up with Dr Andrew Wakefield, the play's hero.[59] He gives her the explanation that she needs: that her child's illness is due to – the MMR vaccine. The play is riddled with factual errors and gives little credence to the scientific data. Despite this the producer denied that the play was factually biased. The writer, Tim Prager, emphasized that much of what had been written 'about the possibility of a link between MMR and autism has been based upon statistics'. (This was meant to be a criticism of those who believe MMR is safe.) Finally, the actress playing the mother had this to say:

I would like a calm and informed debate to come out of [the play]. There is a sort of hysteria coming out of the government at the moment, and you can't go on telling frightened people that they are wrong. You have to understand what the fear is. At the moment, people are just being told 'Shut up and don't worry, have the MMR.' It's very patronising.[60]

When challenged as to her expertise on the matter, the actress said that she too was 'a mother'. A mother: just like those many millions of mothers who have not seen any link between autism and MMR and whose children's lives have been made safer by the vaccine.

The regressive temptation

Notwithstanding its extraordinary achievements, there has been in some quarters increasing dissatisfaction with what scientific medicine has to offer – though the overwhelming majority of people who fall seriously ill still make it their first resort. There are obvious reasons for this. Success is less visible than failure. Things that go wrong – ineffective treatments, untreatable diseases, mistakes, adverse effects of medication and poor care – attract disproportionate attention. But there are other, less obvious, explanations for why increasing numbers of people are turning to so-called 'alternative medicine', either instead of, or more commonly in addition to orthodox science-based medical care. They are worth examining, and challenging, not only because of the present scale of the alternative medicine industry but also because there is a danger of a corrupting effect on clinical medicine – on medical education, and on medical practitioners. This, in turn, may have adverse consequences for the future of scientific medicine which still has a great deal to achieve.[61] The problems intrinsic to alternative medicine are concealed by the muddled thinking which is endemic in pretty well all discussions of the phenomenon.[62] That muddle is seeping into mainstream medical practice.

The rise of alternative medicine

First some (rather extraordinary) facts. In 1990, 60 million Americans spent an estimated $13.7 billion on alternative therapies and their 425 million estimated annual visits to alternative practitioners exceeded all those to US primary care physicians.[63] By 1996, expenditure in the USA had increased to $21 billion.[64] This figure exceeded the total amount spent out-of-pocket in the entire mainstream medical system. Where the USA leads, the United Kingdom follows, and a recent report estimated that about £1.5 billion is spent in the UK on alternative treatments annually, and there are 50,000 alternative practitioners.[65] At present at least 40 per cent of general practices provide some alternative medicine services and there is pressure to make them universally available on the NHS.[66]

This last statistic illustrates something else: although alternative medicine is still presented as if it were a challenge to the authority of a monolithic, unicultural health system, it is actually becoming equally institutionalized. There is now hardly a chemist's shop that does not have a substantial section devoted to alternative medicine and it is sometimes quite difficult to distinguish a shop run by a properly qualified pharmacist from a health shop run by an alternative medicine practitioner. The proceeds from both pass into the same till. The *British Medical Journal* has advocated 'integrative' or 'integrated' medicine which combines orthodox medicine with alternative medicine.[67] A guide published in the *Observer* to the hospitals providing the best care for breast cancer used the availability of alternative treatments – aromatherapy, homoeopathy, reflexology, acupuncture – as one of its criteria of excellence.[68]

Just how respectable alternative medicine has become is reflected in the fact that HRH Prince of Wales, an advocate of homoeopathy,[69] contributed to the special issue of the *British Medical Journal* just referred to.[70] More startling still, he was invited to express his views at the Royal College of Physicians and had a letter published in *The Times*.[71] Medical schools are now including alternative medicine in the curriculum. In the UK, the approach is still reasonably cautious and critical, taking the form of special study modules in which students learn mainly about patient's beliefs and the various kinds of alternative medicine they take.[72] In the USA, where the profession is more willing to provide customers with what they want, so long as the source of reimbursement has been identified, 75 out of 125 medical schools offer education on complement- ary and alternative therapy, which includes advice on prescribing.[73]

The allure of alternative medicine

There is negligible evidence that the effectiveness of alternative therapies is greater than would be expected from a placebo effect – the effect, that is to say, of suggestion. Of course, there is much apparent evidence: anecdotes, patient testimony, endorsements from satisfied customers – the kind of evidence used by the first huckster who sold his first bottle of snake oil off the back of his ox-cart and the first magician to turn his attention to the lucrative business of peddling cancer cures. As we saw in Chapter 3, the only way of making sure that the apparent benefits of a treatment are not due to either suggestion, placebo, bias, chance effects, or to spontaneous recovery, is to carry out a proper trial. The treatment should be compared with an inert placebo or best current therapy in a randomized double-blind controlled trial. In such a trial, neither the beliefs of the patient nor of the therapist can affect the outcome. Proper randomization of patients is necessary to ensure that those receiving the treatment being evaluated are similar in all important respects to those receiving the comparator. Any specific benefits observed under such circumstances will, if sufficient patients are included, probably be real.

The importance of rigorous empirical tests is even greater where, as in the case of most alternative medicine, treatments are biologically implausible or even, as with homoeopathy, physically implausible. At the dilutions used in most homoeopathic remedies, there is a high probability that there is not one molecule of the putatively active material in the treatments given.[74] And those, for example, who profess success with 'healing touch' do not actually touch the patient: the healer runs the palm several inches above the patient's skin, breaking up 'fields of force' unknown to biology or physics. The situation with acupuncture is a little more complicated. There is some physiological basis (and clinical evidence) for the value of acupuncture in the treatment of chronic pain. Acupuncture needles preferentially stimulate certain nerve fibres that then prevent the ascent of nerve impulses associated with pain ascending to the brain. This does not, however, justify its use as a universal panacea for stress, for diabetes, for strokes. What is more, acupuncturists require one to believe ideas about illness for which there is no evidence, other than the sacred texts of Chinese medicine: that there are patterns of energy flow (Qi) throughout the body that are essential for health; that disease is due to disruptions to this flow; and that acupuncture corrects the disruptions.

The lack of a sound theoretical basis for alternative medicines means that there is a pressing need for them to be thoroughly tested in practice. It is therefore regrettable that most alternative therapies have not been evaluated in trials, not even badly designed ones. Where properly designed trials have been performed, the results have been overwhelmingly negative. A recent comprehensive overview of a wide range of alternative medicine therapies in an equally wide range of diseases found that none had performed better than a placebo; that is to say, they had no specific effect beyond suggestion.[75]

This does not impress its practitioners. The failure of trials to demonstrate benefit is, they say, irrelevant because the very conditions under which such trials are performed minimize the chances of detecting the potency of the treatment. And this makes a kind of sense. If Chinese medicine proved to be merely as good as diuretics for patients with heart failure, it would just be another (more expensive) alternative to diuretics, rather than an expression of an alternative vision of illness and of the universe in which illness is manifest. As we shall see, alternative medicine not only offers cures for illnesses; it changes your view of yourself.

There is an irony in the glamour that invests alternative therapies and therapists. As Henry Shenkin has pointed out:

Prior to World War II almost all medical practice was 'alternative medicine' since there was little evidence for the validity of treatment methods, and even orthodox physicians could do little for their patients beyond providing them and their families with empathy and moral support.[76]

'Folk medicine' belongs to the pre-scientific phase of physic out of which scientific medicine has climbed only with great difficulty and only very recently. It is medicine's greatest triumph that it has shed folk remedies and woken from the 5,000- or 10,000-year hegemony of the untested. Alternative medicine is the kind of medicine people took when there was no alternative; when there were no antibiotics, no steroids, no effective treatments for cancer, heart attacks, stomach ulcers.

There are many reasons for the rise of alternative medicine. We have already mentioned one: the limitations of science-based medicine. What is more, alternative therapies are often quite pleasant: having one's feet caressed by a reflexologist who is paying you and your ailments undivided attention in a relaxing setting cannot be bad. The aromas used in aromatherapy smell nice. Treatments that have no pharmacological effects will have no side effects either. In addition, some of those who take alternative medicine without the knowledge or blessing of their orthodox medical advisers feel they are thumbing their noses at a 'powerful' body of opinion. Moreover, by picking and mixing between orthodox medicine and alternative medicine, patients may feel that they are exercising their rights as consumers, and undermining the oppressive authority of the medical profession. In fact, the authority of the practitioner of alternative medicine is more personal, more priestly and, being less evidence-based, more oppressive. He has not submitted his treatments to the democratic tribunal of clincial trials. In moving from orthodox medicine to alternative medicine, the patient swaps the evidence-based impersonal authority of the physician for the unchallengeable personal authority of the practitioner who does not deign to provide evidence: he is one who knows.[77] Not a good basis for advanced consumerism, one would have thought.

Deeper than the desire to cock a snook at the medical establishment is the longing to make a different kind of sense of one's illness. This is particularly important where the illness is incurable, or incompletely curable: the notion that the process which has one in its grip is impersonal or meaningless makes make illness even less easy to bear. While alternative medicine may bring the hope of cure when all hope seems to have been lost, it still offers something even when it fails to deliver – the promise of personal significance.[78] Roy Porter, with characteristic perceptiveness, remarked that medicine has 'offered the promise of "the greatest benefit of mankind", but not always on terms palatable to and compatible with cherished ideals'.[79] Least compatible of all is the third-person approach to the understanding of disease that underlies the success of Western medicine.

When I am told that this ghastly feeling I have had for the last few months and which has interfered with my daily routine is due to an increase in the blood levels of urea because of the failure of kidneys, which have figured so little in my life and in my thinking about myself, this is both good and bad news. It is good news because it means that there may be a way of alleviating my ghastly feeling. It is bad news because it means that I am now, and for the foreseeable future, the site of impersonal biochemical disasters that will have to be corrected again and again by treatments that are as impersonal (and, ultimately as obscure) as those biochemical disasters. By contrast, alternative medicine treats each patient differently. If a dozen patients with diabetes present themselves to an acupuncturist, although they will receive treatments that are superficially more similar, the treatment, so the rhetoric goes, will be 'tailored' to the individual patient.[80]

The impersonality of disease is particularly awful when it is incurable.

When the great German poet Rainer Maria Rilke fell ill with a fatal leukaemia:

he did not want to hear what the disease was called, preferring to regard it as peculiar to himself, and accepting his condition rather 'as an inevitable mystery, which ought not to be examined too closely'.[81]

No wonder, then, that patients seek out practitioners who relate their illnesses to the individual details of their lives; who, in short, *personalize* their diseases. This personal attention minimizes the impersonal aspects of illness. What is in fact biochemical failure is connected with important life events, such as the job, or the relationship with the spouse. This not only gives the disease a personal meaning but also gives patients the feeling they are in control of their illness: if it's about the way I am living, I can change my way of life.

The re-enchantment of disease not only reconnects it with the patient as a person but also with deep and magical general notions, which are nevertheless intuitively sense-making and so reinforce the connection with the person. Alternative medicine invites you to locate your illnesses in the doubly alluring context of your individual self and of exotic notions drawn from distant times and distant places, rooted in world-views that are not disenchanted.[82] An illness becomes a window on to a different, more exciting view of the world, rather than being merely an especially grim expression of the everyday reality that has us in its grip. If, for example, the reason for your backache is not some mechanical process in your body but the fact that your energy balance is out of kilter and this energy balance is a reflection of the sickness of modern times, then there is more to the pain in your back, and to you, than anything your doctor in his surgery could suggest.

Boutique multiculturalism

Alternative medicine has benefited from the notion that scientific medical knowledge, produced by an unprecedented cooperative effort of mankind, is 'monolithic' and the hegemony of 'Western medicine' is a form of intellectual colonialism. Making alternative medicine widely available and drawing on different cultural resources respects 'cultural diversity' as well as 'consumer choice'.

A recent Working Group on Traditional and Complementary Health Systems, established by Commonwealth Health Ministers, seems to have begun precisely from this assumption: that integrating 'Western' and 'traditional' medicines is a good thing. Bodeker[83] has argued for 'communication and mutual understanding among different medical systems' and an 'equitable distribution of resources between complementary and conventional medicine'.

However, the equitable distribution of resources 'between complementary and conventional medicine' is the last thing really sick people in developing countries want. As John Diamond notes:

It is easy for a well-fed metropolitan with time and money on his hands to talk about dealing with his chronic symptoms with ayurvedic medicine or Chinese herbal remedies, but if you go to those countries where they are all they have, you'll find them crying out for good old Western antibiotics, painkillers and all the rest of the modern and expensive pharmacopoeia. A Ugandan dying of AIDS-related tuberculosis doesn't want to be treated with the natural remedies of his forefathers: he wants an aseptic syringe full of antibiotics...[84]

In countries where traditional medicine predominates, there is a high infant mortality rate, people die young and the illnesses that are treated routinely in the West go uncured with much pain and suffering. The maternal mortality rate in Third World countries – even those not riven by famine, civil war and natural disasters – is the most telling testimony to this truth. Given an informed choice, seriously ill people go for Western medicine. Integration of medicine that works with medicine that doesn't (but offers a more attractive story about the patients and their illnesses) is an unaffordable luxury in developing countries.

John Diamond's point is a profound one. Sentimental attitudes towards untested medicines invested with the magic of antiquity and the subversive charm of irrationality are unsustainable except against the background of universal provision of orthodox care for serious illness. I have strong personal reasons for being aware of this.

Thirty years after I returned from a year practising as a very junior doctor in Nigeria, I am still haunted by what I saw there; in particular by the catastrophic influence of traditional medicine and by the consequences of not getting so-called 'Western medicine' to those most in need of it. Let me give one example of the results of the irrationalist, unaccountable, evidence-free medicine that many aficionados of alternative medicine would advocate being reintroduced more widely into the West.

In the part of Nigeria in which I worked, a woman who had given birth to a child was regarded as unclean. (When it was a case of the first child, the mother was expected not to refer to her pregnancy at all because it was a source of shame: it implied that she had engaged in sexual intercourse – a matter of pride, of course, to the father.) Immediately after the birth she was then subjected to an ordeal prescribed by traditional healers: a ritual cleansing that involved sitting in a kind of oven where the temperature often exceeded 100 degrees Fahrenheit. She had to drink very large quantities of a 'cleansing' fluid rich in sodium and potassium. Not infrequently, after pregnancy and childbirth marked by malnutrition and extensive blood loss due to mismanaged labour and post-partum haemorrhage, the mother would be profoundly anaemic. The combination of anaemia, heat stress and salt and water overload had precisely the effect predicted by Western biomedical science: the patient would go into heart failure, something otherwise unheard of in young women without primary heart disease.[85] Many of these women arrived at the hospital mortally ill and required immediate treatment with powerful diuretics and other drugs if they were going to be saved. The effects of such orthodox, science-based treatment were often miraculous.

One night, such a patient came in under my care. About a week before, she had been delivered of a child and she was now gasping her last. When I asked for a syringe of frusemide – the diuretic we used – none was forthcoming. The ward sister who had never been particularly enthusiastic about Western medicine had gone off to her supper and taken with her the key to the drug cupboard (always locked because its contents had the habit of disappearing and reappearing in the local market for sale). There was nothing I could do. The woman expired, drowning in her own secretions, before my eyes. Her grief-stricken husband wanted to take her body away so that he could bury her before sunset; whereupon officious porters set upon him, insisting that (as this was a teaching hospital) she should first of all go to the mortuary so that she could be used for an instructive post-mortem. My final image of this avoidable catastrophe was of the distraught husband, with one or two of his other children around him, walking down the main hospital corridor, his wife's corpse on his shoulder, being waylaid by porters who had been told to prevent him from leaving with her.

This lady was just one statistic out of many millions. Recently, the World Health Organization (WHO) reported a maternal mortality rate of 480 per 100,000 in less developed countries compared with 27 per 100,000 in more developed countries.[86] While the tragedy of a young woman dying in childbirth may occur also as a result of poverty, war, corruption, lack of personal accountability, and the undervaluing and oppression of women, these statistics should give pause to those who advocate day-trips into the world of traditional healers as a corrective to the perceived deficiencies of science-based care.

A more recent example of traditionalist irrationality at work, garnished with an extremely modern paranoia about the alliance between science, big business and covert activity by the American intelligence community, is the hostility in Northern Nigeria to a vaccination campaign to immunize 63 million children in West Africa against polio. It is a key part of the WHO's fifteen-year campaign to halt the transmission of the virus across the world by 2005. According to local clerics and politicians, who are blocking the vaccine campaign, 'it was a US plot to depopulate Muslim lands by causing sterility and spreading AIDS.'[87] Some of the clerics said their own scientists had tested the vaccine and found it to be impure. The persistance of polio – an entirely preventable killer and maimer of children – in Northern Nigeria should give our local anti-MMR campaigners, and those who have regarded the government support for the triple vaccine as a conspiracy between the medical establishment, the pharmaceutical industry and government, an opportunity to see the consequences of the kind of irrationality they would wish to be respected in the UK. It is only because there are strong countervailing forces that they and their fellow citizens are protected from the consequences of these beliefs.[88] Where there is no such protection, the consequences could be catastrophic.

In South Africa, there has been, in recent years, an appalling example of the effects of a government-sponsored attack on the 'hegemony' of Western, science-based medicine in President Thabo Mbeki's refusal to acknowledge that AIDS is a sexually transmitted disease caused by a virus which could be prevented or treated by anti-viral drugs. He was attracted by the maverick ideas of Peter Duesberg, who claimed that AIDS was a lifestyle disease and had nothing to do with HIV. Mbeki liked this notion because it was unorthodox, anti-establishment, anti-pharmaceutical industry and therefore somehow allied with his own 'anti-colonialist' stance. Duesberg's totally discredited ideas also had a veneer of science. Moreover, Mbeki approved of Duesberg's denial that AIDS could be heterosexually transmitted. Given the high prevalence of the disease among heterosexuals in sub-Saharan Africa, Mbeki argued that the conventional story of the sexual transmission of AIDS denigrated 'black people as vice-ridden germ carriers unable to control their lust'. He brooked no dissent: black people who accepted the orthodox understanding were 'negroes of enslaved minds'.[89]

Since he was head of state in a country where the mechanisms of democratic accountability are still not well developed, Mbeki was able to place his ideas at the centre of his government's response to the most terrible crisis South Africa has faced in its history. In particular, he opposed sex education and the provision of anti-AIDS drugs. Doctors, scientists and AIDS activists who disagreed with his views have been – and are – threatened and vilified. When the South African Medical Research Council (MRC) pointed to the scale of the problem, Essop Prahd, Mbeki's 'chief enforcer', launched a campaign against Malegapuru Makgoba, the MRC's president, for playing into the hands of racists. The ANC 'distributed a fat document which claimed that anti-HIV drugs are an attempt to commit genocide against black people and another that compared anti-retrovirals to "the biological warfare of the apartheid era" '.[90]

South Africa's health minister Manto Tshabalala-Msimang has fought the good fight by campaigning (with considerable success) against anti-retroviral drugs, which she wants to phase out in favour of traditional remedies.[91] She approved of a very popular DJ, Fana Khaba, who, on discovering that he was HIV-positive, sought the advice of a sangoma, or traditional healer. He refused anti-retroviral drugs and in early 2004 died a horrible death, having infected dozens of women, including his wife, during his illness.

Of the 70,000 children born annually to HIV-positive mothers in South Africa about half could have been protected from becoming HIV-positive themselves, and suffering a painful protracted death, with a single dose of a cheap anti-retroviral drug. Mbeki has done everything possible to prevent this from happening. Many of the 800,000 non-infant deaths per year from AIDS could also be prevented by making anti-retroviral drugs available but Mbeki's ideological views do not permit it. According to a recent study (suppressed by the South African government, who now maintain that anti-HIV drugs are toxic and will primarily benefit pharmaceutical companies) immediate provision of such drugs could save up to 1.7 million people by 2010.[92] As one of his former supporters, the Anglican Archbishop of Cape Town, Njongonkulu Ndungane, has said, Mbeki's AIDS policies are as serious a crime as apartheid – and, of course, have already killed many more people.[93]

Some readers may greet with incredulity or indignation the suggestion that there is any connection between Thabo Mbeki's iniquitous policies on HIV and AIDS and popping into the chemist's shop for a herbal remedy for a cold or seeking reflexological relief for stress. The difference is, of course, one of scale and degree. Insincere critiques of 'Western Medicine' and dalliance with the world pictures that underpin traditional therapies lie at the top of a slippery slope at the bottom of which lies the unreason and abuse of power that characterizes Mbeki's interference with the health care of the people of South Africa. Very wisely, most advocates of alternative medicine remain at the top of the slope, and are lucky enough to have the luxury of doing so. They do not take the ideas they profess seriously enough to endanger their own lives.

The multiculturalist sympathy for native, traditional and other forms of alternative medicine may be part of a wider trend: the pretence to a relativism that rejects dominant forms of truth, 'reason' and 'rationalism'. I have discussed this at length elsewhere[94] and will not examine it here. As Gellner said, reason is 'a Cosmic Exile' that has only its achievements to commend it. Which is why, when educated people are really worried about their health – notwithstanding their rhetoric about the virtues of ancient remedies (much tried but never properly tested) – they will turn to what is called Western medicine.

'The medicine of humanity'

The *bien pensants* might find it easier to square their own preference for scientific medicine when they, or their loved ones, fall seriously ill, if they stopped calling scientific medicine 'Western medicine'. Their anxiety is in part based on the correct intuition that no single culture or epoch has a monopoly on truth or access to absolute truth. They could spare themselves the discomfort of equating the superiority of evidence-based over evidence-free medicine with 'cultural imperialism' by acknowledging the extent to which 'Western medicine' is the product of streams of thought and inquiry that have had many sources. It is multicultural.

In the successive awakenings of hominid bodily self-understanding, neolithic experimentation, Chinese philosophy and European Renaissance thought have all made significant contributions. While the major advances over the last few hundred years have come from Europe and places where Europeans have dominated, the development of scientific medicine is now a world-wide effort. This is illustrated by the two studies on aspirin and stroke referred to in Chapter 3: both, with their identical findings, were truly international. Good medical science is part of a world-wide consensus.

An even more telling example is the research effort that has gone into understanding the causation, the modes of transmission, the prevention and the treatment of AIDS. This has been truly global, with contributions from scientists from all over the world. What is more, contrary to what politicians such as Thabo Mbeki would say, there are no 'indigenous' ways of understanding the behaviour of retroviruses. Retroviruses can no more be culturally relativized than failing kidneys, diabetes, or piles, though the taboos that surround AIDS and obstruct the fight against it are certainly culturally relative. It was Hegel who famously pointed out that while reason is universal, irrationality and error are local.

It is interesting to see what Roy Porter has to say on this:

Western medicine has developed in ways which have made it uniquely powerful and led it to become uniquely global. Its ceaseless spread throughout the world owes much, doubtless, to western political and economic domination. But its dominance has increased because it is perceived, by societies and the sick, to 'work' uniquely well, at least for many major classes of disorders. (Parenthetically, it can be argued that western political and economic domination owes something to the path-breaking powers of quinine, antibiotics and the like.) To the world historian, western medicine is special. It is *conceivable* that in a hundred years' time traditional Chinese medicines, shamanistic medicine or Ayurvedic medicine will have swept the globe… But there is no real indication of that happening, while there is every reason to expect the medicine of the future to be an outgrowth of present western medicine – or at least a reaction against it. What began as the medicine of Europe is becoming the medicine of humanity.[95]

'The medicine of humanity' says it all. And this encompasses not merely high-powered interventions with expensive drugs or ingenious operations. The bacterial theory of infectious disease which brought in its wake those aseptic procedures and public health measures that have delivered such huge benefits is just as much an expression of 'the medicine of humanity' as are heart transplants. (The scarcely noticed eradication of African river blindness is a recent glorious, light- and life-giving consequence of the scientific approach to a disease that has blighted the lives of people in Central Africa since time immemorial.[96]) The gifts of antibiotics, of the public health and hygiene approach to endemic diseases, of immunization, of safe surgery, of pain relief, of the recognition and treatment of vitamin deficiency are of immeasurable worth.

I ought perhaps to end with a declaration of partiality. I owe my own life at the age of six weeks to orthodox medicine. Because immunization against whooping cough was not available in 1947, I was one among many millions of children who fell ill from this disease. I coughed, vomited, refused food and drink, developed pneumonia, and started to fade away. Had it not been for antibiotics and, more important, intravenous infusions into the tiny vein in my scalp, I would have died. If instead I had been offered reflexology, acupuncture, crystal therapy or homoeopathy, I would have been another statistic in the infant mortality returns of 1947.

Permanent revolution

The high standing of the NHS in the eyes of the public, consistently displayed over a long period, is of course primarily a testimony to the consistent record of achievement of a dedicated health care workforce.

The historical record suggests a less generous estimate of the contribution of governments, politicians and bureaucrats. Notwithstanding their habitual claim that the NHS is granted the highest priority, in practice it has been mismanaged, neglected and starved of resources. Thereby the work of the NHS workforce has been seriously handicapped and services have fallen short of the standards taken for granted elsewhere.

Charles Webster, *The National Health Service. A Political History*[97]

For the whole of my medical career I have lived with oppressive cuts and frustrating rationing. And then in the new millennium came the possibility of a properly funded NHS. But there was a catch: the promised money had to pass through a series of filters, and its expenditure macro- and micro-managed to the nth degree. It was not long before the euphoria vanished: it became apparent that very little of the deluge of cash was going to get through to the front line – or at least my bit of it. Mr Brown's bounty would be like a monsoon reduced by the multiple layers of intervening foliage to sporadic drops on the jungle floor. And it was to be linked to 'modernization', which meant ever-more detailed interference from the centre and, to ensure that this could take place with minimal let or hindrance, there were to be changes in the structure of the health service. In short, it was business as usual.[98]

My older son, who was about three years old when he first heard me ranting about 're-disorganizations' and has now finished a postgraduate degree, asked me whether I really believed that no structural change since I qualified had helped me as a doctor to give better care to my patients. That gave me pause. There had been so many reforms, reorganizations and initiatives, it was difficult to remember even those changes that had been introduced as the 'greatest/most radical/most far-reaching' reforms in the fifty years of the NHS. In the first three years after I had qualified, at the end of 1970, NHS policy was dominated by the run-up to the 1974 reorganization – universally regarded as a disaster – and the pace of change has steadily accelerated since then. The Thatcher–Major years, described by Charles Webster, the foremost historian of the NHS, as 'continuous revolution', have been followed by seven years of near-delirium ('constant white water' as one manager described it to me) under Blair. (The events of 1997–2001 alone occupy over 20 per cent of Webster's history of the fifty-five-year-old NHS.)

Before I could answer my son's question, a certain amount of reflection was necessary, supplemented by reading. The relationship between NHS macro-politics and daily clinical life, between policy wonks and a clinician and medical teacher like myself, was for a long time a distant one. I began to take an interest in health policy only in the Thatcher era when it began to bear down directly and explicitly on my day-to-day practice and on the hopes I shared with my colleagues for improving what we had to offer our patients. It has increased as government has penetrated ever further into the capillaries of the NHS, until the present when we are all of us 'drowning in a sea of parchment'.

A brief history of continuous revolution

For twenty years or so after the NHS was founded, there was little government interference. According to Webster, the story was one of 'resource starvation and policy neglect'. There was concern in the very early years that the NHS was drawing on an open cheque when expenditure appeared greatly to exceed forecasts and allocated budgets. This prompted the introduction of charges for drugs, dentures and spectacles which shocked Labour ranks and led to ministerial resignations. However, the Guillebaud Report published in 1956[99] was reassuring on two fronts: the rising cost of the NHS was more apparent than real; and the service was good value for money. There was no need for drastic changes in either organization or financing.

A stinging attack by Lord Brock, one of the founders of cardiac surgery, in a letter to *The Times* in 1956, on political parties for 'unscrupulously deriving political capital from their support for the NHS... while allowing the UK hospital system to degenerate to a state where it was both derelict and dangerous'[100] pointed to the need for capital investment. The 1962 *A Hospital Plan for England and Wales* resulted. It was over-ambitious and remained unfulfilled forty years later. For example, Phases 1 and 2 of the Swindon hospital build were completed by 1964 but the final phase, due to be completed in the early 1970s, then in 1978, was resumed in 1990, then ground to a halt, was considered for a Private Finance Initiative project, then blocked by legal difficulties and the 1997 general election.

The NHS established by Aneurin Bevan in 1948 had a tripartite administrative structure: local Health Authorities ran a mixture of facilities such as health centres and maternity services; regional hospital boards and boards of governors ran, respectively, non-teaching and teaching hospitals; and executive councils oversaw independent contractors such as general practitioners and dentists. In the late 1960s this was seen to be increasingly unsatisfactory, giving rise to 'persistent and serious problems of duplication, fragmentation, and lack of cohesiveness, all characteristics horribly reminiscent of the defects of the service before the NHS'.[101] After approximately six years of debate and planning, consultative documents, papers Green and White, a radically reorganized NHS, 'mauled and bleeding under the surgeon's knife' was launched in 1974 'on a sea of words'.[102]

The result was recognized at once as disastrous. The three-tier administrative structure – with Regional Health Authorities, Area Health Authorities, and District management teams, managing by 'consensus' – augured confusion and paralysis. This promise was amply fulfilled, especially since the reallocation of jobs seemed to favour the least competent individuals for the most senior posts.[103] A threefold increase in administrative and clerical staff to deal with the new arrangements added to the confusion about who was responsible for what.

I can vividly remember this time, just before I was a consultant; indeed I set a novel in the late 1970s, which captured some of the frustrations.[104] In one scene resuscitation of a patient who has had a cardiac arrest fails because the defibrillator is long beyond its shelf-life. The juniors wonder how they might get another one:

Equipment costs money. The size of the equipment grant allocated to the North Brompton Royal Infirmary could be deduced from its general appearance of unchecked entropy. Revenue and capital, it seemed, had long since deserted this neck of the NHS. A formal request for another defibrillator would not, of course, receive an explicit refusal. That would be far too crude and court dangerous publicity. Instead it would meet the implicit 'No' that is embodied in delay, evasion, obliquity and inaction. This 'No' would be underlined by the unavailability or unidentifiability of any person who could make a positive decision or be held responsible for a negative one. Nick envisaged two blizzards of memoranda – one travelling upwards and the other downwards – between the hospital and the higher reaches of the NHS.[105]

The 1974 reorganization marked the start of an era in which reorganizations begat new reorganizations; where the primary triggers to the next lot of changes were the problems experienced with the last lot. The three-tier system was reduced to two tiers in 1982 (just about the time I became a consultant) and District management teams became statutory authorities – District Health Authorities. Because the NHS was seen to be 'over-administered and under-managed', Margaret Thatcher commissioned Roy Griffiths, deputy chairman and managing director of

Sainsbury's supermarket chain, to cast a businessman's eye on the service. He was struck by the lack of clear lines of accountability and responsibility. (Except in direct patient care: when something went wrong clinically, it was pretty obvious whose fault it was.) He famously announced that: 'if Florence Nightingale were carrying her lamp through the corridors of the NHS today, she would almost certainly be looking for the people in charge.' He recommended a system of 'general management' at every level in the service.

It was not clear that this meant anything other than the end of management by consensus and a concentration of power in the hands of senior administrators – who were now called 'managers'. Doctors would have less say in the development of the service: managers would control the introduction of 'cost improvement programmes' (cuts), would evaluate results and would hold consultants to account.

This assumed its full importance only when the next tranche of reforms, triggered by a sense of crisis in the service, were introduced five years later. A hurriedly cobbled together White Paper, entitled *Working for Patients*, introduced the concept of the internal market. The running of hospitals (and other so-called 'providers') was to be separated from their financing and they would have to compete for business with adjacent, and even distant, hospitals to provide services to be bought by Health Authorities and other so-called 'purchasers'.

The underlying idea was that health care providers wouldn't work hard without the incentive of competition. The split in the NHS between providers – who provided care – and purchasers – who bought it – was underlined by the option available to hospitals to opt out of Health Authority control and become Trusts run as quasi-businesses. The main statutory responsibility of the Trust 'boards', consisting of a mixture of executives and non-executives, was to balance the books. Where their local hospitals had opted out, District Health Authorities had a greatly reduced role – just a few years after they had acquired their statutory function.

This was limited even further when they were instructed not to switch providers too drastically: they were told to maintain a 'steady state', to aim at 'measured change' and to allow spurned hospitals 'a soft landing'. The internal market could not be allowed to work like a real market since hospital Trusts could not be put out of business. Even so, the top managers in both Trusts and Health Authorities were granted the title and status of 'chief executives'. Except as government enforcers (including the enforcement of cash limits), they were not very powerful; indeed their potency had not changed much except compared with a now greatly disempowered clinical staff. For there were other powers in the land: the ever more politicized centre which prescribed in ever more minute detail what hospitals should do and what Health Authorities should demand of them.

The newly empowered centre was the scene of an interesting managerial ballet. At first, a Health Services Supervisory Board and an NHS Management Board was established. This was a response to the Griffiths challenge to find 'someone in charge'. The Supervisory Board, however, was soon got rid of, as it was uncertain as to how 'supervision' and 'management' roles should be defined with respect to one another. This simply moved the uncertainty to the interface between the Management Board and the Department of Health, whose civil servants were deeply unhappy about this new organization. The Management Board was deemed to be' 'a complete and utter disaster' by a well-placed source in 1987.[106] The notion of parcelling off the NHS to an independent corporation was toyed with – an idea that has a recurring appeal to all sorts of people, ranging from insiders such as Lord Porrit[107] to armchair critics such as the *Observer* columnist Will Hutton, as well as, from time to time, politicians.[108] (The attraction to politicians is that it may be possible to separate policy-making from operational matters and credit for novel new ideas from blame for their unworkability or for the lack of resources to implement them.) Instead, *Working for Patients* reintroduced the Supervisory Board under another name: The NHS Policy Board, chaired by the Secretary of State, and an NHS Management Executive, chaired by a Chief Executive. Like the Supervisory Board before it, the Policy Board served no useful function, but it was not abolished. The NHS Management Executive changed its title to a snappier NHS Executive. It became very powerful and somewhat secretive, working closely with the Regional Health Authority offices (that were under its thumb) to favour the implementation of the internal market and pressurize hospitals to become Trusts. Mrs Thatcher's commitment to rolling back the power of the state became, at least in the case of the NHS, merely a commitment to rolling back the visible, accountable power of the state.

The pace of change was now picking up. While the 1974

reorganization had taken six years to plan and execute, the introduction of the internal market and the other changes that, it was claimed, 'were the most far-reaching reforms of the National Health Service in its forty-year history',[109] took three years. Admittedly, there were a few after-thoughts, such as papers on care in the community. As Charles Webster points out, one of the many weaknesses of *Working for Patients* was the focus on hospitals, as if the NHS were a National Hospital Service. This was because hospitals were where the most serious trouble and the most bothersome trouble-makers were to be found. It was 'the deafening chorus of complaint'[110] from hospital doctors, in particular the howl of rage provoked by the case of a child who died while waiting for heart surgery, that caused Mrs Thatcher to act in the late 1980s.

There followed, in rapid succession, a series of quite radical (or at least time- and resource-consuming) changes. Smaller Trusts were amalgamated. Smaller Health Authorities were fused to form bigger ones that served larger populations. Family Health Services Authorities, which dealt with general practice and other aspects of care in the community, were merged (only a few years after they had been created) with District Health Authorities to form single Health Authorities covering both primary and hospital care. And, finally, Regional Health Authorities were eliminated and replaced with even more pointless Regional Offices. By 1996, all of the tiers established in 1974 had been removed and an administrative structure rather like that envisaged in the Crossman Green Paper of 1968 (dismissed at the time) had been created.

By that time, it was universally acknowledged that everyone had had enough. Even the politicians were tired of change. Under Stephen Dorrell's brief reign as the last Secretary of State for Health before the arrival of New Labour, the emphasis was on consolidation and stability. His White Paper *A Service with Ambitions* – dismissed by his ambitious opponent Chris Smith – marked the end of his own career in health care politics. Not long after it was published he was out of office.

New Labour, despite the promises in opposition of bringing to an end the 'continuous revolution' that had marked the Tories' eighteen-year stint, had its own revolutionary ideas. In part these were driven by trying to reconcile two promises: to save and improve the NHS; and to remain within the Tory spending limits. In short, as they came into government, they 'faced the impossible task of providing a comparable level of service, involving similar costs, but with only half the resources available elsewhere among leading western economies'.[111]

Labour put its faith in something called 'modernization', which would somehow do away with the need for actual resources. The circle could be squared, it was thought, by efficiency savings and by fudges. According to their own figures, £1.5 billion a year in administration costs would be released by abolishing the internal market; and the late conversion to the Private Finance Initiative (of which more presently) would enable promises of shiny new hospitals, health centres, and equipment to be honoured without fiscal embarrassment. The most dramatic step was the creation of a brand new administrative tier: the 480 Primary Care Groups (PCGs) would shortly be reorganized into 300 Primary Care Trusts (PCTs). According to the plans later set out in the White Paper, *Shifting the Balance of Power within the NHS*, 75 per cent of the resources made available to the NHS would pass through PCTs. This was the death knell of the Regional Offices (not that anyone would have noticed the difference) and the District Health Authorities. The transitional period was particularly difficult as the mass sackings and re-hirings greatly reduced available expertise in purchasing secondary and tertiary services and in indeed in developing coherent health services overall. (In Greater Manchester in the late 1990s we had thirty unfledged PCGs and eight moribund and warring Health Authorities to turn to for funds for developing neurosurgical, neurological and neurological rehabilitation services.)

Incessant structural change in the early years of New Labour was an attempt to get more for less. In short, trying to solve or conceal under-resourcing by reorganization. This is analogous to treating a patient who is anaemic by operating on their blood vessels and altering the distribution of blood. Vascular surgery under such circumstances is a particularly ill-judged therapeutic strategy because it is associated with considerable blood loss and the result is yet more profound anaemia. In the end, the cover was blown and, as White Paper succeeded White Paper – *The New NHS. Modern Dependable*; *The NHS Plan. A Plan for Investment. A Plan for Reform*; *Shifting the Balance of Power within the NHS*[112] – each heralded as the 'most radical/far-reaching' reform since the creation of the NHS, the emphasis shifted from modernization as the solve-all to 'investment tied to reform and modernization'.

Investment. This was something new. And exciting. Bliss was it in that dawn to be alive, but to be a middle-aged consultant was very heaven. What is more, investment was to be on a grand scale. Tony Blair committed his government to reaching average European spending levels within less than a decade. But the promises were twinned with threats, and the target of the threats was clear: the recalcitrant workforce, most particularly the medical profession, which was, in the new millennium, increasingly being described as 'scandal-hit'. Nobody quite knew what 'reform and modernization' were. There was talk of relocating power and resources 'close to frontline workers', acknowledged to be in touch with the needs of patients and communities, and more talk of new and complex ways of making clinicians and managers accountable, so that they would be shamed into meeting targets and standards. In fact, the closeness of the front line to the centre made the apparent devolution of power to the periphery simply a way of bypassing the old power structures (in particular those in which there was a conspicuous medical lead) in the NHS. The merging of old posts of Permanent Under-secretary to the Department of Health and the Chief Executive of the NHS brought policy and operational matters under the direct control of the Minister.

From then onwards, NHS employees could expect no escape from frenzied interference. And so it has been ever since. The working out of the implications of the recent White Papers has proved immensely complicated and and yet more fundamental changes are being flagged up. The privatization programme – beyond anything the Tories would have dared shout out in their sleep – is getting into gear. The proposal to create Care Trusts (in which health and social services work more closely together, sharing budgets and commissioning of services) is being realized and there are further plans to roll out commissioning beyond the professionals to 'the people'. And there is the still uncompleted 'blue-sky thinking' of the Forward Strategy Team of the Cabinet Office, headed up by Adair Turner. As Mr Blair said after the first few turbulent years of New Labour, the NHS workforce is now 'accustomed to being told every couple of years that they are about to face the biggest overhaul since the beginning of the health service, and that the process of modernization is only entering its stride, and that they are about to face "unsettling times" '.[113] The message was: get used to it; from now on, the only constant will be change.

'If', as Lord Falkland famously said, 'it is not necessary to change, it is necessary not to change.' For change is always costly and sometimes dangerous. The justified concern that the cost of structural change may outweigh any benefits, which guided the thinking of politicians in the first quarter of a century after the creation of the NHS, is now mocked. In the thirty years since the 1974 reforms, the default position has moved from 'Don't change unless you can prove the necessity for change' to one of 'Change at all costs' and to brand anyone who protests as a 'reactionary' or a (to use Mr Blair's famous phrase) a 'wrecker'. It may be useful, therefore, to reflect on some of the drivers to relentless change.

The purpose of changing the way health care is delivered should be to get better, more cost-effective care. This seems pretty obvious and something that all parties, and all stakeholders, would, if asked, agree upon. But there are many many reasons for wanting to alter the administrative structure of the NHS.

Among the most rational are, often small-scale, structural reorganizations in response to medical advances – the discovery of new treatments, the emergence of new disciplines, and the creation of new services. The development of cardiac surgery quite properly led to the formation of specialist units that provided regional services: regionalization ensured the concentration of expertise; the pooling of experience to reduce the period of time during which practitioners are bumping along the bottom of a learning curve; quality control; and the avoidance of wasteful duplication.[114] The amalgamation of smaller units into larger ones – as in the reorganization of neurosciences services in Greater Manchester – prevents wasteful duplication of equipment, permits sub-specialization and allows strategic planning in a way that the competition between cottage-hospital-sized units would not permit.

Reorganization may also be prompted by the perception that existing structures are dysfunctional, that they obstruct progress or ordinary day-to-day working through being over-bureaucratic. This was the driver for the 1974 reorganizations and for some that were undertaken in response to the problems created by that reorganization. There was a desire to simplify the processes by which things get done and/or to rationalize the way resources were spent, not least to deal with the progressive demotivation, even the sense of hopelessness, of the professionals working within the system. This was the rationale behind the removal of the Area Health Authority tier in 1982.

Over the last twenty years, however, the urge to reorganize has become increasingly caught up in issues of control. Much of the rhetoric that has informed organizational change has been about 'shifting the balance of power' (to echo the title of the 2001 White Paper), supposedly from the centre to the periphery. The move towards a more strongly managed NHS not only promised better internal control but, through opening up lines of accountability that reached directly to the top, made it possible to impose tighter external political control on what happened in the service. The absurd ballet around the top tables of the NHS in the wake of the Griffiths Report, the endless navel-gazing around 'management' and 'policy' and 'strategic' boards, testified to preoccupation with top-down control. But it also reflected the political need to separate strategy and policy – which can be visionary and exciting – from implementation and operational matters that are always imperfect, often disappointing and sometimes disastrous.

There is natural antagonism between politicians who have notional responsibility for the health service as a whole and those who are more closely responsible for parts of it. The Minister has to please a macroscopic abstraction – the electorate – while the clinician has to satisfy concrete individuals presenting with serious problems. This contrast is a recipe for mutual misunderstanding, hostility and contempt. In the highly politicized debate about the NHS, the appalling responsibilities carried by clinicians are almost invisible – except where they are deemed to have failed to honour them. To clinicians aware of the complexities of medical care the nostrums of politicians and their advisors seem puerile and often dangerously disruptive and distracting.

The politicians, moreover, are often transient: yesterday's Transport Secretary is today's Health Minister and tomorrow's Secretary of State for Defence or, if things go badly, embittered back-bencher. The workforce the Secretary of State faces is more or less permanent. Not unexpectedly they will have a deeper knowledge and understanding of the real business of medicine than a Minister appointed at a few days' notice. The transitoriness of ministers, and indeed of the administrations of which they are a part, creates another problem. The criteria by which a Minister may be judged to be successful – diminished discomfort at the despatch box, less flak in the tabloids – will be remote from the reality of changes in the delivery of care to the individual patients clinicians meet every day. The Health portfolio is tantalizingly close to being one of the great offices of state, hanging on to its Cabinet status by the skin of its teeth. It could be a lily-pad to political success; but for most of the incumbents it has proved the pinnacle of their career before a lapse back into obscurity.[115] The ministerial agenda consequently has a different timescale from that of most truly beneficially changes. An initiative that does not deliver within a very short time – a Minister's life expectancy, usually a few years, an administration's term of office – might as well not have been launched.[116]

The disempowerment of doctors – who increasingly figure in the political mind as self-interested opponents of reform – has been an important driver to recent structural change in the NHS. This has not always been the case. Although the creation of the NHS is sometimes presented as a triumph of egalitarian and idealistic politicians over conservative, self-seeking doctors, the relationship between the former and the latter in the established NHS was not seen as adversarial in the early years. Apart from the occasional outburst – 'I stuffed their mouths with gold' and such like[117] – Aneurin Bevan, the Minister who presided over the creation of the NHS, seemed to have a benign understanding of the division of responsibilities between his own ministry and the profession. In a speech given a few weeks after he became Minister of Health he said:

I conceive it the function of the Ministry of Health to provide the medical profession with the best and most modern apparatus of medicine and to enable them freely to use it, in accordance with their training, for the benefit of the people of their country. Every doctor must be free to use that apparatus without interference from secular organizations.[118]

When the *NHS Plan* was published in the summer of 2000,[119] the commitment to investment was linked to the requirement for 'reform' in the working practices of those in the NHS. It was repeatedly asserted that clinicians and managers had not hitherto put patients first; that there would be a new era of 'patient-centred' – as opposed to staff-centred – care.

This assault on the moral standing and good intentions of doctors was not the first, of course. In 1988 the then Secretary of State for Health, Kenneth Clarke, irritated by medical opposition to the internal market (subsequently acknowledged to be the disaster doctors said it was going to be), asserted that calls for reform always caused doctors 'to feel their wallets'.[120] Medicine was a closed shop and doctors should be treated no differently from dockers. His successor, Virginia Bottomley, enlisted patients, encouraging them to complain against doctors. She introduced the Patient's Charter, which laid much of the blame for unsatisfactory services at the feet of those providing it. But these initiatives did not make a huge dent in the standing of doctors. Alan Milburn's attack on the profession was more sustained and radical, and also more direct.

This was not surprising in a Minister who came from a political party that, after nearly a generation in opposition, was imbued with fantastical ideas about its ability to transform public services almost overnight. Couldn't this be achieved with the same command-and-control approach that had made the Labour party electable in the first place? It was merely a matter of disciplining those working in the NHS. The fact that medical care has an incredibly complex knowledge, skill and organizational base, and that a public service is not like a political party, seemed to go unnoticed. The huge majority that the government enjoyed reinforced the feeling of omnipotence. The combination of hearts in the right place, linked to brains free of ideological baggage, with a mandate from the people for radical change, meant that anything was possible. Inevitably the failure to deliver on impossible promises in an unrealistic timescale prompted a search for people to blame. Where such good ideas, such plausible rhetoric, such sincere promises, such impressive commands all fail to deliver, this must be due to reactionary forces and 'wreckers' within the system.[121]

One would not have to be over-cynical to think that the driving forces for structural changes in the NHS over the last thirty or so years have been largely: to wrest control of the service from those who are delivering it and to contain costs; to repair the damage caused by earlier structural changes; and to conceal lack of resources. There is, however, a further trigger: inquiries set up in the wake of scandals.

The number, scale and public profile of such inquiries is increasing: of the fifty-nine inquiries that have taken place since 1974, there were two in the 1970s, five in the 1980s and fifty-two from 1990 onwards.[122] In some cases, they have prompted useful action; for example, the inquiry into the abuse and ill-treatment of vulnerable long-stay patients at Ely Hospital led to the setting up of the Hospital Advisory Service by

Richard Crossman. This had a statutory responsibility for inspecting facilities in which the most vulnerable patients were cared for. In the thirty years of its existence, it was an effective champion of better long-stay services for elderly people and people in psychiatric institutions.

Other inquiries, however, have failed to bring about major improvements. It is depressing that the same problems keep recurring. A recent 'Inquiry into Inquiries' noted an 'eerie parallel' between the diagnosis of 'poor clinical leadership, an isolated and inward looking culture, inadequate management structures and systems, and inadequate resources' in the first modern NHS inquiry in 1967 into Ely Hospital 'and the findings of the public inquiry into paediatric cardiac surgery at the Bristol Royal Infirmary in 2002'.[123] This may be because the diagnosis is not accurate or precise enough to be helpful. The increasing tendency to think of inquiries as 'case studies in organizational failure' is reflected in a propensity for inquiries to propose ever more radical organizational changes.

The 2000 Bristol inquiry made nearly 200 recommendations, many of them related to the organization of the service. These recommendations have been used to justify the individual and organizational league tables that have tilted the focus away from the accountability of ministers to the competence of those providing the services. Now it is very much a matter of the Minister holding the profession to account in his role of patient's champion. The professionals have been displaced from that moral high ground from which, for example, paediatric cardiologists in Birmingham in 1987 berated Mrs Thatcher, and Lord Brock (in 1956) and Lord Winston (in 2000) berated the governments of their day.

How beneficial these costly, increasingly frequent and very public inquiries are is unclear. They have all the faults of single case studies subjected to retrospective analysis. They are therefore more likely to generate plausible explanations than identify root causes. As Walshe and Higgins conclude, 'inquiries have not been the subject of much research, and there is a pressing need for some evaluation of how they work and what they achieve.'[124] Without such an evaluation, there is a danger that health care will fall victim to the kind of on-the-hoof, reactive reorganizations that have characterized the evolution of child protection practices over the last fifty years.

Other pressures for change come from the sense that they run things better elsewhere. Service models from outside the NHS – from Europe, from the United States or from the private sector – have seemed attractive. There have been flirtations with different ways of funding and managing the service, and with novel approaches to 'incentivizing' its presumed-to-be-unmotivated staff. The Thatcher reforms of the late 1980s were an attempt to bring in management expertise and styles from the private sector and to utilize transatlantic ideas about the virtues of managed competition within public services. Unfortunately, the focus of her reforms was largely financial, with 'Corporate Governance' (balancing the books) being the prime duty of Trusts and their boards. Clinical Governance – ensuring the quality, as opposed merely to the quantity, of care – became a political preoccupation, and a responsibility of Trusts, only a decade later. Thatcher's internal market was another expensive failure.

On closer inspection the better way of ordering things in Europe or the USA turned out to be either more expensive, less equitable, or both. Alternative approaches to funding were ruled out by the 2002 Wanless Report,[125] the cost-effective virtues of American-style Health Maintenance Organizations (HMO) did not stand up to dispassionate scrutiny. And, when it came to argument by means of anecotes about care, as many stories of appalling care could be unearthed about 'the best health service in the world' (France currently facing bankruptcy) as much as in 'the worst in Europe' (Britain). The 13,000 deaths of elderly people during the August 2003 heatwave in France was in part due to the inability of understaffed hospitals to cope with the demand for care. Too many doctors had gone to the beach.[126]

The most powerful driving force in recent years for reorganization has been successive governments' determination to prove their radical credentials and to place clear water between the present and the past. As Polly Toynbee put it:

Everybody has to think up some super whizzbang new plan so they can go to electors and say, 'We are going to rip it all up and produce wonderful things called Primary Care Trusts (PCTs),' or whatever happens to be the fashion of the day. Every five years somebody has to come up with super-duper new ideas.[127]

As a result, no incoming government is motivated to see whether existing structures can be made to work better.[128] And, as in the case of New Labour, even an idea that is not very new has to be presented as brand new. For change itself is, it seems, such an intrinsic good that the appearance of it has to be maintained. To bring Lord Falkland up to date: 'Even if it is not necessary to change, it is necessary to change.'

Most of the changes that have proved of net benefit have resulted from the introduction of evidence-based methods of caring for patients. Such changes have modest non-clinical costs compared with governments' macroscopic interventions. These are justified. So too are changes designed to cut red tape and to de-bureaucratize management. Unfortunately the scissors that are supposed to deliver such reforms seem themselves to generate more red tape with every cut.[129]

The cost of permaent revolution

It is a strange paradox that having, in the interests of the economy, insisted on rigorous evaluation of clinical or management innovations, the government failed to observe this rule when it came to market reforms.[130]

The bitter lesson that physicians have learnt over the last few centuries is that the intuitive attractiveness of a remedy is no guarantee of its effectiveness or safety. This lesson does not seem to have influenced policies on health. 'Gurus' are more common than robust data; even qualitative evaluations of the costs and benefits of reorganizations are almost unheard of.

Insights sometimes come from unexpected sources. The Chief Economic Adviser to the Department of Health at the time of the introduction of the Thatcher internal market, who was a crucial player in implementing the changes, admitted not only that there was no conclusive evidence of the advantages of the market system, but also that it would not be possible to obtain such evidence, since 'it is the nature of major organization and management changes that they can rarely be proved to be more effective than those they replace'.[131] The difficulty of evaluating large-scale changes makes the responsibilities of those who would impose them even greater. The experience of the disastrous 1974 reorganization, painfully reversed over twenty evidence-free years, should have made policy-makers think twice.

In fact, even minor organizational changes may be difficult to evaluate: their effects may extend beyond their purpose. Again, this places the onus on those who introduce changes to examine both their direct and indirect consequences. If for example, the government decides to introduce publicly available individualized performance figures for surgeons, it should consider the impact this could have on the willingness of surgeons to operate on high-risk cases that could 'spoil' their figures. If data are published apparently showing that operative mortality has improved, it should not be assumed, even less claimed, that this is due to the policy of publishing league tables of surgical performance. It could be due to case selection, the introduction of new, safer treatments, or of other factors such as better pre-operative or post-operative care. The issue of 'knock-on effects' is particularly important in a complex system dealing with an almost infinite multitude of diseases. While the compulsory introduction of a triage nurse in the A & E department reduced the time between the arrival in casualty and being seen by someone, it had no impact on the total duration of stay. The same, or a longer stay was punctuated by an encounter with a nurse whose skills were being wasted in acting as a kind of receptionist.[132]

Sometimes the adverse effects may be quite remote. For example, there is a staffing crisis in pathology laboratories: the combination of low wages, low status and high responsibility makes this a potentially vulnerable area. However, the focus on trolley waits and the length of waiting lists for elective surgery consumes all resources and makes upgrading of staff a low priority, even though an efficient high-quality laboratory service is an essential prerequisite to safe surgery.

Politicians don't like research. The uncritical rhetoric of success and objective evaluation do not always make happy bedfellows. Kenneth Clarke, who preached the doctrine according to *Working for Patients* adamantly opposed a gradual introduction of the internal market with appropriate clinical trials. His view was that once academics get hold of something nothing would happen, a sentiment that is captured in a paper critical of government attitudes to evidence-based policies:

asking for higher standards of evidence of the effectiveness of interventions is sometimes deemed to be a recipe for inaction and doing something is felt to be better than doing nothing.[133]

The present government's promise when in Opposition that there would be change only after consultation and prior experimentation, has proved as empty as the promise that 'permanent revolution' would come to an end. One can understand the disinclination to evaluate when the Opposition, and the press, are so scornful of experiments that do not work. To take an example from outside medicine, the recent experimental introduction of night sittings in law courts to deal with offences 'on the spot' and to clear a backlog has had disappointing results. There proved to be little demand for the facility. This outcome, revealed through responsible evaluation, was used as a basis for point-scoring by the Opposition. No wonder, as Polly Toynbee points out, that 'the one outcome that is never measured in the NHS is the outcome of what politicians do.'[134] There are numerous inspectorates, but no one inspects governments; it sets up inspectorates but does not invite itself to be inspected. The notion that the electorate is that inspectorate is laughable.

There is the period of paralysis when reorganizations are anticipated and when new structures are bedding down. Constant changes therefore make such paralysis seem almost permanent, especially when the next reorganization is usually launched before the last one has started to deliver. The pell-mell of initiatives, of course, also makes the effectiveness of any single initiative impossible to determine.

Costs mount up too because of the need for parallel and shadow organizations during the period of transition.[135] Generous redundancy packages to staff who may then be re-employed in the NHS after a month's pause (often in the same office) will add to the costs. There will be a long learning curve for the incoming managers, and for those who have to deal with new systems and develop effective working relationships with the incomers.[136] Transitional costs often evolve into permanent structural costs. The 1974 reorganization, for example, doubled the number of managers:

A steady stream of paper poured out of the DHSS, refining and developing earlier guidance and creating the impression of a central department determined to control every detail, but hardly able to co-ordinate the work of its own divisions.[137]

One of the most serious, but less visible consequences of reorganizations has been the squandering of clinician time. From the late 1970s onwards, more and more doctors and nurses were caught up full-time or part-time in servicing the new structure or operating the planning system.[138] By the

1980s and 1990s a significant proportion of hospital doctors had some kind of management role. Encouraging clinicians to become involved in management might be seen as precisely what they were asking for, given that they were feeling increasingly marginalized. They were, however, unable to influence big decisions either locally or on a national scale; even less the framework within which those decisions were made. At best, they were involved in helping to implement plans made elsewhere. In particular, they were kept busy writing usually unsuccessful 'business cases' for developing underfunded essential services. Not infrequently, hours and hours were spent formulating bids in pursuit of 'priority money' – usually announced at very short notice – in the hope of catching resources on the wave of a new government initiative. Most of those who chased would, of course, be unlucky; for the bids were always competitive. Those who used the most buzzwords – 'interagency, seamless, inclusive, patient-centred' – and, more importantly, made the cheapest bid, would strike lucky; the rest would be denied the essential upgrade of the Accident and Emergency Department or whatever had been identified as this week's priority.

For many senior doctors, the 1990s was the decade when, finally, the number of hours spent reading textbooks, keeping up to date through medical journals and conferences, was exceeded by the number of hours spent on management briefings and poring over business cases. Most of this activity took the form of trying to read between the lines, forgetting about the urgent clinical case for the resources, and trying to work out the politics behind the bidding process. Many of us had to rush through ward rounds – or even miss them altogether – in order to attend meetings at which spending decisions would be made or planned.[139]

Casuistry has become the supreme clinical art for clinicians and front-line managers anxious to secure resources for her patients. Those who wish to be successful patient advocates must toe the line, or their services and their patients will lose out. One of the key skills has been what one manager described to me as 'the black art' of 'benefits realization' – that of learning to describe in favourable, quasi-quantitative terms the impact of any service development on such things as 'the local health economy' and the 'wider social and material environment'. NHS managers often hire expensive private companies to assist with this spinning and complex numerical juggling.

Since the doubling of the number of administrative and clerical staff in the wake of the 1974 fiasco, the trend has been inexorably upwards. Senior managers in the NHS increased from 500 to over 20,000 in the first five years (1989–94) of the internal market. In the latter half of the 1990s, senior managers increased by a further 48 per cent and managers overall by 24 per cent, while nursing numbers increased by less than 8 per cent and the number of beds fell by 25 per cent.[140] A significant landmark was passed in January 2003: the total of managers, administrators and clerks in the NHS (211,650) exceeded the number of beds (199,670).[141] It is hardly surprising that the cost of hospital administration has increased from £3 billion to £5 billion since 1997, despite the fact that there has been only a 2 per cent increase in treatments.[142]

These recent increases have been driven by the requirement to monitor progress towards the 300 targets and the 600 performance indicators that Trusts have to report on.[143] No wonder the Queen Elizabeth Hospital in Birmingham has 1,300 administrators for its 1,000 beds. This is not, incidentally, an attack on managers as such; as I have already noted, many are as committed, and as energetic in pursuit of excellence, as the best clinicians. At least three out of the ten most impressive people I have met or worked with in my thirty-two years as a doctor have been managers. It is the highly politicized, controlling administrative framework within which they have to work that is at fault.[144] Indeed, it is not the number of managers *per se* that is the problem but the fact that they are reduced to transmitters and implementers of directives from central control.

One time-consuming consequence of continuous reorganization has been the increasingly complex negotiations between the different bodies in health commissioning. The recent birth of Primary Care Trusts (PCTs) means that clinicians have to spend absurd amounts of time courting decision-makers in these organizations.[145] Hospital doctors are disadvantaged because PCTs are both purchasers of care and – in primary care – providers of it; this conflict of interest means that they will earmark resources to meet their own duties and responsibilities before they consider hospital care.

This is the reason, when at last there has been a credible commitment to proper funding, that the resources are not getting through to the 'front line'. The £320 million allocated to cancer care, for example, has not reached hospital wards. In part it has been siphoned off by various bodies needing to pay off old debts accumulated in the years of underspending; in part it has been diverted by PCTs, who have control of 75 per cent of the budget, and who have their own priorities; and in part it has been squandered on paying the people who staff the many new managerial posts created in the wake of successive reforms. The increase in NHS funding of 30 per cent between 1998 and 2003 delivered only a 2 per cent rise in waiting list patients treated, although this was one of the government's key targets.[146] Finding out what has happened to the money itself involves more cost: a brand-new tier of auditors is being appointed to track the billions that are being 'pumped' (the usual phrase) into the NHS. Auditors will, of course, demand more data from hospitals, PCTs, GPs, and this will require more management time – from clinicians as well as from full-time managers.

Charles Webster predicted this consequence of New Labour very quickly:

This unavoidable commitment [to meeting pay rises] together with the cost of meeting the endless stream of directives or financing new schemes such as NHS Direct, goes a long way to explaining why NHS Trusts are left with little discretionary funding to support much-needed expansion or improvement of their front-line services. When, in addition the higher costs of privatized services are taken into account, it is easy to see how higher spending on the NHS could actually result in a diminution of services. New Labour has translated this hitherto unlikely scenario into a real possibility.[147]

All of this explains why, in my last year as a full-time academic clinician, just as in every one of the previous twenty-one years of my consultant life, I face the prospect of more cuts to the service I work in; why I have to fund the specialist nurse who supports my epilepsy clinic from resources I myself have raised from the pharmaceutical industry; why my local evening paper reported (nearly three years after Tony Blair's momentous announcement on television, in January 2000, of a massive hike in NHS funding) that 'Greater Manchester hospitals and GPs are facing a £55.5 million health cash black hole;'[148] and why by 2004 Trusts in England and Wales had a collective debt of £500 million.[149] The newly created Greater Manchester Strategic Health Authority said 'there was simply no more money to bail out struggling hospitals and

Primary Care Trusts (PCTs).' If, as seems likely, they do not balance their books, the PCTs and hospitals will be zero-star-rated and will miss out on extra cash for good performers and could well be taken over by yet more staff parachuted in by the Department of Health (assuming, that is, the star system which has consumed so much time and distorted priority setting remains in place).[150]

Our health service is, with respect to its ever-changing administrative structures and governance, almost 'an organization without memory':[151] the NHS does not know what the NHS knows or has known. Things that are cast aside before they are fully assessed are there to be picked up again and again. The price of non-evaluation is the recycling of the same bad ideas. So while there are very few management structures in the NHS that are more than five years old, many of them are old structures reintroduced in a new guise.

For reasons that will by now be clear, the suspicion that some structural reorganizations have been harmful is difficult to substantiate. Nevertheless a study from Bristol has produced startling evidence of the damage produced by ideologically driven rather than clinically justified structural change.[152] It suggests that competition between hospitals in the period of the internal market was not just wasting an estimated £1.5 billion a year and an immeasurable amount of clinical and managerial time; it actually killed patients. The study compared trends in death rates of patients admitted for heart attacks in the third of the country where there was only one hospital (where the internal market could not work) with the remaining two thirds where there was more than one hospital. Competition was associated with higher death rates; conversely patients had least chance of dying wherever there was least competition. Importantly, death rates diverged only during the period when the market was in force, namely 1991–9.[153]

There are also strong suggestions that the clinical and management culture described by the Kennedy Report on the Bristol tragedy was exacerbated by the internal market. The spirit of 'pressing on regardless' and of 'make do and mend' – of doing things within an inadequate infrastructure – was entirely consistent with the competitive ethos, as was the hope that money would come to the Trust in the wake of increased activity: the money, we were told 'would follow the patient'.[154]

Three areas of reinvention are particularly striking: the number of administrative tiers; the balance between the centre and the periphery with respect to control of priorities and expenditure; and the relationship between the public and private sectors. We saw how the Tories' abolition of the Regional Health Authorities in 1996 brought the administrative structure roughly back to that envisaged in Richard Crossman's Green Paper of approximately thirty years before. Labour introduced new tiers of administration – Primary Care Trusts (PCTs) – shortly followed by another tier – the Strategic Health Authorities which have inherited the aggressive impotence of regional offices.[155] The next step in this expansionist phase may well be the rolling out of health care planning to lower-tier, local bodies – citizens' juries and panels – which will have to be supervised by PCTs, who in turn are supervised by Strategic Health Authorities.

The second type of cycle – the oscillation between centralization and peripheralization of power and control – is difficult to track. Often there is a 180-degree phase shift between the rhetoric and the policy: the politicians who talk most passionately about freeing up local providers (and front-line workers) are those who are most likely to be placing ever tighter constraints on their freedom. The cycle is complex because it has several components that can be varied independently of one another: power and control are often unlinked from accountability and responsibility.[156]

A shocking episode in 2001 at the Bedford NHS Trust, a hospital which had shortly before been awarded three stars, is instructive. Due to a unique and unfortunate combination of circumstances, there was no mortuary space to house the bodies of patients who had died. They were therefore accommodated in the hospital chapel. This pragmatic and respectful solution was construed as an outrage. Photographs of corpses on the floor of the hospital chapel were featured on the front pages of several national newspapers. Within a few hours of the publication of the (truly disrespectful) photographs of the dead, the Secretary of State for Health, angered at this embarrassment, had sacked the Chief Executive of the Trust. It would be difficult to think of a clearer example of centralization of power and the peripheralization of responsibility.[157]

All of which means not only that the out-of-phase cycling of rhetoric and reality as regards central control and local autonomy can be masked, but also that the cycling of untested ideas can occur faster and faster. One of the recipients of the the ministerial benefaction of 'earned autonomy' are three-star Trusts that are to become 'Foundation Hospitals'. Foundation Hospitals are a reintroduction, at a slightly more radical level, of the original Tory vision of NHS Trusts – and the much-despised fund-holding practices. New Labour leaders are now committed (after jeers from the Tories about a two-tier system) to universalizing foundation trust status and extending it beyond providers such as NHS Trusts to purchasers such as Primary Care Trusts (PCTs).

Similar 'opt out' ideas were rubbished by New Labour in opposition a few years back on the (valid) grounds that they squandered resources, they caused a damaging lack of cooperation between parts of the NHS, and they created new inequities. Indeed, the abolition of the internal market was the first major change implemented by New Labour. Seven years later, we have a plan which will 'convert the NHS from a nationalized service into a network of competing providers'.[158] This was more than many members of the Labour party could stomach and there was huge hostility from back-benchers. They were bought off by the warning that a government defeat would be a present to the Opposition; and by a promise that the first wave of Foundation Hospitals would be evaluated by the Commission for Healthcare Inspection and Audit before a second wave could be agreed. Once the Bill had been passed, John Reid then promptly announced a second wave of Foundation Hospitals, which he called 'Wave 1b'.[159]

Recycling of discredited but untested ideas can occur more efficently if the cycling in question occurs within administrations and does not require a change of government. It is even more efficient if it takes place inside the head of one individual: the Secretary of State for Health.[160] To take one example, while in the middle of 2001 Alan Milburn, the then Secretary of State, was declaring that 'thankfully we have one monopoly provider and that is the National Health Service and as long as the Labour government is in power that will remain the case.' A few months later he said he wanted to see the end of the NHS as 'a centrally run, monopoly provider of services', and to encourage alternative providers from the voluntary and private sectors. His U-turning continued at an ever-faster pace until he left office. Fast-track private surgery units set up to clear NHS waiting lists first were, and then were not, to be used for private patients. Private contractors in private finance schemes were, and then were not, going to have managerial responsibility for clinical care. And so on. The extent to which the private sector may provide NHS care has been subject to even more complex recycling. Sometimes the role of the private sector has been strictly controlled and sometimes the magical whizz-kids from the private sector are going to be offered limitless control.

The most interesting ministerial wriggles have been in connection with the Private Finance Initiative (PFI) – paying for capital works in public services through loans raised in the private sector. Charles Webster has set out very clearly the steps by which New Labour has moved from its Opposition position that PFI was a repugnant privatization of the NHS and a betrayal of the Bevanite heritage, to one in which it is central to its modernization policies.[161] It has quickly moved to bring in schemes that the Tories would not have dared entertain for fear of Labour criticism.

The Private Finance Initiative – as a way of modernizing public sector infrastructure without the government having to borrow the capital upfront – took a long time to make an impact in the NHS. The private sector had to be persuaded it wasn't really carrying the financial risks it was supposed to be taking off the public sector. PFI is now in full swing: eight schemes with a total capital value of £1.2 billion had been opened by mid-2002.[162] Some schemes have been initially successful; as in the completion of the final phase of the Swindon hospital after over thirty years of frustration. In others, the story has been rather different. Many schemes require cuts in bed numbers (to make costs attractive), at a time when the government is finally realizing that increased bed numbers are needed. The first eleven completed schemes resulted in a net loss of 3,800 beds.[163] Several initiatives delivered disastrously badly constructed buildings. The virtually uninhabitable and in places frankly dangerous Cumberland Infirmary resurrected the planning mistakes of 1960s tower blocks – with leaking sewage, unusable rooms and no air conditioning – and its occupation precipitated a staffing crisis, as people were reluctant to work there. The savings assumptions built into the PFI business cases are uniformly over-optimistic. For example, the Audit Office found the estimate of annual revenue savings in the Dartford and Gravesend scheme to be about £12 million adrift.

These disasters are, of course, only the beginning; the real problems lie ahead. First, with the emergence of PCTs as the lead commissioners, fledgling organizations are overseeing huge projects. In Enfield, three PFI projects, totalling about £150 million, are being negotiated by the local PCTs who are not sure whether they can afford them; in particular whether the annual leasing charge (key to the PFI deals) may actually suck the area dry of funds.[164] The combination of such huge risks and such inexperience is terrifying. Secondly, there is uncertainty over who will bear the risks if PFI schemes fail and the company building the premises goes bust during or after construction. The transfer of risk to the private sector is largely illusory, as experience elsewhere has shown. Two failed PFI schemes in Australia resulted in the government having to come to the rescue and increase payments to contractors.[165]

PFI schemes are inevitably expensive – though the expense seems to be deferred – as the cost of borrowing in the private sector is greater and private contractors are not charitable organizations. PFI more than doubles the cost of capital as a percentage of the trust's operating income. Deferred immediate costs will be hugely magnified further down the line. These costs will be borne by local health economies whose capacity to bear them is unforeseeable. This is a matter of even greater concern since PFI is being extended from hospitals to primary care and, if the plans for Foundation Hospitals are realized in full, they will be cut adrift from central support in the near future. The problems will be exacerbated by the new method of payment-by-productivity using standard national tariffs. Currently expensive hospitals (usually teaching hospitals dealing with more complex cases in areas of social deprivation) will be financially penalized and will quickly go into the red.[166] The total restructuring of billing methods will, of course, bring its own costs.

Hostility to anyone casting doubt on the wisdom of PFI is merciless. The distinguished academic Allyson Pollock has, in particular, been singled out for execration. The Parliamentary Select Committee on Health, angry at her rational examination of a major public expenditure initiative, rubbished her work and recommended that funding for her research and her department should be withdrawn – a very grave interference with academic freedom and free speech.[167] This is a new departure in the micro-management of the NHS; it is, however, a natural development for a government that, under the banner of giving people local autonomy, has assumed command and control to a degree no previous administration would have even dreamed of.

It is universally acknowledged that our Health Services are the best in the world.

Lord Horder's preface to the *Political and Economic Planning Report of the British Health Services*, 1937[168]

It will be evident that I cannot answer my son's question as to whether *any* of the 'reforms' of the NHS during my time as a doctor have been of net benefit. The only conclusion that can be drawn with confidence is that they have consumed unimaginable quantities of clinical and non-clinical time and money and for that reason alone we may reasonably suspect that they will have killed patients. That patient-care in the NHS has improved out of all recognition since I qualified cannot be taken as evidence of the effectiveness of policy-makers. Most improvements are due to painstakingly evaluated clinician-led advances in medical technologies and the delivery of services supported by dynamic local managers; others are a result of the increased wealth of the nation incompletely reflected in increased resources for the NHS; but none could be safely attributed to structural change. Reorganizations that have delivered better care and improved outcomes have been driven by clinical imperatives rather than been politically inspired. Some of the latter may have brought about improvements, but we simply don't know. One thing is certain: clinician-led advances are now more difficult to implement in a time of ever-changing health policy. It is easier to repair, refit and upgrade the ship in dry dock rather than in the Roaring Forties. Unfortunately successive governments have kept the good ship NHS permanently in the Roaring Forties and the roar gets louder every year.

Clinicians and their patients should rebel and follow Polly Toynbee's advice:

If the Opposition gets up and starts producing amazing new plans, then the NHS – nothing to do with government, simply the professionals – could say, 'You come and bounce it off us first, and we will tell you whether it is a load of rubbish or not'. If it is a load of rubbish, the chances are that Liam Fox, or whoever the next Opposition person is, will all roll over with their tail between their legs. Politicians are quite easy to frighten, because respect is always really with the health professionals more than it is with the politicians. I think it is extraordinary how often you have all rolled over. You should be much more forceful.[169]

At any rate, we should refuse to cooperate with reforms or redisorganizations that have no evaluation built into them. As Iain Chalmers has expressed it:

Evidence of collective uncertainty about the effects of their policies and practices should prompt the humility that is a precondition for rigorous evaluation.[170]

Perhaps the running of the NHS could be devolved from central control to regions – large enough to take a strategic overview that can encompass secondary and tertiary as well as primary care and small enough to be sensitive to local needs – as has happened in Sweden a long time ago and more recently has been implemented in Spain.[171] If this way were to be chosen as the way forward, *the existing structures should be used*. No one could stand another reorganization. Let us see how an adequately funded NHS develops in the absence of major structural change, allowing only small-scale, evaluable changes driven by advances in clinical science. We might be pleasantly surprised.

Anyone planning any more 'far-reaching' changes should reflect on the final paragraph of Brian Watkin's history where he looks back – just before the Thatcher onslaught – on the disaster of the first large-scale NHS reorganization:

Above all the lesson stands out that there is virtue in making haste slowly, in proceeding by trial and error, in making small mistakes in order that learning can take place, rather than one large error that must be defended at all costs lest those responsible lose credit. The trend towards over-centralization and ever-increasing bureaucratic complexity must be reversed, and this will only be achieved if trust is placed in people – people well chosen, well trained, well motivated – rather than in structures and systems.[172]

A quarter of a century on, health care professionals in the NHS can only say 'Amen!'

Zero tolerance

Health care professionals and patients must be more grown up about errors and mistakes. We need a system that recognizes that accountability is not the same as blame. Blame is a serendipitous weapon used to pillory someone who happens to be caught in its sights.[173]

Ian Kennedy

We will pursue every factor, every element, every second of the timeline of the final hours of Maurice's life. We will pursue that relentlessly. That will be our quest from now on.[174]

Robin and Barry Gibb

Complain complain, complain... otherwise nothing will change.[175]

J. Knowsley

Medicine has become ever safer and more effective. Even cardiac surgery, once the last-ditch answer to end-stage illness, is often routine, with excellent outcomes in terms both of survival and post-operative quality of life. This is despite the trend to treat ever more complicated cases and patients receiving cardiac surgery who are getting younger at one end of the scale and increasingly older at the other. During the last eight years, the number of highly complex combined valve and coronary bypass operations performed in the United Kingdom has quadrupled while operative mortality has halved; the proportion of patients undergoing heart surgery who are over seventy-five has risen from 2.3 to 8 per cent. Notwithstanding the opinions expressed by various 'authorities',[176] outcomes in the underfunded NHS are comparable to the best in the world. Death rates in the UK after coronary artery bypass surgery, the commonest heart operation, averaged 2.1 per cent between 1999 and 2001, compared with 2.6 per cent for 2001 in the USA. (Germany, Belgium and the Netherlands had the same mortality as the UK.)

This remarkable story of improvement preceded the Kennedy Report on paediatric cardiac surgery at Bristol, with its nearly 200 recommendations. Nor did it require published league tables naming and shaming hospitals, units and individual surgeons. Even more remarkably, the improvements occurred while claims were abounding that things were bad and getting worse and that doctors, in particular surgeons, should be called to book. In short, blame becomes prevalent as surgeons become less and less blameworthy. Tolerance of error by those who take responsibility for other people's lives is approaching zero.

Of course, complaints are sometimes justified and some doctors deserve public pillory, removal from the GMC register and even custodial sentences. What is not justified is the standing assumption that everything that goes wrong is someone's fault. Where people die under medical care it is usually the underlying illness not the medical care that has killed them. Unfortunately, when medical care is usually of a standard that previous generations would have regarded as miraculous, people find it more and more difficult to accept the notion of a fatal disease.

A little while back, I had a ninety-seven-year-old lady under my care. She had had advanced cardiac failure for several years; despite this she had done quite well until her final illness, when she went into a decline that all our efforts were unable to arrest. Throughout her hospital stay her family quizzed me almost daily as to why she was getting worse. No explanation would satisfy them because, they argued, she had been reasonably well until just before she came into hospital. They were absolutely sure that her deterioration and eventual death were due to bad nursing and incompetent medical care. That life is a disease with a dreadful prognosis, with a 100 per cent mortality rate, was something they were simply not prepared to accept. I was informed, in one of many meetings with family members, that I was simply 'writing her off' because she was old, an accusation that, as a geriatrician who has championed access to full medical care for every one irrespective of age, I bitterly resented, though of course my customer care skills ensured that I saved any expression of this until I returned to my office. Such an attitude of scornful disbelief reflects a wider misunderstanding, beautifully captured by Theodore Dalrymple:

Man is born immortal but everywhere he dies... The belief is now general that Man has achieved such mastery over Nature that, if life turns out to be unfair, human malevolence must be to blame. Death these days is definitely somebody's fault.[177]

From time to time, avoidable errors will occur. It would be astonishing if they did not. The NHS treats 1 million people a day, the annual case load includes 8 million hospital admissions, 14 million visits to the Accident and Emergency department and 45 million out-patient appointments.[178] Medical care is complex and each admission or visit will involve contact with dozens of people: there are over 400 million interactions with health professionals each year.[179] There are innumerable steps in something as simple as taking, and getting the result of, a single blood test. Moreover, given that medicine is a probabilistic art, many decisions will rely upon necessarily fallible judgement.

The number of points at which mistakes could be made, or judgements challenged in retrospect, in a given year in the NHS therefore runs into billions. Not even the most robust systems can pre-empt all of these potential mistakes. The most conscientious practitioners working under ideal conditions will make some mistakes, and, medicine being a serious business, some of these will be serious. A librarian's error may lead to a book being located in the wrong place; a doctor's error may result in death. In many cases, especially with hindsight, medical mistakes will appear to have been avoidable. In some cases, a small minority, they will be culpable; and in an even smaller minority they will result from criminal negligence.

Putting such mistakes into perspective means taking denominators into account: looking at the frequency of actual mistakes as a proportion of the number of transactions that are liable to error. This will correct for the recall bias in which the minority of things that go wrong will be remembered and the overwhelming majority of things that go right forgotten. For the truly astonishing fact is not that clinical errors occur, and that sometimes they are catastrophic, but that they are so rare relative to the number of opportunities for them to occur. While drug administration errors do occur, they are infrequent compared with the total number of drugs that are administered.

A few years ago there was saturation media coverage of the mistaken removal of a healthy instead of a diseased kidney from a patient who subsequently died. The surgeon and the hospital were pilloried and the surgeon was placed on a manslaughter charge on which he was eventually acquitted. Even so, his ordeal was not at an end. Four years after his error, the consultant (and the registrar with whom he was operating) was suspended by the General Medical Council for twelve months, for 'serious professional misconduct'. The GMC commented that in view of the surgeon's previous unblemished record over a long professional career, striking off would be 'disproportionate'.[180]

It subsequently transpired that this was not the first time such an event had taken place in the United Kingdom. An inquiry revealed that three incorrect kidneys had been removed over a ten-year period. The shock this caused in the press would have been greatly mitigated had it been pointed out that during that time a total of 75,000 kidneys had been removed, 74,997 of them correct. This is still three too many and a catastrophe for the patients, their relatives and, it should be added, for the surgeon. But an error rate of 1 : 25,000 was rather less than the massive press coverage of it suggested.[181]

Extensive reporting of medical errors – or errors even glancingly related to medicine[182] – is justified, it is said, because they are in the public interest. It warns patients what is going on in their NHS and puts pressure on clinicians to repent of their mistakes and do better in future. This may be why, as a recent study has found, the rate of medical manslaughter prosecutions has increased dramatically over the last decade. During the 1970s and 1980s only four doctors were charged with manslaughter; while in the 1990s, twenty-eight have been tried.[183] And the pace is quickening. In 2003 alone, five doctors faced 'gross negligence manslaughter charges', including a twenty-three-year-old junior doctor, six weeks into his job, who inserted a feeding tube into the patient's lungs.[184]

Justification for what seems to be a retributive attitude towards error is that society needs to be protected against incompetent practitioners. Similar justification is invoked by many complainants who clog up the expanding Customer Services Departments. The complaint is usually hedged about with statements like 'I know whatever happens can't turn back the clock but I just want to make sure it doesn't happen to anyone else/anyone else's mother.' It is, that is to say, made in a communitarian spirit – but not one that allows for suggestions as to the ways in which the complainant might positively support the hospital.

Complaints will almost certainly increase with the establishment of the Commission for Patient and Public Involvement with its 600 Forums, 1,600 staff and nearly 6,000 members, and dealing with them will also become more complex. Letters of complaint, often the result of collaborative efforts, now include absolutely every possible source of disaffection. One complaint I am currently dealing with invites me to comment on the fact that 'the nurse rolled up her eyes' in response to a request that I did not witness over a year before. The (entirely proper) release of case notes to complainants will provoke further inquiries and inquiries about the response to inquiries. Another case with which I have been only tangentially involved (I simply attended one meeting with the complainants to support the locum consultant who had been looking after the patient) has continued for nearly three years and the end is not yet in sight. The primary charge of unnecessary death of the patient was shown to be unfounded: the medical care was entirely appropriate. But one of the spin-off complaints required a three-page letter of explanation from a consultant haematologist. The complainants had noticed that a report on a blood specimen was dated forty-eight hours after the death. They assumed from this that the blood had been taken after the patient had died and, in the wake of the Alder Hey furore, had concluded that the staff were experimenting on the dead. The actual explanation was that, because the blood test in question was non-urgent, it was dealt with along with others in a weekly batch. The blood was taken while the patient was alive but was not analysed until his death.

I am not complacent about the complaints: many will be justified, some will be serious and many will be both justified and serious. Indeed, for a while I headed up our directorate's Critical Incident Group and we looked not only at complaints and things that had gone wrong but also at things which *might* have gone wrong. (These are referred to in the airline industry as 'near misses'.) Medicine needs to learn from its mistakes and, indeed, like the airline industry, support a culture committed to identifying potential threats to patient safety and good practice. The much-vaunted shift of emphasis in current discussion of medical errors from the culpability of individuals to the dysfunctioning of systems of which clinicians are only a part is particularly welcome. Most people who make mistakes, even terrible ones, are rarely scoundrels, careless of the lives of their patients, idle or ignorant.

This was brought home to me when I was a very junior doctor. A fellow houseman killed a twenty-one-year-old patient by giving intravenous potassium instead of sodium. The phials looked identical, were kept in adjacent boxes and the writing on them was minute and difficult to see at the poorly illuminated bedside of a patient. My friend blamed himself – 'I was in too much of a hurry' he said to me – but it was perfectly obvious that this was an accident waiting to happen. The incident had lavish coverage in the *Evening Standard* with the grieving mother asking why her lovely daughter with her whole life ahead of her had died. The answer was not that she had been deliberately harmed by my friend (whose name was duly printed in a million copies of the *Evening Standard* in the successive issues that covered the coroner's inquest) but that the system had a built-in propensity to disaster. My friend was not reprehensible, and his error did not reflect his overall competence or character.[185]

The extent to which press coverage of the errors of 'named and shamed' doctors really *is* in the public interest may be judged from the fact that, thirty years after my friend's error with potassium, a study of adverse incidents in hospital care showed this is still a major hazard.[186] Vilifying individual doctors may actually inhibit illuminating exploration of the factors predisposing to errors and encourage concealment.[187] By contrast, the use of confidential inquiries that produce a mature analysis of causes of adverse outcomes, and disseminate anonymous information about those adverse outcomes and the lessons to be learned from them, has been signally successful. For example, the Confidential Inquiry into Maternal Mortality, published annually for nearly fifty years, has contributed hugely to the dramatic decline in deaths associated with childbirth. The public execration of the obstetrician in every case of a woman dying in childbirth would have encouraged dishonesty or at least concealment, thereby ensuring that more children would be orphaned at birth than are at present.

There have been similar beneficial effects from the National Confidential Enquiry into Perioperative Deaths, which was set up over twenty years ago by surgeons and anaesthetists to look at the factors determining mortality after operation. Created and led by clinicians, it has had a huge impact, changing practice and improving outcomes.[188] For the most part it has depended upon clinicians filling in forms in their own free time. Its value was recognized by government, who in 1988 started to provide funds. In 2004, it has been expanded to encompass non-surgical hospital patients and primary care. The benefits delivered by this blame-free, non-adversarial approach have been immeasurable.

Punitive attitudes to medical errors or other unsatisfactory aspects of care assume that complaints, threats and menaces are the only way to ensure improvement. One day this may be the case. At present, doctors become doctors mainly because they want to make sick people better. Far from being psychopathically relaxed about their errors, doctors are far too prone to self-blame, a fact that is reflected in the high suicide rates.[189] Acknowledging this would remove much of the spice from medical disaster stories. Discovering that blame is *un*founded will get little or no coverage. One of the most vilified doctors over the last decade, Mr Janardan Dhasmana, the second surgeon in the Bristol heart hospital scandal, was found guilty of serious professional misconduct by the General Medical Council. He was forbidden to operate on either adults or children for three years. The Kennedy Inquiry, however, found Dhasmana's surgical skills to be commendable except in one area and added that he was 'self-critical and aware of his own shortcomings' – a picture that hardly justified Frank Dobson, the then Secretary of State for Health, opining on television that he 'should have been struck off'.[190]

The shift of blame from individuals to the system or the context in which mistakes occur is therefore urgent and overdue. In part this has been prompted by the current Chief Medical Officer (CMO), Liam Donaldson, whose paper *An Organization with Memory*,[191] has been widely applauded by doctors. Even so, the CMO's own attitude towards error is not entirely reformed: the old habits of blame die hard even among the leaders of a 'no-blame' culture. I shall examine his response to the public outcry over the retention of organs at Alder Hey hospital later in the book (see page 188). It is enough to note for the present that he referred sixteen individuals to the General Medical Council. The lives of those who were referred were blighted; many of them were suspended by their Trust 'as a precautionary measure'. This action, which 'combined poor judgement and political expediency',[192] directed a considerable amount of distressing and demeaning publicity at the accused. In the end, the GMC concluded that there was no evidence to take any further proceedings against *any* of the consultants.

It was the CMO's department, furthermore, who subjected the local consultants and managers to a very public flagellation when it appeared (incorrectly) that a serious mistake had been made. It was discovered that twenty-four patients in the North of England had been treated with surgical instruments that had previously been used to treat a patient who, at post-mortem, was unexpectedly found to have Creutzfeld-Jakob disease.[193] The Department of Health, who described the event as 'an appalling incident', excoriated the Trust for not following their own 'crystal clear guidance'. In fact the hospital had followed the guidance in every single respect. As the clinical director said, 'We went by the book and the book was written by the Department of Health.' The Department covered its retreat with 'an inquiry' ordered by the CMO.[194]

It is easy to see why the Chief Medical Officer is so ambivalent about his own (in the present climate quite brave) no-blame approach and the attempt to move towards the much-needed 'new mechanisms of accountability... which go beyond the culture of blame and victimization of professional groups'.[195] As an extremely surefooted medical politician, he cannot be unaware of the political necessity of criticizing the medical profession. 'Who would have thought' asks Allyson Pollock

that a mass murderer such as Shipman or system failures revealed by the Bristol Inquiry could have given politicians such power to regroup the profession along market-oriented lines. In this growing culture of blame, victimization and punishment the aim is to stamp out protest and all scrutiny of the new modernized NHS.[196]

Denial of progress

The almost miraculous work of today's paediatric cardiac surgeons in deftly correcting errors in hearts the size of acorns in tiny babies – while maintaining their life before, during and after these operations using technological support of an unimaginable complexity – is less appreciated than that of the butchers of the past, who hacked crudely at their unanaesthetized patients with commonly disastrous results. The occasional tragic death nowadays of a patient from a routine operation is seen as a greater scandal than the routine death of patients from pretty well all but the simplest operation in the past. Success redefines what counts as failure: today's miracle cure is tomorrow's routine treatment. It is easy to forget the extraordinary progress that has been made.

Even the brightest journalists are prone to such forgetfulness. In 1998 Will Hutton published an article in the *Observer*[197] arguing that Bevan's dream was 'Degraded and Debased by what was happening in the NHS' which he compared to the Kremlin. That Sunday morning I had just returned from a ward round with the specialist registar and senior house officer, seeing all the new emergency admissions in our recently opened £14 million facility for old people, built as part of the expanding teaching hospital. Most of the patients I had seen (within eighteen hours of admission, as we consultants had all voluntarily agreed to some while back) were in their eighties and nineties. Before Bevan it was very difficult for a very elderly person to get into a teaching hospital. My ninety-year-old mother – for whom the NHS has provided a total hip replacement, a coronary angioplasty and one or two other operations, since her late seventies, and who is reasonably healthy on a cocktail of medication – reminded me how her mother, who died of renal failure at sixty, had been denied a hospital bed until the last few hours of her life because she was too old and not able to pay to go privately.

The care of older people is a sensitive, if for many an unglamorous indicator of the progress that has been made in the first half century of the NHS, since they are usually pushed to the back of the queue. When at the outbreak of the Second World War the Emergency Medical Service[198] was established, elderly and long-stay patients were kicked out of major hospitals. Their plight (which had already been pretty terrible) became even worse. They were, according to Charles Webster, 'exposed to humiliating conditions arguably little better than the concentration camps'.[199]

The founding of the NHS prompted a fundamental review of the services for older people. The speciality of geriatric medicine was established. As a result of the labours of a series of energetic and charismatic clinicians, most notably Dr Margerie Warren, supported by sympathetic hospital administrators, their services were progressively improved.[200] What is more, older people are no longer denied acute medical care, high-tech care, or rehabilitation. These advances took time. I can still remember visiting my great-aunt in a long-stay psycho-geriatric ward in the late 1960s. The patients were confined to endless, close-packed rows of beds. The stench of urine, and spectacle of abject, passive misery and pointlessness was overwhelming. The psycho-geriatric wards of today are totally different: very few patients are long-stay, the rooms are pleasant, the emphasis is on diversionary activity and on acknowledging the past and personality of the patient – with mementos around the bed and no smell of urine. The final stages of dementia are still terrible but, with the exception of pockets of bad practice, institutional exacerbation of this naturally occurring tragedy is rare.

By the 1980s, British geriatric care, fostered in the NHS and driven by impassioned advocates, was a model that was copied throughout the world. After that, the developed world caught up and overtook our services in some respects: there is only so much you can do in a Victorian building with limited resources. Progress, however, was sustained in other respects; for example, greater access to ever-more sophisticated treatments.[201] But it would be foolish to suggest that everything is perfect, and in some areas we have gone backwards. The 'massive retreat' of skilled and senior nurses from the bedside has resulted in a decline in nursing standards in some places.[202] And ageism is still alive and well in parts of the NHS – including government White Papers and even National Service Frameworks.[203] But to suggest that 'Bevan's dream is dead' is absurd.

There are many other markers of progress. In the first fifty years of the NHS, infant mortality fell by more than 80 per cent, the proportion of people dying before the age of sixty-five fell from 40 per cent to 7 per cent, and life expectancy rose by a decade. This trend has continued; life expectancy rose by a further year in the first half of the 1990s.[204] In the decade before the NHS was created, an Englishwoman going into labour had a one in 250 chance of dying; now it is one in 10,000.[205]

While most improvements in health and life expectancy between 1900 and 1950 were due to public health measures, social policies, and the alleviation of poverty and privation, in the last half century, the proportion of life expectancy gain due to specific medical care is about 50 per cent.[206] Once a reasonable social welfare and public health infrastructure is in place, and the extremes of poverty have been eradicated, most of the gains are due to medical, or medically guided, care. The period of disability and chronic ill-health before death has shrunk dramatically and is continuing to shrink. More people are living to old age and they spend more of their old age in good health.[207] Beyond life-saving treatments, the NHS has made vast numbers of drugs and operations available to people with a huge beneficial impact: the quality of life of people with cardiac failure, with angina, with Parkinson's disease, with epilepsy, with peptic ulcers, with arthritis of the hips, with renal failure, and many other diseases has been improved enormously. James LeFanu, a medical journalist as well as a doctor and a stern critic of many of his fellow professionals, has stated that 'the achievements of medicine in the fifty years since the War rank as one of the most sustained epochs of human endeavour since the Renaissance.'[208] While it would be absurd to attribute these advances solely to the existence of the NHS, many of those who have worked in the service have made major contributions to the lengthy process of turning biomedical discoveries into better treatments. The NHS, moreover, has made those treatments more widely available than even Bevan could have dreamed of.

There is in some quarters an antipathy to the very notion of progress in human affairs: it seems 'triumphalist'. Even as balanced a medical historian as Roy Porter hesitated to acknowledge without qualification that scientific medicine has delivered results that no other medical tradition can match. There is a fear of Whiggish optimism and of monoculturalism, of a failure to be sufficiently a (spatial and temporal) relativist:

Avoiding condescension equally does not mean one must avoid 'winners' history… but there is good reason for bringing winners to the foreground – not because they are 'best' or 'right' but because they are powerful. One can study winners without siding with them.[209]

There is the influence of postmodern thinkers such as Michel Foucault for whom progress (in particular medical progress) was a cruel bourgeois lie.[210] Those who none the less insist that progress has been made and, what's more, suggest that continued progress will come from the same direction – the humane application of reason and science to human problems – are decried as complacent, blind, shallow; or worse they are irresponsible, in the pay of the pharmaceutical industry, or uncritically upholding of the established order. The immemorial custom of shooting the messenger now has a new spin: it is the bearer of good news who needs to fear for his life.[211]

The most important, and most public, reason for denying progress is political point-scoring, which we have already alluded to. Even in power, politicians may continue their attack on the service to justify the changes they are imposing, arguing that the damage done by the previous administration will take a long time to reverse and that 'root and branch reform' is necessary. Charles Webster described this process in the 1980s:

As the decade wore on, the Thatcher camp became increasingly adept at exploiting the public relations arts, mobilizing the media to spread alarm and build up disenchantment concerning the current state of the health service, and then to instil greater public confidence in the government's chosen market solutions.[212]

Politicians will, of course, emphasize progress if they feel able to attribute it to their own interventions. In 2001, the then Secretary of State chided those who would deny Labour's achievements in health: 'It is easy to forget how far we have come in just four years.'[213] To admit that there was progress before the root and branch reforms that are causing so much disruption would be unhelpful.[214]

An interesting facet of the denial of progress is the denial that there have in the past been any leaders of true worth in the NHS. There were leaders of a sort, but apparently they were of the wrong sort: doctors innocent of the present government's mode of discourse. Their clinically inspired (truly patient-centred) developments were, politically, not very helpful. And so the NHS Plan is committed to delivering 'a step change in the calibre of NHS leadership'. The Department of Health is now busy sending hospital chief executives and senior clinicians to Leadership Centres or on LEO ('Leading Empowered Organizations') courses. Here they can learn how successful institutions such as the BBC[215] are run and can come back empowered to empower others.[216]

The denial of progress and trashing of the past depend on the fact that few of us retain a sense of proportion when it comes to things that matter so much to us. The recent comparison in the *Manchester Evening News* between an over-crowded and a rather over-booked out-patient clinic at an oncology unit with 'Belsen on a bad day' shows how easily perspective is lost. Mrs Rooney's famous cry, in Beckett's *Watt*, when the porter refuses to help her with her luggage – 'Christ, what a planet!' – stands, for all of those moments when we talk about traffic wardens as fascists and respond to a street fight as the end of civilization.

Of all the examples of lack of proportion, this is my favourite. A few years ago, two episodes occurred in hospitals in Cornwall. In the first, a nurse was found to be assisting at an appendicectomy. The patient came to no harm. In the second, a needle had accidentally been left in a baby. A fortnight later the parents discovered the needle and it was removed. The baby came to no harm. There was saturation media coverage of both events. Questions were asked as to 'what was happening in health care and to the NHS in Cornwall'. Two adverse events, out of several tens of millions of events, suggested that nothing was happening either to the NHS or to health care in Cornwall. It is boring to say this. It is much more exciting to suggest that problems at the edge mean rottenness at the core.

Another example, more worrying in view of its source, concerns Lord Desai, Principal Health Spokesman in the Lords when Labour were in opposition. On learning from his GP that he would have to wait ten months for a hearing test he concluded that the NHS compared unfavourably with health care in India since his relatives were better treated there.[217] He probably recognized that it was unlikely that the average poor person in India – 90 per cent of the population – would be treated as well as his relatives. At any rate, he should have done. For the record, this is a recent report from a medical student on an elective in Southern India:

India displays its pathology for all to see. The sight of children's limbs hanging useless from polio, amputees begging from the slurry of the gutter, and eyes rendered sightless by cataracts are commonplace. And that is without the storm clouds of HIV and AIDS, threatening to rain misery on a woefully unprepared people... Infant mortality at one year in rural areas is approaching 50 per cent, with similarly alarming maternal mortality statistics.[218]

Perhaps Lord Desai was aware of all this; but he still drew some pretty far-reaching conclusions: 'We have constructed for ourselves the most appalling health system. The time has come to totally rethink it and look at wild ideas.'

There is another, deep-seated, reason for denying progress. It is connected with the myths about the coldness of technology and the intrinsic inhumanity of scientific medicine. This is a profound misconception. Despite the depersonalization of illness that underpins effective treatment, medical care in, say, a contemporary Western hospital, when compared with what went before it, is a miracle of humanity. It is a triple victory of civilization – over the inhumanity of the human body; over the inhumanity of man to man; and over the natural regression towards uncaringness and indifference that might reasonably be expected to afflict individuals during a lifetime of caring for the sick.

People tend to forget how utterly horrible untreated diseases are. The death of Philip II of Spain – then the most powerful and potentially cosseted man in Europe – should be mandatory reading for anyone who questions whether modern health care, even in diseases still incurable, is of net worth.

On 22 July, Philip was carried to his bed for the last time. Around midnight, he developed a high fever that signalled the beginning of a long, agonizing demise…

For the next fifty-three days Philip was forced to lie on his back, unable to move and unable to be moved or touched without pain. Even the weight of the sheets caused him distress. The gout and arthritis that had plagued him for the past few years continued to torment him and may even have intensified. The dreaded *tercianas* fever caused him to alternate between hot flashes and chills. The sores on his feet and hands also worsened and had to be lanced. He developed a festering abscess above his right knee that also had to be lanced without the aid of any anaesthetic on 6 August. This open wound would not drain properly and had to be squeezed, yielding two basins full of pus each day. Philip's chronic dropsy caused his abdomen and joints to swell with fluid. Bed sores erupted all along his backside as the ordeal progressed. Although at times he lapsed into a fitful sleep or seemed barely conscious, he was troubled by insomnia and never fully escaped from the horror of his condition.

According to all eyewitnesses, the worst torment of all was the diarrhoea, which developed halfway through his final illness. Because the pain caused by being touched or moved was too great for Philip to bear, it seemed best not to clean the ordure that he produced, and not even to change his linens, so many times the bed remained fouled, creating an awful stench. Eventually, a hole was cut into the mattress to help relieve this problem, but it was only a partial remedy. Philip continued to waste away, wallowing in his own filth, tormented by the smell and the degradation of it all. According to one account, he was also plagued by lice.[219]

I have discussed the absurd notion that science-based medicine is somehow cold and brutal because it is not natural, at some length elsewhere.[220] Those who truly believe in the intrinsic inhumanity of science-based medicine forget the inhumanity of nature, mainly because they have had little direct acquaintance with it. Most of the residual barbarities and inhumanities in scientific medicine ultimately owe their origins to the human body itself. When the body goes wrong it informs us of trouble in rather unhuman ways. Death, an outcome that suggests that we are closer to insects than angels, is its most extreme statement. There is nothing specifically human about much of what goes on in the human body: dogs, too, make faeces; goldfish, like us, exchange gases with their environment; flatworms share our proneness to ageing.[221] The humbling truth broadcast by illness is that our bodies are products of evolutionary processes that didn't particularly have us in mind; certainly not our ways of life and preoccupations, which do not belong to the natural order of things. George Orwell expressed this well:

People talk about the horrors of war, but what weapon has a man invented that even approaches in cruelty some of the commoner diseases? 'Natural' death, almost by definition means something slow, smelly and painful.[222]

Scientific medicine, for all its faults, is the bravest and most honest attempt to mediate between the needs of suffering humans and the 'unhuman' body.

If we are to put present discontents with medicine in proportion, we should recognize how (relatively speaking, of course) comfortable both successful and unsuccessful treatments have become, compared not only with disease but with the treatments of the past. It is not difficult to imagine what medical care must have been like in the pre-scientific era. Even if we did not have direct evidence, from literature and painting, we may be pretty sure that with an overwhelming burden of incurable disease, unalleviable symptoms and brutal or poisonous treatments, there would be little emphasis on customer services. Science separates the barbarities of the past from the thoughtful medical practice of the present.

Consider surgery. Up to a century or so ago it was usually unspeakably painful, and often fatal. A good example would be Fanny Burney's mastectomy for breast cancer. The operation was performed without anaesthetic and her account of her agony and terror, and of the knife 'rackling' against her breastbone as the surgeon scraped away the cancerous tissue, is unbearable.[223] Every aspect of the art has been transformed, made not only safer but also less terrifying a prospect, as a result of surgeons' ceaselessly modifying their techniques in the light of scientific understanding and using ever more sophisticated science-based technology.

Take, as another example, abdominal surgery. Diagnosis – and the decision whether or not to operate – requires invasive operations such as laparotomy less often than in the relatively recent past: diagnosis can be made using new painless, non-invasive imaging techniques such as computerized tomographic scanning or endoscopy. If these tests reveal a lesion requiring an operation, this may often be dealt with using minimally invasive methods employing the latest technology for visualization, incision and suturing. Post-operative care – pain control, fluid replacement, nutritional support, the prevention of infection, and nursing – has also benefited enormously from basic biological science. The intravenous drip (an icon for some of modern, depersonalizing medicine) exposes the common error of equating 'hi-tech' with 'nasty tech': infusing pain relief, thirst relief and nutrition, it is infinitely less unpleasant than (the more natural) pain, dehydration and malnutrition it addresses.

Many of these advances are comparatively recent. Returning to breast cancer, it is noteworthy that every single aspect of patient care – diagnosis, communication of diagnosis, surgery (and anaesthesia and post-operative care), the ward environment, and counselling, even the justly dreaded chemotherapy – has been subject to continuous incremental improvement over the last fifty years, in particular over the last twenty years. Which is not to say that there isn't room for much further improvement – both with respect to outcomes and the experience of treatment – but the overall trend towards improvement in all directions is indisputable.

The impotence and crudity of pre-scientific medicine affected those who looked after patients. Nurses were often brutal as well as incompetent; midwives and doctors ditto. Concern for the patient's *experience* of care could come to the fore only when good outcomes were possible. Even when better treatments started to become available, nurses and doctors were not infrequently psychological terrorists, extending the field of their authority beyond that justified by their specific competence, expertise and domain of responsibility. Even in the best-run Nightingale ward, 'the patient as partner' and 'the subjectivity of the patient' did not figure high in the list of health care workers' priorities.

A picture by Pieter Breughel the elder says it all.[224] It is titled *Cutting out the Stone of Madness, or an Operation on the Head*. The patient, tied to a chair, is screaming in unimaginable pain, as villainous-looking doctors attempt to open his head. More telling even than this useless and agonizing procedure are the details in the background: other patients being subjected to the same procedure and one poor creature, naked and squatting on the floor, ignored by everyone. The 'surgery' is presented as a side-show, with grinning and curious onlookers relishing the spectacle of agony and terror and pressing in through the open door. There is neither dignity nor privacy; neither privacy nor compassion. The sterile hush of the clinic or the impersonal care of even the most badly run modern ward would be a thousand times more caring, and more effective, than this.

One does not have to rely on remote historical examples to get some idea of the inhumanity of pre-scientific medicine. Those places in today's world where scientific medicine has made few inroads and traditional practices predominate are windows on to the pre-scientific past. The publicness of treatments in cultures reliant on folk medicines, the lack of anything corresponding to consultation with the patient, compounds the injury of the useless treatments offered. The cognitive gap is often filled with superstitions that give human cruelty free rein. In Chapter 2, I mentioned pre-microbiological notions of impurity and cleanliness in the East that not only encouraged woefully inadequate public health and hygiene but also reinforced iniquitous caste systems which dehumanized large sections of the population. The Untouchables received no care at all, never mind humane and respectful care.

I was recently reminded of the association between inhumanity and pre-scientific medicine when I heard a talk given by a representative of the World Health Organization on attitudes to epilepsy. The speaker explained why those who suffer from epilepsy in India are called 'the burned'. People with uncontrolled seizures (common because few have access to modern drugs) are prone to fall into household fires. Folk wisdom holds that it is dangerous to touch someone who is having a fit, as the condition (or the curse) may be transmitted. Others are therefore reluctant to rescue them from the flames. Many die; hence 'the burned'. In Nigeria, the same anxiety prevents others from rescuing people with seizures who fall into rivers and lakes. Many die; hence the soubriquet 'the drowned'.[225]

A dispassionate scientific approach brings with it a dispassionate kindness. This has been clearly demonstrated by the social history of the AIDS epidemic. The contrast between the attitude of the press, the general public and certain politicians to those who contracted the disease early on in the epidemic – an opprobrium that treated them as objects of moral terror – and the collective response of the medical community, who got on with trying to understand the disease and to help sufferers to the best of their ability – could not have been sharper.

Here, as elsewhere, the medical profession (with certain iniquitous exceptions) took the lead in adopting humane attitudes to those with serious illness.[226]

The essential humanity of scientific medicine (and indeed of science) is not at all popular among many humanist intellectuals, for whom pessmism and a loathing of modernity is an article of faith. When I suggested that there was something intrinsically human about technological medicine in a talk I gave at a Symposium on The Two Cultures in Lisbon, I had an unusual experience that I still remember vividly a decade later. The Chairman, a sociologist, was so angry that instead of treating me, an invited speaker, to the usual courtesies, he launched into a tirade against my naivety, citing the usual suspects, Adorno and Horkheimer, Foucault et al. Unfortunately, he was shouting so loudly that I couldn't hear the simultaneous translation in my headphones and could only guess at what he was saying. His anger and disgust, however, was not in doubt; nor was that of my audience who cheered him when he had finished his tirade. The reason he was so angry was, I suspect, connected with something that José Merquior once said: that humanist intellectuals need to believe that modernity, and its most characteristic manifestation, science-based rationalism in human affairs, is in deep trouble. This will then give them a flattering image of themselves as 'soul doctors to a sick civilization',[227] and a sense of purpose they might otherwise lack.

The task of humanizing medicine is, of course, still incomplete. Progress continues to be made, in parallel with progress in its science base. In my thirty or more years as a doctor, I have seen advances on both fronts. There has been incremental humanization of medical institutions, despite their offering more and more hi-tech interventions and being under ever greater pressure to do so at high speed. In hospitals, I have seen increasing liberalization of visiting hours; the encouragement of parents to stay with their children and a deeper understanding of their needs; improvements in the design of wards (particularly wards for people with dementia); the training of nurses in the sensitive management of disturbed patients; and so on. It is difficult to imagine these advances (and the responsiveness to criticism or the self-criticism that has driven them) taking place where pre-scientific medicine prevails.

Progress will be more difficult so long as we make the wrong diagnosis of the residual ills of medicine and believe that its scientific basis is at odds with its humanity. The miracle of scientific medicine is the development of rational evidence-based treatments in the face of the terror of illness and of the propensity of humans to lie and to deceive themselves. The miracle of humane medicine is the cultivation of intelligent kindness in our dealings with the sick and powerless – in the face of the inhumanity of the human body and the general inhumanity of man to man individually and collectively. Doctors and nurses have to overcome the universal, congenital tactlessness that afflicts humanity, and under difficult circumstances: the continuous exposure to suffering, to needy people, in a context where the needs and the suffering have to be translated into problems to be solved and solved problems are reckoned up as output. For this, something more than 'customer service' and a narrowly contractual approach to care is required.

Those who deny progress have many things in their favour. The collective amnesia of how things were in the past – and an upward calibration of expectation and a downwards regulation of tolerance to imperfections – is the most powerful. Almost as powerful is a lack of balance, so that faults and failings are disproportionately represented in public perception of health care. And then there is a tendency, when thinking about whether progress has been made, to compare how things are with how they should be or how we would like them to be, rather than with how they once were. This plays into the hands of policy-makers who wish us to believe that there are only political solutions to the failings of the NHS, that its failings are so radical that it needs 'saving', and that they are the saviours it needs. To dissolve the myths such politicians feed on, in particular that of the lack of progress of an inhumane health service, it is necessary only to compare the (non-atypical) fate of my mother with (the absolutely typical) fate of her mother and then consider whether, as Will Hutton has claimed, 'Bevan's dream is dead'.

7

Representations and Reality

From grief to grievance

This [the organ retention furore] has been a difficult business for the medical profession. I believe we have been victims of poor and badly applied law, and have been let down by one aberrant pathologist. Our desire to shield patients and their relatives from some of the more distressing aspects of illness and death has been pejoratively derided as paternalism. The long-standing intention to learn and teach, even after a patient's death, has been debased, in many commentators' words, as morbid curiosity or worse.

John Bennett[1]

In the early hours of the morning, when I am most actuely aware of the random brutality of the world and my entire life seems an exposed surface, the fear that something terrible may happen to one of my sons cuts deepest. For a few moments I can begin to imagine what it must be like to be a bereaved parent. All bereavement brings the sense of a shared journey broken off; where it is a child who has died, this must be intensified by the poignancy of the lost future: growing up, love, marriage, a career, having children, making a difference in the world, of preparation for a life that never started.

And there is a sense of responsibility, which, as the melancholic diarist H-F Amiel says, 'mortally envenoms grief'.[2] It is guilt of the survivor: I continue, surrounded by these daily things, consumed by everyday preoccupations, while my child is nowhere and no longer. To be predeceased by one's child is to suffer an inversion of that natural order in which the elders are closer to death. The outrageously unfair survivor guilt of the bereaved parent is worsened by the feeling that one failed in a fundamental duty: I did not save my child; I consented to an operation that killed him; I did not protect him from harm; I might have done more; I watched helplessly while he died. Now I can't hug him, comfort him, take his hand, rock him to sleep. He is nowhere, or somewhere quite alone.

The loss of a child awakens other, unbearable, feelings: that someone so small should have suffered adult-sized experiences; that death and dying should take root in the tiny body and the uncomprehending mind of a child. Charlotte Mew's 'Exspecto Resurrectionem', a poem on the death of her five-year-old brother of scarlet fever, captures this. She asks God to give some ordinary comfort to her little brother:

> Dost Thou a little love this one
>   Shut in tonight,
> Young and so piteously alone,
>   Cold – out of sight?
> Thou know'st how hard and bare
> The pillow of that new-made narrow bed
>   Then leave not there,
>   So dear a head![3]

And so I imagine how it must be, or imagine that I can imagine it. Although I might intuit the sharpest pangs, I can't really think into the endless parched places of grief. The chronic sorrow of a bereaved parent is unnarratable and inconceivable to all who have not suffered from it.

It is the very intensity of such emotions that makes them liable to expropriation. And this is what happened when lawyers, journalists and politicians gathered around bereaved parents in Bristol and Liverpool, as the so-called 'Alder Hey organ retention scandal' gathered momentum towards the end of 1999, and colluded in the transformation of their grief into grievance.

Keeping tissues and organs was done – generally – with good intent and no malice. However, by today's standards the process was informal and implicit. When it became news, the reaction of those in positions of leadership was illuminating. Calm assessment, putting the matter in perspective, explanation and apology were needed. What we got was ministerial incandescence and mass referrals to the General Medical Council.[4]

Timothy Chambers

The story began in 1996 when the mother of a child who had died after surgery at the Bristol Royal Infirmary saw a television programme about paediatric cardiac surgery. This prompted her to request a copy of the medical records. By this means she discovered that her child's heart had been retained. She asked for it back. Her demand prompted the establishment of the Bristol Heart Children's Action Group, who discovered that the removal of tissue from the bodies of children who had died – for medical education, audit, research, and storage for future research – was routine. There was an outcry and this was taken up elsewhere, especially in Liverpool, the home of the internationally reknowned Alder Hey children's hospital, when it was discovered that they were carrying out the same practices. Professor R. H. Anderson, Professor of Morphology at Great Ormond Street Hospital for Sick Children, had spoken, in defence of the practice at Bristol, of the benefits of retaining hearts for study and teaching. To underline the normality of the practice at Bristol, he referred to the collections at other hospitals around the country. He identified the largest collection at Alder Hey.

Within a few days, Alder Hey was besieged by bereaved parents. They demanded to know whether organs or tissue had been retained and in some cases asked for tissue and organs to be returned for burial. Not surprisingly, the hospital was slow in responding to the many hundreds of inquiries it received. This was, after all, a totally unforeseen crisis for an institution whose staff, in common with those in most hospitals, were already desperately overstretched. Mistakes were made in the information given to parents about what had and had not been removed; and there were inadvertent insensitivities – through, for example, muddling up names – that greatly inflamed the situation. Alder Hey parents formed a support group: Parents who Inter Their Young Twice (PITY II). The beleaguered hospital became the object of widespread execration. Its doctors and managers were demonized. Matters reached a climax with the publication of the Redfern Report in January 2001.[5] The hospital, its managers, its medical staff and the medical profession more widely, were engulfed in a tidal wave of national outrage. In an action already referred to the Chief Medical Officer who should have seen the events in a wider perspective (since he had at about the same time commissioned a report on the retention of organs nationally),[6] referred sixteen people to the General Medical

Council for a disciplinary inquiry, the long-term damage caused by this was immeasurable.

Before discussing the furore, it is important to put the incident in a broader context. The behaviour of one pathologist, Dick van Velzen, as described in the Redfern Report, was utterly disgraceful. Otherwise there was nothing exceptional about the retention and storage of organs and histological slides. Every medical school has a pathology museum – and a slide collection – of which it is justifiably proud. There is nothing sinister or ghoulish about such collections. Secondly, most of the actions branded in the media as abhorrent were within the law and the ethical guidelines in force in the period of the van Velzen years. While the scale of van Velzen's collection was far beyond anything either he or anyone else could justify, the collection of organs was not in itself aberrant.

To contextualize, the Human Tissue Act of 1961, in force at the time of the Alder Hey affair, only forbids a post-mortem to be carried out 'without the authority of the person lawfully in possession of the body'. It defined the person in lawful possession in a hospital as 'the hospital manager'. Moreover, there was no obligation to obtain consent for a post-mortem, although actual written consent was customarily sought. Hospital pathologists usually refuse to perform an autopsy without a consent form signed by a relative: in this respect, far from doctors flouting the law, medical practice was in advance of it. As for retention of tissues, the 1961 Act provided for the removal and use of parts of a body after a hospital autopsy, 'for purposes of medical education and research'.[7] A report from the Nuffield Council on Bioethics in 1995 asserted that 'Provided that the terms of the [1961] Act... are complied with, any part may be removed.'[8] The failure to obtain consent from the parents in some cases for the retention of organs was not therefore either illegal or at odds with current ethical opinion.

It is important to remember also that the failure to spell out to parents the precise nature of the retention of organs was not prompted by base motives. Even the Redfern Report acknowledges in its final pages that the practice of organ retention without consent arose from a feeling among the doctors of what would be in the 'best interest of the parents'. The claim that 'such practice was misconceived and was bound to cause upset and distress'[9] has to be set against the judgement that spelling out the nature of the autopsy and what was to be removed was equally likely to cause upset and distress.[10]

The hounding of the medical profession in the wake of Alder Hey shocked many. The GMC found no evidence in respect of the people referred to it by the Chief Medical Officer (CMO) (with the exception of van Velzen) to justify further proceedings. It took four years to arrive at this judgement. Many had in the meantime been suspended from their jobs. The CMO also instituted a search for retained organs, samples and slides in hospitals and medical schools throughout the country. Along with every other academic clinician in the UK, I had to sign a declaration to the effect that my offices, a long way from wards or pathology laboratories, had been personally searched by me and that no specimens had been found.

In this, the CMO had taken his cue from the Secretary of State for Health, whose 'disgust' as he read the 'gruesome' Redfern Report was widely trailed before his statement in the House of Commons. Alan Milburn described the events set out in the Redfern Report as 'the worst disaster to befall the NHS', although, as John Bennett points out, no physical injuries or deaths were caused by them. Milburn made the most of the Redfern Report's reference to 'paternalism', linking it to the general criticisms he had been making of a 'secretive', 'unaccountable', 'arrogant', 'self-centred' profession.[11]

The response of the broadsheets was indistinguishable from that of the tabloids. Tabloids, in their ruthless pursuit of 'the human story', engaged in exploits such as following bereaved parents to the House of Commons and back to Alder Hey hospital to confront managers (who understandably became flustered and sometimes got complainants' names wrong). The broadsheets competed in the production of ghoulish and macabre headlines. The *Independent* devoted most of its front page to a picture of a deserted bare room, which had (presumably) housed some specimens in the Alder Hey, with the headline 'THE BASEMENT OF HORRORS'[12] with its obvious echo of the basement where Frederick and Rosemary West had sexually abused, tortured and murdered young girls.

Unsurprisingly, already angry parents became ever more incensed. Members of the PITY II group became preoccupied with the physical integrity of the bodies of the children they had buried. The discovery of missing parts prompted a second, third and even fourth funeral. In some cases, there were ceremonies for slivers of tissue on slides. By a bitter irony, preoccupation with the retained organs of their children brought home the awful reality of death – and what happens to a body after death – even more clearly. While being distributed among specimen pots is arguably less horrible to imagine than the consequences of either cremation or burial, the retained organs furore forced parents to confront the physical reality of death in a way that is required of few parents. Media outrage suborned the deep and unbearable emotions of bereaved parents to the ephemeral purpose of selling daily papers. Moreover, they used the shocking truth of the physical reality of death to pass judgement on the standing of doctors, and in particular pathologists, who have to deal with it most directly. The implication in the popular press was that those who deal with death are somehow responsible for it.

There was also something else going on. The idea of the death of one's child, of the ordeal leading up to it, and the loss itself, is unbearable enough, and the desire to continue to protect the child can make the thought of a post-mortem really horrifying.[13] Sometimes, when I have requested a post-mortem because I really wanted to be sure that I had not overlooked any treatable condition or missed out on a lesson for the future, it has been refused by the next of kin on the grounds that 'I don't want him to suffer any more'. It would tactless and cruel to spell out the fact that dead bodies cannot suffer and that if they could suffer they would suffer no more from an autopsy than from burial or cremation. Yet superstition about the suffering of dead bodies combined with guilt at failure to protect one's child can make the discovery of an autopsy one does not recall authorizing[14] a real shock.

The parents therefore felt the need to transform their grief into something else, and thereby obtain some kind of relief. Comparatively speaking, grievance is less profound and therefore more bearable; it looks outwards and addresses itself to something that can be repaired – the grieving person is distracted from a tragic loss by a remediable wrong. Attributing blame imports some ordinary sense into something – the death of a child – that eats away at the very roots of a meaningful universe. However, the transformation of grief into grievance makes grief only temporarily more bearable. This became evident when a few parents started to arrange funerals for slides containing microscopic slivers of tissue. Other parents, who had lost children decades before, came forward, wanting to know whether their children's bodies had been buried whole. Anger, like grief, does not have a statute of limitation. A woman broke down when she discovered that some of the organs of a twenty-nine-week-old still-born baby she had given birth to eighteen years ago had been kept in preservative and then incinerated; another woman reported that she had been trying to find her child's organs for over thirty years. Five years after the affair broke, the papers still carry stories of parents who were planning repeat funerals for their children's body parts.[15]

Predictably, the Redfern Report and a subsequent exhaustive survey of every site in England and Wales where organs and tissue samples might be stored, did not satisfy many parents. The need to know what had happened modulated into an unallayable suspicion of a 'cover up'. Concern spread from Bristol and Liverpool to other cities: in Manchester[16] the Retained Organs Commission was contacted by over 700 people.

The Retained Organs Commission was set up in April 2001 in order 'to heal the pain arising from past practice and to re-establish trust between patients, their families and the NHS'.[17] The belief of the chairman of the Commission that 'by working with the profession, families and the Retained Organs Commission, trust can be restored' proved optimistic. In the short term, the Commission simply widened the field of parental anger, and was itself the target of much resentment. In Manchester, its chief executive came under fire from a new parental pressure group, STORM (Stop Organ Retention Manchester). One of the parents called for a judicial review, on behalf of parents, of the GMC's decision not to proceed with cases against most of the doctors referred to the GMC in the Chief Medical Officer's trawl.

For the lawyers, this was a potentially very lucrative tragedy. The lawyer representing the Alder Hey families had a very large number on his books. They were offered £5,000 each and most accepted, but some held out for more. This is, of course, only the beginning: the National Committee Relating to Organ Retention estimates that 134 Trusts are involved and, since the Commission asserts that the same rules apply to adult patients, the overall cost may be of the order of tens or even hundreds of millions of pounds. It is not irrelevant to observe that the legal fees alone could have been spent on life-saving treatment for many hundreds of children especially as it seems unlikely that the sum of money involved (dismissed as 'paltry' and 'an insult' by some parents) along with the return of specimens, slides and organs, will truly alleviate much grief.[18]

The affair has resulted in a set of recommendations for a new kind of consent form required to obtain consent for autopsy, post-mortem biopsy or organ or tissue retention. The form described in pp. 372–5 of the Redfern Report is enormously complex and brutally bureaucratic and would certainly cover future doctors against complaint.[19] It has, however, been suggested that the process of requesting post-mortems should be handled by 'a bereavement adviser'. This personal touch may soften the brutality of the form but bereavement advisers are warned that 'no subject should be avoided and [parents] must be treated with honesty even if the truth is painful' (p. 377). As John Bennett points out, the requirement to spell everything out in stark detail, 'notwithstanding the distress this will often cause to the patient or relative, let alone to the doctor' sits ill with certain aspects of the humanitarian tradition of medicine which have been derided as 'paternalistic'.[20] 'It is for cleverer minds', Bennett says, 'to show how that fits with our additional duty to be sympathetic or empathetic – but it seems that strict compliance with the most stringent interpretation of the law is considered more important'.[21]

The new form may not help patients, of course, as the recent headline in the *Manchester Evening News* – 'Anguish of parents in organ storm' – suggests.[22] The parents in question had contacted the press because they were uncertain whether samples of their babies' organs had been retained and whether they constituted whole organs. The consent form had been used in line with the Department of Health guidelines. The costs meanwhile, quite apart from the time and effort and financial settlements, are not in doubt – and they are still rising. The long-term effects are incalculable.

For the last few years, the lives of many of those who worked at Alder Hey hospital have been almost untenable and this includes clinicians who have to continue their daily work and concentrate on making difficult decisions that affect the lives and health of children under circumstances that are the reverse of straightforward. A fine hospital, which each year treats hundreds of thousands of children – many from the most deprived areas – to a high standard, has been vilified as a place where a scandal took place. This, for example, was from the *Independent*:

A REPUTATION IN RUINS, BUT NOT ENTIRELY LOST

It is Europe's largest children's hospital and carries the symbol of a rocking horse, imploring parents to trust in it...[23]

THE TRUTH ABOUT ALDER HEY

Organs of hundreds of children were hidden by doctors in a hospital cellar. Yesterday their parents learned the full scale of a terrible betrayal.

A veil was lifted yesterday in one of the most gruesome chapters, in the history of the National Health Service...[24]

Developments in clinical services have been hindered as a result;[25] for example, plans for improving children's cancer services.[26] A new building to deal with the increasingly complicated (and increasingly successful) approaches to childhood and adolescent leukaemia was held up as management and medical staff remained beleaguered by a small group of parents and by the collapse of the hospital's fund-raising efforts. Nothing could demonstrate more starkly the principle enunciated earlier that patient advocacy groups are sometimes the enemy of other patient groups.

But the damage has extended far beyond Alder Hey hospital. There is hardly a major children's hospital that has not been targetted by angry parents seeking restoration of organs; indeed, as one solicitor Mervyn Fudge has said, with respect to the 134 hospitals across Britain where claims are outstanding, 'I am sure the rest of the country does not want the perception that justifiable claims are being left behind while Alder Hey progresses.'[27] At the time of writing, some 2,000 parents are in bitter dispute with the NHS at having been offered only £1,000 compensation while the Alder Hey parents got £5,000.[28] As Polly Toynbee asks, commenting on this 'bizarre' example of the compensation culture, 'What price children's organs?'.[29]

There has been a steep falling-off in autopsy rates, and the hospital autopsy in general has almost disappeared.[30] This is dangerous, as the benefit of uncovering mistakes at post-mortem will be lost. 'To stop people dying prematurely, we need to get more real about death,' Phil Hammond has pointed out, adding that:

On one level... the organ retention hysteria amounted to a realization that pathologists collect pathology specimens... Maybe this year we'll discover that surgeons cut you up with knives, bodies are left to rot underground and it gets pretty hot in the crematorium.[31]

Of all the clinical disciplines, pathology is the one that most directly reflects the demystification of the human body that has made scientific medicine so effective and so humane. It expresses the truth under-pinning scientific medicine, the inhuman truth of the human body, and disperses the mist of evasion that characterizes folk medicine and everyday thinking about sickness and health. In essence, the Alder Hey clinicians were blamed for the honest confrontation with the nature and posthumous fate of our bodies that lies at the root of effective medicine. They were made to pay for the fact that, as T.S. Eliot wrote, 'human-kind/ Cannot bear very much reality'.[32]

If people refuse to face this reality, more mistakes will be made because previous errors will go undetected. The fact that van Velzen accumulated specimens on such a vast scale and for no apparent purpose, does not alter the general principle that autopsies are a fundamental part of good medical practice. Falling neonatal autopsy rates[33] are particularly alarming: the decline is due mainly to failure to obtain permission. Doctors' jobs are made more difficult because 'Grief counsellors, nurses or social workers who may be in contact with parents can unconsciously send messages that discourage parents from consenting to an autopsy.'[34] Donations of organs and tissue for research have fallen precipitously. In the six months after the organ retention furore first erupted, tissue donations to the UK Children's Cancer Study Group fell by 40 per cent, according to Cancer Research UK. Given that there could be no more manifestly worthy cause than one in which the words 'children' and 'cancer' are combined, this was a depressing index of public reaction to the affair.

Meanwhile the care of seriously ill children (and of seriously ill adults) is threatened in other, more direct ways. There has been a fall in the organs made available for transplantation. At the height of the Alder Hey crisis, an angry mother received a prolonged round of applause on a radio programme for saying that she hoped that, the next time a doctor requested that the kidneys of a dead person be donated for transplantation, he would be told to go to Hell. Such an attitude not only undermines the deeply humane and difficult work of transplant surgeons, it also stamps on the hopes of other parents, possibly in some cases condemning their children to death. The 30 per cent fall of heart/lung transplants (often for children with cystic fibrosis for whom it is the only hope of life) between 1995 and 2000 speaks for itself.[35] The submission of whole organs such as brains and hearts to specialist centres for much-needed studies has fallen, and even routine diagnostic work such as histology to confirm cancer and tuberculosis is reduced.

There has also been an impact on the discipline of pathology: the fall in recruitment to paediatric pathology services has been catastrophic. As a pathologist has pointed out:

All pathologists have had to absorb personal comments about their chosen profession ranging from the jocular to the malicious. Young pathologists have been reluctant to disclose their profession to friends and relatives and some pathologists have even chosen to leave the profession.[36]

Innocent individuals have been demonized in the press. A pathologist in Nottingham woke up one morning to find that he was the focus of 'a scandal of national magnitude'.[37] He had been smeared by disgruntled mortuary workers wanting to discredit the Trust and its management. They had made unfounded accusations about the disposal of organs and body parts, which were then featured in the *News of the World*. The then Health Secretary at once ordered his suspension, launched an independent inquiry and placed the mortuary workers under protection as 'whistleblowers'. The pathologist's house, his life, his children were besieged by journalists, and he had the appalling experience of watching David Frost discuss 'this latest scandal' on television. A full-length front-page picture appeared in a tabloid under a damning headline.[38] Needless to say, the independent inquiry found no case to answer and the mortuary workers were sacked for gross misconduct. While the allegations, the pathologist said, 'became a national scandal that spread across the world's media within hours and through the internet like a cancer', the exoneration was barely mentioned. He was left feeling defiled and with the fear that the episode left 'a lasting impression of guilt to those unaware of the outcome'.

The case of a consultant pathologist and former head of paediatric and perinatal pathology in a prestigious teaching hospital, who was forced temporarily to flee her job and work as a part-time GP in Wales, is even more disturbing.[39] She had wanted, she said, to be a pathologist who could sit down with parents and explain the post-mortem findings to them; in short to be all that Redfern enjoined. She encountered extreme hostility. One father told her, after she had introduced herself as a pathologist in the context of a request for a post-mortem, that 'he wanted [her] children to die in tragic circumstances': 'he wanted their hearts on his mantlepiece'. She was repeatedly subjected to verbal abuse and asked whether she kept organs in her shed. Her children 'were told in the playground that their mother was probably an organ-snatcher and she chopped up dead babies'.

The public image of an unglamorous specialty, staffed by dedicated and extremely bright people, has been profoundly damaged. It must be difficult for the public to see that

the provision of perinatal and paediatric pathology services is a sign of an enlightened society. It symbolizes the care society attaches to the well-being of its young by trying to find out what makes each pregnancy and infancy go well or badly.[40]

The impending collapse of paediatric pathology – when, in the wake of the acquittal of Sally Clark and others, on appeal, of the charge of murdering their babies, there has been a demand that all sudden infant deaths should prompt a full post-mortem carried out by an appropriately qualified pathologist – is deeply worrying. Applications for training posts have fallen. A fifth of consultant paediatric pathology posts are empty and have little prospect of being filled. Of all the wounds dealt to medical care in the United Kingdom, this may take longest to heal.

Yet there maybe an even more serious consequence. The Human Tissue Bill, hastily and incompetently put together in the wake of Alder Hey, sets out a proposed new legislative framework governing the removal, storage and use of human organs and tissue. It establishes a very demanding but ultimately unclear notion of the consent required for any kind of research on human bodies or the smallest parts of them. The new criminal offences in this Bill are very wide-ranging and custodial sentences figure significantly. A doctor who, through oversight, uses a piece of tissue for a research study other than that spelt out in the initially very complex research consent form, will face up to three years in jail and unlimited fines. The requirements for explicit consent are such that it may be better to give up research altogether if one wishes to avoid acquiring a criminal record.

The legislation against using material for research or training 'not incidental to the diagnostic process' covers blood samples, urine and sputum that would otherwise be disposed of as 'clinical waste'. A foray into a sputum pot, without the legal protection of the minutely documented consent of the patient who coughed up its contents, may lead to loss of liberty, expulsion from the profession and financial ruin. Obtaining such permission, prospectively, in case the materials might be used for the benign purposes of teaching and research, will consume an estimated 450 million minutes of clinician time per year – sufficient to fully staff three medium-sized NHS hospitals.[41]

The proposed legislation is not only impractical and punitive, criminalizing much current research (including the kind of research that was necessary to make sense of BSE and to identify the genes that predispose certain women to breast cancer). It is also a disincentive to much good clinical care. Doctors, uncertain of their position with respect to supplementary testing of diagnostic material, may prefer to run the risk of a serious medical error (which carries with it only the likelihood of being struck off) to a long custodial sentence which will be the result of making errors in the consent procedure. The effect of this opaque and punitive legislation on monitoring long-term trends in infectious diseases using data from stored tissue will be catastrophic.

The Human Tissue Bill – which is currently undergoing revision in the House of Lords and may yet have some of its absurdities removed – is the disastrous legacy of the muddled thinking, displaced emotions and lack of political leadership that allowed the aberrant behaviour of one pathologist to become an indictment of an entire profession by giving the impression that the worst practice was the norm and that the norm was not motivated by anything other than the highest motives.

There is a wise Jewish saying: do not judge people by what they say in their grief. The correlative of this is that one should not treat those who cry out in grief as if they were oracles. The combination of populism in government, of consumerism in society and misplaced egalitarianism has given the outrage of those who have been, or believe they have been, injured by public services increasing influence. This is dangerous. First of all, it is unreasonable to expect grief to bring the wider perspective and overview that is necessary to shape services in a way that will achieve genuine improvements – and without having an adverse effect on other services (the bump in the carpet effect). Grieving parents – even less angry, grieving parents – could not, and should not be expected to consider the adverse knock-on effects of their demands on the present services for other children in the hospital to which their anger is directed, even less to imagine the ripples that will have such detrimental effects on the health of children in other places and future times.

Nor is the elevation of those who grieve, and who are coping with their grief by turning it into anger, to the status of oracles restricted to the sphere of health care. One of the most worrying examples was the Cullen Inquiry into the Paddington rail disaster. Victims were treated as experts on rail safety: their views were widely canvassed and given much air-time. While someone involved in a particular disaster may be able to give useful clues as to what happened immediately before and in the wake of the crash, this hardly amounts to expertise on future strategies for preventing recurrence of crashes or indeed in determining the appropriate level of expenditure to achieve this. When the Cullen Inquiry came to its conclusions, it was as if the intensity of the grief of those affected by the crash, their bravery and articulacy and the coverage this received, gave a special authority to the small amount of data they could contribute.

The recommended installation of the 'Automatic Train Protection System' would cost £3 billion and might prevent up to five deaths a year – half the number of lives lost on the road each day.[42] The same investment in road safety could save many more lives. Switching resources from road safety to rail safety consequently cost lives.

While it may seem heartless to contradict someone whose convictions are forged in grief, it is less heartless than allowing their grief and anger to shape policies: being caught up in an agenda driven by grieving parents will, as the Alder Hey affair has shown, ultimately result in *more* grieving parents. This is no way to commemorate those who have been loved and lost.

'The culture of contempt'

It would be absurd, unfair and, indeed, self-refuting to condemn all journalism. I could not have written this book without extensive use of newspaper reports. While I have usually looked beyond the lay press to professional journals for many facts, I am aware of shining examples of clear thinking, a commitment to accuracy, careful analysis and even-handed judgement, even among journalists writing for mass circulation papers. Names such as Nicholas Timmins and Polly Toynbee spring to mind. Such high-quality, thoughtful reporting is, however, the exception. The media – in particular print journalism, which will be my primary concern – seem ever more at ease with being part of, indeed fostering, 'a culture of contempt'.[43]

There seems to be a preference for bad news over good. This preference goes beyond the reporting of current medical care to coverage of the research that sustains hope for better medical care in future. A recent study[44] compared the characteristics of press releases by the two major British medical journals, The *British Medical Journal* and *The Lancet*, with reports in two newspapers, *The Times* and *The Sun*.[45] While good and bad news was equally likely to be represented in the press releases from the medical journals, bad news was almost twice as likely to be reported in the media.

The research charity Cancer UK has invested a good deal of its resources in research into improving communication between doctors and patients with cancer. Even so, the organization is contacted incessantly by reporters wanting examples of poor rather than good doctor–patient communication.[46] When Professor Lesley Fallowfield, its director, was invited to appear on BBC breakfast television to discuss a paper published in *The Lancet* that had reported on a randomized controlled trial that demonstrated the effectiveness of a communication skills course for oncologists in thirty-four centres throughout the UK, things did not go as she had expected. The item was hijacked by a lengthy report about a patient with a brain tumour who had been given bad news insensitively. Fallowfield was asked to comment on the particular case but was denied the opportunity to discuss the work that was intended to make such experiences less common in future. In only two out of the seven interviews that day was she given any opportunity to discuss the good news in her paper.

The sub-editing of an article on the disappointing results of a trial of the implantation of foetal cells to promote regeneration of the nervous system in patients with Parkinson's disease was recently described in detail by a group who had access to the original piece.[47] The *Guardian* commissioned an experienced health journalist to write a piece setting the study in the context of a general discussion of clinical trials. During the sub-editing process there were numerous significant alterations – ranging from changes of emphasis to sensational embellishments – aimed at making what was a timely, responsible and honest evaluation of a promising technique look like 'Frankenstein science'. The title of the article was changed from 'Clinical Trials' to 'Trial and Error'. Although the manuscript had made no reference to 'human guinea pigs', a sub-title 'Medical research needs human guinea pigs' was inserted, as well as a sentence insinuating that the participants' consent to enter the study had not been fully informed. The conclusion that the treatment had 'failed' was changed: it had 'gone horribly wrong'; and the sub-editor had added that 'the cells appeared to have gone into overdrive... causing the patients to writhe and jerk their heads uncontrollably'.[48] The anonymous sub-editor also removed the journalist's reference to the benefits that accrue simply from being in a clinical trial – close observation, best care from experts who have an interest in optimizing the outcome for the patient. This kind of reporting – or rewriting – may actually endanger the future of a research programme that offers one of the few hopes for patients with this appalling disease.

Challenging scare stories, however, is an almost impossible task. If 'the scientific community' or 'the authorities' try to place the scare in perspective, or suggest that the findings require confirmation, they are accused of 'spin'. Scientists are all too familiar with the way those who misrepresent science have an unobstructed path, while those who attempt to correct misrepresentations will be accused of 'cover-up'.[49] We saw this in the case of the panic over MMR.

A recent article in the *Reader's Digest*[50] is for this reason doubly welcome. Since the magazine does not represent 'government sources' or some other 'discredited' agency, the article cannot be dismissed as 'spin'. It looked at a handful of scare stories: weekly visits to the swimming pool are as harmful to children's lungs as adult smoking; kissing babies may kill them; and eating vegetables can cause cancer of the oesophagus. It then retraced the winding path back to the original scientific articles that demonstrated none of the frightening claims. Proclaiming bad news based on bad or non-existent science not only invokes terror in a population already hypochondriacal about its own health and that of its children. It also distracts from important scientific truths about the path to health and about real risks. There is also the waste of resources in dealing with the consequences of the scares.

The ultimate health scare story must be the one the *Observer* ran in 2001 in 'Why the NHS is bad for us'.[51] The health editor Anthony Browne, 'once a passionate believer in the NHS, tells why he now feels it can never work and is only kept alive by wrong-headed idealism'. The article was remarkable even by the standards of present-day broadtab journalism, where an error or deficiency in the service is always a scandal and scandals are quickly collected into the notion of a 'scandal-hit' health service. Its tone was set in the first few sentences: 'Another lonely death. Another preventable death. Another reason why you must challenge your most deeply held beliefs.' It continued: 'Each year, thousands of British people – the young, the old, the rich, the poor – die unnecessarily from lack of diagnosis, lack of treatment and lack of drugs.' No data are given to back up these remarkable assertions. The facts absent from Browne's article show that, overall, the NHS has provided identical health gains to the USA for approximately half the expenditure, a doubly laudable achievement in view of the obstacles we discussed in Chapter 6.[52] A recent analysis has shown that the UK health service comes top out of nine Western countries in terms of years of life expectancy gained for each 1 per cent of GDP spent on health. The USA is at the bottom and, what's more, Britons on average enjoy 2.5 more years of good health than Americans.[53]

Browne quotes Bernard Kouchner, the health minister of France ('widely thought of as having the best health system in the world'), who describes the NHS as 'medieval' and 'intolerable'. The comparison with the French system is rather unfortunate, where all is not always well (despite over-lavish funding). The scandal of the deaths of elderly people in the summer 2003 heatwave in France, due in part to hospitals being deserted by staff on their August break,[54] also casts an interesting light on the functioning of 'the best health service in the world'. This is just anecdotal information. Perhaps more to the point is that in the analysis of life expectancy gained per 1 per cent of GDP, France is third from the bottom.[55]

Such facts would cut little ice with journalists such as Anthony Browne who can now see that the NHS 'causes misery on a scale seldom seen outside the developing world'. The problem, moreover, is not one that can be solved by adequate resources, for example, by closing half the funding gap between the NHS and the French system that Browne so uncritically reveres. The very principles of the NHS – and by this I presume he means that it is comprehensive, free at the point of use and funded out of general taxation – will, he argues, block any improvement. Those 'who claim that to question the institution's failed principles is somehow unethical have blood on their hands'.

In further support of his case against the NHS, he cites that 'Britain has the worst survival rates for almost all forms of cancer of any Western country.' Even if this were true, there are several reasons why he should not blame the NHS for this, given that it delivers identical health improvements to the US health system at approximately half the cost. He should then ask himself to what extent these cancer survival figures reflect the influence of the *principles* of the NHS and to what extent they reflect the *underfunding* the NHS has suffered from since its inception (expenditure at the time of the article, according to Antony Browne's own figures, is a third less than other European countries).[56] He should ask himself why he feels that adequate funding will not solve the problem. How, also, does he account for the fact that significant gains have been made in the outcomes of many forms of cancer (such as breast cancer) and in the prevention of others (such as cervical cancer) over the last decade, and that age-adjusted deaths from heart disease have fallen by 30 per cent over the last ten years even within an underfunded version of the NHS?[57]

Not to have addressed these questions, and to have relied on patchy evidence in order to make the case for another massive change in the NHS, that is, the dismantling of it, is the height of irresponsibility.

There is another dimension to 'the culture of contempt': the hounding of doctors who are deemed to have failed their patients. The publication of the Kennedy Report on paediatric cardiac surgery in Bristol generated some very striking examples. The Executive Summary of the Report has 102 paragraphs, and very few of them were directly critical of the consultant cardiac surgeons at the centre of the scandal; indeed many are full of praise. 'The story of the paediatric cardiological service in Bristol', the Summary begins, 'is not an account of bad people. Nor is it an account of people who did not care, nor of people who wilfully harmed patients. It is an account of people who cared greatly about human suffering and were dedicated and well-motivated.' It then emphasizes how most of the factors that led to the poor results lay outside the consultants' control:

It is an account of health care professionals working in Bristol who were victims of a combination of circumstances... at the time than any individual failing. Despite manifest good intentions and long hours of dedicated work, there were failures on occasion in the care they provided to very sick children.

It is an account of a service offering paediatric open-heart surgery which was split between two sites and had no dedicated paediatric intensive care beds, no full-time paediatric cardiac surgeon and too few paediatrically trained nurses.

It is an account of a time when there was no agreed means of assessing the quality of care. There were no standards for evaluating performance. There was confusion throughout the NHS as to who was responsible for monitoring quality of care.[58]

Only after having highlighted the powerlessness of the consultants to make their patients safer and their own lives easier, does the Report go on to make direct criticism:

It is an account of a hospital where there was a 'club culture'; an imbalance of power with too much control in the hands of a few individuals.[59]

The Summary contains hardly any other direct criticism.

Yet, the tabloids had their own interpretation of Sir Ian Kennedy's findings. The *Daily Mirror*'s headline was 'CLUB OF DEATH'.[60] The no-blame culture, which focuses on systems rather than individuals, holds little attraction for the media. The Kennedy Report's recommendation that 'learning from error, rather than seeking someone to blame, must be the priority' has had little influence, as another couple of examples illustrates.

At the beginning of 2002, Iain Duncan Smith, then leader of the Tory party, raised the case of a ninety-four-year-old lady, Mrs Rose Addis, who had been admitted to Whittington Hospital following a fall. When her relatives visited her (after a delay of forty-eight hours) they had been shocked by what they found. Allegedly, Mrs Addis was in a severe state of neglect and 'caked in blood' from injuries sustained in the fall. They at once lodged a formal complaint. Without waiting for a response from the hospital, they also contacted Mr Duncan Smith, her daughter's constituency MP. When the latter raised the matter in the Commons, he demanded a public apology from Tony Blair and quoted Mrs Addis's daughter as saying: 'If my poor mother had been a dog she would have been treated better.' The patient's grandson, who was described as 'a journalist', took a photograph of Mrs Addis, showing her unkempt, confused and bruised from her fall. The photograph was widely published in the national press.[61]

On further inquiry, it became apparent that Mrs Addis had not been mistreated: she had simply resisted being washed by the staff. According to a patient in the adjacent cubicle, Mrs Addis was confused and the doctors and nurses had been extremely attentive and courteous despite much abuse from her. Any attempt to have washed and changed her clothes without her permission would have been an assault. Had the family materialized a little earlier, they might have been able to help the nurses to persuade the patient of their good intentions.[62]

The care given to Mrs Addis was also defended by the Chief Executive of the Trust, by the Medical Director James Malone-Lee, and by the Prime Minister. Ian Duncan Smith then attacked the Prime Minister and the Chief Executive for betraying confidential details about a patient. This was followed by a complaint from the same grandson who had sent her photograph to the national papers. He asserted that it was 'an absolute disgrace' that Downing Street had intruded into Mrs Addis's privacy. Press attention then switched to Professor James Malone-Lee, who had defended the care the patient had received.

Although he was frequently described in the press as a surgeon, James Malone-Lee is Professor of Geriatric Medicine and and a man whom I admire enormously for his research into the problem of urinary incontinence in older people. This is not a glamorous area but one that is immeasurably important to the many patients who suffer from it.[63] He has devoted his professional life to the care of elderly people. So far as the press (notably the *Evening Standard*) was concerned, this was a man who had wrecked a wonderful bad-news story; what was more, he had defended the management line against the interests of the patient. It was discovered that he was a 'Labour party activist'. According to the Tory central office, Malone-Lee's defence of the staff at the Whittington Hospital typified the way that anyone who criticized public services should expect to 'be pilloried by local management working within the Labour rebuttal machine to sustain a culture of deceit'.[64] Liam Fox, the Conservative health spokesman, accused him of 'manipulating his position [as medical director] and manipulating staff to his own political ends'.[65]

Malone-Lee's Labour party 'activism' amounted to dishing out a few leaflets and signing a letter along with fifty-nine other doctors in 1997 warning that voting for the Tories would mean the end of the NHS. This was not very exciting, so certain journalists decided to subject Malone-Lee's life to more detailed scrutiny. They approached people at a pub near the hospital to find out whether he had a drink problem or drank there at lunch-time; and they contacted hospital staff to find out if he had ever had an extramarital affair.[66] They turned up nothing. Needless to say they did not report his work on urinary incontinence in old age. This was not perceived to be a 'story'.

The treatment of James Malone-Lee sent a signal to the medical profession: if you challenge the coverage of medical issues by the press and, in particular, deny them a tasty circulation-boosting scandal, you had better watch out. The impact of the misrepresentation of the Whittington Hospital on the morale of the staff and the recruitment of nurses may be readily imagined. Meanwhile, Iain Duncan Smith ordered his party colleagues to find more 'Rose Addis-style' controversies.[67]

Comparatively speaking, Professor Malone-Lee got off lightly and unlike the pathologist Geoffrey Hulson referred to earlier (see page 196), he has not suffered lasting damage.[68] For a journalist who scents a good story will not shrink from exploiting it to the limit, as consultant psychiatrist Anthony Farrington disovered when Roy Whiting was convicted of the murder of Sarah Payne.[69] It was claimed that, some five years earlier, Dr Farrington had given his opinion in court that Whiting 'had no paedophile tendencies'. According to the media, this had contributed to the decision to give Whiting a more lenient sentence for abducting a nine-year-old at knife-point. As a result Whiting had been freed to commit Sarah Payne's murder. This claim was first made in the *Daily Mail*, accompanied by a full-length photograph of the psychiatrist. Two days later, *Daily Mail* columnist Simon Heffer declared that Farrington ought to have Sarah Payne's death on his conscience. This triggered a siege, in which practically every national paper, and many local ones, demanded interviews, frequently doorstepping Farrington with photographers. A common ploy was to threaten him with even more unfavourable coverage if he did not oblige them, hinting that major hatchet jobs were being prepared by other papers, so that it would be in his interest to give his story to them.[70]

Farrington's torment was exacerbated by the fact that he was not able to speak out so long as the Whiting trial was pending or in progress for fear of prejudicing the trial. He had to suffer the misrepresentation of his expert opinion, the trashing of his professional competence, without being able to speak out. This inability to respond, to defend oneself, to set the record straight – because of patient confidentiality, gagging clauses or legal requirements – is one of the most unbearable features of the ordeals suffered by doctors when they are 'exposed' by the press.

Only after the trial was Farrington able to point out that he had never said that Whiting did not 'have paedophile tendencies': this was an interpretation placed on the report by Whiting's defence barrister, Philip Marshall. What Dr Farrington had said was that Whiting did not meet the diagnostic criteria which would have justified the court making a hospital order – an entirely accurate statement of fact. As for matters of opinion, his report had predicted that Whiting was likely to reoffend. The judge in the Sarah Payne case had commented on how right the psychiatrist had been in his initial assessment.

Being cleared of all blame still does nothing to restore a damaged reputation. Christopher Ingoldby, a surgeon at Pinderfields Hospital, was suspended following the death of a patient on the day of surgery the previous year.[71] An ad hoc committee convened in 1998 by the present Chief Medical Officer, Sir Liam Donaldson (and subsequently shown by a judicial review to have been flawed) paved the way for a process that continued until November 2001, when all forty-seven charges against him were dropped.[72] This was the GMC's judgement:

We have considered the evidence from your professional colleagues as to your competence, skills and good character, as well as testimony from a number of former patients that you are a caring and considerate doctor. Consequently, we do not find the charges of serious professional misconduct proved.[73]

Too little, too late. After four years, the surgeon's reputation had been irreversibly damaged.

> The purest treasure mortal times afford
> Is spotless reputation: that away,
> Men are but gilded loam, or painted clay.[74]

He and his family had been through an unspeakable ordeal and he was financially ruined. He received no apology.

The ordeals of James Malone-Lee, Anthony Farrington and

Christopher Ingoldby carry a warning: you practise under the sword of Damocles. As was said with respect to the Ingoldby case, 'the risk of complaints is now so high that it is no longer a reasonable assumption that if a doctor is suspended, he or she must have done something wrong'.[75] This does not, of course, protect doctors referred to the GMC (whose names are now made public while they are awaiting their hearing) from press innuendo. What overall effect this will have on recruitment to the medical profession remains to be seen, but if, as seems distinctly possible, it may make surgery in particular a very unattractive career option, the world will be a less safe place.

While many journalists may begin with the dream of righting injustices and bringing scoundrels to book, and so making the world a better place, a preoccupation with scoops, exclusives and exposés soon takes precedence. Janet Malcolm's extraordinary assertion that 'Every journalist who is not too stupid or full of himself to notice knows that what he does is morally indefensible'[76] seems, in the light of the behaviour of some journalists, to be not so extraordinary after all.

One of the greatest journalistic exposés in the last fifty years was the Watergate scandal: it established new role models and aspirations among journalists and this had a deeply corrupting effect on its practitioners. The story of the fearless young investigators propelled to world fame by their exposure of wrongdoing in high places increased the glitter of the prizes for those who hit lucky. The delicious pleasures of being on the moral high ground were combined (almost uniquely in life) with the most unswerving pursuit of self-interest. The assumption of misdemeanours wherever there is power, combined with the certainty that where misdemeanours are not found or are denied there must be 'a cover-up', has, over the last thirty years become the default position.

Even in my own hospital, world famous for its research and pre-eminent in some of its specialties, it has become a matter of honour for the health correspondent (whom we christened 'Fearless T _ _ _ _') steadfastly to refuse to report any of the good news – the establishment of new services, new discoveries in medical science – and endlessly to ferret for scandals such as cockroaches in the junior doctors' accommodation!

Watergate intoxication is only part of a very general trend in journalism.[77] Steven Barnett divides postwar political journalism into four phases: the age of deference, the age of equal engagement, the age of journalistic disdain, and the age of contempt. Andrew Marr describes the long-term impact of the 'culture of abuse' on political journalism:

It is acid. It is eating away at the thoughtful culture of public discourse, burning out nuance, gobbling up detail, dissolving mere facts. And that, in turn, cannot help a struggling democracy.[78]

Nor can such reporting help a health service struggling to take advantage of the fact that, for the first time, it has begun to move towards reasonable levels of funding.

As Peter Riddell has pointed out, the broadsheets now slavishly follow the tabloid agenda. The way political stories are about putative scandal and misconduct, rather than policy or procedure, mirrors the press coverage of medical issues. Cut-throat competition for circulation in a declining newspaper market, especially in the tabloid sector; relaxation of the regulatory environment; and reduction of advertising revenue which has made circulation wars even more intense – these are some of the factors driving down standards. It is why attempts by scientists, clinicians and others to communicate with and educate many journalists are worthy but futile. 'The whole truth set in context' is not a priority.

The way in which the press abuses its own freedom has started to be challenged. Onora O'Neill, in her Reith lecture, 'Licence to Deceive',[79] points out that:

journalists have largely escaped the revolution in accountability that has imposed rigorous regimes of regulation and audit on so many professions and institutions. Reporters write a lot about others' trustworthiness, but often make it hard for the rest of us to check their trustworthiness... [The] media, in particular the print media – while deeply preoccupied with others' untrustworthiness – have escaped demands for accountability... Outstanding reporting and accurate writing mingle with editing and reporting that smears, sneers and jeers, names, shames and blames... In this curious world, commitments to trustworthy reporting are erratic: there is no shame in writing on matters beyond a reporter's competence, in coining misleading headlines, in omitting matters of public interest or importance, or in recirculating others' speculations as supposed 'news'.

Our present culture of suspicion, O'Neill points out, 'cannot be dispelled by making everyone except the media trustworthier'. Untrustworthy media may bring about the very thing they report: 'the intrusive methods that we have taken to stem a supposed crisis of trust may even, if things go badly wrong, lead to a genuine crisis of trust.'

Steven Barnett's talk, in the article cited earlier, of a 'crisis in journalism' possibly provoking a crisis in democracy, may be a little apocalyptic, perhaps even a touch journalistic. (The contagion, as I myself have found, is strong.) What is more probable is that the culture of contempt, of an unaccountable watchdog journalism supposedly holding everyone else to account, and focusing on personality and scandal rather than analysis of facts placed in perspective, could result in a steady decline in the morale, recruitment and retention of staff in the NHS. By this means, the very crisis talked up in the press could be brought about.

As collective consciousness becomes ever more expropriated by the media and the media become more tabloidized, popular debate may no longer be deep enough to accommodate the real issues and challenges of medicine, none more important than that of carrying responsibility for the life and death of others. It is to that responsibility that, in our discussion of the present discontents of medicine, we now, finally, turn.

The unbearable heaviness of responsibility

The sometimes unbearable nature of the responsibilities borne by doctors, given the inevitability of occasional error, is not generally appreciated. This failure to communicate the particular cross they have to bear is a tribute to the profession and to the demeanour of calm authority, often mocked as 'paternalistic', that it has always aspired to assume before anxious patients. A commitment to open, shared worry, or a shared panic, would benefit no one.

That this burden, so central to medicine, can be almost invisible was brought home to me in the decade when I was Dean of Admissions for Manchester Medical School. We used to ask prospective medical students what they felt were the greatest stresses of a life in medicine – as a preliminary to asking how they would cope with them. For every twenty students who referred to 'the long hours' hardly one spoke of the burden of responsibility.

Everyday medicine has the habit of taking even the most responsible and cautious practitioner up to and beyond the limits of his or her confidence and certainty. We are always operating on the margins of knowledge when we apply general principles to individual situations: these margins lie at the centre of ordinary practice. To make things worse, while we need routines and the automatic pilot to get us safely through the complexities of medicine, anyone who allows routines to dull their vigilance will soon be punished. The unusual presentation will be missed, the rare disease overlooked, the signal lost in the noise, and error will result.

The practice of medicine is about making countless decisions for which one has ethical, legal and personal responsibility: the decisions for which one is answerable to the patient, her supporters, the public at large, the law and, above all, to oneself are of many kinds: to reassure or not; to wait and see or to investigate and treat; to do this test or that; to prescribe this tablet, that one, or none at all, in this dose or that; to operate or not. Decisions are often made under difficult circumstances: inadequate information, distraction, hurry, preoccupation with other decisions. Even in ideal circumstances, they are still complex and difficult. Clinical medicine is always about probabilities, about making definite, often irreversible, decisions with incomplete certainty. The general templates we bring to our practice from our knowledge and experience never quite fit the problems presented by the individual patient. The mesh of evidence internalized by the most assiduous evidence-based practitioner is still sometimes quite coarse, leaving a penumbra of uncertainty around the singular patient. While there are many 'Must-dos' and 'Must-not-dos', quite a lot of medicine is about doing what one 'Probably-ought-to-do' and avoiding what one 'Probably-ought-not-to-do'. A doctor's sense of the relevant probabilities is a synthesis of objective knowledge, personal experience and tacit clues provided by the patient. This still leaves a gap: every medical procedure is to some extent an experiment. Being a good doctor is, as much as anything, about learning how to handle uncertainty in the way that gives the best outcome for the patient.

I still feel this even in the area where I have most claim to expertise – epilepsy in older people. It might be expected that, as I have been interested in this small area for nearly twenty years, have run a specialist clinic for over five years, have given countless lectures on the topic and written endless overviews for books and journals and have audited the outcome of my treatment and reflected on cases where things have gone wrong, I should always be confident about the advice I give to my patients and the prescribing decisions that I make. Mostly this is true, but I still agonize over how to manage some patients. I am sometimes struck by the contrast between the confidence of the advice in the chapters I have written on epilepsy, the clarity of my letters setting out the decisions, and the uncertainty I felt when I was with the patient, arriving with him or her at a management plan.

There are many less favourable situations for decision-making than a relatively calm specialist clinic: the over-filled clinic with a waiting room full of angry patients, rushed ward rounds when patients have numerous, often interacting, problems, the Accident and Emergency Department, are some commonplace examples. Hindsight is a potent tool for transforming a reasonable decision that turned out to be wrong into an eccentric or negligent action. Sometimes a series of decisions – where to insert this tube, which incision to make, where to place this stitch – has to be made under the worst possible circumstances:

Aorta clamped, blood pressures rise on either side of the operating table as the surgeon unpacks four sets of sterile surgical instruments before she gets one that is complete. Surgical supplies are subcontracted out with the laundry and the catering.

Meanwhile the locum consulant anaesthetist waits for cross-matched blood and the patient has an infarct on the table. The agency theatre staff struggle to orientate themselves to the ways of the hospital and the surgeon. They prove clumsy and inept assistants. Minutes tick by. NHS cost-cutting measures put an end to the sandwich lunch for theatre years ago and so the surgeons and the theatre team work through their hypoglycaemia. The surgeon has just spent twelve consecutive days of working and spent the last night emergency operating… Another two patients in A & E now need surgery.

The team emerges exhausted after eight hours operating and no food. Washing is out of the question – the showers are dirty and there are never any towels: these fell victim to another cost-cutting exercise when laundry and cleaning services were contracted out. The patients take their chance in ITU. One dies. Yet another bad statistic for the surgeon and hospital.[80]

All physicians carry a burden of responsibility that at times seems insupportable, when uncertainty becomes an agony of indecision, and errors of omission and commission may haunt one for years. Even so, we acknowledge that the gravity of the decisions surgeons take daily, and their naked exposure to the consequences, places them in a different league. I have huge admiration for the courage – the 'grace under pressure'[81] – of surgeons. To open up the body of an anaesthetized patient is to assume an awesome responsibility. The life of a surgeon requires a moral confidence that few, if any, jobs require in modern life. The peculiar nature of surgery – that it is literally hands on (or indeed hands in) – such that its consequences are as immediate as is possible in this world, makes it stand out starkly from other professions.

Most doctors, in contrast with many other professionals (including those in health care), remain on the front line, dealing directly with patients, listening to them, examining them, carrying out procedures, providing comfort, to the end of their careers.[82] They cannot be promoted out of reach of blame. They have to find ways of coping with their errors. The most effective way for a conscientious clinician to deal with things that go wrong is to try to improve his service, at the very least to reduce the chances of it going wrong in future.

Medical life is dogged by a sense of inadequacy, by guilt and self-blame. When a patient dies and one believes, rightly or wrongly, that he might have been saved had things been managed differently, one is put into the role of a guilty survivor. The usual reassurances – 'nobody is perfect', 'a woman who made no mistakes made nothing', 'you can't win them all' – seem obscenely inadequate to such a despair. A death cannot be glossed over by Christmas-cracker aphorisms. Doctors who make mistakes feel frightened, guilty and alone. The threat of litigation makes talking it over almost impossible.

Medicine is a desperately serious, sometimes grim business. There is the daily spectacle of suffering, of disability, of despair and death. Even so, it is the sense of responsibility that makes the deepest impact. This is well captured in this passage from Peter McDonald, a surgeon:

When an anastomosis leaks or when a diagnosis is reached too late and the patient perishes, only a hard man would not feel moved... Nights without sleep, suicidal thoughts and feelings of shame follow such events until the rush of saving more lives diminishes them. But as one wise old consultant said to me, these feelings never go away.[83]

Reading this reminds me of a colleague who used to wake some nights clutching his wife, shouting 'Stop the bleeding!'.[84] To face the challenges of surgery day in and day out, to know that at any time a routine operation can go badly wrong and you will find yourself at the end of a harrowing and exhausting day trying to explain to shocked, uncomprehending and grieving relatives what has gone wrong, takes a very special kind of person.[85] One of the founding fathers of cardiac surgery spoke of how such experience 'leaves its mark on the surgeon and inevitably influences his life permanently'.[86] Marc de Leval, a world leader in paediatric cardiac surgery, dedicated an international lecture to 'Robert M', his first operative death as a cardiac surgeon, twenty-three years earlier.

While it is surgeons who are most nakedly exposed, the picture painted by Peter McDonald will be familiar to all clinicians who have not prudently removed themselves to a place of safety far from front-line responsibility.

Milan Kundera explored what he called in his most famous novel 'the unbearable lightness of being':[87] our lives seem to pass through us, and we pass through our lives, like water through sand. Those who have to carry the unbearable heaviness of responsibility might wish for such problems. I have always found that, when I am worried about a patient, I cannot take radical ideas seriously: I feel nailed to what philosophers call the 'natural standpoint' and to my everyday life; I am pinned to my particularity by the nag of concern for the other person who has trusted her life to me. Responsibility presents itself as a guarantor of the stubborn reality of the world as it appears to common sense. It emphasizes the indissoluble link between myself and the accidents of my life and my world.[88] Such responsibility is something that cannot be captured in the shallows of much public discourse about medicine. The contract between physician and patient is an existential contract that sits uneasily with the business plans, ticked boxes, service level agreements and targets that dominate the image of medicine as it is understood by those remote from the front line. A doctor is more than (to employ the usual jargon) 'a service provider'.

It might be thought that the increasing emphasis at present on teamworking would spread the burden of responsibility. This is not how things are, nor, perhaps, how they should be. There is no easy way of evading responsibility for mistakes: it is individuals not teams who make diagnoses, write prescriptions, decide that operations are necessary and carry them out. There are acts, central to clinical medicine, that are not the products of seamless teamworking and attibrutable to a nebulous collective. Taking responsibility for a mistake does not, as Launie Lyckholm points out, stop at 'quality control'.[89] Taking responsibility for a mistake is a defining moment in the life of a doctor.

Doctors also have a propensity to shoulder blame for errors even when the problem is at least in great part a system fault. This was evident in a recent death of a three-year-old during a routine operation. The tragedy was due to equipment failure: the continued use in the NHS of an out-of-date anaesthetic machine capable of giving fatal overdoses of nitrous oxide. Even so, the doctor insisted on taking personal responsibility.[90] As has been pointed out, the Bristol and other very public inquiries into error, demonstrate how 'other professions dive for cover when blame is apportioned'.[91] A surgeon who accidentally removes the wrong kidney is personally charged with manslaughter: he cannot hide behind a blurred group decision and collective responsibility. The hospital Trust that made it possible for him to do this does not face a charge of corporate manslaughter. Corporate responsibility for medical error cannot, of course, alleviate individual guilt unless physicians are encouraged to stop blaming themselves for every calamity that befalls their organization.[92] As Allyson Pollock has pointed out, we doctors 'work in teams, but are blamed as individuals'.[93]

To embark on a career as a doctor is not only to commit oneself to a life of service, but also one of frequent worry and blame. Up to one third of doctors who are sued become clinically depressed.[94] Few people are prepared to carry such burdens; at any rate, other careers will seem more attractive to many talented people, and certainly less demanding. This raises a deeply worrying question: will it be possible to find people willing to be the clinicians of the future?

There are good reasons to support this concern. The upbringing and education of children in recent years has (quite properly) emphasized encouragement and praise and the withholding of criticism. While this may build up inner security and self-confidence, it may equally not equip the future adult to deal with responsibility and the blame that attaches to it when things go wrong. Despite the greatly improved conditions under which they work, and much greater support from seniors, junior doctors qualifying in 1995 are reportedly less happy with their career choices than doctors who qualified in 1974.[95]

There are also problems with training that may make the consultants of the future – in particular the surgeons – less able to cope. The public are increasingly averse to being spoken to, diagnosed by, prescribed for, and operated on by junior doctors. The consultant-led service is being replaced by the consultant-delivered service. This, as Anthony Daniels has pointed out, is problematic:

Everyone who comes under the knife wants his surgeon to be as highly trained and experienced as possible: but how is that surgeon ever to come by that training and experience unless he practises on people while he is untrained and inexperienced?[96]

The shift in emphasis in training from 'learning on the job' to 'leaving the job in order to learn' also reduces the opportunities for the confidence-building experience of taking responsibility. Many trainees, and in particular surgeons, already feel ill prepared for consultant responsibilities.

This may be another reason for increasingly defensive medicine: endless diagnostic tests (as evidence that one has taken due care) and countless referrals to colleagues (as evidence that one has taken the patient's problems seriously, though actually designed to spread the blame) may be the order of the day. Notwithstanding what I said earlier, the move towards teams, and shift-working, will help doctors to shoulder only a proportion of the blame when anything goes wrong, a diagnosis missed, accidental poisoning with medication, a surgical disaster.

Personal responsibility, the very heart of medicine, may therefore be weakened in future. The 'customer services' aspect of care, which has assumed increasing importance, will displace wise decision-making, or the capacity to reach through empathy into those places where suffering and frightened patients are exiled by their illnesses. Those able to take responsibility in the deepest and most burdensome sense – to be answerable for dealing with terrifying symptoms and to be able to respond to, and witness together with the patient, what they are going through – may be relics of the past.

The Kennedy Report was called 'Learning from Bristol'. The lesson that upcoming generations may learn from Bristol and other similar events is that only a fool would take on the responsibilities of a surgeon or, indeed, of any doctor: fewer and fewer people may be willing to take another's life into their hands.[97]

Conclusion

The paradox that while medicine, doctors and the NHS are delivering health care and outcomes that previous decades, never mind previous generations and previous centuries, could not have dreamed of, all three are enduring sustained attacks that physicians in their worst nightmares could not have imagined is a matter of the deepest concern. That the results of so much intelligence, passion, commitment, humanity, self-sacrifice and ordinary conscientiousness should be the object of so much disdain from powerful voices within society is not only profoundly depressing, it is also very worrying. As I approach my sixtieth birthday, conscious that ahead of me may lie one or two medical woes, I feel the world is going to become less safe or comfortable for ill people. It is possible that when I fall ill with a searing pain in my abdomen, requiring the skill and courage of a surgeon to act on rapidly taken decisions and the care and attention and intelligence of a nursing team to conduct me back to health in the post-operative period, there will be fewer people to respond to my needs. Instead of surgeons, we shall have people armed to the teeth with degrees in media studies, sharpening their pens in anticipation of a catastrophic outcome that they can report on from the moral high ground cushioned from responsibility. Instead of nurses, there will be individuals trained to deconstruct the authority of my surgeon and his discourses, or PR experts giving out press releases from my hospital or taking advantage of my unhappy outcome to enhance the market opportunities of their own private organizations.

I hope that the story set out in the preceding chapters will do something to avert this fate; for my aim has been to look into present discontents and to think beneath the reflex responses of various parties whose interests do not necessarily coincide with those of the sick person who requires help. We must first of all acknowledge the achievements of medicine. It will not help us if we find that, in our hour of need, we are surrounded by MBAs and not MBs, by PR consultants and not RGNs, by media specialists who will be delighted to assist us when we want to make a story out of how things have gone wrong but have not the foggiest idea about how to make them go right.

Above all, we must separate the remediable from the irremediable in illness and our treatments of it. We need to recognize that no human communication, least of all between someone who has fallen ill of a disease they have never heard of, affecting a body whose contents and function are opaque to them, can be entirely satisfactory. We must work towards an 'ideal speech situation' but not regard it as a scandal when it is not fully achieved. We must also recognize that the time a patient needs may be more than can ever be given, without treating this as grounds for indictment of those who care for her but who also have other patients to look after and even, dare one say it, lives of their own to live. We should also acknowledge that waiting is built into the very structure of illness, being necessary even for the illness to differentiate into a recognizable disease. The feeling of powerlessness that this waiting induces should not be blamed on those who are trying to alleviate the illness.

Obsession with power in medical care should not prompt relentless, unfair criticism of the medical profession who have for the most part used their power for that most benign of ends: the development of treatments for illness and of services to deliver them. Nor should it encourage an uncritical view of those who wish to disempower clinicians. Politicians have their own aspirations to power. 'Patient advocates' – who are sometimes advocates for themselves or for a small sub-group of patients with whom they identify, and are often unaware of the fate of other patients – should not escape scrutiny. In the scramble for resources, including the doctor's time and attention, one patient, or patient group, is often directly or indirectly the enemy of another patient or patient group. Free-ranging distrust of clinicians will be self-defeating: it will bring about the very untrustworthiness it complains of.

The enemies of progress must be identified even, or especially, when they come dressed in the clothes of reform. Those who prefer their own undigested and unreflected-upon experience to the well-founded views of experts could bring many things grinding to a halt. Denial of progress, the result of collective amnesia of the past, lack of proportion, a tendency to compare how things are with an unachievable ideal rather than how things were in the past, and to blame treatments and scientific medicine for the inhumanity of the illnesses the human body suffers from, will get in the way of rational thought about how things might be further improved. Such denial – which as well as being demoralizingly untrue, will, if unchallenged, take away any sense of direction – should be treated with history lessons, denominators, and instruction about the biological roots of the human person. Interminable reorganization of the way care is delivered in the NHS, which is time- and resource-consuming, costs lives, and saps the morale of those in the service, must be met with sustained opposition based upon informed scepticism of the justification given for it. Reorganization intended to conceal under-resourcing, or to subject those who deliver care to ever-tighter and burdensome regulation, must be exposed for what it is. Zero tolerance of error must not itself be tolerated as it will foster poor practice, with defensive medicine that will subject some patients to excessive investigation and treatment and deny others (the old, the frail) any treatment at all for fear of a bad outcome.

Perhaps the most serious obstacle to progress is one that I have not discussed, because it deserves more space than I can give it here: hostility to research. Animal rights activism, misapplication of the notion of human rights to 'protect' people against entering clinical trials, suspicion towards those who want to improve our present treatments or evaluate existing ones and an ever-thickening bitumen of bureaucracy will, if unchallenged, strangle the much-needed research effort. But this is the theme for another book.

Journalists and lawyers who misrepresent doctors' intentions should not go unchallenged. The task of trying to instil a sense of responsibility in all journalists, by making clear the consequences of unfair treatment of individuals in a position of responsibility, should not be shirked. We must, finally, acknowledge those who are prepared to take responsibility for the difficult decisions that have to be made when we fall seriously ill and who use their hard-won skills in making us better − often at the expense of their own ease and comfort and family life.

PART THREE

Destinations

Although the metaphysical roots of therapeutics lie several million years back, in the awakening of the hominid body to self-consciousness, the beginnings of a naturalistic understanding of illness are less than 3,000 years old. A truly scientific approach to understanding the ailing body began only 500 years ago. Fully fledged scientific therapeutics is less than a century old. Medicine is an absolute beginner and its progress hitherto has been astounding.

Grounds, one might think, for optimism. Many commentators, however, foresee a gloomy future for the quiet art. Roy Porter fears that medicine has run its course:

For centuries medicine was impotent and thus unproblematic. From the Greeks to the First World War, its tasks were simple: to grapple with lethal diseases and gross disabilities, to ensure live births and manage pain. It performed these with meagre success. Today, with 'mission accomplished', its triumphs are dissolving in disorientation.[1]

When as wise a historian as Porter expresses fears about the future of medicine, we are forced to take notice.

Is pessimism about current health trends in the developed world, where scientific medicine has encountered fewest obstacles, justified? On the basis of past and present performance there are many reasons to be cheerful. Whether things will continue to improve – and the future of medicine will be as remarkable as the past – will depend on the profession. Self-evidently, clinicians will be central in ensuring that advances in biomedical science translate into more effective treatments. The pressures I have described in previous chapters may reduce doctors to sessional functionaries – servile, self-interested and self-protecting. This is of the utmost concern, as a vision-free profession, delivering on contract according to printed directions, seems unlikely to lead medicine to the better future that science will make possible.

Some may also be disheartened by the thought that, whatever advances medicine makes, birth remains a one-way ticket to the grave and that, what's more, the two fundamental aims of reducing suffering from illness and postponing death may be in conflict. I do not believe the latter to be the case. It is possible, at least in principle, to define an achievable and desirable ultimate aim of medicine: to ensure a 'health span' that approximates very closely to the span of a long life.

Far from having run its course, medicine has clear, non-contradictory goals. Though it cannot, of course, prevent man-made and natural disasters, those goals are attainable if we have the collective will to bring them about and do not allow present discontents, based largely upon misunderstandings, to cloud our vision or disable its sense of its mission.

8

'Meagre Increments': the Supposed Failure of Success[1]

What an ignominious destiny if the future of medicine turns into bestowing meagre increments of unenjoyed life!

Roy Porter[2]

It hardly needs to be said that one of the fundamental aims of medicine – indeed, directly or indirectly, of much human endeavour – is to postpone death. One of the least surprising consequences of decreased mortality is that the population is ageing. Of course, the proportion of older people in a population is affected by factors other than survival: migration into and out of the country, changes in fertility. The latter has been dramatic, with the Victorian and Edwardian UK family of five to ten children being replaced by the late-twentieth-century family of one to two children. The increase in the number of elderly people relative to the population as a whole has therefore been significantly greater than the increase in their absolute numbers. While the population of England and Wales rose by 20 per cent in the second half of the twentieth century, the numbers of those between 0 and 4 years rose by only 9 per cent, while those over 80 rose by 240 per cent. These trends are set to continue, with the sharpest proportionate increases occurring in the oldest old. According to one estimate, between 1991 and 2031 we may anticipate an 8 per cent increase in people between 60 and 74, a 43 per cent increase in those aged between 75 and 84 and no less than a 138 per cent increase in those aged over 85. Already, middle-aged people in the USA have, on average, more living grandparents (yes, grandparents) than children.[3]

That the majority of people are enjoying a full lifespan is cause for rejoicing.[4] Between 1901 and 1999 deaths in 0–4 year-olds have fallen from 37 per cent to 0.8 per cent as a proportion of all deaths, while deaths over 75 in England and Wales have increased from 12 to 64 per cent.[5] Good news, one would have thought.

Many commentators, however, including some who are themselves old, see the ageing of the population as a near disaster. For over twenty-five years, there has been talk of 'the failures of the success' of medicine.[6] Foremost among these supposed failures is the belief that increased life expectancy is almost inevitably bought at the cost of an increased burden of disease. As Roy Porter has put it, the age of infectious diseases that resulted in premature death has given way to the age of chronic disorders: 'longer life means more time to be ill.'[7] More time to be ill, perhaps; but are people ill for a longer time?

There are many reasons for expecting that this might be so. First, most chronic disabling diseases have an almost exponential relationship to age: strokes, Parkinson's disease, dementia, osteoarthritis, chronic respiratory problems, cardiac disease all show this relationship. For example, the chances of being disabled from a stroke increase nearly a hundredfold between the ages of 45 and 85.[8] A study published by the Office of Population Censuses and Surveys (OPCS) in 1988 also confirmed this exponential relationship between chronic disability and increasing age.[9] Perhaps the most alarming fact in that study, given that the greatest proportionate increases in the population are anticipated in the over 75s, was that the curve flicked up sharply at around age 75.

The OPCS data refer to a population studied in the middle 1980s. Since then some surprising things have happened. First of all, what everyone knows has been officially acknowledged: the vast majority of people in later life enjoy excellent health or have health problems that are sufficiently under control not to be a barrier to the enjoyment of a reasonably full life. The consequence of this is that 'a fresh map of life'[10] has had to be drawn. Added years are *not* being bought only at the cost of added troubles: increased life expectancy does not amount to 'meagre increments of unenjoyed life'. The increments are far from meagre; and the evidence that they are enjoyed is getting stronger. Here are a few indicators of how things are going.

The General Household Survey has shown encouraging trends in disability in older people in the United Kingdom. For example, the proportion of men over 85 able to bathe, feed and get to the toilet without help rose from 69 per cent to 79 per cent between 1980 and 1991. The proportion of women rose even faster – from 64 per cent to 80 per cent. The proportion of years over 85 in which people were not significantly dependent on others rose between 1980 and 1991 from 69 per cent to 80 per cent for men and from 67 per cent to 82 per cent for women. The longer-term trends are even more impressive; for example the proportion of men over the age of 85 unable to dress, wash, walk around the house and get on and off the toilet without help fell from 45 per cent in 1976 to 18 per cent in 1994. This is particularly surprising, given that the population we are talking about is the 'oldest old' – those who are on the steepest part of the curve linking age and disability.

There are equally cheering data from America, where accountants have a firmer grip on the health of the nation through monitoring health care expenditure. Kenneth Manton's longitudinal studies have shown that not only is the population living longer but also that the prevalence of disability at each age is falling. Even more cheering is the finding that the rate at which the age-adjusted prevalence of disability and chronic ill-health in older people is falling is itself accelerating.[11] Particularly gratifying are the marked declines in age-adjusted risks of dementia, stroke and chronic heart disease.

Hospitalization is another marker of serious ill-health in old age. Here, too, the news is positive. Richard Himsworth[12] examined the number of days spent in hospital in the last fifteen years of their life by people who died at different ages. The total days of in-patient care for people who died at 90 was only about double that of people who died at 45; and there was hardly any difference when people who died in their seventies were compared with those who died in their nineties: the extra twenty years of life was not bought at the cost of a disproportionate increase in hospital care.

Findings on health care expenditure are equally encouraging. One study in the States found that the average Medicare spend for those who died at 70 was $35,000 compared with $65,000 for those who died at 100+. This looks worrying until one realizes that, since Medicare begins at 65, the average yearly expenditure is $7,000 for those who die at 70 compared with $1,800 for the centenarians.[13] The very long-lived get years of extra life more cheaply: in this, as in so many other things, there are economies of scale.

Moreover, the idea that resources are increasingly being squandered on futile attempts to keep people alive is unfounded. As Henry Shenkin has pointed out,[14] there is no evidence that medical care in the last year of life is becoming more aggressive, or more highly technological. The proportion of total Medicare dollars spent on individuals remained stable in the twelve-year period between 1976 and 1988, despite rapid technological advances; moreover, the payments in the last two months of life, proportionally, did not increase. In fact, only about 3 per cent of those Medicare beneficiaries who die incur the very high costs suggestive of aggressive care at life's end. Such increases as are incurred in health care expenditure in old age overall simply reflect the availability of new treatments, and the appropriate expectation of older people that they will benefit from them. While the total volume of need for health care has increased, age-specific health care requirements, like age-specific disability rates, have actually fallen and are continuing to fall.

The improved quality of life in old age goes beyond gross markers of health gains. Older people have access to more resources than their predecessors: more nutritious food, better housing, and more user-friendly technologies such as mobile phones and accessible alarms, and a variety of sources of home entertainment.[15] Yet these goods are still inequitably distributed; and individuals who have been socially deprived in earlier years will often be doubly jeopardized in old age, being more likely to be malnourished, underheated and subject to a variety of restrictions. The social gradients of health and life expectancy in Britain, and the key role of poverty in determining health, are now fully appreciated.[16] But for the majority of old people, life has never been so good.

The optimistic tone of the preceding paragraphs may provoke disbelief. Surely the longer people live, the more likely they will be 'a burden' or (more politely) 'a challenge' to themselves, to their friends and relatives who find themselves transformed into (willing or unwilling) carers, to medical and social services and to the economy as a whole? Do not old people cost money, time, effort, patience – and all in aid of sustaining them through 'meagre increments of unenjoyed life'? Do we not read daily of the burden placed on society by old people: hospitals overrun by gravely ill octogenarians, who survive their five days' wait on a trolley in Casualty, only to have dreadful experiences in hospital and be readmitted again and again; harrowing tales of carers crushed by the demands of caring; panic in the Treasury as health and social care budgets spiral out of control?

The dissociation between the public perception of old age and the reality of life as an old person is arresting, given that the majority of old people are in good health and enjoying a quality and style of life that their predecessors (at any age) would have found unimaginable. The amount of time that older people spend waiting in A & E departments on hospital trolleys is of course outrageous and if it makes government ministers uncomfortable, this may be no bad thing. But it is a tip to which an iceberg of the wrong size is attached.

The number of old people on trolleys in hospitals is a not a marker of the underlying health of the older population. It is not even a measure of the demands (or the per capita demands) made by older people on health care services. At best it reflects the discrepancy between the need for one sort of health care and the capacity to meet that need. The pressure on hospitals, felt particularly acutely in A & E departments, is less a reflection of the deteriorating health of an ageing population than of a rising expectation of care (i.e. of good health) and the increasing ways that are available to meet those expectations. The failure to meet that expectation is almost wholly due to the decimation of hospital beds over the last few decades. At any rate, it tells us nothing about what being old is like and less than nothing about what it might be like in future.

Porter's characterization of medicine as having 'accomplished its mission' is way off target. We still have many unrealized opportunities for applying basic scientific understanding to new ways of preventing, postponing and treating diseases (in particular those that contribute hugely to ill-health in old age); and in making sure that those new technologies (some of them very simple) are universally available to people who want them.

As everyone knows, health throughout life can be improved by simple 'lifestyle' measures: increased exercise, weight control, drinking in moderation, and not smoking. There is now an understanding of how healthy activities can be promoted. For example, whether or not older people take exercise is less dependent on the impulse to undertake it than on the presence or absence of barriers to doing so and on a sense of self-worth and the control they have over their health.[17] (Older people who feel unwelcome, or out of place, in a gym that is anyway difficult to access, may be discouraged from regularly working out.) The beneficial effects of something as simple as moderate exercise on cardio-respiratory reserve, muscle and bone strength, balance, mental function and self-confidence are astonishing, and they extend even to frail individuals in extreme old age.[18] Elderly cohorts of the (medium-term) future will be better educated than their predecessors and there is plenty of evidence that better educated populations tend to be more amenable to public health messages.

There are even more unrealized benefits for people who have risk factors for various chronic disabling diseases. The commonest cause of severe disability in old age is stroke. We now know how to prevent over 50 per cent of strokes, by measures such as controlling high blood pressure, adequately treating high blood sugar and raised cholesterol, giving aspirin for people at high risk and anticoagulants for people with certain cardiac arrhythmias. Unfortunately, very many who could benefit from such treatment are untreated. Again and again, researchers find that the 'rule of halves' applies: half of those who have the risk factor (such as high blood pressure) are not aware of it; half of those in whom it is detected are not treated; and half of those who are treated are not treated adequately. Even here the news, in the UK at least, is good. In the one of the few policy developments that responded to medical advice, there are now ambitious and promising preventive medicine initiatives built into National Service Frameworks.[19] These will help more people to reduce their risks of stroke and other major threats to quality of life. It is not unreasonable to anticipate a major decline in the incidence of strokes and indeed a reduction of the severity of other conditions, such as Alzheimer's disease, which are made worse by them. Similar strategies will make inroads into the prevalence of other chronic disabling diseases, such as coronary heart disease. Universal availability of a 'polypill' combining blood pressure medications, aspirin, folic acid and fat-lowering drugs – all in modest enough quantities to cause few side effects – could reduce heart attacks as well as stroke by 80 per cent.[20] About a third of those who took the polypill would benefit, gaining on average about eleven years of life free from stroke and heart attack.[21]

We may be equally optimistic about improvement in the treatment of illnesses that are currently unpreventable. New strategies for conditions such as Parkinson's disease and Alzheimer's disease will come from a deeper understanding of the underlying mechanisms. Treatments which address the end-stage of a long series of pathological processes, such as the use of cholinesterase inhibitors for Alzheimer's dementia, which already affords modest but worthwhile gains, will be supplanted by much more potent treatments that address the problem further up the causal chain. More precise diagnosis and sub-typing of conditions will enable tailored treatments to be given earlier in the course of the disease before secondary adverse events take place.

Even if some new treatments do not materialize (and there have been many disappointments, particularly in the area of repairing neurological damage, such as occurs chronically in multiple sclerosis and acutely in stroke), there are still huge gains to be made from optimizing treatments that are already available. There have been numerous studies showing that older patients are often given inappropriate (and not infrequently contraindicated or adversely interacting) drugs, sometimes in wrong doses.[22] Often when the correct drugs are prescribed in appropriate doses, they are not taken because of a lack of concordance of views between doctor and patient. The new science of pharmacogenomics, using genetic profiling to tailor treatment to the individual rather than to the disease alone, will increase the number of people able to benefit from treatments and reduce the number of nasty surprises from hitherto unpredicted adverse effects. Gentler, more sophisticated health technologies for both diagnosis and treatment, suitable for older and frailer people, are also already available. For example, miraculously accurate scans rather than 'open up and see' surgery for diagnosis and minimal access surgery using laparoscopic techniques are already extending the range of people who can benefit from treatment.

Just how much can still be achieved is illustrated by the social gradients in health and life expectancy: in the UK in the 1990s the life expectancy of a working-class male was on average five years less than that of a (biologically very similar) male doing a professional or clerical job. There is much slack to be taken up.

On the other side of the coin, there is evidence that older people are sometimes denied treatments – supposedly on the grounds that they cannot benefit from them or that the benefits are outweighed by the risks – simply on the basis of age. 'Age changes and age infirmities', Wingate Todd wrote, 'are so interwoven that it is not easy to separate the former from the latter.' This is dangerously true. A slipshod doctor, presented with an old lady suffering from aches and pains, or shortness of breath, or difficulty with memory, is tempted to collude with the general lay perception and pronounce 'It's your age, dear' rather than diagnose osteoarthritis, cardiac failure or the adverse effects of medication. Inadequate care is seemingly expedient, because it is superficially cheaper to pronounce a problem untreatable, on the basis of an inexpensive glance at the patient's date of birth, than to investigate and treat it. Yet the cost of early treatment, which may prevent or postpone disability, may be less than the cost of long-term social support at home or in residential care.

The temptation to regard the diseases that come with age as part of 'the ageing process' is understandable given that increasing age is associated with greater burden of disease. There is a crucial, but difficult, distinction here, however. Interestingly, the confusion occurs less readily in the case of rich patients, who will pay more to have specific diseases diagnosed and treated rather than be pronounced untreatably old. It was no coincidence that one of the oldest people in the United Kingdom to receive a total hip replacement (for a fractured neck of femur) in the 1990s was the Queen Mother. Sometimes, it is genuinely difficult to separate an informed and wise clinical judgement that aggressive treatment may be inappropriate (where, for example, background ill-health from concurrent conditions may make an invasive procedure dangerous) from clinical prejudice (the assumption that age automatically reduces the likelihood of benefit). It is equally difficult to separate clinical prejudice from the ageist position that older people are less deserving of expensive care than younger patients.

Even where the underlying biology of a disabling chronic disease cannot be addressed, there is now increasing understanding of the extent to which recovery is possible, given the right environment and the right inputs. This is particularly true of diseases that cause damage to the brain, possibly the single greatest scourge of old age. New techniques have shown how the 'soft-wired' nervous system is able to reorganize on a microscopic and macroscopic scale, to bring about dramatic improvements, and how those improvements may be promoted.[23] Other techniques, such as the use of stem cells and synthetic equivalents of the factors that make nerves grow, are, after many years of disappointment, looking increasingly likely to deliver within the next decade.[24]

There are other favourable trends, too. Because of better nutrition, health and safety at work, and education, people are entering old age in generally better health. There is therefore more capacity to withstand disease when it strikes. There are progressive improvements in intra-uterine health, which is recognized as one of the major determinants of illness in later life. The wider availability of labour-saving devices, of communications systems and user-friendly efficient methods of domes-tic heating and lighting, will make it less likely that impairments will translate into frustrating disability and dependency. A progressive improvement in the quality of old age, in which the health span of a long life approximates the lifespan ever more closely, is feasible. Why, therefore, does public opinion remain resolutely gloomy about the present and doom-laden about the future?

Of course no one wants to grow old and the price of a long life is that one should spend a considerable amount of it in a state in which one is viewed, and views oneself, as 'old'. Even in a society that values older people for their wisdom, those old people are faced with the knowledge that they have less time to live. Cicero cites four reasons in *De Senectute* 'for the apparent misery of old age': 'first it withdraws us from active accomplishment; second it renders the body less powerful; third, it deprives us of almost all forms of enjoyment; fourth, it stands not far from death.' While the first three may no longer be necessary accompaniments of advancing years, the fourth is inescapable; indeed, we may define ageing as the sum of those intrinsic processes in the organism that lead to increased probability of death from natural causes.

Thus defined, ageing starts younger than we think: it begins in our early teens and is continuous thereafter. To avoid ageing, one would have to die at about thirteen, after which mortality rises inexorably.[25] To grow old, as Simone de Beauvoir said, 'is to define oneself' and being defined is privative as well as positive. The ascent to seniority prunes possibility: the old are what they are and, to a lesser extent, what they have been, though past achievements rarely compensate: they belong to the past. Even for those who have had successful lives, the accumulation of experience, connections and possessions may seem an inner obesity rather than an increase of spiritual substance, and the many-paged CV a mere waste product, when the future is looking more explicitly finite than it did at earlier stages in one's life. No wonder we prefer to think of ageing as a problem (with the implication of solubility) rather than as the common and permanent condition of humanity.

Against this, Peter Laslett has argued that 'the passage of time should not be looked upon as the enemy of hope, for life is what you make of it.'[26] Ageing, far from being a problem, is a solution: it enables a long life to be possible without the penalty of a protracted period of decline, so that medicine can deliver on its twin aims of postponing death and reducing the burden of misery due to ill-health.[27] The view that added years have been, and will be, bought only at the cost of added woe, while at odds with the facts, is entirely concordant with prior expectation and the sense of how things should be. The most obvious conclusion to be drawn from the demographic revolution – that we should be rethinking our sense of the course of life – has to combat ingrained prejudice. The notion of the Third Age as a period of health, often as long as childhood plus adolescence, free of the anxieties of child care and the pressures of work, is still not fully accepted.[28]

While biological processes are at the root of ageing, they take place in economic, political and cultural contexts: a significant component of the state of being old is socially constructed rather than biologically determined. It is others, with their attitudes, stereotypes and laws, who translate wrinkles into incompetence, unattractiveness and, ultimately, evidence of valuelessness. The privileged status accorded to children is inversely mirrored in the underprivileged status of the old. The pioneering geriatrician Nascher pointed out that 'the idea of economic worthlessness instils a spirit of irritability if not positive enmity against the helplessness of the aged.'[29] This spirit is expressed in all sorts of ways; for example, finding the hell of dementia funny and describing its sufferers as 'ga-ga'.

Readers will recall Liz Kendall's article describing how she 'fell foul of the NHS'. Its inadvertent messages have been a rich resource for this book.[30] When she tells us of her visit to her GP, we are able to see everyday ageism at work. She looks around the waiting room at the people who are holding her up by being in the same queue as herself. She wonders what is wrong with them:

There was the usual smattering of coughs, colds and sniffles, mothers trying to keep their children under control and a pensioner with a bandaged knee.

She finds it difficult to imagine that a 'pensioner' (an individual defined by his economic status as a non-producing consumer) can have anything serious enough to justify blocking her own access to the GP:

I suspected many people were there less because of ill-health and more because they were lonely or struggling to make ends meet.

She should, of course, be aware that the chances of having an illness warranting medical attention increases, rather than decreases, with age. Perhaps she is; but this is not the same as accepting that the person who has it also warrants such attention.

That the prejudices of those who, like Ms Kendall, populate the think tanks that have played such a prominent role over the last two decades,[31] are liable to turn into policies, does not augur well for older people. Some recent documents emanating from the government have been spattered with anti-ageist rhetoric (no one thinks of himself or herself as ageist) while being loaded with ageist policies. The National Service Framework for Older People is a case in point. It contains specific targets for limiting the numbers of older people entering acute hospitals, on the very dubious grounds that many of them should not have been there in the first place.[32] Those of us who protested[33] were reassured that this was not meant to deny older people care but to give them care in a more appropriate and user-friendly setting. These reassurances have proved to be empty, as recent evidence has shown: older people are increasingly denied access to specialist in-patient care when they fall acutely ill.[34] Many have argued that people in great old age have a lesser entitlement to health care than younger people because they have had 'a fair innings', irrespective of the health gains that might be made available to them or of the fact that they have made the greatest contribution both socially and financially.

There is an even greater crime than being helpless and useless when one is old, and that is failing to withdraw from positions of influence and productivity. The old are seen as ageing trunks blocking the sunlight from young saplings. Of course, the rich and powerful can resist socially constructed ageing: politicians can be young at seventy-five, while lesser workers were (until recent concerns about the burden of pensions) were commonly made redundant at fifty-five. It is assumed that, as one gets older, one will become more incompetent at the highest level – if not paralysed, at any rate foolish. Madness and old age are conflated in the ghastly portmanteau term 'senile'. Alzheimer's disease is regarded simply as an extreme version of anecdotage in which the scripts, anyway boring and irrelevant, have become yet more mangled.

Even those who do not wish to marginalize older people may be anxious about the costs of keeping them healthy enough in order to be active and productive. After all, health improvements do not happen spontaneously: resources will be needed to ensure that the improved health of older people more than offsets their increasing numbers. Where will these resources come from, especially since it is predicted that by 2040 there will be only two people of working age for every pensioner? According to the most recent statistics, the next thirty years in the UK will see a large rise in the dependency ratio (children under fifteen and older people over 65 per hundred of working age) from the current level of 52 to 63.[35]

As soon as one challenges the assumption built into the statistics that people over 65 are (necessarily) 'dependent', the question answers itself. And it does so even if one does not take into account the increase in unit productivity in the population as a whole, and the fact that healthy older people will have less need for chronic care. The age of retirement, after all, is socially not biologically determined. Adjustment of the age of retirement in line with average life expectancy could solve the 'economic crisis'. As Kenneth Manton has pointed out:

Each year of increase in the normal retirement age for Social Security has a large fiscal impact. Thus, if the normal retirement age could be increased to age 70 or 72 – because the physiological status now at those ages is equivalent to the physiological status at age 65 in, say, 1982 – then a large portion of the fiscal burden of population ageing could be addressed.[36]

One area in which it is difficult to reap economies of scale is personal social services, and hands-on caring. Increasing involvement of older adults in this area may, however, be entirely appropriate. At present, such care is often provided by young people who have little alternative opportunities for employment and who, out of inexperience, or resentment, may sometimes be poor carers. At any rate, the solution to the economic problems of an ageing population, being largely self-inflicted because of the assumption of non-productivity in old age, lies within our own hands.

Since all of this is pretty obvious, something must be getting in the way of straight thinking. Is doom and gloom about the increasing numbers of older people more the result of prejudice against the state of being old, which makes younger people not only expect old age to be littered with disasters but considers it proper that it should be so? There are reasons for thinking this might be the case.

For most of the population, the old, in particular the very old, are 'other'. Everyone either is, or has been, young. We have known the condition from the inside. In contrast, no one 'has been' old in the past tense. And the policy-makers and the most influential voices in society tend to be below pensionable age. Older people are, therefore, ripe targets for stereotyping in public discourse. This may underpin a resentment that goes even deeper than concern about any actual burden elderly people may place upon the young and questions the very point of an old person. If older people are not ill all or most of the time, perhaps they should be, as befits their station in the ante-room of extinction. A perfectly fit ninety-five-year-old, who enjoys travelling around the world, may awaken a certain amount of intergenerational envy: such happy continuation is unseemly, she has had her share of life and the fruits of the earth; she is not merely 'hanging on' but a hanger-on. This kind of prejudice is behind the brutal and contradictory utilitarianism of the 'fair innings' argument, which is still being used to underpin ageism in access to health care. (I say 'contradictory' because it is rarely applied consistently: there are different definitions of a fair innings for the rich and powerful compared with the poor and powerless; the tiaraed member of the Royal Family compared with the pensioner with the bandage on his knee.)

Perhaps there is a yet deeper basis for this: a sense of the pointlessness of 'just continuing' year after year. Being old underlines the ultimate futility of existence in two ways: the old are a reminder of our own mortality; but they are also living on beyond the motivating forces that both drive and sustain us for most of our lives. Living beyond career and child care, beyond the promises of a future self that is better, and better off, than the present self, old people are stripped of the standard narratives of development and progression. The trajectory of life has flattened, and this can seem like preparation for the terminal drop; a period of treading water between the end of aspiration and the beginning of expiration. But human beings, however, invent their own meanings, and there is no reason why, as at any stage in life, there should not be new narratives beyond those dictated by biology or economic necessity.

In conclusion, if we are to think rationally about the demographic revolution, we must acknowledge all these anxieties, and recognize, too, that old age is potentially the time when our ability to create meanings is least tethered to external constraints. Survival in good health in old age offers the possibility of a new kind of life beyond the traditional, sometimes unchosen narratives of ambition, development and personal advancement and the biological imperatives of survival, reproduction and child-rearing.

This has yet to be widely appreciated. Peter Laslett, profoundest of social gerontologists, has pointed out that 'nearly all the attitudes and institutions appropriate to an era of transformed age relationships have yet to come into being.'[37] Fostering these attitudes may be in the present interest, as well as the future interest, of the not-yet-old. As Grimley Evans has argued, far from being 'a social incubus the new caste of older people freed from the tangling nets of employment and patronage could be the grey guardians of all our freedoms'.[38] Those who have no hope or expectation of preferment may be more willing to speak out.

Until we learn to think a little more deeply on what being old means in terms of human potential, there is the danger that a long life and a healthy old age will not even seem worth striving for. It may be an appropriate time to ask the shocking and liberating question: What is the point of being old?

If the story of medicine so far is 'the failure of success', one could wish human affairs had many more such failures.[39]

9

The End of Medicine as a Profession?

If I had to identify an overriding reason for writing this book, it is my fear that medicine may be reaching the end of its course as a profession. It is not the only profession under threat.[1] Teaching, nursing and the law[2] are all, for various reasons, losing their distinctive characteristics, those very things for which they have traditionally been valued. No profession is an island: they all interact closely and the decline of one will hasten the decline of the others.

What distinguishes a profession from a business or a trade, perfectly honourable though the latter may be? Professions are associated with an expertise based upon a body of knowledge and a set of skills refined through experience and a deeper form of common sense and nous. But this is also true of many trades that have contributed to the well-being of society but are not counted as professions. There are other things, inseparable from the moral character of the practitioner: honesty, reliability, beneficence, a sense of personal responsibility, integrity and independence. These qualities are depended upon by a patient seeking help with matters that are deeply personal and of the utmost seriousness. Whatever it is that makes doctors competent has to be supplemented by the things that makes them caring: it is not just a matter of providing items of service against a contract, a costed menu.

Professions are associated with a 'calling'. There is a variety of more or less common features to found in someone who has a calling: going the extra mile (beyond the printed directions, or indeed anything that could be defined contractually); not being in too much of a rush to get home and being willing to be available out of hours in a way that is unconnected with remuneration; genuine compassion; an imaginativeness in thinking about ways of caring for people that could only come from really wanting to help as opposed to merely delivering on contract; and a willingness to carry the burden of worry and the personal risk that comes from taking responsibility. Underpinning all of these characteristics is an accountability to conscience that goes beyond strict legal liability and the duty of care defined by one's job description. It cannot be captured in the number of reimbursable or remunerable activities one engages in; it goes beyond 'accountantability' (sic). A person who has a calling is driven by the desire to make things, and people, better.

Such virtues are not, of course, confined to professionals. I know many home helps and other paid carers who work beyond their contracted hours and help their clients in ways that go far beyond the confines of their job descriptions. But these virtues seem intrinsic to, rather than incidental to, a calling. The cynic may say that 'going the extra mile', 'doing explicit good', are luxuries one can afford if one's work is not merely a means to survival, and one is not working all hours simply to make ends meet. That is true. It is equally true that the sense of calling, even in the most committed professional, will inevitably be intermittent. Sometimes one wants to change the world and sometimes one just wants to get to the end of a day's work. This is simply human: it would be unreasonable to expect professionals always to be inspired by their job and constantly gnawed by the desire to do it better. It is necessary, however, that the sense of calling should be felt from time to time and that the drama, the privilege, the challenge of medicine should be at least implicit at other times.

Many commentators have observed how character – as opposed to technical skill – is underplayed in the discussion of the medical profession. 'The virtuous doctor' will go the extra mile, 'beyond obligation even to self-sacrifice'.[3] The exercise of judgement is another key element of professionalism and is also linked with character: if one lacks integrity, one will avoid the responsibility that comes from the exercise of judgement. True professionals may quite properly exercise their judgement in two connected ways: they may deviate from the script if the printed directions do not seem to them to fit their patient; and they do not simply present patients with a range of options and ask them to choose. To do so is not to eschew paternalism but to abdicate responsibility. A sense of personal responsibility for what happens to the patient, which goes beyond anything that can be written down in a job description, lies at the heart of medicine. It makes the physician the patient's advocate, fighting on his or her behalf for what he or she wants. It is an equal part of responsibility sometimes to give patients advice they may not want.

The right to self-regulation is one of the distinguishing features of a profession and is of the greatest significance because it reflects the trust invested in it by society at large. Individual practitioners can be trusted with unsupervised responsibility because they have a well-developed sense of internal accountability. According to John Bunker, self-regulation, in part justifed by the profession's unique body of knowledge and skills, gives the profession as a whole authority 'to determine the qualifications and numbers of those trained for practice', 'the terms, conditions and goals of practice itself' and 'the ethical and technical criteria by which… practices are evaluated' and confers 'the exclusive right to exercise discipline over their members'.[4] To this, Bunker says, 'there should be added the right to a major but not unique authority over and responsibility for the organization and delivery of services'.[5]

At the heart of a profession, then, is a justifiable autonomy expressed in self-regulation and in having a say in the mode of delivery of care. This is the compliment that society pays to the professions it trusts and values. It is this that is under threat and, as I shall argue, if this goes, much else will go along with it and the world for sick people will be a much colder and less safe place.

I have no doubt that we shall have at least as many physicians in 2020 as we have now. Quite likely we shall have many more, as gains in unit productivity free up a greater proportion of the national wealth for health care. Will those physicians be professionals in the way we understand the term at present? Will they have the same values? Or will medicine have become a business, its practitioners tradesmen, and health care just another service industry?[6] There are reasons for thinking that this may be the case, perhaps the most important is a loss of standing.

To some extent doctors have only themselves to blame: they have become victims of their own honesty. When doctors started entering patients in clinical trials run by other people and used the outcomes of such trials to guide their own practice, they colluded in the erosion of their personal authority. As they have become more committed to looking critically at their practices and outcomes – through audit, peer review, benchmarking, formal clinical trials (that are sensitive to outcomes, including adverse effects, that matter to patients), overviews and meta-analyses that put individual clinical trials in perspective – the public has become increasingly aware of the fallibility of medicine and, ironically, less aware of the benefits that are, in fact, immeasurably greater than they have ever been.

Paradoxically, the increased presence of technology in medicine has also contributed to the decline of authority. Technology is no individual practitioner's intellectual property. Whereas a diagnosis I make using my clinical acumen is somehow my own, the one that I read from a report manifestly is not my own. Moreover, the multiplicity of technologies means that diagnoses and treatments are distributed through very large numbers of people working with varying degrees of success in loose associations or teams. The guardian of a particular technology, such as a CT scanner, is likely to be seen 'merely' as a technician.

This is to overlook the role of clinical acumen even in present hi-tech medicine. It requires a good deal of knowledge, experience and good sense to arrive at possible diagnoses and even more nous to put them in perspective. I often remind medical students that anyone can arrive at a diagnosis – hypochondriacs do it on an hourly basis. The art of medicine is to entertain diagnostic possibilities and order them according to a well-informed sense of probability, based upon general knowledge and careful observation. When the CT brain scan was first introduced in the 1970s, it was hailed as 'the automatic neurologist', that made diagnosis on the basis of clinical observation and judgement a thing of the past. This euphoria was short-lived when neurologists were increasingly being referred patients with problems such as 'CT-negative' headache. Knowing what to do when the tests are negative or inconclusive, and not being misled by positive test results, require as much clinical skill as did making diagnoses in the absence of sophisticated tests in earlier times. This is overlooked and the public view tends to be that diagnostic and treatment decisions can somehow be taken off the shelf. The personal contribution of doctors is unfortunately visible only when they are in error.

Because the body of collective knowledge to which doctors have ceded personal authority is sometimes fallible, and certainly incomplete, especially in its application to individual cases, much of medicine consists of dealing with, or dealing in, uncertainty – which may be 'well-informed'.[7] What the patient brings to the decision-making process is personal preference and, sometimes, knowledge of his or her own previous experience of treatment. The doctor brings the body of objective knowledge and accumulative experience of treating many patients – which, of course, encompasses the experience of patients themselves. This asymmetry is healthy and justifies the doctor's salary and authority. For some, however, because the doctor cannot be 100 per cent certain in any individual case whether there will be a balance of benefit, the greater knowledge of the doctor is seen to be unfounded and his or her authority regarded as illegitimate. The end of 'Doctor knows best', widely proclaimed in the media in the wake of the Kennedy Report on Bristol, combined with a general resistance to trusting professionals, has modulated into 'Doctor doesn't even know better'.

The patient as client or customer in the shopping mall of medical care will see the doctor as a vendor rather than as a professional. There will be an increasing emphasis on the accoutrements that make the first experience, or the first encounter, customer-friendly. The key to the doctor-as-salesman will be the emphasis on those aspects of customer care that give the patient the feeling of 'empowerment' – only weakly correlated with the actual empowerment that comes from effective evidence-based medicine. The almost robotic standardization of the way doctors are taught to interact with patients – even down to when doctors should move from open to closed questions, when and how often they should use techniques to indicate they are listening, and the bodily posture that should be adopted – will make the professional, with a deep compassion and the ability to make and stick by difficult unpopular advice, an ever-rarer bird. The doctors of the future will be easy-going and friendly conformists, relentlessly reasonable and entirely clubbable. This is not exactly reassuring because, as George Bernard Shaw said, 'The reasonable man adapts himself to the world; the unreasonable one persists in trying to adapt the world to himself. Therefore all progress depends upon the unreasonable man.'[8]

The doctor who willingly gives up authority and who is able without thinking to assume the relaxed user-friendly mode of automated openness and the postures of 'caringness' may well do so out of less than noble motives. A disinclination to contradict a patient (or a patient's advocate) may have less to do with the patient's welfare than with the doctor's. Grotesquely, this may extend to the very point of death. In an earlier chapter I referred to a recent study in America that found that the decision to carry out cardio-pulmonary resuscitation was often made in the knowledge that it would be futile, by physicians who wanted to avoid litigation or criticism.[9] In a consumer-led society, with a high level of distrust in the professions and a hostility to authority, I can testify to the power of the opprobrium of a patient's relatives to force one down a track that is at odds with one's sense of the right thing to do. This will become more common if doctors, too, are consumers and import consumerist values into their work.

We reflect the values of the society in which we have grown up. Doctors reared in a consumerist society will be consumers too. This is already being reflected in an expressed unwillingness to work long hours and, in particular, to do the unpaid work that earlier generations accepted as the norm.

When, in 2002, hospital consultants rejected the new contract offered by the Department of Health, there was an interesting difference between the reasons given by younger doctors and those given by older doctors. The latter did not want clinical priorities in their work to be subordinated to political priorities; the former were worried about the incorporation of anti-social hours into the normal working week. They did not want to follow in the path of their seniors and demanded 'a better work–life balance'. This in part reflected the (long overdue and greatly to be welcomed) feminization of the profession, in that rightly or wrongly, women still carry the greater burden of child-rearing. What is more, they and their children expect to spend more 'quality' time together: it is no longer acceptable for middle-class children to be fitted around the busy working lives of their parents. But it is not only women who want a life outside of medicine. An increasing proportion of male doctors are planning to work part-time. The very emphasis on 'feely-touchy' values in medicine will encourage the new generation of doctors to value them in their own relationships and their lives. A doctor who cultivates sensitivity to others' feelings at work may find it more difficult to be absent from birthday parties, school football matches and domestic crises.[10]

Many, perhaps most, of those who worked in the NHS in the decades following its establishment, assumed that their job would be a way of life: it was going to be hard, rarely fun and sometimes sheer grind. It was, however, serious and deeply worthwhile. This was what a calling was about. The notion of work as 'creative fun' had not yet taken hold in the collective consciousness. Doctors in the 1950s found working all hours an improvement on war-time service – working all hours and being shot at. The notion of a 'life–work balance' had not entered their vocabulary.

Since then, social attitudes have changed dramatically. One could grossly over-simplify the sequence of events by dividing the changes into two phases: the 1960s and 1970s said it was perfectly OK to be selfish; Thatcher's children in the 1980s learned that it was almost a responsibility to be selfish. A more recent generation, perhaps, has built on this with the notion that it is more important to be cool and successful than to be truly useful and to help people in grave need. The tabloidization of the national consciousness has inculcated an ethos which accepts as role models empty characters in whom surface is more important than substance. Of course, this is a great over-simplification and overlooks some of the healthier trends: the exposure of well-heeled hypocrisy preaching the virtues of self-sacrifice and service to those who serve their interests; the challenging of illegitimate authority; a culture of openness and accountability. Even so, it seems that the emergent social ethos is hardly compatible with a life of caring for and worrying over others, especially in public service where it may be rewarded by low status, continuing criticism and the possibility of public execration.[11]

Societies get the doctors they deserve and an aggressively consumerist society will breed defensive consumerist physicians. John Saunders has pointed out that:

As the practice of medicine becomes more like just another industry, it is easy to narrow the concept of service to that of personal convenience. Too many patients suffer because doctors are unwilling to work beyond contracted hours.[12]

This unwillingness is becoming more evident. (I am aware that seniors have always doubted the commitment of their juniors. My own consultant was unimpressed by my alternate nights off duty when I was a 104-hour-a-week houseman.) Even so, given wider social trends, it would be astonishing if those coming into medicine were as willing as previous generations to tolerate the stresses of medicine, its many worries, its sometimes distasteful aspects.

It is often forgotten how distasteful much of medicine is. What is frequently represented as an enjoyable exercise of power is often a triumph of humanity or objectivity over repulsion. Moreover, for much of their time, doctors are dealing with people who are at their least engaging, or even articulate; the 300,000 consultations that comprise the life of an average GP, the 3,000 highly pressured ward rounds and equal numbers of out-patient clinics of a consultant's life, would – leaving aside the nagging anxieties and the moments of terror – be tedious to those who expect conventionally 'interesting' lives. And this is hardly alleviated by the increasing burden of documentation that contemporary practice requires. Without a sense of service, a concern for human suffering, a compassion that can withstand all the frustrations, upsets, irritations and shocks of an ordinary working day in medicine, it would be intolerable – and would not be tolerated.[13]

At the same time, intolerant consumers with their rising expectations judge doctors ever more severely. A recent issue of the *British Medical Journal*[14] was devoted to the qualities necessary to make a good doctor. It compiled a daunting list of virtues: not only competence in every department, but also listening skills, an ability to tune into every spoken and unspoken worry, and to be caring and compassionate, to have tireless commitment, infinite willingness to learn from mistakes, an ability to take criticism, integrity, decisiveness, cultural sensitivity, tolerance and so on.

Since few people are likely to have all of these characteristics all the time, one can imagine doctors having to be ever-more accomplished actors, concealing behind a mask of 'communication skills' and the rhetoric of 'holistic care' a heart of stone. The imperative to exhibit how much one cares, to mobilize the external markers of caringness, is ignored at one's peril. Evidence from the United States suggests that over 90 per cent of medical litigation 'is prompted by the patient's perception that the doctor did not care about them'.[15] Expectation of a more satisfying and personal attention from physicians in the face of an ever-more contractual and impersonal medical system will make huge demands upon doctors' powers of simulation. The same regulatory bodies which distrust doctors to behave decently and humanly – and assume that in the absence of such regulations, and ever-tighter guidance backed up with increasingly stark threats, they will regress to an inhuman unworthiness – also expect them to be superhumanly selfless.

I am not alone in worrying whether we shall attract to the profession in the future those who had the professional values that fuelled the progress of the past. Adrian Bull (of PPP Healthcare plc) has this to say:

There are still places all through the NHS where, because of the strong sense of vocation and commitment of individuals, beacons of excellence shine all over the place, but that is down to vocationalism. As we see the rise in consumerism, one of the problems is the fall in the vocationalism. People no longer go into the professions out of a sense of public service duty and vocation; they go in because it is another career option, and so we have lost that balance.[16]

There could be no clearer example of the contradiction between rising expectation of the virtues of doctors (respect, true caring, empathy) and the decline of altruism in the society from which doctors are recruited than the challenge, issued to the medical leaders at a summit meeting organized to consider 'the profession's core values', by Sir Maurice Shock, former rector of Lincoln College, Oxford. The medical profession, he asserted, needed to recognize that society is changing: 'gone is "the social contract" and the "rights of man"; instead we have the "sales contract" and the "rights of the consumer".'[17]

A medical encounter governed by the 'sales contract' and the 'rights of the consumer' doesn't seem to fit with patients' wishes for a doctor who cares, who is compassionate and empathetic. Compassion and empathy are hardly what one expects in a garage or a supermarket. If what Shock says is true, then doctors, themselves drawn from a narrowly contractual, consumerist society, and who presumably share its general view of what the medical profession is, will have to straddle two value systems. They can do this only by developing an expertise in feigning the values of the past (still expected of the doctor) while acting in accordance with the new values that shape the expectations of the present. The non-technical aspects of the relationship between patient and doctor will be a meeting of the naked consumerism of the patient and the consumerism of the doctor concealed under a thick carapace woven out of the verbal (and, it mustn't be forgotten, non-verbal) signals of 'caring for the person beneath the consumer'.

Such deception will be necessary to conceal how far medicine has progressed in its journey from a calling to a business, and to what extent doctors are preoccupied with making a sale on behalf of the Health Maintenance Organization (HMO) or working to meet the targets that will determine their managers' well-being and hence their own. Meanwhile, the patient-as-customer will feel free to criticize the doctor for those little things that annoy customers, such as being kept waiting for five minutes past the appointed time.[18] This will further reinforce the doctor's sense of medicine as a business, a service industry, rather than as a calling, a response to human vulnerability.

The more ill the patient is, of course, the less satisfactory a business relationship will be. The less ill, however, are more numerous, more easily angered at the interruption to their lives, and more vocal. It is they who will have the most influence on changing the character of medicine into a set of ever-more shallow transactions divorced from awareness of human suffering. But the seriously ill will find that 'Have a nice day' does not easily modulate into 'Have a nice death'. Dying, terrified, depressed patients will not get the doctors they need because a society whose overriding values are consumerist will not produce them.

Consumerism in patients who see the doctor as addressing their customer rights, and in cynical self-protecting doctors who want a life but do not want to antagonize their customers, will push the profession from a calling to a business. To lament this is not to question the value of business: without business there would be no health service, no drugs to prescribe, no diagnostic tools, nothing. As the son of a scrupulous businessman who underwent considerable personal sacrifice to put me through medical school, it would ill-behove me to be sniffy about business. Nevertheless, there remains a difference between a calling and a business: a calling you enter for what you can put into it; a business for what you can get out of it, though this does not preclude taking pride in the quality of one's work. A profession is somewhere between the two: to it you bring a passion to help others informed by a trained intelligence; and out of it you get a good salary and status.

The move from the calling to the business end of the professional spectrum may in some cases be desirable. One has only to think of examples of great healers who were driven by a sense of calling – and made the lives of their patients and of those who worked with them hell – to worry about 'our terrible notions of duty'.[19] Mother Teresa ran a chain of appallingly managed institutions, putatively for the dying. Despite attracting huge funding and enjoying world-wide fame, they were badly equipped and patients were treated very poorly indeed. Her vanity, inseparable from her highly publicized sense of having been called by God, did not require her to learn anything about evidence-based medicine – with horrific consequences for the dying, and many who should not have died. Nor did she encourage such approaches in the nuns who staffed the homes.[20] The divergence between high standards of medical care and a sense of being called to serve the sick is illustrated by the work of another megalomaniacal self-publicist, Albert Schweitzer. The nuns working in his leper colonies bitterly resented the discovery of Dapsone. Their patients started to be cured and they lost the substrate upon which their sense of mission could operate. Bruno Bettelheim is a secular example of a man called to save his patients – in this case children with autism. A terrifying autocrat, his evident sense of service and image of wisdom made it impossible for his authority (and his discredited ideas about the causation of autism, which spread so much shame and guilt among a generation of parents) to be challenged.[21]

Against the background of such extreme examples, consumerism could operate as a liberating force. Those who have a calling may resist being called to account, except before the tribunal of their God or their conscience. The question still remains, however, whether medicine can do without *any* sense of being a calling, whether a narrowly contractual relationship between doctor and patient will deliver what seriously ill people really want or need. Medicine that has become entirely a service industry, staffed by doctors (and nurses) who are technicians skilled in customer care skills, may be too shallow to accommodate the depths of serious illness and the fear of such illness.

Some of the changes currently under way in the organization of medical care may further undermine the notion of medicine as 'a way of life' and turn doctors into sessional functionaries. Increasingly, patients are looked after by teams. There are often good reasons for this. People vary in their range of competencies: the multidisciplinary team, encompassing nurses, doctors, therapists, social workers and others, helps to make sure that all the patient's needs are met. But there are also less laudable reasons: where there are not enough doctors, nurses or doctor's assistants fill the gap and increasingly the drive towards 'teamworking' comes entirely from outside, motivated by a restriction on working hours.

The European Working Time Directive, implemented in August 2004, will mean that full shift-working will become the norm in UK medicine. In hospitals, this means junior doctors will work with a variety of colleagues in a series of loose associations. The camaraderie of the mess, of being 'in it' together and building up shared memories and experience, and the confidence that comes from knowing each other's strengths and weaknesses, will be denied the trainee of the future. Close working with a senior doctor, who may provide mentorship and a role model, will also be a thing of the past. Already, juniors pass through and between units so quickly, and there is such dissociation of the working patterns of individual members of teams, that in recent years I have found myself having to provide references for doctors with whom I have done as few as a dozen ward rounds and with whom I have been on call perhaps only three or four times. The professional of the future will be an isolated member of an ever-extending network of rapidly changing teams. This will also dilute the sense of personal responsibility for patients who pass through several teams during their hospital stay.

The increasing intrusion of third parties – governments or insurance agencies – into the patient–doctor relationship may also change the attitude of doctors to their work. The notion of doctor as advocate, fighting on behalf of the patient, sits very uncomfortably with the interminable external reviews of the doctor's performance to monitor the extent to which care meets government guidelines. Health Maintenance Organizations (HMO) may point the way to the future, though the cost-containment measures are often counter-productive. As David Mechanic has pointed out, what is elegantly called 'utilization management and review' is enormously expensive.[22] The increasingly tight control of what doctors can and should do for their patients, and the attempts in the United Kingdom by the government to bind doctors into politically determined targets (some of which, it has to be said, correspond to good practice) means that the practice of medicine will be ever more robotized: diktats will shape care. The values of the professional will be subsumed into the printed directions of clinical care as set out by non-clinicians.

Recent directives to physicians in an Ohio Kaiser Permanente HMO have prohibited them from discussing proposed treatments with patients prior to authorization by the 'utilization review group', or even allowed the patient to be aware of the authorization procedure. Here, as in other contexts, current practice in the USA gives us a glimpse of a possible future for the UK.[23] It isn't easy, as Rowan Williams has pointed out:

to sustain the humane vision of medicine (or anything else) when the rules of our humanity are apparently being rewritten to suit the imperatives of management and profit.[24]

The present government is in the process of removing control of postgraduate medical training from the control of the Royal Colleges. The Postgraduate Medical Education and Training Board is a government body which will determine the content of training curricula and the duration of training. I have already alluded to the pressures to reduce the duration of training of surgeons. The 30,000 hours' training for a consultant that was customary before 1995 will fall to about 6,000 hours.[25]

A few years ago, I attended a meeting addressed by a very senior civil servant from the Department of Health. He was discussing the workforce crisis and alluded to his previous experience in the Home Office when he was involved with the prison service, that also had a staffing crisis. There was, he said, an urgent need to cut training programmes in order to get 'boots on the landing' (that is to say, minimally trained bodies to do the job). Getting 'boots on the landing' has now become a prerequisite for the training 'reforms' driven by the government. This short-term consideration is overriding the need for a medical profession that will continue to lead medical research, the development of new treatments and new ways of delivering them, and protect the citizenry from unacceptable interference with their medical care. The doctor as intellectual leader, as clinical pioneer, and as advocate for the patient and the service, as the midwife of the future as well as the servant of the present, may well become a thing of the past. Medicine as a learned profession may prove to be a luxury that societies aiming to maximize the immediate utility to be gained from its servants cannot afford.

David Mechanic's recommendation that 'the medical community must commit to making physicians effective and reliable advocates by... developing and teaching advocacy models in the curricula of medical schools and continuing medical education programs'[26] shows how damaged the professional ethos has become in the USA. We are not far behind in the UK. The consultant contract rejected in 2002 was an attempt to link consultant salary progression over a twenty-year period with meeting management targets, the latter being determined centrally.

The contract for General Practitioners is even more prescriptive. Remuneration is largely tied up with meeting over a hundred quality markers or standards.[27]

Not all the standards in the contract are bad; indeed most of them are evidence-based. The direct link to reimbursement, however, underlines the assumption that has driven target-setting: that without external impetus – carrots and sticks, the promise of money and the threat of sanctions – the profession would not actually care for the health of the population. Targets, moreover, are at odds with the genuinely holistic, 360-degree solid angle awareness of the patient that is the mark of the good clinician. The new contract, with a salary that is pegged to a bill of fare (including whether or not one wants to provide out-of-hours cover), will have no room for idealism; nor will there be any place for unreimbursable activity such as providing comfort – staying up all night with a dying patient, talking to a bereaved wife, simply being 'there' for a patient – that GPs in the past aspired to, subscribed to in principle, and sometimes engaged in.

The statement of values drawn up by the Royal College of General Practitioners in 1985, in the middle of the Thatcherite managerial onslaught on the NHS, now seems poignantly antiquated, a time capsule from an earlier epoch of professionalism.[28] The values are as dated as the assumption that the doctor is male. Here are some of the key statements.

- The doctor tries to render a personal service which is comprehensive and continuing.
- In his practice arrangements he balances his own convenience against that of his patients, takes into account his responsibility to the wider practice community and is mindful of the interests of society at large.
- He subjects his work to critical self-scrutiny and peer review, and accepts a commitment to improve his skills and widen his range of services in response to newly disclosed needs.
- He sees that part of his professional role is to bring about a measure of independence: he encourages self-help and keeps in bounds his own need to be needed.

Given that bad societies are unlikely to produce good doctors and selfish societies unlikely to generate an ever-extending cadre of selfless physicians, one wonders where such doctors will come from.

When accountability is transformed into accountantability, combined with an ever-increasing risk of litigation, the relationship with the patient will be utterly transformed and the attitude of the doctor degraded. At the very least, care will (like the nursing care in long-term facilities) be reduced to 'tick-box' medicine, in part parcelled out to other professionals, in which prescribed 'care pathways' (billable, remunerable, defensible) are adhered to – despite the fact that, even in those areas where they are widely accepted to be most appropriate, they have been found to result in worse outcomes.[29]

The term 'defensive medicine' is a desperate euphemism for a profound corruption of the patient–doctor relationship that will make the much-derided notion of a grateful, trusting patient and doctors doing their best and 'giving over the odds' seem quite attractive. An obstetrician who has a low threshold for performing Caesarean sections to avoid litigation, and personal ruin and disgrace, has lost his or her professional soul. Where he or she ignores the evidence pointing to the safety of a lower operative rate for fear of being outsmarted by a claims lawyer, the first plank of professionalism – the knowledge base – has been abandoned.

Yet this is what is happening: it is becoming almost impossible to live with uncertainty (the essence of good clinical decision-making) because uncertainty will be trumped by the certainties of the courts and the media, who will not hesitate to deploy the superior wisdom of hindsight. The doctor who informs a patient of every possible risk, however remote, of a treatment or investigation and gets the patient to sign that he has understood all of these risks, and leads the patient to expect the worst, may be acting in the new spirit of transparency and partnership, but is more likely to be giving his own fears priority over those of the patient. The doctor who always eschews reassurance in case it might be false and chases down every symptom with a battery of tests he does not really believe in may have abandoned paternalism for something worse – inhumanity.

An unforgiving society will encourage doctors to transfer the risks associated with uncertainty and the fears of a bad outcome from themselves to patients. Knowing that a bad outcome will always make the decisions that lead up to it seem like the wrong ones – even negligent – doctors will act in such a way that they could not be what faulted even by an unreasonable person. Evidence-based medicine (EBM) the glory of the profession, will give way to LPM (lawyer-proof medicine) or GRM (grievance-resistant medicine).

As I suggested earlier, the fundamental injunction of Hippocrates – 'First do no harm' – will, since optimal care informed by the intention to do no harm will not necessarily prevent harm from being done, be displaced by one yet more fundamental: 'First cover your ass and damn the harm.' Ironically, the principle of informed consent will be undermined, because the patient will not truly know the primary reason for the investigation or intervention.

These changes are liable to make medicine an unattractive career. While, as was noted in Chapter 4, it is unclear whether or not fewer bright people are being attracted into medicine,[30] there is a question mark over how many will stay the course. There is mounting evidence that doctors are increasingly unhappy with their professional life. The rising levels of job dissatisfaction are striking. Of doctors graduating in 1974, the majority were reasonably content with their lot, though the prospect of the early retirement many were planning may have had something to do with this. In contrast, 25 per cent of the 1995 cohort had only a lukewarm desire to continue in medicine and only 13 per cent still had a strong desire to be doctors.[31] These alarming figures may in part be due to the greater expectations of happiness, and specifically of job satisfaction, of the more recent generations; but they will also be due to alterations in the working life.

In the USA, where morale among doctors is also low, the most important factor is loss of professional independence. What made medicine a profession in the modern sense of the term, in the autonomy they enjoyed in their everyday work, meant that they were not 'organization men'. Ronald Dworkin observes:

They did not have to be backslappers or joke-tellers or handshakers; they did not have to get along with their boss or be shrewdly political... They answered to no one but their patients.[32]

Now they 'must please some faceless bureaucrat without a medical education before ordering a test'. They are forced to become organization men; and, since 'they get little more out of their work than a paycheck, the money is much more important to them and they increasingly try to make more of it'. This is what happens 'when the medical profession is shorn of its transcendent qualities – its mystique, its notion of duty, its code of honour – and made into a rational, economic enterprise'.[33]

The trade-off between lost independence and boosted salary is very evident in the recent GP contract just referred to in the UK where salary is almost entirely built up of items of service for which points, translated into salary increments, are earned. This may not be sufficient incentive or compensation; for the majority of doctors, who do not participate in private practice, the salary, while comfortable, is not large when compared with that of others in much less stressful and responsible jobs that require less training. While consultant final salaries are often very impressive, these are typically reached only in a person's middle fifties. There are easier ways of earning more money.

For hospital doctors, the most profound change in working life may be the least remarked: loss of collegiality. Since the mid 1970s there has been a determined, and, as we have seen, wholly successful endeavour to undermine the power and standing of the consultant body. This has gone in parallel with the erasure of its symbols: consultants' dining rooms, medical staff committees that anyone takes seriously, medical societies have all vanished or have a different significance. Whereas doctors used to attend their local medical societies to combine a bit of education with socializing with colleagues, they now attend meetings largely to acquire a sufficient number of Continuing Professional Development (CPD) credits. A meeting that is not accredited for CPD will be unattended. Add to this the increase in consultant numbers, the tangential relationship of sessional or part-time doctors to their parent institutions, and the valuing of family over professional life, and it is easy to see why collegiality has all but vanished. Hospital consultants scarcely ever meet outside of formal business; and the mutual education that used to take place when we discussed problems over lunch is a thing of the distant past. Instead of sharing our worries about a patient with, say, kidney problems in informal conversations with the local kidney expert, we simply refer patients on via faxed or e-mailed forms. If we want to learn about renal diseases, we travel 200-plus miles to hear an expert from another centre talk about them at a time when we no longer need the information, but do need the CPD credits. And with this atomization of the profession, something else – the consultant body as the glue that kept a hospital going – has gone.

Just how important that was will only become apparent long after it has vanished.

Roy Porter's observations are highly pertinent:

Once medicine proved effective, the scourge of pestilence was forgotten, and the physician no longer had to be thanked and could be disparaged as a figure of authority, a tool of patriarchy or a stooge of the state.[34]

Ronald Dworkin's reference to the 'mystique' of the medical profession, 'its notion of duty, its code of honour' may elicit an unsympathetic response. Isn't this precisely the 'club culture' that was seen by some as the key to the problems at the Bristol Children's Hospital? Is not a self-directed and self-regulated profession likely to become merely self-interested and unaccountable? Is not the 'mystique' of the profession merely mystification to distract from other things, such as corruption?

It would be foolish, lacking in insight or hypocritical not to acknowledge the contribution of the profession to its own disrepute. In the USA, doctors were often venally spendthrift, over-investigating and over-treating, not infrequently in order to boost their incomes; in the UK a small minority of lazy, incompetent or greedy doctors neglected their duties in favour of private practice and/or the golf course. In short, they abused the trust that had given them professional autonomy. Some of the distrust directed towards some members of the profession was, in short, well earned. What was not deserved was the generalization of that distrust to the entire professional body. What was not justified was the assumption that the worst were the most representative.

It is interesting to look at the changing views of the American sociologist Eliot Freidson who, in the 1960s and 1970s, wrote some of the most penetrating and hostile critiques of the medical profession. The burden of his argument was that doctors had misused the legitimate authority that came from their knowledge and expertise. A corrupt minority was able to get away with a variety of malpractices, including fleecing the system and poor medical care; and the medical profession, an extremely powerful force within a provider-dominated health care system, had utilized the privilege of self-regulation to support highly self-interested restrictive practices. A couple of decades later Freidson had changed his tune. With remarkable honesty, he noted that the legal, economic, political and managerial pressures now threatened the core values of the profession.[35] In the USA, these pressures have not lessened over the last decade, and in the UK, as we have seen, external control over doctors has tightened to an astonishing degree in the last twenty years. The present government has started to remove self-regulation from the profession. A new Council for the Regulation of Healthcare Professionals was established in April 2003 to oversee decisions made by individual regulatory bodies. It has the power to force changes to, and indeed to regulate, the GMC. This is not merely a theoretical power. Recently at great public expense, it has (unsuccessfully) challenged decisions made by the General Medical Council.[36] The most impressive elements of self-regulation – audit and peer review – have been turned against doctors as instruments to discipline them through public humiliation.

The changed views of a sociologist who first blew the whistle on the failure of self-discipline within the profession, and now highlights the fact that the forces of government regulation (predominant in the UK) and the market forces of competition (predominant in USA) threaten professionalism, cannot be dismissed as self-interest. Loss of individual autonomy does not undermine professionalism, he points out, where it is a question of subordinating one's practice to established standards: autonomy is given 'to fellow professionals in a professionally controlled system'. Professionalism is, however, undermined when loss of autonomy involves 'subordination to those trained solely as managers'.[37]

The danger of external control is even greater when the controlling body is not business but the government. Emile Durkheim famously argued that the independent professions are the most important 'intermediary bodies' between the individual and the state. 'These secondary groups,' he pointed out, are not only 'indispensable to prevent the state from oppressing the individual', they are also 'necessary to keep the state sufficiently independent of the individual'.[38] As another sociologist, Anthony Giddens, has put it:

the sphere of the authority of the occupational associations [i.e. the professions] offsets the possibility of state autocracy. If the power of the state is not counterbalanced by other agencies, it readily becomes detached from the interests of those in civil society: 'it is out of this conflict of social forces that individual freedoms are born'.[39]

The professions both insulate the individual from the naked power of the state and the state from being driven by a mob consisting of an aggregate of individuals. The idea of direct government management of a disempowered medical profession by an empowered Secretary of State is deeply disquieting: it cannot be good either for the health of the nation or for the nation's health. Those sceptical of Durkheim's analysis may look to the example of a deprofessionalized medical workforce, predominantly female and of low status, and under the thumb of government and its regional arms, in the late unlamented Soviet bloc.

While this interpretation of the wider political significance of the deprofessionalization of medicine may be thought of as apocalyptic, its potentially disastrous impact on the medical care of the future is less far-fetched. The recent rejection of the first version of the new consultant contract (negatively spun as arising out of laziness and/or greed) was prompted, in the case of senior doctors at least, by the sense that it would be the death knell for professional leadership of medicine. As surgeon Peter McDonald put it eloquently, rejection was driven by:

the feeling that we were to become shift workers pushed around by managers ignorant of what our patients need... There was also the suspicion that somehow targets would be paramount, and more important than the survival of a few emergency patients or the integrity of our profession.[40]

As Onora O'Neill put it:

Each profession has its proper aim, and this aim is not reducible to meeting targets following prescribed procedures and requirements. The culture of accountability provides incentives for arbitrary and unprofessional choices.[41]

In short, something central to professionalism was at stake.

Health care systems in the UK and beyond will have less and less capacity to support innovators. A physician caught in the crossfire between customers with an insatiable appetite for care and attention and external forces such as governments and insurance managers, interested primarily in trying to contain costs or to achieve targets, may have little time to think of the big picture or the nobler aspirations of her profession. Doctors will have disincentives to be original thinkers. Their supposed conservatism, their resistance to beneficial change, much spoken of by the present government, will become a reality. Instead of being initiators, they will simply submit to imposed changes, irrespective of whether they judge them to be of benefit to patients.

Nor can innovation be left to academics who, it might be thought, would have the time and freedom not available to full-time clinicians. Academic medicine is in crisis world-wide, in part because of the obstacles that regulatory bodies are placing in the way of clinical research. In the UK, the situation is exacerbated by current policies of increasing the number of medical students while decreasing the number of academic posts in established teaching hospitals. The number of clinical lecturers in the UK has fallen by a third since 2000.[42] Over 20 per cent of academic posts remained unfilled, with little prospect of attracting candidates of a suitable calibre to them.[43]

As we shall see in the final chapter, while the profoundly worthwhile mission of medicine is incompletely achieved, it *is* achievable. But this will not happen of its own accord. It will have to be accomplished by the combined efforts of many talented individuals, genuine leaders who have vision, energy and the willingness to take risks. It will rely on the physician-scientists to translate discoveries in basic biomedical and other sciences into treatments that will benefit patients; and it will rely on clinical pioneers willing to set up the services that will deliver those new treatments. Such characters will not be drawn from the ranks of 'boots-on-the-landing' government trainees, with curtailed undergraduate education in increasingly teaching-only institutions, who become consultants of a kind after a drastically pruned postgraduate training, and who will pursue career advancement through assiduously matching clinical priorities to those identified by their political masters. To quote Onora O'Neill again:

If we want a culture of public service, professionals and public servants alike must in the end be free to serve the public rather than their paymasters.[44]

If we widen the scope of 'public' to include the present and future members of the planet, the full significance of the deprofessionalization of the medical profession, with the world-wide demoralization and disempowerment of physicians,[45] will become clear. If medicine becomes deprofessionalized, losing its sense of direction in thickets of regulation born of bureaucratic distrust, and society loses sight of those very values that drove the profession to its present heights of achievement, mankind will lose a group of people who, hitherto, have been some of its most effective leaders in the battle against human suffering, frailty and vulnerability.

It's as simple as that.

10

'Everyone Has To Die Some Time'

What do you want to treat all those old people for? Everyone has to die sometime.

Edward Tallis (aged 92)

Vulnerant omnes, ultima necat ('All of them wound, the last one kills').

Inscribed on a sundial and referring to the hours.

In the practice of medicine, knowledge returns to the body from which it originated.[1] We engage with our own bodies via the most abstract and distant modes of apprehension: knowledge liberates us from the prison of organic life, so that, as a consequence, our daily lives are largely made up of activities which cannot be explained in simple biological terms. However, this liberation is temporary. While our bodies understood biologically are not a sufficient explanation of our knowledge and the kind of lives we live, they are a necessary condition of both. We transcend our bodies but cannot float free of them. We are tied indissolubly to the vicissitudes of our flesh. Notwithstanding our ingenious remedies, human life, no less than animal life, will forever remain a fatal disease with 100 per cent mortality.

Does this mean that medicine is, ultimately, futile? If everything goes wrong in the end, are all our efforts in vain? Not if one believes that it is better that things go wrong as late as possible and that as little as possible goes wrong on the way. This response raises more questions. Is it possible to lengthen the course of life without lengthening the course of human suffering? And what counts as a worthwhile extension of human life? Is any finite extension of human life of any purpose – since all deaths, however late, will be equidistant from immortality?

We have dealt with the first question. Extension of life does not necessarily mean increased suffering on the way to a postponed death. Even so, it is difficult to escape the habits of thought that lead to pessimism. I can remember as a teenager, when I was deciding what to do with my life (and before Chekhov had cured me of my Schopenhauerian pretexts for giving way to despair and idleness or apathy dressed up as nihilism), thinking about the futility of human endeavour in general and medicine in particular. If you prevented a child dying of diphtheria, then she would perish as a teenager of TB. If you were able to avert this fate, she would be saved for breast cancer in middle age. If you found out how to cure breast cancer, she would die of a heart attack in her sixties. If you rescued her from that, she would be increasingly likely to have a stroke; and if a stroke didn't get her, she would be preserved for a long and horrible death from Alzheimer's disease.

The finding that increasing life expectancy is not accompanied by prolonged ill-health is encouraging but may not have allayed the worries of those to whom it seems obvious that, if you don't die of a disease at once, you will die of it later; or you will die of something else – probably worse. The clever doctors who stop you perishing from (a relatively cheap and attractively quick) heart attack are simply saving you up for a (very expensive and appallingly prolonged) dementia. So one fundamental aim of medicine – to postpone death – will inescapably be in conflict with another fundamental aim – to alleviate the suffering associated with bodily ills. That they are *not* in conflict is due to something called 'the ageing process'.

We have to pick our words and deploy our concepts with care when we talking about 'ageing'. Because it is used as an excuse by ageist scoundrels wanting to deny health care to older people, we must look critically at the notion that there is such a thing as 'pure' or physiological ageing distinct from the diseases that occur with increasing frequency with age. Suppose all diseases occurring commonly in old age could be cured or prevented, would we, in the absence of death by accident, violence or starvation, enjoy indefinite extension of life? Or would we still die of ageing itself? Alternatively, is ageing actually the sum of sub-clinical disease processes that have not advanced far enough to assume the distinctive features of 'decay' categorizable according to the International Classification of Diseases?

This question is more complex than it might initially appear. Sub-clinical diseases likely to be mistaken for ageing would need to be multiple to have sufficient combined impact. One could argue that the general increase in vulnerability necessary to fall victim to a multiplicity of diseases is precisely what ageing is. Secondly, one might expect low levels of disease to cause visible deterioration or death only in an organism that had been brought near to the threshold by other changes – presumably those of ageing. For an organism near the threshold, less disturbance is required to produce visible dysfunction. What is more, because of the gradual decline of adaptive and compensatory mechanisms, lesser perturbations would be required to produce irreversible consequences. A disease is sub-clinical only so long as it has not been recognized by a clinician.[2] There may be failure to reach the threshold of clinical recognizability, even where there is a good deal of damage, because an aged body is less likely to produce characteristic (usually adaptive) responses. Illness may therefore present as non-specific decline. Biological ageing is characterized by the merging of the manifestations of distinct diseases: the features that characterize, and so sharply differentiate, illnesses in youth may be partly lost in great old age. We might postulate a point of convergence between ageing and disease, where disease elicits no specific features, presenting with general decline.

The conceptual difficulties in sharply demarcating ageing from disease are compounded by empirical ones. There are few symptoms and signs that fully meet the criteria for a 'true' ageing process: one that occurs universally and exclusively in very late life. Conditions that seem to meet those criteria are often trivial (and scarcely life-threatening), such as wrinkling of the skin; or developmental, such as the menopause which has only incidental dysfunctional consequences. Just to make things more complicated, some significant pathology comes close to universality, for example, age-related deterioration of the retina of the eye, osteoarthritis, benign enlargement of the prostate, which will happen to everyone who lives long enough. But no one is going to suggest that these can be dismissed as 'mere' ageing with the implication of therapeutic inactivity.

The uncertainty surrounding the characteristics of 'pure' ageing processes – if they exist – in part reflects the methodological problem of defining study populations in which to look for them. To detect the effects of ageing, it is necessary to compare healthy young people with healthy old people. But is a perfectly healthy centenarian a freak of nature? Should we be studying average or ideal ageing? And comparing centenarians with twenty-year-olds will not necessarily give us information about pure ageing: they will differ in other respects than chronological age, for example, education and nutrition in the first twenty years of life.

One way of resolving this is to follow a cohort of individuals over decades. Researchers and grant-giving bodies are, for obvious reasons, less than keen on this more rigorous approach, though there are some very important longitudinal studies. And even these studies are not without their problems. There is the task of deciding which deleterious changes observed are to be classified as disease-related and which are to be classified as age-related. There is often no sharp demarcation between changes that are typically attributed to age and those that are given a specific diagnostic label; for example the pathological changes seen in Alzheimer dementia are also seen in normal brains, the only difference being one of distribution and quantity (though this may change when more robust molecular markers are identified).

Biological gerontologists (less worried perhaps about the clinical, social and political implications) entertain no doubts about the reality of physiological ageing; for them it is a process of decline, distinct from the effects of disease or trauma or privation, intrinsic in and essential to organisms. It is reflected in the huge differences in the lifespans of organisms. Biologists have sought to understand ageing within the gene-centred perspective of recent (neo-Darwinian) evolutionary thinking.

From the evolutionary point of view, there is little point in an organism surviving beyond its reproductive years. After that, the body may be disposed of. After all, the 'point' of an organism is to ensure replication of genetic material. Old, post-reproductive organisms are just so much clutter, competing with younger ones for resources. This – which might support the idea of programmed self-destruction to clear the planet of old organisms – is a touch simplistic. Peter Medawar refined it by suggesting that ageing happened because natural selection does not operate on organisms after their reproductive years, so that it doesn't matter if deterioration then occurs. There is no evolutionary requirement to weed out designer faults that do not interfere with reproduction.[3]

Tom Kirkwood, in his compelling and ingenious Disposable Soma theory, has developed these ideas further. He has argued that organisms have finite resources, which have to be shared between the energy of reproduction (creation of more genetic material) and of repair (keeping the organism going so that it can reproduce).[4] Too little resource allocated to repair will mean that the organism will fall apart before it reproduces itself; too much, and energy which should be going into making more of the species will be wasted in shoring up an organism that will anyway be doomed to die of accidents or predation. Species that are usually eaten by predators will be better advised to invest in copious reproduction than in meticulous self-repair. A successful organism will inevitably choose a cut-off point at which no more resource should go into repair. Beyond that point, ageing will result. The failure of repair mechanisms may be quite complex and the result of a variety of strategies used by organisms in the allocation of resources between reproduction and repair. Ageing theories, within this conceptual framework, are not therefore necessarily monocausal.

The central argument of the Disposable Soma theory acknowledges that, as Kirkwood puts it, 'the interest our genes have in keeping us going does not happen to coincide exactly with our own.'[5] Genes have an interest in keeping us going until we have reproduced to our maximum, but no interest in keeping us going afterwards. Old age is biologically superfluous. Kirkwood's theory is attractive not only because it leads to testable consequences but also because it suggests that ageing is not, as some have thought, the unmodified consequence of the Second Law of Thermodynamics, in accordance with which disorder or 'entropy' in closed systems tends to increase. According to this law, highly ordered, complex structures such as organisms are very improbable and thermodynamically unstable. We should expect them to fall apart. The fact that longevity is determined by the allocation of resources between reproduction and repair, suggests that decay is not inevitable. We may think of organismal self-repair as marking the difference between ageing as a biological phenomenon and as an inevitable physical process.

So what is the significance of ageing for our discussion of the ultimate aims of medicine and, more particularly, whether the aim to postpone death is in conflict with the aim to reduce suffering by treating or preventing chronic disease? Put very simply, the ageing process is the explanation of the seemingly paradoxical finding that increased average life expectancy is occurring in parallel with decreased levels of age-adjusted disability. In order to understand this surprising finding, we need to form a clearer idea of the overall consequences of ageing for the organism as a whole.

Ageing has been defined as 'a progressive, generalized impairment of function' which results in 'an increased probability of death'.[6] To see how the former leads to the latter, it is necessary to understand the notion of the 'adaptive capacity' of an organism. Nearly 150 years ago, Claude Bernard, the great physiologist and one of the founding fathers of experimental medicine, enunciated the principle that, for higher organisms at least, the condition of survival was the constancy of what he called 'the internal environment'. Survival depends on the exquisite regulation of a vast number of parameters, such as blood pressure, levels of salts, sugar and a variety of other substances in the blood, body temperature, and the total amount of fluids in the different body compartments. The capacity to hold these parameters steady, so that organs can perform their functions (including regulating these self-same parameters), was later called 'homoeostasis'.

Although these regulatory mechanisms can cope with most of the contingencies of everyday life, they have their limits. The body can adapt to a hot climate by mobilizing mechanisms for eliminating heat, such as dilatation of the blood vessels in the skin and sweating. It can deal with shortage of water by conservation mechanisms such as increasing the concentration of unwanted substances in smaller volumes of urine. But sooner or later the unprotected desert traveller with insufficient water will die. Likewise, mechanisms to maintain the blood pressure, and so ensure continuing perfusion of tissues with blood-bearing oxygen and nutriments, can withstand quite an impressive loss of blood but not a catastrophic haemorrhage.

The outcome of all the processes we can plausibly gather under the heading of 'ageing' is progessive narrowing of the capacity to adapt to events that threaten homoeostasis: this narrowing (or 'homoeostenosis') means that the size of the adverse event – disease, trauma, exposure to adverse climatic conditions – necessary to result in irreversible changes leading to the death of the organism is much smaller than it would be in a younger person. Homoeostenosis, a reduced adaptive capacity, is in essence what 'frailty' is. It is associated with an increased probability of death and, equally, with a death that comes more easily: in extreme old age, relatively minor pathological events or external upsets may be fatal. The death of an extremely frail person is less brutal, because more easily achieved, than that of a person with homoeostatic mechanisms intact.

Frailty is not itself unpleasant: it is quite distinct from decrepitude and not associated with the symptoms characteristic of specific diseases, such as nausea, pain or breathlessness. This is because ageing is, as the definition just given emphasizes, *generalized*. It is a global decline in organ systems.[7] It is *focal*, out-of-synch, declines that are caused by specific diseases. The out-of-synch declines – due to diseases which affect particular organs – are associated with symptoms and these may be very severe before they tip a person over into irreversible loss of homoeostasis. The later in the course of ageing that the pathological process occurs, the less savage the illness will have to be in order to exceed the limit from which individuals can bounce back.[8]

This, then, is how ageing comes to the rescue: death occurs more easily from pathological processes, so that living with very severe disease is ever less likely as the individual becomes biologically more aged. As John Grimley Evans has put it:

By delaying the onset of disabling diseases to later ages when intrinsic ageing has raised fatality by reducing adaptability, the average duration of disability before death will be shortened. In brief, we shall spend a longer time living and a shorter time dying.[9]

Thus is the seeming circle squared and the paradoxical decrease of disability before death is explained.

There are excellent data supporting this theoretical argument. One study showed that men who died in their late sixties had, on average, 3.8 years of dependency before death, whereas the number of years of dependency for men who died at eighty-five plus was 3.2.[10] For women, the differences were even more striking: those who died in their late sixties had on average nearly nine years of impairment before death, whereas those who died at eighty-five plus had just under five years of impairment before death. As Grimley Evans has said, more years of living and fewer years of dying.[11]

The notion of a healthy old age therefore depends upon postponing dependency or the onset of severe chronic disease by more years than death is postponed. If death is postponed by ten years and the onset of disabling diseases by fifteen years, the period of disability before death will be reduced by five years. Supposing, however, we find methods of 'treating' ageing. Will they spoil this attractive prospect? Theories such as Kirkwood's raise the possibility of significantly modifying ageing by identifying and restoring failing cellular repair mechanisms. Treatment for ageing will simply be an extension of the emergent molecular medicine approach to diseases. The requisite biotechnology does not seem too remote.

Research into fundamental ageing mechanisms and the development of treatments for ageing, however, lags behind that of treatments to prevent or postpone or mitigate chronic disease. And it always will do, for several reasons. First, as already noted, focal diseases declare themselves, and the search for candidate mechanisms and treatments to address them is (relatively) easy compared with something as global and ill-defined as ageing. Secondly, there is unlikely to be a single cause for ageing; there are many mechanisms promoting repair and they may fail in different ways, in different combinations and with a multiplicity of consequences. It will be necessary not only to address them all but also to examine the effects each has on the others, if one of them is strengthened. Thirdly, evaluating the effects of anti-ageing strategies, particularly if they have to be deployed comparatively early in life, will take much longer than evaluating the effects of treatments for specific diseases. The demographer Kenneth Manton has predicted quite modest increases in overall life expectancy over the next fifty to sixty years. He suggests an average life expectancy of ninety-five to a hundred years. Even taking current potential anti-ageing strategies into account, this seems about right. Most importantly, this is entirely consistent with the eventual compression of morbidity at the end to a few months or even weeks.[12]

The key to well-founded optimism is this: assuming that there is such a thing as physiological ageing, death by old age (with a nudge from pathology) will – in the interim between the conquest of pathology and the conquest of ageing – be preferable to death from severe illness at younger ages. Frailty, as the precursor or predisposing condition to death, will be plausibly less unpleasant, not being itself associated with intrusive symptoms such as pain, nausea, shortness of breath and gross disability. We may envisage extreme old age as a subtle and progressive reduction in life-space as if the gap between life and death had been narrowed.

The image of death-by-ageing-plus-minor-pathology as the end-result of gradual but harmonious failure of all organs is attractive. It might be more conscious, more metaphysical, than death typically is at present. While we may agree with the sentiment of Dylan Thomas's 'Do not go gentle into that good night', we do not want to go kicking and screaming either. Instead, we may hope for a relatively dignified decline through a series of grey-scale gradations of evening to oblivion.

> Bends to the grave with scarce perceived decay
> While resignation gently slopes the way.[13]

Or, if that seems too passive and accepting, then (in the words of my colleague, Professor Mark Ferguson), 'bop till you drop'.

Some may worry that the price of achieving this goal will be the 'medicalization' of old age. If 'medicalization' means the identification of preventable or treatable illnesses leading to evidence-based treatment, so that the constraints arising from ill-health are minimized, then, as Shah Ebrahim has argued, let's have more of it.[14] And if the rhetoric of anti-medicalization leads to older people being offered unsatisfactory and unpleasant social solutions (such as nursing home care) for inadequately treated or undiagnosed medical problems, medicalization should be encouraged even more vigorously. This is particularly so if concerns about medicalization are a smokescreen for (usually misguided) attempts at cost-containment through rationing medical care. Being sentenced to a few years in a nursing home is both more profoundly medicalizing in the undesirable sense and more fiscally burdensome than receiving prompt treatment to prevent disability.

Good medical care, in short, de-medicalizes old age, particularly as medical management is becoming ever-less brutal: less invasive diagnostic tests and operative treatments, with better post-operative care; drugs chosen on the basis of the impact on quality of life as well as on the target medical problem; and so on. There is no reason why experiences of medical treatment will become ever-less intrusive and unpleasant while its outcomes become more satisfactory.

Grounds, then, for optimism all round.[15] The pessimists, though, are not routed. One doom-laden scenario – death through progressive disability due to chronic degenerative disease – may be making way for another, in which the key element is the return of infectious diseases. For some, the evidence that this is happening is available already, irrespective of any man-made contribution either through the escape of a genetically modified superbug from a laboratory or the deliberate reinfection of the world through the terrorist activities of a suicide bio-bomber who has dosed himself up with smallpox. There is no space to deal with their arguments here.[16]

Notwithstanding humanity's rather patchy record of pursuing its own best interests, and the panics that unhelpfully undermine the efforts of those trying to serve those interests, there is no reason why we should not look forward to an ever-more healthy world. We have the tools, the technology and (in places) the intelligence and common sense. Sven Lomberg has persuasively argued that food production and energy production should keep up with population growth without necessarily deforesting or polluting the planet or leaching it of the resources that future generations will require.[17] Not everyone is entirely persuaded by this[18] but there is no doubt that negotiating the future will become easier if population growth is arrested and unit consumption by those (including the present author) who already consume more than they need is reduced. The path to sustainable growth world-wide will include sustainable non-growth in places where affluence is driving an ever-upward spiral of consumption. Learning how to disengage from consumption – a process that will include celebrating what we have already and learning how to make more of it – is going to be key to the future health of the world.[19]

Whether the world outside of medicine, and natural and man-made catastrophes, ultimately defeat the medical mission of a long life and a natural death at the end of a healthy old age, we cannot tell. And pre-cisely because we cannot tell, we must proceed as if a good outcome is at least possible.[20] If the present generation does not believe in – and hope and strive for – a better future, and falls prey to helplessness and despair (or, more likely, a comfortable selfishness, for the cost of pessimism is not borne by those who give seminars advocating it), then the future will be no improvement on the present. If, on the other hand, there is a collective belief in a better future that is worth striving for, to be achieved by a thousand, a hundred thousand, incremental changes, there is a chance that it may come about.

This argument is as much as anything a reflection of my own professional background. As Grimley Evans remarks:

It is in the nature of a geriatrician to be a constructive optimist. That is to say, he believes that things can always be made better but are unlikely to become so spontaneously.[21]

Like many geriatricians, I ended up in my discipline by accident. I can recall my first ward round on a geriatric ward in a crumbling Victorian building in 1980. The most enduring memory was of a wild-haired bedfast woman with dementia, in a toxic confusional state, picking her nose with faeces-caked fingers. The sense of impotence and of the futility of medical care was overwhelming. If ever there was a time to sink back into self-serving nihilism, and self-justifying apathy, that was it. Twenty years later, the proportion of old people who suffer such a terrible end and the duration of the suffering of those who do is much reduced. Health promotion, illness prevention, more effective and more humane treatment in better surroundings, have diminished the sum total of human misery even at the end of life. There is still some way to go and occasional scandals that spur clinicians and managers to take action, and which prompt journalists to take up their pens with circulation-boosting stories, show us how far we have yet to go. We are, however, well under way and there is a clear direction, with a definable goal.

When we think about the possible futures of our lifespan, health span and our health in old age, it seems to me that there are three possible scenarios: the 'Nightmare scenario'; the 'Receding horizon model'; and the 'Approaching asymptote scenario'.[22] Each graph on page 272 represents the average level of disability or chronic illness severity at a given age.

The first curve represents the present situation; what (I hope) we shall come to look back on as 'the bad old days', rather as I now look back on the early 1970s when I first became a doctor or, indeed, the early 1980s when I became a consultant. In this graph, we see that Mr and Mrs Unisex Average live a pretty healthy life, free of chronic illness or significant disability until, say, their late sixties. Then problems start to pile up until, eventually, death supervenes at a unisex average of approximately seventy-five years of age. The period between the onset of significant illness and death is what we have in our sights; and the aim of medicine as defined above is to reduce the shaded area of person years of medically unsatisfactory life.

The possible futures of old age

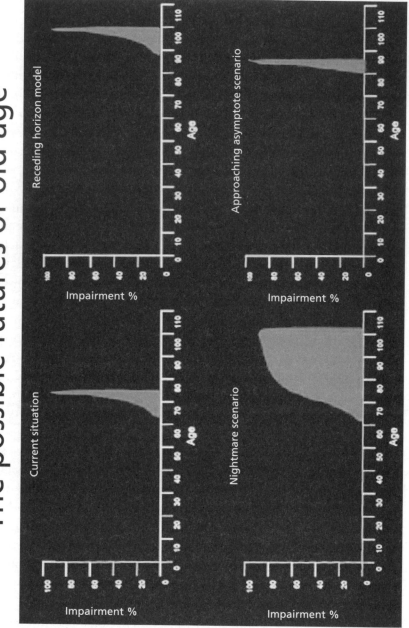

According to the Nightmare scenario, serious illness begins at about the same time but, thanks to the unwise wonders of modern medicine, Mr and Mrs Unisex Average are 'kept alive' much longer: a longer life is bought at the cost of a longer death and medicine adds to the sum total of human woe. In accordance with this scenario, it would not be unusual to have a long Fourth Age in life entirely spent in an acute hospital and a significant portion of it on a ventilator.

The second future scenario – the Receding horizon – is the result of two matched changes: the postponement of the onset of chronic ill-health – its progression to each level of severity – and the postponement of death. While there is a satisfying gain in life expectancy, the target of a health span that approximates to the lifespan retreats as fast as the age of onset of chronic illness advances. The shaded area of medically unsatisfactory life remains unchanged.

In the final future scenario the Approaching asymptote – the onset of chronic illness is postponed much more than death, because at very late old age death occurs easily. There are gains in life expectancy but greater gains in healthy active years of life: the period of chronic illness before death is therefore shortened and the ideal of a long life in which the health span approximates the lifespan ever more closely – so that the shaded area progressively thins – itself comes nearer. It will never be fully achieved because, as my father pointed out, you have to die of something and that means some illness – months, weeks, days before death.

The evidence given earlier does not suggest that the Approaching asymptote scenario is impossible or even unlikely. The twin aims of medicine, those of postponing death and of minimizing suffering due to illness, are therefore not in conflict. A health span that is all but coterminous with lifespan is a goal that is both supremely worthwhile and achievable: there is so much to gain if we get the future of medical care right.

The discussion of medicine should not be hijacked by those whose motives have little to do with the achievement of this future. A skewed public perception, informed by journalists with one eye on pleasing an editor, who has to please a proprietor with both eyes on circulation; informed by lawyers who are remote from the terrible, miraculous and deep truths of illness, caring and curing; and by politicians whose idea of the long term is the space between elections – will inevitably threaten the future of medicine. If its achievable and worthwhile goals are to be realized in practice, medicine will need *true* leadership – not the kind that is acquired at a government leadership centre. Where is this to be found if not in the profession that has taken medical science, its application in clinical practice, and the delivery of care, to their present heights? This would be a leadership by practical visionaries who can look beyond the present, or even the near future; of a learned profession that has not been trained in accordance with a government-inspired curriculum designed to produce 'boots on the landing' but that has always known more than it could put into practice. Those who seek to undermine the influence and standing of doctors may well delay or deny this achievable future, where the ultimate aims of medicine converge at single point.

Envoi

While some of us are lucky enough to pass our lives on the leeward side of history and fortune, we all live on the windward side of time. However death is postponed and palliated – by means of medicine, public health, technology and social reforms – birth remains a one-way ticket to the grave.

> Thou know'st 'tis common: all that lives must die,
> Passing through nature to eternity.[1]

If disease does not destroy us, external events – accidents, war, natural disasters – will bring about our demise. And for complex organisms, the increasingly difficult task of coping with the accumulated internal wounds of an ageing body will eventually prove impossible.

The best we can hope for is harmonious decline. Not even the quasi-immortal sea anenome – safe from predators in the ocean depths and therefore strongly committed to self-repair – will survive the heat death of the universe.

Medicine, which owes its ultimate orgins to the extraordinary self-apprehension of the human body, will encounter unsurpassable limits. Even in the absence of all fatal diseases, when life expectancy is determined by entirely external, environmental risks, average lifespan might rise to at most 600 years.[2] Passing 'through nature to eternity' (or to nothing) will remain the condition of 'all that lives' whatever breakthroughs medicine engineers.

Death will always be premature – at least for the one who is dying. A late death is never late enough. Is there ever a right, a non-tragic, time to die? According to Paul Valéry's 'M. Teste' there is a time to let go with equanimity:

The *natural* or true death would be the total exhaustion of the possibilities of the system of an individual man. All the inner combinations of his capacities, incomplete in themselves, would be exhausted. He has told himself everything he knew.[3]

The natural death – as opposed to what Valery calls the *ordinary* death of 'a man surprised and slightly shocked, impolitely interrupted by some trifle in an interesting conversation' – is not yet available on the NHS. And clinicians, even in the private sector, are far from bumping against the parameters set by the the the properties of the human organism. But, if any human endeavour seems worthwhile, that of one day assuring that everyone can enjoy a physiological old age and attain a natural death, must rank highest. Meanwhile, there is little to suggest that the extended, if not entirely physiological, old age already made possible for many by medical and social advance is a cause for regret.

Medicine is not, of course, an end in itself. Nor does it prescribe the ends of life. Like good government, it liberates people to pursue their own ends. The role of medicine is to restore us to a normal Tuesday free from pain, nausea, itch, or intrusive impairments. What we then do with a normal Tuesday is up to us. If medicine is doing its job properly, it should figure less and less in people's lives and our health should not become an all-consuming preoccupation, as if a healthy body were an alternative to a full life rather than merely the foundation stone for it.[4] Equally, there should be limits to medicalization,[5] though drawing these limits is very difficult and, both those who place certain woes inside, and those who place them outside medicine are often vulnerable to bitter criticism.

Painless decline will be a less opaque metaphysical window than physical suffering; for to suffer is to be nailed to the particular. Good physic will not blunt our awareness of the essential tragedy of transience but purify it, winnowing it from the distractions that dominate decline and death at present. We shall die, as we live, more like humans than animals, ourselves rather than anonymous organisms to the end.

We could rephrase the goal of medicine – 'making the health span coterminous with the lifespan' – as that of pushing the vestiges of inhumanity from the human body and liberating human beings to live long and fully human lives.

The ultimate aim of medicine is to make the human body less inhuman.

Notes

Introduction

1. The history of tribal or traditional medicine and, until relatively recently, of Western professionalized medicine.

Part I Origins

1. William Butler Yeats, 'Death' from *The Winding Stair and Other Poems* (London: Macmillan, 1933).
2. Dylan Evans, 'Pain, Evolution and the Placebo Response', *Brain and Behavioural Sciences*, 2002, 25: 4.

1 The Medicine-taking Animal: A Philosophical Overture

1. And in some cases as bits of the material world. Brain scanning, for example, approaches that most sacred of all organs as if it were a physical object.
2. The interested reader may wish to consult my trilogy *Handkind*, published by the Edinburgh University Press. The parts that deal with the origin of knowledge out of sentience are 'Getting a Grip on the Conscious Human Agent' in *The Hand: A Philosophical Inquiry into Human Being* (2003) and the third volume: *The Knowing Animal: A Philosophical Inquiry into Knowledge and Truth* (2005). The transformation of the consciousness of the organism into a subject is addressed in the second volume *I Am: A Philosophical Inquiry in First Person Being* (2004). Our different kinds of relationship to our bodies are examined in the same volume: see 'On Being, Suffering, Having and Using a Body'.
3. For a reasonably accessible account (and critique) of Heidegger's views, the reader may wish to consult Raymond Tallis, *A Conversation with Martin Heidegger* (Basingstoke: Palgrave, 2002).

4. For a brief summary of the evidence for fleeting self-awareness in higher primates, see Gordon G. Gallup, 'Self-recognition in primates: a comparative approach to the bidirectional properties of consciousness', *American Psychologist*, 1977, 32: 329–38.

5. Karl Popper, Preface to *Objective Knowledge: an Evolutionary Approach* (Oxford: Oxford University Press, 1972).

2 The Miracle of Scientific Medicine

1. Jean Starobinski quoted in Roy Porter, *The Greatest Benefit to Mankind: A Medical History of Humanity from Antiquity to the Present* (London: Harper Collins, 1997), p. 43.

2. The penetration of biomedical science into medical practice is variable. See, for example, V.P. Pomeroy and R.C. Tallis, 'Neurological rehabilitation: a science struggling to come of age', *Physiotherapy Research International*, 2002, 7(2): 76–89.

3. For the anthropological and historical background here, I have drawn on Roy Porter's masterpiece, *The Greatest Benefit to Mankind*, op. cit.

4. Ibid., p. 33.

5. Hippocrates, *On the Sacred Disease*, quoted in J. D. Spillane, *The Doctrine of the Nerves* (Oxford: Oxford University Press, 1981).

6. Lewis Wolpert, *The Unnatural Nature of Science* (London: Faber, 1992).

7. James Buchan, *Frozen Desire. An Inquiry into the Meaning of Money* (London: Picador, 1997), p. 7.

8. See Adam Smith, *The Wealth of Nations* (New York; Modern Library, 1937), pp. 11–12.

9. J. Oeppen, *Science*, 2002, 296: 1029–31.

10. Andrew Achenbaum, *Crossing Frontiers: Gerontology Emerges as a Science* (Cambridge, Cambridge University Press 1995), p. 1.

11. Sue Kelly, Karen Dunell, John Fox, 'Health trends over the last 50 years', *Health Trends*, 1998, 30(1): 10–15.

12. Office for National Statistics (ONS): *Health Statistics Quarterly*; no. 9 (London: HMSO, 2001). Cited in Emily Grundy, 'The Epidemiology of Ageing' in *Brocklehurst's Textbook of Geriatric Medicine and Gerontology*, edited by Raymond Tallis and Howard Fillit (Edinburgh: Churchill Livingstone, Elsevier Science Limited, 2003). Unless otherwise indicated, the statistics given in the next few paragraphs are derived from Grundy's chapter.

13. As did Thomas McKeown in his famous *The Modern Rise of Populations*. A short account of McKeown's views appears in his lecture, 'The role of medicine: dream, mirage or nemesis?' (London: Nuffield, 1976).

14. See J.P. Bunker, 'Medicine matters after all', *Journal of the Royal of Physicians*, 1995, 29: 105–12.

15. See Raymond Tallis, *Enemies of Hope: A Critique of Contemporary Pessimism* (London: Macmillan, 2nd edn, 1999).

16. Bunker op. cit.

17. Office of Health Economics, *Compendium of Health Statistics*, 14th edn, 2002. Summary statistics compiled by Peter Yuen.

18. Kenneth Calman, 'Health and health services: changes over the last seven years', *Health Trends*, 1998, 30(1): 5–7.

19. J. Ciment, 'WHO celebrates triumph over river blindness', *British Medical Journal*, 1999, 319: 1090.

3 The Coming of Age of the Youngest Science

1. Lewis Thomas, *The Youngest Science. Notes of a Medicine Watcher* (London: Penguin, repr. 1995)

2. Ernest Gellner quoted in Raymond Tallis, *Enemies of Hope. A Critique of Contemporary Pessimism* (London: Macmillan, 2nd edn, 1999), p. 488.

3. As David Blake, an orthodox practitioner, was told when he visited a Chinese herbalist: 'It was only Western medicine, which had a much poorer historical base, that required the scientific proof that I appeared to request.' D.R. Blake, 'Alternative prescribing and negligence', *British Medical Journal*, 2003, 236: 455.

4. Theodore Porter, *Trust in Numbers. The Pursuit of Objectivity in Science and Public Life* (Princeton, NJ: Princeton University Press, 1995), p. 204.

5. This is not yet fully understood by governments wishing to publish league tables comparing outcomes in different hospitals. Better results may simply mean more successful discrimination against high-risk patients. Discrimination may occur naturally. For example, in Scotland mortality rates from heart attack are greatly influenced by deaths outside hospital. If the most seriously ill patients die before reaching hospital, the hospital will have better results. (A.H. Leyland, F.A. Boddy 'League tables and acute myocardial infarction', *The Lancet*, 1998, 351: 555–8).

6. International Stroke Trial Collaborative Group. 'The International Stroke Trial (IST): A Randomised Trial of Aspirin, Subcutaneous Heparin, Both, or Neither among 19, 435 Patients with Acute Ischaemic Stroke', *The Lancet*, 1997, 349: 1569–81.

7. (CAST) Chinese Acute Stroke Trial, 'CAST: Randomised, Placebo-Controlled Trial of Early Aspirin Use in 20,000 Patients with Acute Ischaemic Stroke', *The Lancet*, 1997, 349: 1641–9.

8. The reader who wants to know more is strongly recommended to consult I. Chalmers, L.V. Hedges, H. Cooper, 'A Brief History of Research Synthesis', *Evaluation and the Health Professions*, 2002, 25(1): 12–37.

9. Archibald Cochrane, '1931–71: A Critical Review, with particular reference to the medical profession', *Medicines for the Year 2000* (London: Office of Health Economics, 1979), pp. 1–11.

10. Of which more presently.

11. Iain Chalmers, 'Invalid health information is potentially lethal', *British Medical Journal*, 2001, 322: 998.

12. Quoted in Iain Chalmers, 'Trying to do More Good than Harm in Policy and Practice: The Role of Rigorous, Transparent, Up-to-Date Evaluations', *The Annals of the Academy of Political and Social Science*, 2003, 589: 22–40.

13. The story of Southall's persecution is set out in the *Guardian*, 16 October 2001, pp. 6–7.

14. Including the claim that he was referring children whose parents had been caught on video smothering them in order to make 'phenomenal' amounts of money in expert witness fees and using children in care for his research and entrapping parents. (The *Guardian* ibid.)

15. Iain Chalmers and E. Hey, 'Investigating allegations of research misconduct: the vital need for due process', *British Medical Journal*, 2000, 321: 752–5 (and 1348–9, for follow-up correspondence).

16. Quoted in Iain Chalmers and Edmund Hey, 'Learning from Bristol: the need for a lead from the Chief Medical Officer', *British Medical Journal*, 2001, 324: 280–1)

17. Iain Chalmers, – see note 12.

Part II Contemporary Discontents

4 Communication, Time, Waiting

1. *Improving Communication between Doctors and Patients*. A Report of a Working Party (London: Royal College of Physicians, 1997).

2. General Medical Council, *Tomorrow's Doctors*, 1993.

3. Christopher Rudolf, quoted in P. Barkham, 'The Shipman Report', *The Times*, 20 July 2002, p. 15.

4. The quotation continues: 'apart from the fact that he killed my father'.

5. Liz Kendall, 'How I fell foul of the NHS', the *Observer*, 24 February 2002.

6. My repeated reference to what is an ephemeral piece of journalism may strike some readers as somewhat selective. In fact Kendall's article, like one or two others which I repeatedly cite, say much more about what is 'out there' than

many other more extended analyses. Kendall – whom I would have had to invent had reality not done the work for me – is more informative through what she betrays than what she says.

7. And this is certainly the case with respect to communication between members of the ever-expanding team of health and social care workers. We are repeatedly enjoined to 'communicate more' because mistakes and sub-optimal care result from lack of communication. In practice, if everyone communicated with the recommended frequency, there would be less, not more, successful teamworking. In one of Samuel Beckett's novels, *Watt*, there is an episode in which 'the committee exchanges glances'. This takes up many pages of description. With e-mail – that effortlessly includes dozens of members of the many teams of which we are a part – everyone is drowning in 'communication'.

8. See Kathryn Montgomery Hunter, *Doctors' Stories: The Narrative Structure of Medical Knowledge* (Princeton, NJ: Princeton University Press, 1991).

9. I remember a Clinico-Pathological conference when the rather nervous houseman presenting the case described the patient as 'a very nice young man'. The pathologist said, 'Yes, I could tell he was a nice man from his intestinal biopsy.'

10. 'If you let the patient talk and don't interrupt, she will tell you the diagnosis' is a standard claim.

11. W. Langewitz, M. Denz, A. Keller, A. Kiss, S. Ruttiman, B. Wossmer, 'Spontaneous talking time at start of consultation in out-patient clinic: cohort study', *British Medical Journal*, 2002, 325: 682–3.

12. Roy Porter, *The Greatest Benefit to Mankind. A Medical History of Humanity from Antiquity to the Present* (London: HarperCollins, 1997), p. 10. I return to this in Chapter 6 when alternative medicine is considered.

13. Polly Toynbee, 'Between aspiration and reality', *British Medical Journal*, 2002, 325: 718–19.

14. Liz Kendall, the *Observer* op. cit.

15. Ibid. I am not sure that it is true that we have a full knowledge of the track record of the providers of goods and services in all other parts of our lives. We know relatively little about the quality of food in a new restaurant, the success rate of the garage in sorting out problems, the efficiency of the lawyer we hire to convey our house. In most cases, we find out as we go along.

16. 'The duties of a doctor registered with the General Medical Council', London, no date. This has been most recently reiterated in General Medical Council, *Confidentiality: Protecting and Providing Information*, General Medical Council, April 2004.

17. Salford Royal Hospitals Trust, *Trust Policy on Informed Consent*, 2002.

18. Ibid.

19. Peter Marks, 'The evolution of the doctrine of consent', *Clinical Medicine*, 2003, 3: 45–7.

20. Jo Knowsley, 'I went to hospital for a routine operation only to wake up and be told: "Sorry, it's gone wrong". In the week Ministers admitted that one in ten patients is a victim of medical errors, my harrowing experience reveals the true depth of the crisis in the NHS', *Mail on Sunday* Review, 23 June 2002, 5, pp. 49–51.

21. As Ms Knowsley points out, 'thousands are carried out every week'.

22. This has been anticipated: the Trust Policy warns doctors that 'by itself a signed consent form is no guarantee that adequately informed consent has been obtained and does not protect staff from allegations of failure to inform, or from an action in negligence.'

23. See Chapter 5.

24. See Chapter 7.

25. *Learning from Bristol.* The report of the inquiry into children's heart surgery at the Bristol Royal Infirmary 1984–1995 (London: The Stationery Office, 2000). Otherwise known as the Kennedy Report.

26. Michael Balint, *The Doctor, the Patient and the Illness* (London: Pitman, 1957).

27. David Black and Mike Pearson, Editorial 'Average length of stay, delayed discharge and hospital congestion', *British Medical Journal*, 2002, 325: 610–11.

28. Office of Health Economics, *Compendium of Health Statistics*, 14th edition, 2002. Summary statistics.

29. Not only do they have to get 'signed up' but they have to write a report on each episode of CPD, identifying the different headings under which their clinical skills, knowledge or attitudes have benefited.

30. Since patients often write to wards and to teams, many consultants have to resort to borrowing the cards from the wards or from colleagues to photocopy for their 'portfolios'. A colleague of mine suggested that we should include pictures of the occasional gift we receive from grateful patients. A bottle of Famous Grouse would certainly cheer up a rather dreary document.

31. This is at a time when the conduct of research is getting more and more difficult. For a variety of reasons, doing clinical research is now rather like trying to run up a vertical sand-dune.

32. My ward round lasted about half an hour longer after I decided to do precisely this and since, following a complaint that my writing was at some places difficult to read, I have foresworn cursive. This is not only half an hour of my time but also – when they are free to accompany me on the ward round – half an hour of junior doctor time and nursing time.

A recent edict from the Government that older people should be subject to a Single Assessment Process, so that every aspect of their care is gathered together in the one place and all the professionals – social workers, doctors, district nurses – involved in their care should know everything about them, has worrying ethical implications with respect to confidentiality and will also add to time pressures. It is unlikely to deliver much: many boxes will be ticked and few people really helped, as Grimley Evans and I have pointed out. (J.G. Grimley Evans, R.C. Tallis, 'A new beginning for health care for elderly people?', *British Medical Journal*, 2001, 322: 807–8.) Other government guidelines instruct GPs to restructure their patients' records so that other professionals can easily access patient information. They 'will have to trawl patients' notes and translate the medical jargon into something more generic that everyone can understand'. It is estimated that this will take about an hour per patient. (Fintan Coyle, Commentary, *Geriatric Medicine*, February 2000, p. 9.)

33. This and other statistics are taken from W.R. Burnham, 'Federation of the Royal Colleges of Physicians Census 2000', *Clinical Medicine*, 2002, 2(1): 7–8.

34. At present the overwhelming majority of consultants take less than the minimal entitlement of study leave (Audit Commission Medical Staffing Review Acute Hospital Portfolio, 30 August 2002). Given that postgraduate education is often a refreshing break from postgraduate work, and that revalidation will depend on doing in full the prescribed amount of CPD, this is likely to change.

35. Melanie Powell, 'I don't want any more money, Mr Milburn. I want a life outside of work', *Independent on Sunday*, 3 November 2002.

36. Productivity is already falling in surgery. The number of operations per surgeon fell by an average of 20 per cent between 1994 and 2001 (Zoe Morris, 'Surgery in NHS down by 20%', *Hospital Doctor*, 30 May 2002). It is the result of an almost permanent mismatch between available surgeon time, anaesthetist time, theatre time and specialist theatre staff time; the reduction of junior doctors' hours and their not being allowed to carry out parallel lists; more time spent on junior training; and the blocking of surgical beds by acute medical admissions.

37. W.R. Burnham op. cit. This must be one of the many reasons why the NHS gives such extraordinary value for money. As Charles Webster pointed out, 'finance ministers in France and Germany gaze enviously at the UK record of comparable outcomes from half the spending' (*The National Health Service. A Political History*, new edition, Oxford University Press 2002, p. 254). Can doctors really be so idle, given that we have half the number of doctors per head of population?

38. *Fifth Report on the Provision of Services for Patients with Heart Disease, Heart*, 2002; 88 (Suppl 3), pp. 1–56.

39. I will return to this when I consider the possible demise of medicine as a profession in the penultimate chapter of this book.

40. Audit Commission Survey, 2001. The so-called New Deal was signed in the early 1990s!

41. Some of my colleagues have spent a very significant proportion of their free as well as their paid time trying to square the circle in drawing up junior rotas that will comply with the law without jeopardizing patient safety and negotiating them with said juniors and consultant colleagues. This typifies the utterly tedious labour that occupies a vast amount of consultant time, taking them away from patients. A recent judgement – 'Implementation of the European Working Time Directive for Specialist Registrars: Acute Hospital Medicine', (Royal College of Physicians, Commentary, Supplement, November 2003) – is that there are insufficient trainee doctors to construct full-time shifts for middle-grade cover. There will be loss of continuity of care, of teaching and training, or the sense of being part of a team.

42. NHS Executive, *General and Personal Medical Statistics England and Wales: 1st October 1999* (Leeds: NHS Executive, 2000). This figure is continuing to rise. See Frith Rayner, 'Are male doctors the endangered species?', *Hospital Doctor*, 30 May 2002, pp. 18–19, and Janis Smy, 'Is this the consultant of the future?', *Hospital Doctor*, 19 February 2004, pp. 20–4. Smy reports that the latest figures show that 70 per cent of Southampton medical school intake is female. In Newcastle and Leeds it is 80 per cent.

43. Isobel Bowler and Neil Jackson, 'Experiences and career intentions of general practice registrars in Thames deaneries: postal survey', *British Medical Journal*, 2002, 324: 464–5. This has been supported by a more recent survey (reported in Smy, op. cit.) that found that 75 per cent of women will not want to work full-time for at least part of their careers.

44. Secretary of State for Health, *The NHS Plan. A plan for investment. A plan for reform* (London: Stationery Office, 2000).

45. A BMA survey carried out in 2001 revealed that the younger the GP, the more likely he/she was to plan to work part-time. This is in part a reflection of the relationship between age and gender: while only 20 per cent of GPs aged fifty-five to sixty-four are female, women comprise 76 per cent of those under thirty. A recent Royal College of Physicians survey of trainee specialists in hospitals – *Royal College of Physicians Commentary*, May/June 2003, p. 41 – found that 40 per cent approaching the end of their training expressed a preference for working part-time.

46. See note 35.

47. I.C. McManus, 'Medical school applications – a critical situation', *British Medical Journal*, 2002, 325: 786–7.

48. It is perhaps important not to read too much into short-term trends. In 2004, there was an overall increase in applications to medical schools of about 20 per cent (Professor David Yates, personal communication). And the increase in intake is in fact ahead of government targets (Jane Potter, 'Government hits medical school intake target early', *Hospital Doctor*, 18 March 2004, p. 13). It

remains to be seen whether the increased intake stays the course. At any rate, it will not fully compensate for the impact of the European Working Time Directive referred to earlier. What is more, the increase in applications may be a consequence of the fact that many more sixth formers have predicted 3 'A' grades at A level. The population from which applications arise has grown dramatically.

49. E. Ferguson, D. James, L. Madeley, 'Factors associated with success in medical school and in a medical career: systematic review of the literature', *British Medical Journal*, 2002, 324: 284–5. There is also evidence that students with lower entry are more likely to leave medicine altogether: see I.C. McManus, Eleni Smithers, Philippa Partridge, A. Keeling, Peter Fleming, 'A levels and intelligence as predictors of medical careers in UK doctors: 20 year prospective study', *British Medical Journal*, 2003, 327: 139–42.

50. The Research Assessment Exercise (RAE) assesses academic institutions according to the quality of their research and allocates funds on the basis of this.

51. Paul Smith and Zoe Morris, 'More pain for medical schools?', *Hospital Doctor*, 30 May 2002, p. 11.

52. Rhona Macdonald, 'Survey shows serious shortage of medical academics in the UK', *British Medical Journal*, 2002, 324: 446.

53. The palm for lunacy must go to a scheme launched in 2001–2 to parachute in doctors from abroad to perform elective operations. It involved a huge amount of effort and resource. In the three months after it was launched it yielded five visiting teams: one assisted at some operations and none of the others was involved in any operations (Amena Salim, 'Are doctors responsible for failure to recruit foreign teams?', *Hospital Doctor*, 10 October 2002). A team arrived at Birmingham City Hospital in order to carry out eye operations but left without performing any after it transpired that they were unsuitable.

Shortly after, another team of ophthalmological surgeons also brought over from Germany walked out in mid-session. They arrived an hour before the first operating list was due to start – scarcely time to familiarize themselves with the hospital never mind the patients – carried out two out of a planned five operations, and then abandoned the three remaining patients who had already been prepared for surgery (Amena Salim, 'Visiting surgeons walk out in mid-session', *Hospital Doctor*, 24 October 2002). An NHS consultant had to be called in to take over the list after completing his own.

A parallel scheme to recruit 1,000 'clinical fellows' from abroad (including parts of abroad that themselves have a shortage of doctors) has also yielded much publicity but little clinical care. Eight months after the scheme was launched, forty-five fellows – none in the targeted specialties identified by the government in launching this very costly scheme – had been appointed after the processing of 413 applicants. In a separate global scheme, out of 5,000 doctors who had expressed an interest in working for the NHS nineteen were recruited.

54. Janis Smy, 'Is this the consultant of the future?', *Hospital Doctor*, 19 February 2004, pp. 20–4.

55. H. Philip, Z. Fleet, K. Bowman, *The European Working Time Directive – interim report and guidance from the Royal College of Surgeons of England Working Party* (London: Royal College of Surgeons, January 2003).

56. Joanna Chikwe, Anthony de Souza, John R. Pepper, 'No time to train surgeons', *British Medical Journal*, 2004, 328: 418–19.

57. G.J. Morris, D. Clark, J. Torkington, D.J. Bowrey, R.E. Mansel, 'Training in the Calman era: what consultants say', *Annals of the Royal College of Surgeons of England*, 2002, 84 (Suppl): 345–7.

58. Melanie Newman, 'College wants to use larger animals in surgical training', *Hospital Doctor*, 18 March 2004, p. 14.

59. Isobel Allen, 'Doctors under stress', *BMA News Review*, April 1996, pp. 32–4.

60. W.R. Burnham op. cit.

61. B. Sibbald, C. Bojke, H. Gravelle, 'National survey of job satisfaction and retirement intentions among general practitioners in England', *British Medical Journal*, 2003, 326: 22–4.

62. Department of Health, *Investment and Reform for NHS Staff – Taking forward the NHS Plan*, 2001. According to the government-commissioned Wanless Report, the NHS will need 62,000 new doctors by 2010.

63. We shall return to this issue in later chapters. For the present, it is interesting to note the proposal, in a recent 'modernizing' document – *Modernizing Medical Careers* (Department of Health, 2002) – to reduce the years of training. A doctor could become a consultant by twenty-seven years of age (Amena Saleem, 'Majority of consultants could soon be appointed in their twenties', *Hospital Doctor*, 20 February 2003). This is suggested at a time when the experience a trainee might pack into a year will be rather less. The European Working Time Directive, which will require full-shift systems, will mean that those who are on nights will lose out on specialist training, which takes place mainly in the day. It will reduce daytime activities of senior trainees from 29.5 to 6.15 hours per week (79 per cent down). They will therefore need more years of training to get the same training experience – from 6 to 8.45 years for surgical training.

64. Recent studies have shown that average consultation times should be increased by nearly 100 per cent: G.K. Freeman, J.P. Horder, J.G.R. Howie, A.P. Hungin, A.P. Hill, N.C. Shah, A. Wilson, 'More care and more options and more genuine discussion of those options with informed patient choice inevitably leads to pressure of time', *British Medical Journal*, 2002, 324: 880–2.

Meanwhile, access to GPs – one of the cornerstones of the NHS Plan – has got worse since the Plan was launched. The proportion of people waiting more than two days to see a GP increased from 13 per cent in 1998 to 23 per cent in 2003 (S. Leatherman and K. Sutherland, *The quest for quality in the NHS. Mid-term evaluation of the ten-year quality agenda* (London: Nuffield Trust, 2003)). One response is to increase throughput by reducing time made available for each patient. This is being explored in Central Control: Jo Revill, 'Doctors ordered to slash time for patients', the *Observer*, 20 April 2003.

65. K. Walshe, 'The rise of regulation in the NHS', *British Medical Journal*, 2002, 324: 967–70.

66. I owe this phrase to Professor John Grimley Evans.

67. *Fifth Report on the Provision of Services for Patients with Heart Disease Heart*, 2002, 88 (suppl 3).

68. D. Robinson, C.M.J. Bell, H. Moller, I. Basnett, 'Effect of Government's two week target on waiting times in women with breast cancer in south-east England'. *British Journal of Cancer*, July 2003; 89: 493–496.

69. When triage nurses were first introduced into Casualty departments, they seemed to spend much time doing nothing. At any rate, they did little triaging and no nursing. I caused considerable offence by describing them as 'government greetings clerks'. They seem to have disappeared: we have another government with another set of initiatives.

70. In addition to the competition between priorities and posteriorities that are not important to the minister but are clinically of the greatest importance, there are also struggles between one priority and another. Government and clinicians are both agreed that they would like to see both more care for more patients and better care for all. The more (quantity) and the better (quality) are, however, in conflict. See Zoe Morris, 'A struggle between two priorities', *Hospital Doctor*, 14 March 2002.

71. Daniel K. Sokol, personal view, 'How (not) to be a good patient', *British Medical Journal*, 2004, 328: 471.

72. P. Bower, M. Roland, J. Campbell, N. Mead, 'Setting standards based on patients' views on access and continuity: secondary analysis of data from the general practice assessment survey', *British Medical Journal*, 2003, 326: 258–60. Foolishly, the Department of Health is trying to encourage more general practices to offer 'advanced access': no appointment systems; no waiting when you get to the surgery either; and a long enough appointment to be fully heard and sorted.

73. Roland Barthes, *A Lover's Discourse. Fragments*, translated by Richard Howard (New York: Hill and Wang, 1978), p. 40.

74. This is the opposite of the 'benumbed waiting' in which, according to Ryszard Kapuscinski in *The Shadow of the Sun* (translated by Klara Glowczewska,

New York: Vintage, 2002), so many people in Africa pass their lives, at least in part in response to the hopeless chaos of civic life (see pp. 15–18).

75. Jo Revill, 'Doctors ordered to slash time for patients', the *Observer*, 20 April 2003.

76. NHS Direct is due to expand its capacity from 6 million to 16 million calls per year. This is despite the fact that there is no evidence that it takes pressure off GPs (Rachel Chapman, Gillian Smith, Fiona Warburton, Richard Mayou-White, Douglas Fleming, 'Impact of NHS Direct on general practice consultations during the winter of 1999–2000: analysis of routinely collected data', *British Medical Journal*, 2002, 325: 1397–8). An earlier study, which had been funded by the Department of Health and actually published (though too late) showed that NHS Direct had no effect on the use of emergency ambulances or emergency departments and, at best, had a very small effect in flattening the rising curve of demand on out-of-hours GP services (though this may have led to more demand in-hours). J. Munro, J. Nicholl, A. O'Cathain, E. Knowles, 'Impact of NHS Direct on demand for immediate care: observational study', *British Medical Journal*, 2000, 321: 150–3.

77. Recently our local paper carried a front-page story criticizing a GP who had not immediately carried out a blood test on a teenage girl who had presented with a sore throat. A fortnight later, when her sore throat had failed to respond to simple treatment, he did a blood test which showed leukaemia. 'Why did my daughter have to wait?' asks angry mother. The answer, which would not have satisfied the angry mother but should have stopped a responsible newspaper from pillorying a competent GP, was that in 99.9 per cent of cases sore throats do not have serious causes and do not warrant immediate blood tests. The signal of a serious disease takes time to emerge from the noise of minor illness.

5 Power and Trust

1. Jo Knowsley, 'I went to hospital for a routine operation only to wake up and be told: "Sorry, it's gone wrong." In the week Ministers admitted that one in ten patients is a victim of medical errors, my harrowing experience reveals the true depth of the crisis in the NHS', *Mail on Sunday Review*, 23 June 2002, pp. 49–51.

2. In the United Kingdom, nurses have much more autonomy than in many other countries. For example, in France, nurse-led clinics, nurse prescribing and nurse consultants are unthinkable. A recent paper, reporting the popularity of British junior doctor posts among German trainees, pays tribute to the accessibility, generosity and kindness of senior doctors and the contrast with Germany, where medical training is much more hierarchical and seniors are

often unapproachable. As the author of this paper (Marcus Simmgen, 'Why German doctors enjoy British medicine', *Clinical Medicine*, 2004, 4(1): 57–9) comments, 'In the UK, advice from even very distinguished doctors is easy to obtain and there is rarely any hesitation in engaging in an educative conversation.' His main complaint was lack of equipment, and the frustation (which, needless to say, his seniors shared) this caused.

3. W.R. Burnham, 'Federation of the Royal Colleges of Physicians Census 2000', *Clinical Medicine*, 2002, 2(1): 7–8.

4. *GMC News*, issue 18, June 2003, p. 1.

5. The change has been quite dramatic. Between 1992 and 2002, the number of female consultants in England increased from 2,688 to 6,116. In non-surgical specialties, women account for between 25 per cent and 40 per cent of the consultant workforce. (Data from the British Medical Association.) Female consultants find it irritating that patients at first assume that 'the lady' who has come to see them is a nurse or a pharmacist rather than a doctor.

6. 'Clinical freedom was the right of doctors to do whatever in their opinion was best for their patients. Medical care is [now] to be limited to what is of proved value.' J.R. Hampton, 'The end of clinical freedom', *British Medical Journal*, 1983, 287: 1237–8.

7. Roger Dobson, 'Sharing of uncertainty can unnerve patients', *British Medical Journal* 2002, 325: 1319.

8. Brian Capstick, 'The future of clinical negligence litigation?', *British Medical Journal*, 2004, 328: 457–60.

9. The hurry of doctors who are perceived to be in power is often interpreted as another exercise of their power. It seems to say, 'You are not the only thing on my mind. I am one, you are many.'

10. Out-patient waiting times are a government target and she will herself have added to her pressures by fitting in extra patients to please a worried GP or someone whose problems seem urgent.

11. H.R.H. Patel, C.N. Luxman, T.S. Bailey, J.D.M. Brunning, D. Lemmel, L. K. Morrell, M.S. Nathan, R.A. Miller, 'Outpatient clinics: where is the delay?', *Journal of Royal Society of Medicine*, 2002, 95: 604–5.

12. 'How doctors deliver the curt words that mean life or death', the *Observer*, 10 November 2002, p. 10.

13. For a discussion of the hypocrisy of postmodern deconstructions of scientific and medical truth, see Raymond Tallis, *Enemies of Hope. A Critique of Contemporary Despair*, 2nd edn, *passim* (London: Macmillan, 1999). When Foucault was knocked down in the street, he was rushed to hospital, where he seems to have received excellent care. His friends, however, were horrified because the hospital did not seem to know who he was!

14. The outgoing President of the Royal College of Surgeons identified the

inability to introduce improvements in the services they provide, as well as lack of clinical independence, as the main cause of the steady deterioration in hospital doctors' morale. Norman Browse, 'Clinicians must lead', *British Medical Journal*, 1996, 313: 1268.

15. This is in part a reflection of the rule that prioritizing some things means posteriorizing others; but it is also because the NHS is not equipped to spend the billions that have been promised to those developing services. Owen Dyer has argued that 'NHS lacks the capacity to absorb the government's extra billions' (*British Medical Journal*, 2002, 325: 734) It is too used to saying 'no'. The analogy of driving blood down a furred-up vascular tree into atrophied organs seems applicable. However the money has disappeared. Where it has gone will be apparent when we discuss 're-disorganizations' in Chapter 6.

16. Those hoping to develop specialist services are now even more frustrated, as a result of yet another ill-thought-out reform, which has moved commissioning of services to Primary Care Trusts (PCTs) that are even more inexperienced and fragmented than the old Health Authorities (see Chapter 6.)

17. The political class's love affair with the consultancy seems to have peaked. There was a period in the late 1980s and early 1990s when one was visited by 'consultants' almost weekly. Their ignorance of the NHS and of health care beggared belief: we had to spend many hours (away from patients) briefing them on elementary things, illustrating the old adage that a management consultant is someone who steals your watch and charges you for telling the time. Most were amazed that we managed to achieve what we did with so little support. The typical outcome of a visit was a glossy brochure full of recommendations which we had no resources to act on and a big bill. Now we have think tanks whose inanities translate almost directly into policies, they have a vested interest, of course, in suggesting 'big ideas': the number of such ideas they suggest is their performance indicator.

18. Frith Rayner, 'Will Wanless Report make a difference?', *Hospital Medicine*, 2 May 2002, p. 8.

19. Billroth, the great pioneer of gastro-intestinal surgery was stoned in the streets of Vienna following the death of his first three patients who underwent the partial gastrectomy operation he introduced. Partial gastrectomy was the mainstay of treatment – saving many lives and much unhappiness – until the 1970s. This is a risk that all medical pioneers run, especially in the present day. The mobbing of the Bristol heart surgeons shows how close all surgeons – not only pioneers – are to this kind of barbarous 'customer feedback'.

20. This list was inspired by a letter, 'So who are the real NHS innovators, Mr Blair?' by M.C.T. Morrison, *Hospital Doctor*, 4 April 2002, p. 19.

21. I have focused on consultant-initiated innovations. An equally long list could be generated for primary care. General practice has been particularly

impressive in developing ways of making the service more patient-friendly, of handling uncertainty, of communication and of rethinking the patient–doctor relationships. See, for example, Marshall Marinker, 'What is Wrong and How We Know It: Changing Concepts of Illness in General Practice', in I. Loudon, J. Horder C. Webster (eds), *General Practice under the NHS 1948–1997* (Oxford: Clarendon Press 1998).

22. The dismal story of interminable 're-disorganizations' is told in more detail in Chapter 6.

23. See Chapter 6.

24. The story of the rise of geriatric medicine is told in John Brocklehust, 'Geriatric Medicine: History and Current Practice in Europe', in Raymond Tallis and Howard Fillit (eds), *Brocklehurst's Textbook of Geriatric Medicine and Gerontology*, 6th edn (Edinburgh: Churchill Livingstone, 2003). We shall revisit this story in Chapter 10.

25. It is some consolation to see that the government is finally admitting to having second thoughts about targets. (John Carvel and Rebecca Smithers, 'Labour in retreat on targets', the *Guardian*, 10 February 2004.) Giving hospitals star ratings, largely based on their achievement of targets, which always looked simplistic where they were not actually irrational, and promoting perverse incentives, is also due for the chop. None other than Professor Sir Ian Kennedy, the chair of the supreme regulatory body for the NHS, the Commission for Healthcare Audit and Inspection, has described the system of star ratings as 'fundamentally flawed' (Jo McCarroll, 'Jubilation at scrapping of ratings – but what next?', *Hospital Doctor*, 19 February 2004, p. 6.)
A recent study has shown that three-star hospitals perform no better than zero-star hospitals in terms of the quality of care for patients or outcomes – where accurate data are avilable (K. Rowan, D. Harrison, A. Brady, N. Black, 'Hospitals' star ratings and clinical outcomes: an ecological study', *British Medical Journal*, 2004, 328: 924–5). In most cases, outcome data are not accurate (K. Gill, S.A. Black, C.P.R. Corbett, 'Misleading mortality data in league tables', *Annals of the Royal College of Surgeons of England*, 2003, 85 (Suppl): S244–7).

26. Peter Langhorne and Martin Dennis, *Stroke Units: An Evidence-Based Approach* (Oxford: Oxford University Press, 1998).

27. *Summary Report on the National Sentinel Stroke Audit 2001/02* prepared on behalf of the Intercollegiate Stroke Working Party by Clinical Effectiveness and Evaluation Unit, Royal College of Physicians, London, July 2002. Summarized in Anthony G. Rudd and Michael Pearson, 'National Stroke Audit', *Clinical Medicine*, 2002, 2(6): 496–7.

28. Hazel Blears, an outstandingly honest politician, admitted when she was Public Health Minister that it is the Department of Health, with its endless

stream of directives and its inability to respond to genuinely new ideas that would improve patient care, that obstructs innovation in the NHS. See 'Minister admits NHS stifles innovation', *Hospital Doctor*, 16 May 2002.

29. K. Walshe and J. Smith, 'Cause and Effect', *Health Service Journal*, 11 October 2001, pp. 20–3.

30. A recent study of doctors carried out by the hospital managers' organization concludes that doctors are *too* self-critical and, far from gathering round in a corrupt club when things go wrong, support their colleagues very poorly. *British Medical Journal*, 2002, 324: 835–42. Ironically, managers use these observations to lay the blame at the doctors' door for their low morale. In short the paper criticizes doctors for being too self-critical.

31. I am grateful to Professor Irving Taylor (personal communication) for this list.

32. For those looking for a cure for insomnia, here is a more complete list:

a) **National**: General Medical Council revalidation procedures; UK Council for Regulation of Healthcare Professionals; National Clinical Assessment Authority; National Care Standards Commission; Commission for Health Improvement; National Patient Safety Agency; Cancer Accreditation Teams.

b) **Hospital**: Clinical Governance Committee; Continuing Professional Development Committee; Professional Advisory Panel; Clinical Audit Committee; Annual Consultant Appraisal; Junior Doctors Hours Action Team; Pre-Registration House Office and Senior House Officer Reviews for Postgraduate Team; Specialist Registrar Review for Postgraduate Dean and Royal College of Surgeons.

c) **University**: Internal Quality Assurance Committee; Staff Review and Development Committee; Annual University Appraisal; Quality Assurance Agency; Research Assessment Exercise; Peer Review of Teaching; Research Governance Committee.

By the time you, the reader, comes to read this, more will have been added.

33. *Daily Mirror*, March 1995. Personal communication from Dr Val Broadbent the doctor persecuted by the press.

34. Leonard Leibovici and Michel Lievre, 'Medicalization: peering from inside medicine', *British Medical Journal*, 2002, 324: 866.

35. Roy Porter, *The Greatest Benefit to Mankind: A Medical History of Humanity from Antiquity to the Present* (London: HarperCollins, 1997), p. 718.

36. Some have suggested that the very use of the term 'patient' is disempowering, recommending alternative terms such as 'user' and 'client'. This has been debated by J. Neuberger and R. Tallis, 'Do we need a new word for patients?', *British Medical Journal*, 1999, 318: 1756–8.

37. Rhona MacDonald, 'Lessons from medicine's shameful past', *British Medical Journal*, 2004, 328: 411.

38. Alan Milburn, 'Redefining the National Health Service', speech to the New Health Network, 4 February 2002. Tell this to the surgeon who has got out of his bed night after night, or the physician who works 59 hours a week on a 37.5-hour contract, or a nurse who again and again is late picking up her children because there is too much to do on the ward, to the GP who will have seen a total of 250,000 patients in his forty-year career, or a manager who comes in Sunday after Sunday to implement the latest government initiative. In the most recent survey of NHS staff (reported in *Hospital Doctor*, 8 April 2004), 75 per cent of staff said they routinely worked more than their contracted hours. Twelve per cent worked more than ten hours of unpaid overtime in an average week. Finally, in a recent survey of 1,001 doctors, 77 per cent of respondents reported that their job prevented them from spending adequate time with their family (*Hospital Doctor*, 8 April 2004, pp. 10–11).

39. This in part explains why, as Theodore Dalrymple has pointed out in *Mass Listeria. The Meaning of Health Scares* (London: André Deutsch, 1998), p. 61, that 'trust in the medical profession seems to be inversely proportional to the scientific basis of its practice: it was accorded the most authority when it least deserved it.'

40. For example, the highest levels of overall satisfaction with the NHS are amongst older people, who actually receive the vast majority of care (Michael Calnan, editorial, 'Are older people still grateful?', *Age and Ageing*, 2003, 32: 125–6). Interestingly, these high levels of satisfaction in older people have not changed over twenty years. It may be that the more serious your medical problems, the more likely you are to put the imperfections inevitable in any service in perspective.

41. This illustrates Theodore Dalrymple's observation (in 'Wronged by our rights', the *Spectator*, 24 April 2004) that 'People who stand on their rights are seldom concerned with the rights of others. There is no logical reason why this should be so, but it is a fact of human psychology. "It's my right!" is not a call of freedom but of egotism.'

42. Secretary of State for Health, *The NHS Plan. A plan for investment. A plan for reform* (London: Stationery Office, 2000).

43. E. Simpson and A.O. House, 'Involving users in the delivery and evaluation of mental health services: systematic review', *British Medical Journal*, 2002, 325: 1265–8. M.J. Crawford, D. Rutter, C. Manley, T. Weaver, K. Bhui, N. Fulop, P. Tyrer, 'Systematic review of involving patients in the planning and development of health care', *British Medical Journal* 2002, 325: 1263–4. Nor do patients necessarily want to be involved. A recent MORI poll (quoted by Frank Dobson, ex-Secretary of State for Health) found that only 22 per cent of people wanted to have a greater say in the development of their local health service and 51 per

cent did not want to have a greater say. Perhaps they recognized that running a hospital is a complex, technical and managerial business.

44. I recall an exquisitely embarrassing occasion when a new branch of the Stroke Association was opened in a northern town and the Mayor who was doing the honours said that it was, indeed, about time that '*heart attacks* received the attention they deserved'.

45. Sir Donald Irvine in *Risk and Trust in the NHS*, edited by Hugo Foxwood (London: The Smith Institute, 2002), p. 74.

46. As Theodore Dalrymple has pointed out, 'Information without perspective is a higher form of ignorance.' *Mass Listeria. The Meaning of Health Scares* (London: André Deutsch, 1998), p. 34.

47. And this will certainly get in the way of the increasingly efficient, throughput-dominated NHS of the future. Any aspect of quality, including kindly, properly paced explanation and listening and counselling – which no one can quarrel with – is at odds with the Government's target-based demands for ever-increasing quantity. Patients want quality in health care when they reach the doctor *and* quantity that ensures that everyone, including themselves, gets all the health care they want.

48. 'Mixed verdict in NHS staff survey', *Hospital Doctor*, 8 April 2004, pp. 10–11.

49. John Carvel, 'Chaos ahead for foundation hospitals', the *Guardian*, 21 January 2004, p. 5.

50. Hazel Blears, 'Communities in control: public service and local socialism', *Fabian Ideas*, 607, Fabian Society, June 2003. It is worth again recalling the recent MORI poll in which 51 per cent of those polled said they would *not* like to have a greater say in designing and running their health services and only 22 per cent showed any interest at all.

51. 'Trust me, I'm a patient', Cristina Odone, *Observer*, 22 December 2002. The sub-editor obviously didn't like the doctor-friendly tone of the article because he sub-headlined it 'Doctors have to respect that we know more about our health' and lifted the following passage out of context – 'Mute and docile as children, we once did the medic's bidding' – whereas Odone's point was that the pendulum has swung too far in the opposite direction.

52. The survey of 200 GPs cited by Odone found that half would like to tell their patients to wash before coming to see them; two thirds wanted to be able to inform their patients that they were overweight; and half believed that their patients did not take the medication they recommended.

53. Francesca Robinson, 'Where have all the doctors gone?', *Hospital Doctor*, 22 February 2004, pp. 22–6.

54. Melinda Letts in *Risk and Trust in the NHS*, edited by Hugo Foxwood (London: The Smith Institute, 2002).

55. This topic is brilliantly handled by Onora O'Neill in her 2002 Reith Lectures, 'Called to Account' (London: BBC Publications, 2002). Many of the points in this chapter echo those she made there. See also Raymond Tallis, 'The reluctance to trust in trust', *Times Literary Supplement*, 30 January 1998, pp. 5–6.

56. A poll carried out by MORI for the BMA showed that the trust in the profession actually rose in the twelve months following the Bristol and Alder Hey inquiries, rising by 2 per cent to an extraordinary 89 per cent. Even after being reminded of these episodes, 84 per cent of the public placed doctors at the top of the list of the professions they trusted. These data are quoted in Ray Dunne, 'Trust me…', *Hospital Doctor*, 2 August 2002. Even more encouraging are the results of a MORI poll in 2004, which found that 92 per cent of the public trusted doctors to tell the truth. This is much higher than any other professional group and the highest since the poll began in 1983. The least trusted groups were journalists (20 per cent), politicians (22 per cent) and government ministers (23 per cent) ('Doctors trusted more than any other group', *British Medical Journal*, 2004, 328: 726).

It is also worth putting the problems of the medical profession in perspective. There are 200,000 doctors registered with the General Medical Council, 120,000 in active practice. Less than 4,000 a year are referred to the GMC, mostly for non-clinical issues. Action is taken against only 800 and less than 200 are taken off the Register.

57. Department of Health (2000) National Survey of NHS Patients, April 2000, www.doh.gov.uk/public/nhssurveys.htm

58. Onora O'Neill, 2002 Reith Lectures, op. cit., Lecture I 'Spreading Suspicion'.

59. The interested reader might want to read Raymond Tallis, *Enemies of Hope: A Critique of Contemporary Pessimism* (London: Macmillan, 2nd edn, 1999), especially Part II, 'Marginalizing Consciousness'.

60. As Onora O'Neill, op. cit. says, 'a crisis of trust cannot be overcome by a blind rush to place more trust.'

61. *The Times* ('Health care watchdog chief broke inquiry rules', 12 November 2002) delightedly pointed out that when the medical director of the Government's Commission for Health Improvement was herself medical director of a trust, she failed to ensure that all perioperative deaths were recorded and referred to the National Inquiry on Perioperative Deaths. The finger of blame has a habit of pointing back at the blamer.

62. Made possible to an undreamed-of extent by modern information technology.

63. Onora O'Neill, op. cit., Lecture I.

64. Jonathan Asbridge, 'Modernizing regulation – can we still trust health professionals?', *Risk and Trust in the NHS*, edited by Hugo Foxwood (London: Smith Institute, 2002), p. 41.

65. Clara MacKay, ibid., p. 44.

66. Kieran Walshe, 'The rise of regulation in the NHS', *British Medical Journal*, 2002, 324: 967–70.

67. C. Hood, C. Scott, O. James, G. Jones, T. Travers, *Regulation Inside Government: Waste Watchers, Sleaze Busters and the Quality Police* (Oxford: Oxford University Press, 1999).

68. 'Labour new health quangos to be axed', *The Times*, 26 November 2003.

69. The evidence is that its methods of inspection – a 'process by which a ragbag of reflections (including variable attempts to to capture the patient experience) are convertted to global and quantified assessments' – are flawed. *The NHS Improvers: A Study of the Commission for Health Improvement*, 2004, *www.kingsfund.org.uk*

70. Many doctors, who in the past felt confident that they would be supported in ensuring that patients in unbearable torment in the final stages of a terminal illness were given adequate pain relief, even if it hastened the end, now feel very anxious. For this reason, the new Patient (Assisted Dying) Bill, currently being considered by a Select Committee of the House of Lords, is being welcomed by some of us. We no longer feel that humane care is an adequate defence against, for example, pro-life activists who wish to impose their values and beliefs on dying patients.

71. John Saunders, 'Perspectives on CPR: resuscitation or resurrection?', *Clinical Medicine*, 2001, 1: 457–60.

72. C.A. Marco, E.S. Bessman, C.N. Schoenfeld, G.D. Kelen, 'Ethical issues of cardiopulmonary, resuscitation: current practice among emergency physicians', *Academic Emergency Medicine*, 1997, 4: 898–904.

73. As Saunders, op. cit. points out, 'autonomy is not enhanced where one choice offers no reasonable prospect of a particular outcome.'

74. Clara MacKay, op. cit., p. 45.

75. Kenneth Minogue, *Times Literary Supplement*, 27 June 2003, p. 15.

6 Enemies of Progress

1. Rose Shepherd, 'Nil by mouth', *Observer Magazine*, 29 February 2004, p. 27. This was said in support of the wonderful benefits of so-called 'health foods'.

2. By, for example, pointing out that while fraud in science does occur, it is episodic rather than structural and less pervasive than in any other walk of life (and certainly than in the alternative medicine industry); that mistakes, too, occur but, along with fraud, are sooner or later corrected or found out; and that the double-blind randomized controlled trial is the best way of bypassing the vested interests of drug companies, as many high-cost disappointments experienced by them attest to.

3. Quoted in I. Chalmers, L.V. Hedges, H. Cooper, 'A brief history of research synthesis', *Evaluation and the Health Professions*, 2002, 25 (1): 12–37.

4. As a teacher used to remind me, 'the plural of anecdote is not data.' Even less is the plural of selective anecdotes a database.

5. And is being still further refined. See, for example, M. Landray and G. Whitlock, 'Evaluating treatment effects reliably', *British Medical Journal*, 2002, 325: 1372–3.

6. This is a particularly dubious claim. The triple vaccine is out of patent and drug companies stand to gain more by supporting a regime of single jabs.

7. A.J. Wakefield, S.H. Murch, A. Anthony, J. Linnell, D.M. Casson, M. Malik et al., 'Ileal-lymphoid-nodular hyperplasia, non-specific colitis, and pervasive developmental disorder in children', *The Lancet*, 1998, 351: 637–41.

8. This became clear only five years later in an extraordinary twist to a by then extraordinarily twisted tale. See below.

9. E. Middleton and D. Baker, 'Comparison of social distribution of immunisation with measles, mumps, rubella', *British Medical Journal*, 2003, 326: 854.

10. B. Taylor, E. Miller, C.P. Farrington, M.C. Petropoulos, I. Favot-Maynaud, J. Li et al., 'Autism and measles, mumps and rubella vaccine: no epidemiological evidence for a causal association', *The Lancet*, 1999, 353: 2026–9.

11. Brent Taylor, Elizabeth Miller, Raghu Lingam, Nick Andrews, Andrea Sommins, Julia Stowe, 'Measles, mumps and rubella vaccine in children with autism: population study', *British Medical Journal*, 2002, 324: 393–6.

12. K.M. Madsen, A. Hviid, M. Vestergaard et al., *New England Journal of Medicine*, 2002, 347: 1477–82.

13. A. Patna, I. Davidkin, T. Turki et al., 'Serious adverse events after measles – mumps – rubella: vaccination during a fourteen-year prospective follow-up', *Paediatric Infectious Disease Journal*, 2000, 19: 1127–34.

14. For a beautiful analysis of muddled public debate about MMR: see Paula McDonald, 'False syllogisms, teddy bears, causality and MMR', *Prescriber*, 2003, 14(22): 77–82.

15. N. Andrews, E. Miller, B. Taylor, 'Recall bias, MMR and autism', *Archives of Disease in Childhood*, 2002, 87: 493–4.

16. Corri Black, James A. Kaye, Hershel Jick, 'Relation of childhood gastro-intestinal disorders to autism: nested case-control study using data from the UK General Practice Research Database', *British Medical Journal*, 2002, 325: 419–21.

17. Paula McDonald, op. cit.

18. Anna Donald, *British Medical Journal*, June 2002, Overview of MMR evidence.

19. Beezy Marsh and Tahira Yaqoob, 'I won't let our baby have MMR jab, says Livingstone', *Daily Mail*, 3 July 2002. In fact a study from the south of England

has refuted the 'Livingstone-whack' hypothesis. There was no association between immunization with MMR and the subsequent incidence of serious bacterial infection – in fact it went down (*Archives of Disease in Childhood*, 2003, 88: 222–3).

20. Claire Hindley, 'MMR Jab Ruined My Life', *Manchester Evening News*, 19 January 2002.

21. Nor was the significance of the fact that Mr Lloyd's son (who is now fit and well) 'is joining others in a huge lawsuit against a number of manufacturers'. For the law, needless to say, has had its eyes on the potential rich pickings from the presumed association between MMR and autism. Approximately 600 parents who believe their children's woes are due to MMR are being represented by one firm of lawyers.

22. Lorraine Fraser, 'Parents pay to bypass MMR in NHS surgery', *Sunday Telegraph*, 10 November 2002. Some of these clinics have now been closed for unsafe practices.

23. The fact that single vaccines imported to meet the rising demand had not been licensed for import or tested for toxicity ('Dogma on MMR does not work', *Observer*, 10 February 2002) seems also, until the end of 2001, to have escaped the attention of their advocates.

24. Data provided by the NHS reported in *Evening Standard*, 31 October 2003. Nationally there was a fall from an overall 92 per cent in 1998 to just under 80 per cent in early 2004. In some parts of Ken Livingstone's London, the rates were as low as 60 per cent (data from James Meikle, 'Demand for full MMR inquiry', the *Guardian*, 23 February 2004, p. 7).

25. Lynda Lee Potter, *Daily Mail*, 3 July 2002, p. 11. It seems to me more insulting to parents to think that they would be more influenced by the example of one person than by the objective data made available to them.

26. 'Who can we believe these days?', the *Observer*, 10 February 2002, p. 27.

27. Overlooking that it was medical scientists who demonstrated the link between thalidomide and birth deformities.

28. Editorial, 'Dogma on MMR does not work', the *Observer*, 10 February 2002.

29. Nick Hornby, 'Why parents are angry', the *Observer*, 10 February 2002, p. 27.

30. Roger Dobson, 'Parents' champion or loose cannon?', *British Medical Journal*, 2002, 324: 386.

31. N.P. Thompson, R.E. Pander, A.J. Wakefield 'Is measles vaccination a risk factor for inflammatory bowel disease?', *The Lancet* 1995, 345: 1071–4. The ethical case for these invasive procedures on young children – along with even more invasive lumbar punctures – is currently being investigated by the General Medical Council.

32. Editorial, 'Time to look beyond MMR in autism research', *The Lancet*, 2002, 359: 637–8.

33. Maxine Frith, 'Measles alert in MMR crisis', *Evening Standard*, 3 July 2002, pp. 1–2.

34. Peter English, 'General practitioners' two roles are not in conflict with MMR immunisation', *British Medical Journal*, 2002, 324: 734.

35. 'Health Promotion England MMR Factsheet 3', MMR Information Pack for Health Professionals. Nobody, incidentally, has said sorry for the deaths.

36. M.C. Nelson and J. Rogers, 'The right to die? Anti-vaccination activity and the 1874 smallpox epidemic in Stockholm', *Social History of Medicine*, 1992, 5: 369–88.

37. 'Theodore Dalrymple, *Mass Listeria. The Meaning of Health Scares* (London: Andre Deutsch, 1998), p. 108. This is clearly illustrated in a series of articles by Melanie Phillips, published in March 2003 in the *Daily Mail* ('MMR – The Truth', 11, 12, 13 March). She points out that many of the experts who have supported MMR vaccine have links with drug companies who manufacture vaccines. She fails to record that Andrew Wakefield is acting on behalf of parents in an upcoming court case over MMR – of which more presently. When it comes to vested interests, we should not overlook the fact that Professor John O'Leary – whose observations of fragments of the measles virus in samples of intestines from children with autism were crucial to Wakefield's case – himself runs a company called Unigenics which has received £800,000 from the UK legal aid fund for this work, which may well be flawed (Brian Deer, 'Fresh cast on MMR study data. Court told of contamination fear', *Sunday Times*, 25 April 2004, p. 11).

38. Brian Deer, 'MMR: the Truth Behind the Crisis', *Sunday Times*, 22 February 2004.

39. Editorial, 'Misled over MMR', the *Observer*, 22 February 2004.

40. Francis Elliott, ' "Misconduct" inquiry for doctor in MMR scare', the *Observer*, 22 February 2004.

41. Jeremy Laurance, 'MMR. The facts, claims, realities and the unanswered questions', the *Independent*, 24 February 2004, p. 1.

42. Editorial, 'This carefully orchestrated campaign must not be allowed to stifle real debate on MMR', the *Independent*, 24 February 2004.

43. On the same grounds one would question the establishment view that pneumonia may be caused by bacteria and strokes may be caused by problems with blood vessels in the brain.

44. 'Dogma on MMR does not work', the *Observer*, 10 February 2002.

45. The total deaths from definite or probable v CJD in the UK – whose origin still remains uncertain – was 141 between 1996 and April 2004. (Edinburgh: CJD Surveillance Unit)

46. Marco Angelini, Notes for a talk at meeting of Philosophy for All group, January 2003.

47. Raymond Tallis, 'Apocalypse Soon?', *Times Literary Supplement*, no. 4855, 19 April 1996, pp. 25–6.

48. Theodore Dalrymple, *Mass Listeria* (London: Andre Deutsch, 1998).

49. In practice, only 'if children came into contact with the kind of quantities of apple juice in which they were more likely to drown than drink, that is to say 24, 000 cartons per day' might they develop cancer – and then only if they were biologically like mice (Dalrymple, ibid., p. 108).

50. Sven Lomberg has made some effort to place environmental scares in perspective in his brave book, *The Sceptical Environmentalist* (Cambridge: Cambridge University Press, 1999).

The pleasure of moral indignation may be extended when scares are found to be groundless; for the 'whitewash' will confirm a widely held suspicion that the government and scientists are colluding in a cover-up. Such was the fate of the investigators who examined the supposed outbreak of illness occurring in Cornwall as a result of the accidental spillage of alumnium into the water supply. The two reports – Lowermoor Incident Health Advisory Group, *Water Pollution at Lowermoor, North Cornwall* (Truro: Cornwall and Isles of Scilly District Health Authority, 1989) and Lowermoor Incident Health Advisory Group, *Water Pollution at Lowermoor, North Cornwall*, second report (London: Stationery Office, 1990) – resulted in vilification of the experts. (I had a particular interest in this because I was in Cornwall when the spillage happened and I and my family drank the contaminated water.)

Subsequent studies a decade later vindicated the reports: hospital admissions and mortality were lower in the area affected than in the rest of Cornwall and the country (P.J. Owen, D.P.B. Miles, G.J. Draper, T.J. Vincent, 'Retrospective study of mortality, after a water pollution incident at Lowermoor in north Cornwall', *British Medical Journal*, 2002, 324: 1189).

51. Bill Durodie, 'Plastic Panics. European Risk Regulation in the Aftermath of BSE', in Julian Morris (ed.), *Rethinking Risk and the Precautionary Principle* (Oxford and London: Butterworth-Heinemann, 2000). Durodie's examples of the power of the Green lobby to raise scares about harmless toys, and harmless substances, and to get products banned at huge cost to business and to the scientific community, are terrifying.

52. According to the then Consumer Policy and Consumer Health Protection Commissioner, Emma Bonino, 'pressure from public opinion and interested bodies has often appeared to be the strongest driving force to guarantee that all necessary measures to protect public health are effectively taken' (Durodie ibid., p. 14).

53. Durodie, ibid., p. 15. I draw attention to this problem as a Europhile. I do

not believe that there is anything specific about the EU in this regard. What we may call the 'Health and Safety Executive culture', a product of a litigious society, is forcing absurd decisions on many large organizations. This may be why the Commission's own Consumer Committee proposed the application of the precautionary principle 'even where there is no known scientific uncertainty'.

54. Sometimes the scale of the threat may be measured directly – as Lomberg has attempted to do in *The Sceptical Environmentalist*, op. cit. The grave danger that comes from ascribing special authority to those who have been victims will be discussed in Chapter 7 in the section 'From Grief to Grievance'.

55. Annabel Ferriman, 'Advocates of PSA testing campaign to silence critics', *British Medical Journal*, 2002, 324: 255. This story continues in Australia: Professor Alan Coates, chief executive of the Cancer Council Australia, who stated that he would not choose to have the PSA test as a routine screen, has been accused of showing (amongst other things) 'contempt for men and their families' (Simon Chapman, 'Fresh row over prostate screening', *British Medical Journal*, 2003, 326: 605).

56. Equally unbalanced is the concern over the dangers associated with the very effective anti-smoking drug Zyban, which has been associated with sixty-three deaths. But this is in a population of 540,000 individuals who have used it, who are anyway at risk from fatal cardiovascular and respiratory disease from smoking – which kills half of those who take it up.

57. 'MMR row "misreported" by press', Daniel Forman, *epxNews*, 19 May 2003.

58. Jenny Hope, 'New autism jabs fear', *Daily Mail*, 14 January 2003.

59. Max Wells and Sarah Boseley, 'Calls to axe TV drama on MMR', the *Guardian*, 3 December 2003, p. 9.

60. Ibid.

61. John Diamond, in his lucid, passionate and very funny *Snake Oil and Other Preoccupations* (London: Vintage, 2001) questions the very category of alternative medicine: 'There are interventions one can make that have some effect on illness and there are interventions one can make which have no effect at all. The former count as medicine, the latter don't' (p. 13).

62. Including, inexcusably, the special issue of *British Medical Journal* devoted to 'Integrated Medicine', of 20 January 2001. There are, however, several excellent accounts of the phenomenon – well-informed, insightful and sympathetic. I have found four short contributions particularly helpful: John Diamond's *Snake Oil*, which I have already mentioned; Henry Shenkin, 'If It's Different from Orthodox Medical Care, It's Got Be Better', *Myths in Medical Care. Causes and Effects* (Danbury, CT: Rutledge Books, Inc., 2000), pp. 178–95; Ronald W. Dworkin, 'Science, Faith and alternative medicine', *Policy Review*, 108, August September 2001; and John Saunders, 'Alternative, complementary,

holistic...', *Philosophical Problems in Health Care*, ed. D. Greaves and H. Upton (Brookfield, VT: Avebury, 1996), pp. 103–25.

63. D.M. Eisenberg, R.C. Kessler, C. Foster et al., 'Unconventional medicine in the United States: prevalence costs, cost and patterns of use', *New England Journal of Medicine*, 1993, 328: 246–52.

64. Ronald Dworkin, op. cit.

65. BBC 1, *Six O'Clock News*, 2 March 2004.

66. K. Thomas, M. Fall, G. Parry, J. Nichol, *National Survey of Access to Complementary Health Care via General Practice*, Final Report to the Department of Health (Sheffield: University of Sheffield, 1995).

67. Op. cit., note 62.

68. The *Observer* 'Guide to Breast Cancer Treatment', published as a supplement, 29 September 2002.

69. As are many other members of the Royal Family.

70. HRH Prince Charles, 'Personal View: The best of both worlds', *British Medical Journal*, 2001, 322: 181.

71. HRH Prince of Wales, 'When our health is at risk, why be mean? Alternative medicine needs and deserves more research funding', *The Times*, 29 December 2000, p. 28.

72. D.K. Owen, G. Lewith, C.R. Stephens, 'Can doctors respond to patients' increasing interest in complementary and alternative medicine?', *British Medical Journal*, 2001, 322: 154–8.

73. M.S. Wetzel, D.M. Eisenberg, T.J. Kaptchuk, 'Courses involving complementary and alternative medicine at US medical schools', *Journal of the American Medical Association*, 1998, 280: 784–7.

74. Benveniste, who published a study in *Nature*, putatively demonstrating differences between homoeopathic dilutions and ordinary water, claimed that the former had the molecular 'memories' or 'ghosts' of the homoeopathic substances that had once been in the potion. This is contrary to anything known to physicists.

75. D.M. Eisenberg, 'Advising patients who seek alternative therapies', *Archives of Internal Medicine*, 1997, 127: 61–9. There are occasional isolated reports of benefits. For example, a recent study showed that patients with chronic headache with no underlying cause had some real benefit from acupuncture. A.J. Vickers, R.W. Rees, C.E. Zollman et al., 'Acupuncture for chronic headache in primary care: large, pragmatic, randomised trial', *British Medical Journal*, 2004, 328: 744–7. The design of the trial was not such as to rule out a placebo effect.

76. Shenkin op. cit. (see note 62), p. 185.

77. This is why alternative medicine practitioners may not benefit from being embraced by the medical profession. The gain in respectability may be more than offset by the loss of status attached to being rejected by the medical

establishment. Moreover, if alternative medicine is 'integrated' into conventional care, it will lose a good deal of the aura it derives from being 'exotic'.

78. This may not take obvious forms. Alternative medicine practitioners are adept at finding diseases where orthodox practitioners, perhaps reluctant to medicalize human unhappiness that does not seem to stem from pathology, can find none. This may be a unique example of the effectiveness of the homeopathic principle of 'treating like with like'. The alternative medicine practitioner who finds an illness that physicians cannot find is somehow supporting, acknowledging or validating you. Where there is no disease but only unfounded belief in disease, this will also respond very well to another unfounded belief.

79. Roy Porter, *The Greatest Benefit to Mankind: A Medical History of Humanity from Antiquity to the Present* (London, HarperCollins, 1997), p. 8.

80. The contrast between the endless variety of 'orthodox' medicine – with a multitude of different remedies for the multitude of different diseases – and the monotony of the remedies offered by alternative practitioners, has never been sufficiently remarked upon. This monotony is overlooked because the wares of different kinds of practitioners are lumped together in health shops. It is forgotten that a given practitioner will have a very narrow range of responses to the vast panoply of disease. What is more, exponents of one particular brand of alternative therapy often have little time for purveyors of other non-orthodox alternatives. The closed-mindedness orthodox practitioners are accused of is very much alive and well in the ranks of alternative practitioners.

81. Donald Prater, *Ringing Glass, The Life of Rainer Maria Rilke* (Oxford: Oxford University Press, 1986). p. 403.

82. Ronald W. Dworkin, 'Science, Faith and alternative medicine', *Policy Review*, 108, August/September 2001.

83. Gerard Bodeker, 'Lessons on integration from the developing world's experience', *British Medical Journal*, 2001, 322: 164–7.

84. John Diamond, op. cit., pp. 36–7.

85. N.M. Davidson and E.H. Parry, 'The etiology of peripartum cardiac failure', *American Heart Journal*, 1979, 97: 535–6.

86. World Health Organization United Nations Children's Fund, *Revised 1990 estimates of maternal mortality: a new approach by WHO and UNICEF* (Geneva: WHO, 1996).

87. Fiona Fleck, 'West Africa polio campaign boycotted by Nigerian states', *British Medical Journal*, 2004, 328: 485.

88. It is worth noting how close the successful WHO campaign has come to wiping polio from the face of the earth. Since 1988, WHO has immunized 2 billion children in 200 countries and the infection rates in those countries have fallen from 350,000 cases when the campaign began to 782 last year. Not one

new case of this ghastly crippling disease has been recorded in twenty-two countries across eastern and southern Africa since October 2002. Meanwhile, 400 Nigerian children have contracted polio in the last six months (Declan Walsh, 'War on polio obstructed by radical clerics', *Independent on Sunday*, 21 March 2004, p. 21).

89. This and other facts are taken from an article by Chris McNeal, the *Guardian*, 1 November 2002, pp. 4–5.

90. Ibid.

91. Liz McGregor, 'DJ's AIDS death highlights pain of South Africa', the *Observer*, 29 February 2004, p. 25.

92. Rory Caroll, 'South Africa "stalling" on AIDS', the *Guardian*, 15 July 2003, p. 13.

93. The lack of drugs is, of course, only part of a picture in which irrationality and the abuse of power go hand in hand. The refusal of Mbeki to acknowledge that underuse of condoms and the absence for many women of any control over how, when and with whom they might engage in sexual activity, plays an even greater part. Multiculturalist sentimentality about 'traditional' beliefs has yet to engage with many unacceptable practices. 'Traditional' societies often subordinate the rights of individuals to the needs of others compounding the catastrophic influence of myth, legend and magic thinking in addressing medical problems. The tradition from which 'traditional medicine' springs is one of unaccountable authority.

94. Raymond Tallis, *Enemies of Hope: A Critique of Contemporary Pessimism* (London: Macmillan, 2nd edn, 1999).

95. Roy Porter, *The Greatest Benefit to Mankind*, op. cit., pp. 6–7. This passage is particularly impressive because, throughout his book, Porter is trying to avoid a Whiggish or triumphalist account of the progress of medicine. At the same time, he is sufficiently honest not to be able resist the facts.

96. J. Ciment, 'WHO celebrates triumph over river blindness', *British Medical Journal*, 1999, 319: 1090.

97. Charles Webster, *The National Health Service. A Political History* (Oxford: Oxford University Press, new edn, 2002). I am enormously grateful to, and have been heavily dependent upon this wonderful book. I have also profited from Brian Watkin's lucid, persuasive and wise account of the first twenty-five years of the NHS – *The National Health Service: The First Phase 1948–1974 and After* (London: George Allen & Unwin, 1978).

98. I used to think that the Tories were the greatest threat to the NHS. I no longer believe this. The enduring legacy of New Labour has been to increase funding and then, by virtue of distrust-fuelled over-regulation, to get in the way of increased resources translating into benefits for patients. After New Labour, both the friends and enemies of the NHS will believe that it is an 'unworkable idea'.

99. See Watkin, op. cit., pp. 34–8.

100. Webster, op. cit., p. 44.

101. Webster, ibid, p. 61.

102. Watkin, op. cit., p. 152.

103. Watkin's account of this on pp. 147–51 is a wonderful – and terrible – eye-opener.

104. Raymond Tallis, *Absence. A Metaphysical Comedy* (London: The Toby Press, 1999).

105. Ibid., pp. 124–5.

106. Unnamed source cited in Webster, op. cit., p. 173.

107. See Watkin, op. cit., p. 135.

108. Recent events at the BBC in the wake of Lord Hutton's inquiry may make the Corporation model less attractive.

109. Margaret Thatcher introducing *Working for Patients*. Quoted in Webster, op. cit., p. 190.

110. In 1963, at the end of his three-year term as Secretary of State for Health, Enoch Powell wrote in *A New Look at Medicine and Politics* (London: Pitman Medical, 1966):

One of the most striking feature of the National Health Service is the continual deafening chorus of complaint which rises day and night from every part of it… The universal Exchequer financing of the service endows everyone providing it as well as using it with a vested interest in denigrating it, so that it presents what must be the unique spectacle of an undertaking that is run down by everyone engaged in it.

111. Webster, op. cit., p. 230.

112. It was interesting that the Department issued this last document 'for consultation' in August 2000 and set 7 September as the deadline for responses. On 7 September, the government launched the next stage of its plan – the Strategic Health Authorities – demonstrating the fictional nature of the consultation process. Nick Bosanquet, 'Brave new NHS. Across the great divide: discussing the undiscussable: Getting real', *British Journal of Health Care Management*, 2001, 7(10): 395.

113. Webster, op. cit., p. 238.

114. The fact that this has not always been successful, as the Bristol heart hospital inquiry showed, should not distract from an overall success story: the Bristol problems took place against a background of almost miraculous improvement in survival figures nationally at a time when more and more complex cases were operated on.

115. Kenneth Clarke was – in this respect as in many others – an exception.

116. Recently there has been a trend for large, ambitious initiatives, such as

National Service Frameworks, to have intermediate targets and 'early wins' built into the plans.

117. This was Bevan's famously cynical observation when he obtained the hospital consultants' commitment to the NHS by a generous system of distinction awards to compensate for loss of private earnings and to reflect professional excellence.

118. Quoted in Watkin, op. cit., p. 40.

119. Secretary of State for Health, *The NHS Plan. A plan for investment. A plan for reform* (London: Stationery Office, 2000).

120. Understandably, he judged doctors' motivation by his own. As for his motivation, we may judge this from his career since ceasing to be the Secretary of State for Health. As Deputy Chairman of British American Tobacco, he has a key role in overseeing the dissemination of smoking to new markets in countries which as yet have fewer regulations and fewer smoking-related deaths.

121. It is, characteristic of command-and-control governments with 'Big Plans' to start paranoiacally believing in 'wreckers' when the Big Plans don't work.

122. These data are taken from a thoughtful paper by Kieran Walshe and Joan Higgins, 'The use and impact of inquiries in the NHS', *British Medical Journal*, 2002, 325: 895–900.

123. Ibid., p. 895.

124. Ibid., p. 899. Indeed, *The Report of the Independent Inquiry into Paediatric Cardiac Services at the Royal Brompton and Harefield Hospital* (London: Royal Brompton Hospital, 2001), observed that 'there was no precedent nor guidelines to draw on to help us run the Inquiry. This is surprising, given the number of non-statutory reviews conducted in the NHS' (quoted in Iain Chalmers, Edmund Hey, 'Learning from Bristol: the need for a lead from the Chief Medical Officer', *British Medical Journal*, 2001, 324: 280–1). Not only surprising, but disgraceful, given the cost of inquiries and the anguish they cause those who are investigated.

125. Derek Wanless, *Securing Our Future Health. Taking a long-term view*, April 2002 (Crown Copyright, 2002).

126. Anthony Browne, 'Why the NHS is bad for us', the *Observer*, 7 October 2002. The facts about the excessive number of deaths of elderly people in 2003 in France are in *British Medical Journal*, 26 August 2003.

127. Polly Toynbee, 'Modernising Health Care – the Patient', in *Risk and Trust in the NHS*, edited by Hugo Foxwood (London: Smith Institute, 2002), p. 79.

128. The role of 'independent think tanks' has been a crucial force behind the introduction of an endless succession of 'super-duper new ideas'. Producing such ideas is their *raison d'être*. No think tank mindful of its own survival is going to suggest that 'nothing needs to be done' or 'all that is lacking is resources' or that 'the problem is essentially clinical and beyond our expertise'.

129. As illustrated by the instruction reported to me by Gill Morgan, the Chair of the National Association of Health Service Managers: 'We have overprescriptive demands at the centre. We must address this problem by reorganizing at the periphery.'

130. Webster, op. cit., p. 204.

131. C.H. Smee, 'Self-Governing Trusts and GP Fundholders: The British Experience' in R.B. Saltmann and C. von Otter (eds), *Implementing Planned Markets in Health Care: Balancing Social and Economic Responsibility* (Buckingham; Open University Press, 1995). Quoted in Webster, op. cit., p. 204. There is an interesting ambiguity here: does he mean that it is not possible to prove things one way or another or that, when things are looked into, they rarely prove to be of benefit?

132. There is a particularly irony in a recent development that was seen to be of sufficient importance to be discussed on television. Kettering Hospital had produced a miraculous improvement in its waiting times in the A & E department by shedding the triage nurse and arranging for patients to be seen straight away by a consultant. The miracle was so striking, Kettering was invited to teach University College Hospital how to do it, with comparable effects. The impact on the other duties the consultant had was, of course, not evaluated. See also S. Turner and T. Collinson, 'When is an emergency department not an emergency department?', *British Medical Journal*, 2002, 325: 901.

133. G. Davey Smith, S. Ebrahim, S. Frankel, 'How policy informs the evidence', *British Medical Journal*, 2001, 322: 184–5.

134. Toynbee, op. cit., p. 79.

135. In the case of the recent replacement of Health Authorities by Primary Care Groups and then Primary Care Trusts (PCTs) the transitional period was three years.

136. An almost continuous process in the Department of Health, where people out of touch with the pressure of delivery that they impose on those in the real world jealousy guard portfolios and fiefdoms whose boundaries were constantly being redrawn from above. In my years as informal adviser on health care of the elderly to the Chief Medical Officer, I was never able to work out any of the structures, though I was given many hours of patient tutoring.

137. Watkin, op. cit., p. 150. This was before the era of e-mails and word processors.

138. Ibid., p. 161.

139. Interestingly, this practice could be construed as being in breach of the first 'duty of a doctor registered with the General Medical Council': 'make the care of your patient your first concern.' In a condition of permanent structural change, however, it is necessary also to try to discharge one's duty of care to future patients.

140. Maurice Slevin, *Resuscitating the NHS: A Consultant's View* (London: Centre for Policy Studies, 2003).

141. Jonathan Carr-Brown and Lois Rogers, *The Times*, 2 January 2003, from which I have also obtained the dismal statistics that follow.

142. Data from a leaked Cabinet document reported in the *Sunday Times* (David Leppard and Robert Winnett, 'How extra spending failed to improve the public services', *Sunday* Times, 25 April 2004, pp. 6–7). According to the same leaked document, productivity in hospitals has fallen by 15 to 20 per cent since 1997.

143. Hospitals have also been swamped by a new breed of administrator: patient pathway managers, who have little or no experience of health care, and who are paid £35,000 to £40,000 a year trying, as one observer pointed out, 'to work out what they are doing'. There are other new types of managers emerging: 'information analysts', 'service planners', 'access managers' and 'programme facilitators' whose salaries, ranging up to £60,000, far exceed that of most of the doctors and all of the nurses delivering patient care – that is to say, doing the real, serious business of the NHS. The increasingly managed NHS is, to use the title of Harriet Sergeant's book, *'Managing not to Manage'* (London: Centre for Policy Studies, 2003).

144. Because every document that is generated by the Trust has to be checked against central guidelines, we have to document that our documents meet documenting standards. For this a 'Document control coordinator' has been appointed to our Trust.

145. Michael Barber, the head of the Prime Minister's Delivery Unit, worried that the extra billions going into the NHS could go to waste, identified the 'weaknesses of Primary Care Trusts (PCTs) and Strategic Health Authorities' as a key factor (*Evening Standard*, 8 January 2003). Terrifyingly, it has been suggested by Nigel Edwards, the Policy Director of the NHS Confederation, representing NHS managers and Trusts, that Primary Care Trusts (PCTs), being new organizations, 'needed more investments in managerial capacity… The paradox is that the NHS is under-managed.' (quoted in Rosemary Bennett and Nigel Hawkes, 'No. 10 tells Milburn not to squander NHS cash', *The Times*, 9 January 2003). The notion of a 'Delivery Unit' is another fantasy   it delivers nothing, while demanding more and more paper.

146. 'Bill of Health', unsigned editorial, *The Times*, 11 March 2003, quoting a Reform group think tank. It is now recognized, also, that PCTs, who are charged with determining local priorities, have proved a serious obstacle to implementing National Service Frameworks. For example, their local decision-making has got in the way of the National Cancer Plan, aimed at improving cancer outcomes (*Six O' Clock News*, BBC1, 25 March 2004), demonstrating how their discretion reintroduces the 'postcode' lottery that national standards were supposed to eradicate.

147. Webster, op. cit., p. 225.

148. *Manchester Metro News*, 13 December 2002, p. 1.

149. Leppard and Winnctt, *Sunday Times*, op. cit.

150. I have not, of course, mentioned all the costs of the new organizations. For example, the Commission for Patient and Public Involvement has been established to oversee 600 or more patient forums to give 'users' a direct voice in the the delivery of health care and independent support in filing formal complaints when things go wrong. Nearly 6,000 voluntary members are required and this will generate a huge bill for expenses and administration. In Luton, where, as elsewhere, there was little interest from the ethnic minority community in involvement in patient forums, despite a 25 per cent ethnic minority population, and only three or four people turned up to meetings, two community empowerment officers were appointed and then ten from each of Asian and Afro-Caribbean groups turned up. 'Pilot Fright', the *Guardian*, 15 January 2003.

151. With apologies to Sir Liam Donaldson, Chief Medical Officer, for inverting the title of his *An Organization with a Memory*.

152. Carol Propper, Simon Burgess, Denise Gossage, Competition and Quality: Evidence from the NHS Internal Market 1991–9', Bristol University Centre for Market and Public Organization/03/007 Bristol: 2003.

153. This study is not without its problems. For example, the mortality rate in hospital may rise if mortally ill patients get to hospital quicker; they will die there rather than in the community. An increased mortality rate may therefore result from a more efficient service. A study in Scotland has shown the extent to which in-patient mortality rates are influenced by the mortality before reaching hospital (A.H. Leyland and F.A. Boddy, 'League tables and acute myocardial infarction', *The Lancet*, 1998, 351: 555–8). Even so, this natural experiment is the nearest we have to an evaluation of these particular 'reforms'.

154. *Learning from Bristol. The report of the inquiry into children's heart surgery at the Bristol Royal Infirmary 1984–1995* (London: Stationery Office, 2000). The Kennedy Report specifically identifies 'managing the transition from the known (the old NHS) to the unknown (Trust status)' as a major factor in the poor management of paediatric cardiac surgery at Bristol (Executive Summary, para. 26). The Chief Executive met 'the principal obligation of balancing the books' but showed no clinical leadership: clinical governance was to be discovered later.

155. Thus reaching a state of affairs not too different from that envisaged in Kenneth Robinson's Green Paper of 1967, which proposed strategic Health Authorities without regions. (I owe this melancholy observation to Nick Bosanquet, 'Across the great divide: discussing the undiscussable: Getting real', *British Journal of Health Care Management*, 2001, 7 (10): 395.)

156. A recent report from the NHS Alliance has described the notion of a

'primary-care led NHS' as empty rhetoric. 'Minerva', *British Medical Journal*, 2003, 327: 1356):

The Department of Health is entirely insulated from Primary Care Trusts (PCTs) by a so-called 'top table' of senior officials and strategic Health Authorities… We have created a managerialized NHS that effectively excludes the voices of front-line clinicians and lay people.

157. Actually, another, even more disgraceful example springs to mind. Frank Dobson, the then Health Secretary, stated on live television that Janardan Dhasmana, one of the paediatric cardiac surgeons at the Bristol children's hospital suspended by the GMC, should have been struck off. The following day he was sacked. The subsequent inquiry found him virtually blameless. At the time of writing, he is still without employment ('Surgeon is cleared of blame over Bristol', *Hospital Doctor*, 2 August 2002, p. 1).

158. Krishna Guha and Nicholas Timmins, 'Milburn set to increase local control of health care', *Financial Times*, 15 January 2003.

159. Owen Dyer, 'Reid accused of breach of promise over foundation hospitals', *British Medical Journal*, 2003, 327: 1306.

160. Malcolm Dean, 'A season of U-turns for UK health politics', *The Lancet*, 2002, 359: 589.

161. See Webster, op. cit., pp. 225–9. Indeed, it is arguable that the combination of Foundation-style opt-out and PFI will re-create a health service not too different from the arrangements that were in place before the NHS was established.

162. These and other data are in Seamus Ward, 'PFI is here to stay', *British Medical Journal*, 2002, 324: 1178.

163. The first fifteen schemes have been associated with a reduction of about 30 per cent in overall hospital bed capacity without compensatory capacity being created elsewhere (Matthew G. Dunnigan and Allyson M. Pollock, 'Downsizing of acute hospital in-patient beds associated with the Private Finance Initiative in Scotland: a case study', *British Medical Journal*, 2003; 326: 905–8). This has taken place four years after the National Bed Inquiry called for an *increase* in overall bed capacity, after thirty years of progressive bed losses.

164. John Carvel, 'The big PFI gamble', the *Guardian*, 21 October 2002.

165. Allyson Pollock, Jean Shaoul, Neil Vickers, 'Private finance and value for money in NHS hospitals: a policy in search of a rationale?', *British Medical Journal*, 2002, 324: 1205–9. Much of the discussion that follows is drawn from this paper and other work by Professor Pollock. Already at least ten NHS hospitals built with private sector funds are facing deficits – totalling more than £40 million (Jo Revill, 'NHS hospitals sink into debt to pay off PFI', the *Observer*, 14 March 2004, p. 11).

166. Kieran Walshe, 'Suspended sentence', *Health Services Journal*, 11 March 2004, pp. 16–17.

167. See, for example, 'Wyres crossed', *Private Eye*, 30 June 2002, p. 26.

168. Quoted in Watkin, op. cit., p. 3.

169. Polly Toynbee in *Risk and Trust*, op. cit., p. 80.

170. Iain Chalmers, 'Trying to do more good than harm in policy and practice: the role of rigorous, transparent, up-to-date, evaluations', *The Annals of the American Academy of Political and Social Science*, 2003, 589: 22–40.

171. Richard Smith, editorial, 'Oh, NHS, thou art sick', *British Medical Journal*, 2002, 324: 127–8.

172. Watkin, op. cit., p. 163.

173. Ian Kennedy quoted in Anne Gulland, 'Doctors must be free of the "confetti of interference" ', *British Medical Journal*, 2002, 325: 1190.

174. The brothers of Maurice Gibb and fellow members of the pop group the Bee Gees, quoted world-wide on the day after the former's death following emergency intestinal surgery that had to be carried out shortly after he had had a heart attack (*Metro*, 14 January 2003).

175. Jo Knowsley, *Mail on Sunday*, Review, 23 June 2002, pp. 49–51.

176. Including the *British Medical Journal*, which cites the Bristol cardiac surgery report as its sole datum in support of the claim that outcomes in the NHS are worse than elsewhere (Richard Smith, 'Oh, NHS, thou art sick', *British Medical Journal*, 2002, 324: 127–8).

177. Theodore Dalrymple, *Mass Listeria. The Meaning of Health Scares* (London: Andre Deutsch, 1988), p. 1.

178. Data taken from Malcolm Dean, 'A season of U-turns for UK health policies', *The Lancet*, 2002, 359: 589.

179. Nigel Edwards, Mary Jane Kornacki, Jack Silversin, 'Unhappy doctors: what are the causes and what can be done?', *British Medical Journal*, 2002, 324: 835–8.

180. Owen Dyer, 'Doctors suspended for removing wrong kidney', *British Medical Journal*, 2004, 328: 246.

181. Here's another example. A recent study in a large teaching hospital reported that it had received about 1,000 complaints in a year. However, only 100 complaints were about clinical care. Others, for example, concerned the quality of the food or the attitude of a porter. During the year in question, there had been 5.89 million clinical interactions with patients – taking a very conservative estimate of an average of about six interactions per out-patient visit or in-patient day – making a clinically related complaint rate of about one per 50,000 interventions. (I am grateful to the Chief Executive of the hospital in question for these data.)

182. At the beginning of 2003, at a time when the UK was moving towards

war with Iraq, the first item on the national evening news was a story of a woman who had given birth to a baby with a congenital heart defect. The baby was taken by emergency ambulance to Guy's Hospital for the cardiac surgery. The mother herself, with whom the various 'options' had been discussed, had gone to the hospital by public transport. It was understood that she might have come to harm, as she had only recently been delivered of her child. The Chief Executive of the hospital was interrogated for a full five minutes about this episode, during which he repeatedly apologized to the parent and assured everyone that the (very junior) midwife would be 're-trained', but quite properly refused to promise that she would be suspended.

183. Francesca Robinson, 'Doctors behind bars', *Hospital Doctor*, 4 December 2003, p. 24.

184. Jon Holbrook, 'The criminalization of fatal medical mistakes', *British Medical Journal*, 2003, 327: 1118–19.

185. As was pointed out by the coroner, who sympathized with 'the shadow that had been cast over the life of a promising young doctor'.

186. For full reference to this and other studies see CMO update 38 May 2004 (www.dh.gov.uk/cmo)

187. See Anon, 'An error of omission', *British Medical Journal*, 2001, 322: 1236–40.

188. Susan Mayor, 'Changing practice', *British Medical Journal*, 2004, 328: 248.

189. S. Lindeman, E. Laara, Hakko et al. 'A systematic review of gender-specific suicide mortality in medical doctors'. *British Journal of Psychiatry* 1996; 168: 274–9.

190. The Inquiry criticized one omission: failing to tell the parents of a young patient about a staff meeting at which doubts had been expressed about whether to perform a particular operation.

191. Expert Group on Learning from Adverse Events in the NHS, *An Organization with Memory* (London: Department of Health, 2000).

192. D.A. Hughes, 'Consultants at Alder Hey look to the future', *British Medical Journal*, 2001, 323: 1064.

193. Editorial, 'Think before condemning', *British Medical Journal*, 2002, 325: 1045.

194. The Department of Health is not the only watchdog that specializes in blame and has had more than once to eat its words. The Commission on Health Improvement (CHI), which is responsible for identifying and publicly reporting on poor practice or results, claimed in December 2000 that Chesterfield and North Derbyshire Royal Trust had surgical mortality figures 100 per cent higher for elective surgery and 29 per cent higher for emergencies than the naotional average. But it had made an elementary error and in fact the results in the Trust were 6 per cent *better* than the national average. In the meantime,

the local and national press had covered this 'scandal' lavishly, much to the dismay of the staff. Unsurprisingly, the local newspaper did not attempt to correct the impression when the true figures were accepted by CHI. What was worse, the CHI forgot to change the figures on its own website, still adding that the Trust needed to provide an explanation of its higher mortality and should take steps to address this (John Camm, *Hospital Doctor*, 27 September 2001).

195. Ibid. The benefits of a blame-free approach go beyond medicine. The accusatorial trends of victims wanting criminal prosecutions in the case of the Southall rail crash (and others) can delay evidence being given to find the root cause of the accident and to implement recommendations that would prevent a recurrence (B.M. Hutter, *Regulation and Risk: Occupational Health and Safety on the Railways* (Oxford: Oxford University Press, 2001), pp. 284–5).

196. Allyson Pollock, 'We work in teams but are blamed as individuals', *GMC News*, issue 10, February 2002, p. 2.

197. Will Hutton, 'The Disgrace that is the NHS: Nye Bevan's dream is degraded and debased', the *Observer*, November 1999/2000.

198. In part, the Emergency Medical Service was inspiration for a nationally coordinated health service, and was set up in anticipation of huge casualties from aerial bombardment.

199. Charles Webster, *A Political History of the National Health Service* (Oxford: Oxford University Press, 2nd edn, 2001), p. 6.

200. This extraordinary story has never been fully told but a a flavour of it may be gleaned from the chapter by John Brocklehurst, 'Geriatric Medicine: History and Current Practice in Europe', in Raymond Tallis and Howard Fillit (eds), *Brocklehurst's Textbook of Geriatric Medicine and Gerontology*, (Edinburgh: Churchill Livingstone, 6th edn, 2003).

201. Anyone, incidentally, who would wish to deny the leadership role of consultants in the past, and that they have been innovators and a force for good, rather than self-interested opponents of reform, should look at the evolution of the care of elderly people. The low status of elderly people in society at large, which rubs off on those who care for them, may surely protect the consultants – who were advocates for them and, at considerable personal cost, developed ever improving services – against the charge of unmitigated self-interest.

202. Myles Harris and Janet Warren have examined this in Digby Anderson (ed.), *Come Back, Miss Nightingale: Trends in Professions Today* (London: The Social Affairs Unit, 1998). This has been an unfortunate and unlooked-for result of the attempts to improve the status of nursing:

Washing the sick would not teach you much about accounting or forward planning. The three obligations of the nurse based on the corporal works of mercy – to comfort, feed and bathe the sick, the most important parts of nursing, and essential to patient's survival – suddenly came to be seen as embarrassing reminders of the days when nurses were merely dumb helpmeets of a male medical profession. (p. 17)

203. *National Service Framework for Older People*, April 2001.

204. Life expectancy increase in the 2nd half of the 1990. Kenneth Colman 'Health and Health Services: Changes over the last seven years.' *Health Trends* 1998, 30 (1) 5–7.

205. See Roy Porter, *The Greatest Benefit to Mankind: A Medical History of Humanity from Antiquity to the Present* (London: HarperCollins, 1997), p. 711.

206. John Bunker quoted in Digby Anderson (ed.), op. cit., p. 87.

207. See Chapter 8.

208. James Le Fanu, 'Successful but devalued: the medical profession – a British View' in Digby Anderson, op. cit., pp. 95–106.

209. Porter, op. cit., p. 12.

210. This and the general propensity to pessimism and irrationality is discussed (and criticized) at length in Raymond Tallis, *Enemies of Hope: A Critique of Contemporary Pessimism* (London: Macmillan, 2nd edn, 1999).

211. As Bjorn Lomberg discovered when he published *The Sceptical Environmentalist* (Cambridge: Cambridge University Press, 2001), criticizing what he calls 'the litany of woe' from which many working within and outside NGOs have earned a pleasant living.

212. Webster, op. cit., p. 164.

213. Alan Milburn, 'Redefining the National Health Service', speech to the New Health Network, 4 February 2002.

214. One of the most spectacular examples of this came not from a politician but from Sir Donald Irvine, the previous President of the General Medical Council. In his Duncan Memorial Lecture given in 2003 at the Liverpool Medical Institute – 'Patient-Centred Professionalism – Decision Time' – he seems to divide the history of UK medicine into two unequal halves: before 1995 (about the time he himself became President of the GMC), when doctors were self-serving, self-centred and unaccountable; and after 1995, in the wake of scandals and increasing regulation that he introduced, improvements started to take place and the interests of patients, rather than doctors, were placed at the centre of health care. The story of gradual, incremental improvement in both the technology of health care and the user-friendliness of its delivery over the preceding fifty years seems to have passed him by.

215. Whether recent developments in the wake of Lord Hutton's report condemning the BBC's management structures will prompt a change of role model remains to be seen.

216. Claire Sanders, 'Leo makes managers kings of the jungle', *Times Higher Education Supplement*, 27 September 2002.

217. Anthony Browne, 'Labour peer joins attack on "flawed" NHS', the *Observer*, 3 February 2002.

218. 'Personal View' *British Medical Journal Careers Supplement*, 2001, 325:150.

219. I have taken this story from Theodore Dalrymple's *Mass Listeria. The Meaning of Health Scares* (London: Andre Deutsch, 1998), pp. 78–80. The passages come originally from Carlos M.N. Eire, *From Madrid to Purgatory* (Cambridge: Cambridge University Press, 1996).

220. Raymond Tallis, *Newton's Sleep. The Two Cultures and the Two Kingdoms* (London: Macmillan, 1995). See especially 'Anti-Science and Organic Daydreams', pp. 55–67.

221. See Paul Valery, *Monsieur Teste* (translated by Jackson Mathews (London: Routledge & Kegan Paul, 1973), p. 49): 'We are made of many things that know nothing about us. And this is how we fail to know ourselves' (p. 49).

222. George Orwell, 'How the Poor Die', in *The Collected Essays, Journalism and Letters of George Orwell*, vol. IV, *In Front of Your Nose*, 1945–50, edited by Sonia Orwell and Ian Angus (London: Penguin Books, 1970), pp. 261–72.

223. I owe this example also to Theodore Dalrymple, op. cit., p. 81.

224. It is on the cover of Roy Porter's *The Greatest Benefit to Mankind*, op. cit.

225. This example is particularly poignant because it is now 2, 500 years since Hippocrates' scornful dismissal of the superstitions surrounding epilepsy. It was one of the most influential attacks on supernatural accounts of disease. In his *On the Sacred Disease*, he advocated a rational and naturalistic approach to the problems experienced by people with seizures (most of which come from other people's attitudes).

226. Indeed, many doctors are appalled at the ignorance and insensitivity of the world at large and are often angered at the casual cruelty and denigration of chronically ill, old, or psychiatrically disturbed individuals in the press and the world outside hospitals.

227. J.G. Merquior, *From Prague to Paris* (London: Verso, 1986), p. 260.

7 Representations and Reality

1. John R. Bennett, 'The organ retention furore', *Clinical Medicine*, 2001, 1: 167–71. I have been greatly assisted by Dr Bennett's article.

2. Henri-Frederic Amiel, *The Journal Intime*, translated by Mrs Humphrey Ward (Macmillan: London, 1889), p. 9.

3. Charlotte Mew, 'Exspecto Resurrectionem', quoted in Penelope Fitzgerald, *Charlotte Mew and Her Friends* (London: HarperCollins, 1984), p. 10.

4. Timothy Chambers, 'Trust me – I'm a philosopher', *Clinical Medicine*, 2003, 3 (1): 83–4.

5. Royal Liverpool Children's Inquiry, *The Royal Liverpool Children's Hospital Inquiry Report* (London: The Stationery Office, 2001) www.rlcinquiry. org. uk (It is also called the Redfern Report after the QC who led the inquiry.)

6. Department of Health, *Report of a Census of Organs and Tissues Retained by Pathology Services in England Conducted by the Chief Medical Officer* (London: The Stationery Office, 2001).

7. Quoted in Bennett op. cit., p. 168.

8. Nuffield Council on Bioethics, *Human Tissue: Ethical and Legal Issues* (London, April 1995). There is an exception: 'where the deceased has specified a particular part (in which case it appears that only that part may be removed). The part may then be used for the purposes indicated by the deceased or the person lawfully in possession of the body.'

9. *The Royal Liverpool Children's Hospital Inquiry Report*, op. cit., p. 444.

10. A 'personal view' by a consultant, who was sympathetic to the needs of the parents for information, admitted that 'It was hard to get a balance between a frank and honest revelation of all information available and compassionate and supportive counselling of parents in deep distress. We came under some criticism for providing families with unsolicited and upsetting information.' (Gillian Derrick, 'Lessons we can learn from organ retention', *British Medical Journal*, 2003, 327: 996).

11. There is evidence that Alan Milburn, on this as on other occasions, was 'briefing journalists behind the scenes to the effect that the profession needed taking to task' (Caroline White, 'Doctors under fire', *British Medical Journal*, 2002, 324: 55).

12. Jeremy Laurance, the *Independent*, 31 January 2001. Laurance spoke of hospitals 'taking and keeping organs... for decades with scant regard for the law'. In fact, no laws were broken.

13. In the very moving accounts of individual parents' feelings in the Redfern Report, one expressed 'a primal need to protect Sean even in death'.

14. The Redfern Report quotes parents who did sign consent forms for autopsies and further examination but who stated that they did not realize what they had agreed to. 'When they ask you to sign the form you are in so much turmoil you could sign your life away and would not know it' (p. 18).

15. For example, a *Manchester Metro News* item (boasted as an exclusive), 'Gerard's Second Funeral' (Chris Osuh, 19 December 2003), concerns a child who had died seventeen years before. The article quotes the child's mother: 'I can't wait to get our son's heart back. At the moment our son is not whole. I can't bear the thought of his heart being in a jar as a peep show – it's a blot on his memory.'

16. These facts are drawn from *Manchester Metro News*, 4 October 2002 – front-page headline 'CHILD ORGANS: THE "COVER-UP" '; 8 November 2002

– 'WHAT HAPPENED TO MY BABY'S HEART?'; and 29 November 2002 – front-page headline 'I WILL HAVE TO BURY MY BABY AGAIN'.

17. Margaret Brazier, 'Restoring Trust After Alder Hey', *Hospital Doctor*, 30 May 2002. The Commission board included two bereaved parents, who discovered that organs had been retained from their children, and representatives from the law and the medical profession. It was chaired by a professor of law.

18. The NHS medical negligence bill doubled between 1997 and 2001 (A. Ferriman, 'NHS faces medical negligence bill of £2.6 billion', *British Medical Journal*, 2001, 322: 1081).

19. I do not exaggerate when I speak of brutality. The proposed Human Tissue Bill, put together in haste (see below), insists that permission to remove tissues post-mortem from a child's body should be given *by the child*, so long as it has been established that he or she is mentally competent. No sensitive doctor would wish to carry out any research that involves discussing with a child the disposal of its bodily parts after death.

20. The charge of paternalism is so universal, it is hardly surprising that the Redfern Report describes the behaviour of certain female managers as well as that of doctors of both sexes as 'paternalistic'.

21. Bennett, op. cit., p. 170. The Redfern Report is over-long, anecdotal, poorly organized and lacking in intellectual rigour. Populist outrage, hindsight, the retrospective application of standards created in the wake of the furore, have displaced judicial wisdom.

22. 'Anguish of parents in organ storm', *Manchester Evening News*, 29 November 2002.

23. Ian Herbert, the *Independent*, 31 January 2001.

24. Jeremy Laurance, the *Independent*, 31 January 2001. In an article written four days before, Laurance had promised 'Grim revelations undermine trust in doctors' (*Independent*, 27 January 2001).

25. David Hughes, 'Consultants at Alder Hey look to the future', *British Medical Journal*, 2001, 323: 1064.

26. Sarah Grant, 'Alder Hey's doctors speak out on life under a cloud', *Hospital Doctor*, 7 February 2002.

27. Quoted in Bennett, op. cit., p. 171.

28. Clare Dyer, 'Thousands of families to sue over retained organs', *British Medical Journal*, 2004, 328: 184.

29. Polly Toynbee, 'Be robust about risk', the *Guardian*, 25 February 2004.

30. See Bennett, op. cit., p. 170.

31. Phil Hammond, 'The death of the autopsy', *NHS Magazine*, June 2002, p. 28.

32. From T.S. Eliot, 'Burnt Norton', *Four Quartets, Collected Poems 1909–1962* (London: Faber, 1963).

33. M. Brodie, A. Laing, J.W. Keeling, K.J. McKenzie, 'Ten years of neonatal autopsies in a tertiary referral centre: a retrospective study', *British Medical Journal*, 2002, 324: 761–3.

34. It is also potentially a dangerous business for the doctor seeking consent. Recently, a young consultant in paediatric intensive care (not the kind of job where it is desirable to have additional stresses and distractions) was cleared by the GMC of serious professional misconduct years after he had been wrongly accused by parents of a child of lying to them about the replacement of organs removed at post-mortem. He was subjected to a huge amount of adverse publicity both locally and nationally.

35. Cited in Bennett, op. cit., p. 170.

36. Carl Gray, 'What Alder Hey has done to alter pathologists' lives', *Hospital Doctor*, 16 August 2001, p. 23.

37. Geoffrey Hulson, 'A Tabloid Story', *British Medical Journal*, 2003, 326: 231.

38. The *Guardian* printed a piece on his dress sense that suggested that he was not 'upright and disciplined' and 'ill-equipped to deal with the difficult times ahead and in desperate need of a suit' (Quoted by Hulson, ibid).

39. Ray Dunne, 'Trust me…', *Hospital Doctor*, 2 August 2001, p. 18.

40. T.Y. Khong, 'Falling neonatal autopsy rates', *British Medical Journal*, 2002, 324: 749–50.

41. Peter Furness and Richard Sullivan, 'The Human Tissue Bill. Criminal sanctions linked to opaque legislation threaten research', *British Medical Journal*, 2004, 328: 533–4.

42. Paul Marston, 'Rail Safety system "will take 15 years to install" ', *Daily Telegraph*, 29 March 2001.

43. This is a modification of a phrase ('the age of contempt') used by Steven Barnett in his important essay 'Will a Crisis in Journalism Provoke a Crisis in Democracy?', *Political Quarterly*, October 2002, 73 (4): 400–408.

44. Christopher Bartlett, Jonathan Sterne, Matthias Eggar, 'What is newsworthy? Longitudinal study of the reporting of medical research in two British newspapers', *British Medical Journal*, 2002, 325: 81–4.

45. It is interesting that the researchers yoked these two rather different newspapers.

46. Lesley Fallowfield, 'Bad news from research really is headline news', *British Medical Journal*, 2002, 325: 774.

47. Iain Chalmers, Ulrich Trohler, Ben Toth, Iain Milne, 'Assessing the effects of treatments: what's needed to inform the public?' Background paper for an informal discussion, UK Cochrane Centre, NHS Research and Development Programme, 2 April 2001.

48. There had been worsening of the involuntary movements in one or two

patients, but these are a feature of the disease and a frequent side effect of its conventional (drug) treatment.

49. K.J. Petrie, S. Wessely, 'Modern worries, new technology and medicine', *British Medical Journal*, 2002, 324: 690–1. Incidentally, exaggerating the benefits of developments in medical science is just as unhelpful. 'Breakthrough' stories can discredit science as much as 'scandal' stories. Unfortunately the terrain in between, where most science takes place, is not a circulation-boosting zone.

50. Lucy Wildman, 'Health scares that worry you sick', *Reader's Digest*, May 2002, pp. 92–3.

51. Anthony Browne, 'Why the NHS is bad for us', the *Observer*, 7 October 2002.

52. The reader will recall the impressive data on coronary artery bypass grafts – usually used as an indicator of the quality of cardiac surgery – given in Chapter 6. And the observation by John Bunker that health improvements in the last fifty years are about the same as those in the USA and achieved at about half the cost. A very recent study places Britain in third equal place in cancer death prevention over the last twenty-five years out of fifteen European countries and the 24 per cent fall in death rate from breast cancer is the fastest in Europe. All of this has taken place despite interference and underfunding. More recent studies – *Winning the War on Heart Disease* (reported in *The Times*, 25 March 2004) – shows that the rate of decline of coronary mortality exceeds that in any other European country.

53. Harvey Cole, 'Public sector productivity', *Prospect*, January 2004, p. 13.

54. Alexander Dorozynski, 'Heat wave triggers political conflict as French death rates rise', *British Medical Journal*, 2003, 327: 411.

55. Cole op. cit.

56. There has recently been some catching up in UK health expenditure. But this has been so recent that it would be unfair to have expected that it would be reflected in indices of health, particularly those that refer to the pre-catching-up period. According to Office of Health Economics, *Compendium of Health Statistics*, 14th edn, 2002 (summary statistics compiled by Peter Yuen), per capita health care expenditure in 2000 was approximately 20 per cent more in France, 35 per cent more in Germany and 180 per cent more in the USA. (Figures in pounds are 1,126 in UK, 3,057 in US, 1,596 in US and 1,366 in France.)

57. Some of the data from the most recent Wanless Report are less encouraging, with respect to socio-economic variations in health and life expectancy in the United Kingdom. This later Wanless Report argues for more work on the contributions of housing, diet, lifestyle factors, and exercise as major contributors to mortality and chronic ill-health. Even so, the *trends* in both cancer and heart disease are looking impressive. WHO figures for mortality trends between 1990 and 1999 show greater reductions in cancer mortality (18

per cent) in the UK than in the other countries examined in the Wanless Report. What is more, there was a 41 per cent fall in mortality rate from coronary heart disease in those under sixty-five compared with a 31 per cent EU average during the same period. Quoted in Mark Gould, *British Medical Journal*, 2004, 328: 10.

58. Sir Ian Kennedy, Executive Summary, *Learning from Bristol: The report of the inquiry into children's heart surgery at the Bristol Royal Infirmary 1984–1995* (London: the Stationery Office, 2000).

59. Ibid.

60. Jill Palmer and Oonagh Blackman, *Daily Mirror*, 19 July 2001.

61. Given Mrs Addis's confusional state, she would not have been able to give informed consent for her humiliating exposé in the mass media. Publishing the photograph seems to me as ethically indefensible as that of using Mrs Addis's case as political ammunition.

62. Polly Toynbee, 'Hospital Dramas', the *Guardian*, 25 January 2002, p. 21.

63. See, for example, James Malone-Lee, 'Urinary incontinence' in Raymond Tallis and Howard Fillit (eds), *Brocklehurst's Textbook of Geriatric Medicine and Gerontology*, (Edinburgh: Churchill Livingstone, 6th edn, 2003).

64. Michael White, Jeevan Vasagar and John Carvel, 'Blair calls for truce as health row spirals', the *Guardian*, 25 January 2002, p. 1.

65. Liz Bratby, 'Whittington Medical Director "Would Do It All Over Again" ', *Hospital Doctor*, 2 May 2002, pp. 18–19.

66. Frith Rayner, 'Media terror for doctor who dared to defend staff', *Hospital Doctor*, 31 January 2002, p. 3.

67. Paul Waugh, 'Tory leader tells party to uncover an new NHS scandal', the *Independent*, 28 December 2002.

68. Geoffrey Hulson, 'A Tabloid Story', *British Medical Journal*, 2003, 326: 231.

69. Raj Persaud, 'A scapegoat for Sarah Payne?', *British Medical Journal*, 2002, 324: 56.

70. This is becoming common practice. See Ameena Salim, 'More doctors face the glare of increased media scrutiny', *Hospital Doctor*, 22 January 2004, p. 3. The weekly rate of inquiries to the Medical Defence Union about media intrusion exceeds the monthly rate ten years ago.

71. Christopher Ingoldby, 'I felt I was thrown to the wolves', *Hospital Doctor*, 7 March 2002.

72. Only one of the charges referred to poor surgical practice: the others referred to patient selection and the choice of investigations.

73. Quoted in Ingoldby, op. cit.

74. William Shakespeare, *Richard the Second*, Act 1, Scene i.

75. Editorial, 'Stop the blame culture wrecking more careers', *Hospital Doctor*, 7 March 2002.

76. This is the opening sentence of her book *The Journalist and the Murderer*, quoted by Ian Jack in 'The Flash of a Knife', the *Guardian*, 7 February 2004, pp. 4–6.

77. See Steven Barnett, op. cit.

78. Andrew Marr, 'The Lying Game', the *Observer*, 24 October 1999, p. 30.

79. Onora O'Neill, 'Licence to Deceive', Reith Lectures, London, 2002.

80. Allyson Pollock, 'Comment: We work in teams but are blamed as individuals', *GMC News*, issue 10, February 2002, p. 2.

This illustrates in passing how the malign influence of the previous administration's privatizations reaches into the very capillaries of the service, making clinical medicine more difficult. After twenty years of putting out services to private tender, the filthy hospital has become the norm. This doesn't matter because the underpaid ancillary workforce does not cause the government any trouble. The total disregard of the physical working conditions of those who deliver care is a constant across governments. A recent Department of Health proposal that junior doctors on call at night could be housed in airline-type seats rather than having rooms of their own is shocking but not at all surprising.

The Bristol Royal Infirmary Final Report (the Kennedy Report) vividly captures the circumstances under which the cardiac surgery team had to work:

There seems to have been an overriding sense of pressing on and hoping that one day the service would be moved onto one site, that the new hospital for children would be built, that the new surgeon would arrive, and that all would then be well.

Facilities for parents, and necessary medical equipment for children, had to be funded through the good offices of a charity, The Heart Circle.

There can hardly be a clinician in the land who does not recognise this picture – described as one of 'make do and mend' by Kennedy.

81. Ernest Hemingway applied this description of courage first of all to bullfighters.

82. When, worried about the emergent policy of creating new barriers to the admission of older people to acute hospitals (as they were deemed to be inappropriately occupying beds), I had a meeting with an extremely senior Department of Health civil servant, I brought with me a list describing the twelve new patients I had seen on my Sunday emergency ward round the previous day. It would have been unsatisfactory, and in some instances dangerous, to manage these patients in the proposed 'community' facilities. My interlocutor was not interested.

83. Peter McDonald, 'Traumatic truth of surgery life', *Hospital Medicine*, 21 March 2002, p. 12.

84. I have carried much responsibility and agonized over decisions and

mistakes in my career, but I would never have the qualities required to make a surgeon. Such qualities inevitably have their drawbacks. The personality of an individual willing and able to take the risks of carrying out difficult operations may actively unsuit him to the caution verging on paranoia of anyone providing a service in a society increasingly dominated by litigation.

85. A recent survey showed that surgeons were four and a half times more likely to be suspended than physicians.

86. Quoted by Marc de Leval, 'Facing up to surgical deaths', *British Medical Journal*, 2004, 328: 361–2.

87. Milan Kundera, *The Unbearable Lightness of Being* (London: Faber, 1984).

88. Such a feeling or responsibility has no place in the world as seen by many in the humanities, for whom empirical truths are treated with disdain, the notion of the self is deconstructed, and 'hard facts' dissolve into social constructions informed by nebulous communities of power.

89. Laurie Lyckholm, 'There is no easy way round taking responsibility for mistakes', *British Medical Journal*, 2001, 323: 570.

90. Comment, 'Don't blame doctors for system failures', *Hospital Doctor*, 18 April 2002.

91. Charles Essex, 'All teams need a leader', *Hospital Doctor*, 30 January 2003.

92. Wayne Lewis, 'Move from "I" to "we" represents a paradigm shift in responsibility', *British Medical Journal*, 2001, 323: 570.

93. Pollock, op. cit.

94. 'Safety and quality in health care: what can England and Australia learn from one another?', *Clinical Medicine*, 2003, 3: 68–73.

95. Health Policy and Economic Research Unit, *BMA Cohort Study of 1995 Medical Graduates* (London: BMA, 2001) reported by Isobel Allen in *British Medical Journal*, 28 September 2002.

96. Anthony Daniels, 'Medicine put under the knife', *Sunday Telegraph*, 15 December 2002. The notion, fostered by the present Government, of the patient sitting with the GP choosing the surgeon with the best track record for her operation – and actively choosing against junior doctors – carries dire implications for training and also elevates selfishness ('I shall leave the less good surgeons to operate on others') to a moral principle. This is another illustration of how every patient is directly, or indirectly, the enemy – or at least a threat to the welfare – of other patients.

97. The difficulty of recruiting surgeons and the recent rise in the number of surgeons taking early retirement (Jeremy Laurence, 'Surge in consultants retiring hits NHS reform', the *Independent*, 27 January 2003) suggest that this anxiety may be well founded.

Part III Destinations

1. Roy Porter, *The Greatest Benefit to Mankind: A Medical History of Humanity from Antiquity to the Present* (London: HarperCollins, 1997), p. 718.

8 'Meagre Increments': the Supposed Failure of Success

1. This chapter draws, quite heavily in places, on several articles I have published previously, including 'Going, going, gone', *London Review of Books*, 1996, 18(7) pp. 26–7; 'Finding the True Significance of the Demographic Revolution', *Times Higher Education Supplement*, 9 July 1999; and 'When I'm sixty-four: Age Concern', *Telegraph Magazine*, 17 February 2001, pp. 55–7. It owes much to the thinking of J.L. Fries and to the writings and personal inspiration of John Grimley Evans.

2. Roy Porter, *The Greatest Benefit to Mankind: A Medical History of Humanity from Antiquity to the Present* (London: HarperCollins, 1997), p. 718.

3. Andrew Achenbaum, *Crossing Frontiers: Gerontology Emerges as a Science* (Cambridge: Cambridge University Press, 1995).

4. It is a cheering fact that most demographic projections have proved to be rather conservative, with estimates of survival having to be revised upwards as the future gets closer.

5. Emily Grundy, 'The epidemiology of ageing' in Raymond Tallis and Howard Fillit (eds), *Textbook of Geriatric Medicine and Gerontology*, (Edinburgh: Churchill Livingstone, 6th edn, 2003).

6. E.M. Gruenberg, 'The failures of success', *Milbank Memorial Fund Quarterly*, 1977, 55: 3–24.

7. Porter, op. cit., p. 716.

8. J. Bamford, P. Sandercock, M. Dennis, J. Burn, C. Warlow, 'A prospective study of acute cerebrovascular disease in the community: the Oxfordshire Community Stroke Project 1981–6. 2. Incidence, case fatality rates and overall outcome at one year of cerebral infarction, primary intracerebral and subarachnoid haemorrhage', *Journal of Neurology, Neurosurgery and Psychiatry*, 1990, 53: 16–22.

9. Jean Martin, Howard Melzer, David Howard, *The Prevalence of Disability Among Adults*, OPCS surveys of disability in Great Britain (London: Office of Populations Censuses and Surveys, 1988).

10. Peter Laslett, *A Fresh Map of Life. The Emergence of the Third Age*, (London: Macmillan, 2nd edn, 1996).

Nicholas Craft of the London School of Economics (personal communication) has estimated that the expected length of retirement has increased by between fourfold and eightfold since 1870 and that nearly all of this is due to increased life expectancy rather than earlier retirement. The average length of retirement increased by five years (from ten to fifteen years) between 1981 and 2001. Lifetime leisure (or non-marketable work) has increased since 1870 by between 50 per cent and 80 per cent of waking hours. This amounts to some extra 130,000 hours, 61 per cent of which is due to decreased mortality.

11. K.G. Manton and Gu XiLiang, 'Changes in the prevalence of chronic disability in the United States black and non-black population above age 65 from 1982 to 1999', *Proceedings of the National Academy of Sciences, USA*, 2001, 98: 6354–9.

12. R.L. Himsworth and M.J. Goldacre, 'Does time in spent in hospital in the final 15 years of life increase with age at death? A population based study', *British Medical Journal*, 1999, 319: 1338–9. Studies in Europe confirm these cheerful findings; for example R. Busse, C. Krauth, F.W. Schwartz, 'Use of acute hospital beds does not increase as the population ages: results from a seven-year cohort study in Germany', *Journal of Epidemiology*, 2002, 56(4): 289–93.

13. J. Lubitz, J. Beebe, C. Baker, 'Longevity and Medicare expenditure', *New England Journal of Medicine*, 1995, 332: 999–1003.

14. I am grateful to Henry A. Shenkin's 'Medical Care at the End of Life Squanders Resources: Reality or Myth?', *Myths in Medical Care* (Danbury, CT: Rutledge Books, 2000) for these data. This marvellous book is required reading for anyone who likes to see received ideas exposed to critical scrutiny and empirical testing.

15. Increasingly, it seems (to parody Shakespeare), 'our little life is rounded with a soap'.

16. Wanless Report *Securing Good Health for the Whole Population: Population Health Trends*, www.doh.gov.uk/wanless/index.htm

17. See David C. Kennie, Susie Dinan and Archie Young, 'Health promotion and physical activity' in *Brocklehurst's Textbook of Geriatric Medicine and Gerontology* op. cit.

18. A. Young, 'The health benefits of physical activity for a healthier old age', in A. Young and M. Harries (eds), *Physical Activity for Patients: An Exercise Prescription* (London: Royal College of Physicians, 2001), pp. 31–42.

19. *National Service Framework for Older People* (London: HMSO, April 2001).

20. A. Rodgers, 'A cure for cardiovascular disease?', *British Medical Journal*, 2003, 326: 1407–8.

21. N.J. Wald, M.R. Law, 'A strategy to reduce cardiovascular disease by more than 80%', *British Medical Journal*, 2003, 326: 1419–23.

22. Including studies conducted by my own group, e.g. C. Lindley, M. Tully, V. Paramsothy, R.C. Tallis, 'Inappropriate medication is a major cause of adverse drug reactions in elderly patients', *Age and Ageing*, 1992, 21: 294–300.

23. V.P. Pomeroy and R.C. Tallis, 'Neurological rehabilitation: a science struggling to come of age', *Physiotherapy Research International*, 2002, 7(2): 76–89.

24. *Restoring Neurological Function: Putting the Neurosciences to Work in Neurorehabilitation*, A Report of the Academy of Medical Sciences (London: March 2004).

25. See Figures 2.4 and 2.5 in Grundy, op. cit.

26. Peter Laslett, op. cit. And also, to some extent, what others make of it.

27. J. Fries, 'Aging, natural death and the compression of morbidity', *New England Journal of Medicine*, 1980, 303: 130–5.

28. Even harder to accept is that, from such elders, remote from the stereotypes of decrepitude, may come a new understanding of life. 'Old men ought to be explorers', T.S. Eliot said in 'East Coker', *Four Quartets*. Old men and old women, in reasonable health, attendees of the University of the Third Age, now can be.

29. Quoted in Andrew Achenbaum op. cit.

30. 'How I fell foul of the NHS', Liz Kendall, the *Observer*, 24 February 2002.

31. Ms Kendall's latest suggestion from the Institute for Public Policy Research (*Sunday Times*, 19 July 2003) is that the work of overstretched GPs could be taken over by 'health care practitioners', who would do relatively unskilled tasks such as taking histories and examining patients(!), 'information brokers' who would tell patients what they wanted to know about their diseases, and consultant pharmacists who would manage the medicines of patients with chronic illnesses. No doubt these new barefoot clinical assistants would be directed towards pensioners with bandaged knees rather than younger, more important people, such as assistant directors of think tanks, who would expect to see a doctor.

32. *National Service Framework for Older People*, op. cit.

33. J.G. Grimley Evans and R.C. Tallis, 'A new beginning for health care for elderly people?', *British Medical Journal*, 2001, 322: 807–8.

34. Age Concern, British Geriatrics Society and David Black, 'Medical aspects of intermediate care', *Clinical Medicine*, 2003; 3: 9–10.

35. Office of Health Economics, *Compendium of Health Statistics*, 14th edn, 2002. Summary statistics compiled by Peter Yuen.

36. K.G. Manton, 'The future of old age' in Raymond Tallis and Howard Fillit (eds), *Brocklehurst's Textbook of Geriatric Medicine and Gerontology* op. cit.

37. Laslett, op. cit.

38. John Grimley Evans, 'Ageing' in Marshall Marinker and Michael Peckham (eds), *Clinical Futures* (London: BMJ Books, 1998), p. 182.

39. The optimism of this chapter and of Chapter 10 will have to be drastically modified if the present upward trends in the prevalence of obesity at all ages continue. Here, as elsewhere, our collective fate lies in our own hands. Everyone

knows what should be done. If action is not taken, it is possible that, for the first time for many generations, life expectancy will fall and the period of disability before death will increase.

9 The End of Medicine as a Profession?

1. This chapter has been strongly influenced by the excellent essays in Digby Anderson (ed.), *Come Back, Miss Nightingale. Trends in Professions Today* (London: The Social Affairs Unit, 1998), where the decline in many professions – nursing, teaching, the law – as well as medicine is examined.

2. This is discussed in Fernand Keuleneer's essay 'The lawyer as hired gun' in Anderson, ibid., and in Andrew Philips's brilliant brief meditation 'Are the liberal professions dead, and if so, does it matter?', *Clinical Medicine*, 2004, 4: 7–9.

3. John Saunders, 'The good doctor and Aristotle's good man', *Advances in Bioethics*, 1998, 4: 279–94.

4. Quoted in John P. Bunker, 'Medicine: an American view' in Digby Anderson, op. cit.

5. Ibid.

6. I do not presume to criticize service industries. The snobbish attitude of the professions towards 'trade' and 'business' is unforgivable and uncritical – as is the hostile attitude of many doctors to accountants as 'bean counters'. Without bean counters, there would very soon be no beans. What I am concerned about are the implications of making health care a purely service industry.

7. Iain Chalmers, 'Well informed uncertainties about the effects of treatment', *British Medical Journal*, 2004, 328: 475–6.

8. George Bernard Shaw, *Man and Superman*, Act IV (London: Penguin, 1971).

9. C.A. Marco, E.S. Bessman, C.N. Schoenfeld, G.D. Kelen, 'Ethical issues of cardiopulmonary resuscitation: current practice among emergency physicians', *Academic Emergency Medicine*, 1997, 4: 898–904. This study was referred to in Chapter 5.

10. It is significant that the possibility of waiving the European Working Time Directive of 2004, and so of postponing a potential workforce disaster for the NHS, has been welcomed by senior doctors, but has been opposed by junior doctors (Melanie Newman, 'Working time definition row', *Hospital Doctor*, 8 April 2004, p. 6).

11. The issue of status is precipitating a crisis in the nursing profession. A recent motion at the annual conference of the Royal College of Nursing has proposed removing nurses further from hands-on care. The proposers argue that 'nursing must decide whether educated and well-qualified nurses should carry out complex aspects of nursing and delegate the "touchy-feely" bits to others... We

are moving towards a situation where, if you are interested in providing basic nursing care, you would be better becoming a health care assistant rather than a nurse.' (Sarah-Kate Templeton, 'Nurses are "too clever" to care for you', *Sunday Times*, 25 April 2004, p. 4).

12. Saunders, op. cit., note 2, p. 290.

13. The non-glamour applies also to academic medical life. The years it takes to acquire the skills to contribute one grain to the antheap of clinical knowledge may not appeal to future generations more used to instant gratification.

14. *British Medical Journal*, Special Issue: 'What's a good doctor and how do you make one?', 2002, 325.

15. Jonathan Martin and Jane Dacre, 'Professional attitudes: why we should care', *Clinical Medicine*, 2002, 2: 182–5.

16. Adrian Bull, *Risk and Trust in the NHS*, edited by Hugo Foxwood (London: The Smith Institute, 2002), p. 78.

17. Quoted in Martin and Dacre, op. cit., p. 183.

18. Readers will remember the survey that found that 33 per cent of patients thought being detained in the waiting room for more than five minutes was too long while 71 per cent thought a ten-minute delay was unacceptable (M. Roland et al., *British Medical Journal*, 2003, 326: 258–60).

19. Arthur Hugh Clough, 'Amours de Voyage':

> I tremble for something factitious,
> Some malpractice of the heart and illegitimate process;
> We are so prone to these things, with our terrible notions of duty.

20. Robin Fox, *The Lancet*, 17 September 1994. According to one of Mother Teresa's disciples, 'such systematic approaches [that is, correct as opposed to botched treatment] are alien to the ethos of the home. Mother Teresa prefers providence to planning: her rules are designed to prevent any drift towards materialism.' Nothing could be more materialistic than the effective science-based medicine that alleviates unbearable suffering – or more humane.

21. He shot to fame with a theory of autism which attributed it to an indifferent 'refrigerator' mother. This theory has now been discredited with overwhelming evidence of a biological causation. While he was alive, his views in certain circles were unassailable. See Matt Ridley, *Nature via Nurture. Genes, Experience and What Makes us Human* (London: Fourth Estate, 2003).

22. D. Mechanic, M. Schlesinger, 'The impact of managed care on patients' trust in medical care and their physicians', *Journal of the American Medical Association*, 1996, 275: 1693–7.

23. Ibid.

24. R. Williams, *Monmouth Diocesan Newsletter*, 1998, 121: 5, quoted in John Saunders, 'Validating the facts of experience in medicine', *Medical Humanities*

ed. M. Evans and I. Finlay (London: BMJ Books, 2001) p. 223–235.

25. Joanna Chikwe, Anthony de Souza, John R. Pepper, 'No time to train surgeons', *British Medical Journal*, 2004, 328: 418–19.

26. Mechanic, op. cit., p. 1696.

27. It is hardly surprising that another government initiative, the 'university for the NHS', which will be linked to the introduction of appraisal and personal development plans for staff throughout the service, including doctors, whose training needs will be assessed and linked to revalidation, has been treated with a certain amount of suspicion.

28. 'What sort of Doctor? Assessing Quality of Care in General Practice No 23 (London: Royal College of General Practitioners, 1985) p. 2.

29. *Stroke*, January 2003. J Kwan, P Sandercock, 'In-hospital care pathways for stroke' Cochrane Database of Systematic Reviews 2002: CD 02924. This is not a call, in the name of clinical freedom, for wilful deviation from established best practice. Nor do I doubt that in many cases the use of tick-box prompts may guard against a failure to achieve minimal standards of good care. Instead, it is a cry for freedom not to be robotically confined to clinical pathways laid down by those remote from the care of the patient.

30. While 'widening access' (so that the profession more faithfully reflects society as a whole) is a good thing, it will not benefit society if it is driven primarily by the need to fill the ranks of an increasingly unattractive profession.

31. Health Policy and Economic Research Unit, *BMA Cohort Study of 1995 Medical Graduates* (London: BMA, 2001). Reported by Isobel Allen in the *BMJ*, 28 September 2002.

32. Ronald Dworkin, 'The Cultural Revolution in Health Care', *The Public Interest*, Spring 2000, 139: 35–49.

33. Ibid.

34. Roy Porter, *The Greatest Benefit of Mankind: A Medical History of Humanity from Antiquity to the Present* (London: Harper Collins, 1997), p. 718.

35. Eliot Freidson, *Profession of Medicine: a Study of the Sociology of Applied Knowledge* (New York: Dodd, Mead, 1970).

36. Clare Dyer, 'New Council takes GMC to High Court for undue leniency', *British Medical Journal*, 2004, 328: 541.

37. Eliot Freidson quoted in John Bunker, 'Can professionalism survive in the market place?', *British Medical Journal*, 1994, 308: 1179–80. I have been heavily dependent on this thoughtful piece.

38. Quoted in Raymond Aron, 'Emile Durkheim', *Main Currents in Sociological Thought*, vol. 2, translated by Richard Howard and Helen Weaver (London: Weidenfeld and Nicolson, 1968), p. 95.

39. Anthony Giddens, Introduction to *Emile Durkheim. Selected Writings* (Cambridge: Cambridge University Press, 1972), p. 19.

40. Peter McDonald, 'Milburn's error is to blame doctors', *Hospital Doctor*, 28 November 2002.

41. Onora O'Neill, 'Called to Account', Reith Lectures (London: BBC, 2002).

42. Melanie Newman, 'Would the last one to leave academic medicine please turn off the lights?', *Hospital Doctor*, 4 March 2004, pp. 20–3.

43. Rhona Macdonald, 'Survey shows serious shortage of medical academics in the UK', *British Medical Journal*, 2002, 324: 446.

44. Onora O'Neill, op. cit.

45. N. Edwards, M.J. Kornacki, J. Silversin, 'Unhappy doctors: what are the causes and what can be done?', *British Medical Journal*, 2002, 324: 835–8.

10 'Everyone Has To Die Some Time'

1. That scientific medicine does not quite fit into the place from which it came is one of many reasons for the enduring attractions of the ideas underlying some brands of alternative medicine.

2. This highlights another problem with differentiating ageing from disease: namely that neither is strictly what philosophers call 'a natural kind'. The identification and classification of disease is subject to a good deal of 'disciplinary construction'; and the boundaries of decremental changes that do not count as disease must likewise be relative to what counts as disease to experts.

3. Peter Medawar, 'An Unsolved Problem in Biology' (London: H.R. Lewis, 1952).

4. Refined over many years but set out very accessibly in his popular book, Tom Kirkwood, *The Time of Our Lives* (London: Weidenfeld & Nicolson, 1999).

5. Ibid., p. 63.

6. Quoted in Kirkwood, ibid, pp. 34–5.

7. See Kirkwood, op. cit.

8. This is particularly liable to be true as many of the symptoms of illness – such as the malaise associated with viral infections or the pain associated with inflammation – are themselves the products of adaptive responses, which are blunted in the biologically aged.

9. John Grimley Evans, 'Ageing', in *Clinical Futures*, edited by Marshall Marinker and Michael Peckham (London: BMJ Books, 1998), p. 174.

10. John Grimley Evans, 'Implications for Health Services', *Philosophical Transactions of the Royal Society of London*, Series B 1997; 352: 1887–1893.

11. Grimley Evans, op. cit. Just how important this (achievable) postponment of the onset of disabling diseases is may be illustrated by the case of dementia.

A recent study (Professor Martin Knapp, LSE) suggested that there would be a 66 per cent increase in the number of people with Alzheimer's disease and other forms of dementia by 2031. (Nigel Hawkes, 'Growing elderly population doubles dementia care costs', *The Times*, 23 January 2003) because of the increase of the ageing population, especially the number of people in their nineties. The report, however, also points out that even modest success in developing drugs to delay the onset of the condition would greatly allay the burden of disease, and treatments that reduced the percentage of people with dementia by one point would be sufficient to offset the increasing burden of care. Modest gains in delaying the onset and progress of the disease could turn a bad news story into a good one.

12. K.G. Manton, E. Stallard, B.H. Singer, 'Methods for projecting the future size and health status of the US elderly population', in D. Wise (ed.), *Studies of the Economics of Ageing.* (Chicago: University of Chicago Press, 1994).

13. Oliver Goldsmith, *The Vicar of Wakefield.*

14. Shah Ebrahim, 'The medicalization of old age', *British Medical Journal*, 2002, 324: 861–3.

15. An optimism that, as I have already emphasized, will be justified only if the present growing epidemic of obesity is dealt with. Since everyone knows what to do, I remain optimistic. Our fate lies in our own hands.

16. Readers might like to read my sceptical account of this and other less numerate panics in Raymond Tallis, 'Apocalypse soon?', *Times Literary Supplement*, 19 April 1996, pp. 25–6.

17. Bjorn Lomborg, 'How healthy is the world?', *British Medical Journal*, 2002, 325: 145–6.

18. There are opposing views – as Lomberg has discovered to his personal cost. The contrary view is ubiquitous. A succinct presentation of this position, which he describes as 'systemic optimism', is presented by Anthony J. McMichael, 'Commentary: Gilding the global lily', *British Medical Journal*, 2002, 325: 1465–6.

19. See Raymond Tallis, 'The difficulty of arrival', in *Newton's Sleep* (London: Macmillan, 1995) and Raymond Tallis, 'The work of art in an age of electronic reproduction' in *Theorrhoea and After* (London: Macmillan, 1999).

20. A more detailed version of this argument is given in Raymond Tallis, *Enemies of Hope: A Critique of Contemporary Pessimism* (Macmillan: London, 2nd edn, 1999).

21. John Grimley Evans, 'Ageing', in *Clinical Futures*, edited by Marshall Marinker and Michael Peckham (London: BMJ Books, 1998), p. 181.

22. The diagram is reproduced from R.C. Tallis, 'Medical advances and the future of old age' in *Controversies in Health Care*, edited by Marshall Marinker (London: BMJ Books, 1994), pp. 76–88.

Envoi

1. William Shakespeare, *Hamlet*, Act 1, Scene 2, lines 72–3.
2. R. Walford, *Maximum Lifespan* (New York: W.W. Norton, 1983).
3. Paul Valery, *Monsieur Teste*, translated by Jackson Matthews (London: Routledge & Kegan Paul, 1973). This rather intellectualist view seems to leave out sorrow for those who are left and from whom one is parted and concern for those who are yet to reach fulfilment.
4. Ronald Dworkin, 'The New Gospel of Health', *The Public Interest*, Fall 2000.
5. Ronald Dworkin, 'The Medicalization of Unhappiness', *The Public Interest*, Summer 2001.

Index

The figures in italics indicate a graph.